WOMEN'S TRAVEL WRITINGS IN INDIA
1777–1854

WOMEN'S TRAVEL WRITINGS IN INDIA 1777–1854

*Edited by
Katrina O'Loughlin
and Michael Gamer*

Volume II

LONDON AND NEW YORK

First published 2020
by Routledge
2 Park Square, Milton Park, Abingdon, Oxon OX14 4RN

and by Routledge
52 Vanderbilt Avenue, New York, NY 10017

Routledge is an imprint of the Taylor & Francis Group, an informa business

© 2020 selection and editorial matter, Carl Thompson, Katrina O'Loughlin, Michael Gamer, Éadaoin Agnew and Betty Hagglund; individual owners retain copyright in their own material.

The right of Carl Thompson, Katrina O'Loughlin, Michael Gamer, Éadaoin Agnew and Betty Hagglund to be identified as the authors of the editorial material, and of the authors for their individual chapters, has been asserted in accordance with sections 77 and 78 of the Copyright, Designs and Patents Act 1988.

All rights reserved. No part of this book may be reprinted or reproduced or utilised in any form or by any electronic, mechanical, or other means, now known or hereafter invented, including photocopying and recording, or in any information storage or retrieval system, without permission in writing from the publishers.

Trademark notice: Product or corporate names may be trademarks or registered trademarks, and are used only for identification and explanation without intent to infringe.

British Library Cataloguing-in-Publication Data
A catalogue record for this book is available from the British Library

Library of Congress Cataloging-in-Publication Data
A catalog record for this book has been requested

ISBN: 978-1-138-20272-6 (Set)
eISBN: 978-1-315-47317-8 (Set)
ISBN: 978-1-138-20277-1 (Volume II)
eISBN: 978-1-315-47305-5 (Volume II)

Typeset in Times New Roman
by Apex CoVantage, LLC

Publisher's note
References within each chapter are as they appear in the original complete work

Printed in the United Kingdom
by Henry Ling Limited

CONTENTS

Introduction   1

Harriet Newell, *Memoirs of Mrs. Harriet Newell* (1815)   17

Eliza Fay, *Original Letters from India* (1817)   147

INTRODUCTION

In bringing together *Original Letters from India* (1817) and *Memoirs of Mrs. Harriet Newell* (1815), this volume presents two highly influential works of travel writing published just at the close of the Napoleonic Wars and the War of 1812. At first glance, few writers would appear to have less in common than the Briton Eliza Fay (1755/6–1816) and the American Harriet Newell (1793–1812), whose differences extend beyond the national and generational to those of temperament and world view. Fay was an ambitious and opinionated Londoner who made at least five voyages of business to India; Newell, by contrast, was a pious young American missionary from rural New England who made only one trip and died just six weeks after her arrival in West Bengal – thereby becoming the first American missionary, male or female, to die abroad. Newell eschewed assemblies and balls as the '*extravagances*' of a vain world; Fay believed a deck of cards to be one of the most valuable things one could travel with, easing the monotony of long sea voyages and providing welcome distraction at awkward dinner parties and gatherings among near-strangers.

One suspects Fay would have had even less patience with Newell's proselytizing than Newell with Fay's gambling ('in the evening we sat down to vingt-un, at a rupee a fish.... I lost only a dozen' (p. 301)). In fact, we know exactly how Fay felt about the missionary calling. In her first voyage, travelling between Leghorn and Alexandria, Fay encountered a Franciscan Friar from Rome on a mission to Jerusalem. She found him a figure at once romantic and ridiculous:

> no man can be better calculated for the hazardous office he has undertaken. Figure to yourself, a man in the prime of life (under forty), tall, well made, and athletic in his person; and seemingly of a temperament to brave every danger: add to these advantages a pair of dark eyes, beaming with intelligence ... and, you cannot fail to pronounce him irresistible.
>
> (p. 177)

Finding him in possession of 'all the enthusiasm and eloquence necessary for pleading the important cause of Christianity', Fay seems almost prepared to forgive 'such ridiculous superstitions, as disgrace the Romish creed' until the friar exhorts her to give up – 'as a libation to the bambino (child) Jesus' – her morning coffee. Fay's outrage is palpable: 'Professing my disbelief in the efficacy of such a sacrifice, I . . . excused myself from complying'. The incipient friendship is abruptly ruptured over Fay's 'obstinate heresy'. The Reverend Father wishes Fay to the devil and, having made an entertaining anecdote of the encounter for her correspondents, Fay smartly consigns the missionary to the same place (p. 177).

Comparing each woman's first experiences on the Indian subcontinent – Fay's in 1780 and Newell's in 1812 – the similarities between them become more striking. Both arrived in Calcutta as very young women, both were recently married, and both were negotiating new lives in extremely difficult circumstances. Both were members of the emerging middle classes, received formal education, and married men of higher education still. More powerfully perhaps, both Fay and Newell shared what we might call a vocation, a singular sense of purpose and profound personal commitment to projects conceived by their husbands, but in which they had important roles to play. Both, then, are professional wives in companionate marriages, even though their very different convictions and callings would probably seem as alien to each other as they initially appear to us. For Fay, her object was the establishment of her husband Anthony's legal career and the couple's economic future in Calcutta, the new centre of administration in Anglo-India. For Newell, it was the ministry of faith. She testifies in her diary: 'I have confessed Christ before the world – I have renounced my wicked companions – I have solemnly promised, that denying ungodliness and every worldly lust, I will live soberly, righteously, and godly, in this present world' (p. 38).

As two adjacent diary entries show, Harriet Atwood's meeting with Samuel Newell gave a powerful focus to her desired spiritual practice:

> Oct. 23 [1810]. Mr. M. introduced Mr. N[ewell] to our family, He appears to be an engaged Christian. Expects to spend his life, in preaching a Saviour to the benighted Pagans.
>
> Oct. 31. Mr. N. called on us this morning. He gave me some account of the dealings of God with his soul. If such a man who has devoted himself to the service of the gospel, has determined to labour in the most difficult part of the vineyard, and is willing to renounce his earthly happiness for the interest of religion; if *he* doubts his possessing love to God; – what shall I say of *myself*?
>
> (p. 53)

Harriet Atwood's vocation was powerfully shaped by a renewed Christian spiritualism among the communities of Massachusetts in the first decade of the century and by the convictions of the man who became her husband. Almost two generations older, Eliza Fay's travels were equally shaped by her husband's personal ambition – at least initially. Irish by birth, married, and admitted to the bar in

London, Anthony Fay sought a position at the newly established Supreme Court of Calcutta. Eliza Fay, by her own admission

> undertook the journey with a view of preserving my husband from destruction, for had I not accompanied him, and in many instances restrained his extravagance and dissipated habits, he would never, never, I am convinced, have reached Bengal, but have fallen a wretched sacrifice to them on the way, or perhaps through the violence of his temper been invoked in some dispute, which he was too ready to provoke.
>
> (p. 242)

Fay's fears seem entirely borne out by the details of her narrative. Reactive, short-tempered, and regularly inclined to 'lose all self-command' (p. 221), Anthony Fay in the course of their journey manages to lose their passports and then their money, quarrels with almost everyone the couple meets (and depends upon), short circuits his legal career, and finally abandons his wife at Calcutta to shift for herself after a year. By comparison, Eliza Fay is shrewd, observant, and resourceful: what begins as his career and journey becomes hers. Although she never enjoyed in her husband the 'beloved friend' (p. 89) and 'most affectionate partner' (p. 88) that Newell found in hers, Fay was also determined not to be the '*self* devoted victim' (p. 230) that observers more than once took her to be. Over the next three decades, and as a single woman, she established a millinery business at Calcutta, opened and then sold a private boarding school in England, and traded in her own ship as a merchant between India, Britain, and America.

Both Fay and Newell share a self-discipline and self-actualization through travel and writing that deserve greater attention. As young women actively making choices that are determined for and by them, both are creatures of a particular moment in Anglo-American history, and remarkable 'speculators' in the gendered possibilities before them. In direct and related ways, both women derived their opportunities from British domination of the Indian subcontinent at the turn of the nineteenth century, where two centuries of lucrative trade with Europe had remade the relationships of people, objects, and power along different meridians. The India Regulating Act of 1773 transmuted commercial dominance into administrative power and created the conditions of possibility for both couples' travels. While the Fays sought the new professional opportunities created by British courts at West Bengal, the Newells wished to bring Christianity to vast multicultural and multi-faith communities in the wake of British conquest. Both speculations – one economic and one religious – were made possible by the consolidation of British rule in India and the establishment of Calcutta as its administrative centre. West Bengal (particularly Calcutta and its near-neighbour Serampore) is therefore a point of critical convergence and space of possibility for the two writers and their texts.

To claim that the Fays and the Newells benefitted from British dominance in India is not to suggest that their relationships with the East India Company or the British Government were either straightforward or smooth, however. This is another remarkable connection between the two narratives: both came up very directly against the Company at key stages of their journey. Although so very different, both are part of a growing group of what one contemporary dubbed 'vagrant Europeans' in India who plagued the Company from the late eighteenth century.[1] These rogue traders, speculators, and 'sectarian missionaries',[2] who neither worked for the Company nor observed its (declining) authority, were perceived as a direct threat to its monopoly and effective rule.

Attempting to capitalize on opportunities from outside the Company's jurisdiction – Fay describes their venture as 'a noble opportunity of making an ample fortune' (p. 256) – the Fays had not applied for the appropriate permits to travel prior to their journey. This might account for the unusual overland route they pursued, their avoidance of English ships, and their systematic misrepresentation of themselves as either French or Danish to avoid detection by various authorities in Egypt and India. Arriving in West Bengal, Anthony Fay simply presented himself to the Supreme Court and requested work. In doing so he shrewdly calculated that his legal qualifications and nationality might prevail.[3] But while his wife carefully courted the acquaintance of leading families in the government of British India (notably the Hastings, Chambers, and Impeys at Calcutta), Anthony Fay became increasingly active in anti-governmental circles, until – as Fay herself revealed in frustration – 'no hope remains of his *ever* being able to prosecute his profession here' (p. 255). At this point, the Fays separate, Eliza Fay moves in with the Chambers, and Anthony Fay leaves the historical record. His shadowy behaviour has led at least one commentator to suggest that he was operating as a spy at Calcutta, gathering evidence to be used against either the Governor General or the East India Company in Britain.[4] Such a prospect certainly presents the Fays' ill-starred first voyage in a rather different light and raises important questions about Eliza Fay's knowledge of key events, and how she arranges them in her narrative.

Like the Fays, the Newells also arrived at Calcutta unannounced and unwelcome. Attempting to undertake mission work in West Bengal, they disembarked to discover America at war with Britain and their work banned by the East India Company.[5] They thus found themselves in the middle of a conflict they neither expected nor fully understood: aligned with the British Baptist missionaries William Carey and John Thomas, and in direct opposition to the East India Company, which believed that mission work caused disaffection among Indian citizens and undermined British authority. The real political and ideological gulf operating between Company and Mission in these years is captured most powerfully in the distance between British Calcutta and Danish Serampore, where the Dissenting missions had been forced to remove. As Karen Chancey shows, the missionary debate in which the Newells became ensnared was fuelled by wider power struggles for which West Bengal had become an incendiary focal point: conflicts between Dissent and the established Church of England; and between the British Crown and the East India Company over who was ultimately to control India, religiously and politically.[6] Harriet Newell's narrative foregrounds the complex reality of Christian missionary work in British India, which sometimes was in concert with, and sometimes worked against, the cultural and territorial imperialism of the East India Company and British Government. The perception of a twin threat posed by imperial and evangelical expansion at this period is brilliantly captured in David Hopkins' urgent publication of 1809, *The Dangers of British India from French Invasion and Missionary Establishments* (London, 1809), which imagines imperial France and evangelical Christianity as unlikely co-conspirators bent on undermining British supremacy in India. It is these regional manifestations of global conflicts – the struggle for dominance over the rich territory and trade of India – which connects Fay and Newell's narratives in unpredictable ways.

As unorthodox women travellers and writers working at the edges of British imperialism, Fay and Newell occupy a liminal space in both early nineteenth-century travel to India and historical discourses of life and travel writing. On the margins of dominant cultural, colonial, and faith discourses – however orthodox Harriet Newell subsequently becomes in Protestant circles as the first missionary martyr – their travel accounts provide an oblique perspective on Anglo-American culture and India during the Romantic period. Understanding the broad cultural forces that constitute British India in the Romantic period requires that we recognize the details and small acts of agency of those who travelled there. These are lives in the making; like the genre of travel itself, Fay and Newell are people in motion, shaped by and shaping the historical moments through which they move.

While the texts comprising the four volumes of *Women's Travel Writing in India* are presented in the order of their publication – so that Newell's *Memoirs* precedes Fay's *Original Letters* – we reverse this order of introduction here because, in dealing with the earlier period 1779–1796, Fay provides important contexts for understanding Newell.

Eliza Fay

Eliza Clement was born in 1755 or 1756, probably at Rotherhithe and one of four children of Edward Clement, a shipwright. We know little of her early life and education before her marriage, on 6 February 1772, to Anthony Fay at St Dunstan-in-the-West (Fleet Street, London). We know even less of her husband Anthony Fay, other than that he was born in Ireland, was violent-tempered, and had legal and perhaps political ambitions, gaining admission to Gray's Inn in 1772 and (with Edward Clement's help) Clement's Inn and Lincoln's Inn in 1778. Eliza Clement was just 16 or 17 when she married; six years later and with the full support of her family, she and her husband sailed for India.

Fay had travelled before. Her letters reveal that, prior to embarking with Anthony, she had made the passage from Dover to Calais at least three times, had visited Paris, and had glimpsed Queen Marie Antoinette at Versailles. But this was a voyage of a different order, made at a time of momentous global events. Fay's first letter is dated 18 April 1779 from Paris; just one week earlier, France (then an ally with the American colonies in their War of Independence) had signed a secret treaty with the Spanish to bring them into that war, effectively expanding the Anglo-French conflict into a global one. Enemy aliens in France, the Fays hoisted a French flag on their arrival in port, and then waited restlessly for passports before striking out overland for Leghorn. Theirs was an unusual route to India; the voyage would normally be made by sea and directly from London. The Fays were travelling frugally and perhaps rather naively (they thought, for example, that the Alps were a single high pass rather than an extended mountain range). Their plans changed more than once as they travelled via Lyons, Pont de Beauvoisin, Chalons sur Soane, and Lanneburg, then over Mont Cenis to Turin, Genoa, and Leghorn. At each step, their itinerary was shaped by their letters of introduction and the remittances they carried.

From Leghorn the couple took a passage in first the *Hellespont* and then the *Julius* to Alexandria. From there they travelled again by water to Cairo, where they were caught up in a dangerous dispute about trade movements through Egypt.[7] The Ottoman Porte and British East India Company had both forbidden British trade through Suez and the Red Sea at this period. But, as Fay explains, 'there never was a law made, but means might be found to evade it' and rogue traders – anxious to use the route to cut travel times and avoid duties – negotiated agreements with local beys for passage (p. 188). It was in this climate and immediately prior to the Fays' arrival, that a caravan of British merchants from the ship *Nathalia* had been plundered and left to die on the overland journey between Suez and Cairo, apparently in recrimination. Making the same journey over the desert in reverse, without the protection of the Company and with realistic fears for their own safety, Fay hides the details of the attack from her family until her arrival at Suez. Boarding the same ship *Nathalia*, only recently returned to its owners after being impounded and stripped, the Fays sailed for India, arriving at the trading port of Calicut on the Malabar coast on 5 November 1779. There they found themselves, once again, enemy aliens on another front of the global Anglo-French War, caught between their Englishness, their putatively Danish ship, and a French Captain. They were promptly imprisoned at the abandoned English Factory by the Governor Sardar Khan on behalf of Hyder Ali, the Sultan of Mysore. After 15 weeks of incarceration in primitive accommodations, they managed to scrabble a release with the assistance of a local Jewish merchant, Mr Isaac, and departed Cochin for Madras and finally Calcutta.

Arriving in West Bengal over a year after they had left Dover, Eliza presented her letters of introduction to Mrs Warren Hastings, the wife of the first Governor General of India; Anthony, meanwhile, presented himself to Sir Robert

INTRODUCTION

Chambers, Second Judge of the newly-formed Supreme Court, and Philip Francis, who had been appointed to the Supreme Council at Calcutta in 1773. We note these introductions because they nicely delineate the two sides of yet another political foment into which the Fays stumbled. In this instance, it was the growing animosity between members of the Council and Court at Calcutta, tensions that were to lead eventually to the impeachment of Warren Hastings in 1788. Acquainted with most – and intimate with some – of the members of the highest administrative and trade circles at Calcutta, the Fays were nothing if not close to the action. At one moment, Fay describes an amateur production of *Venice Preserved* acted by leading civil servants and starring Captain Call, the 'Garrick of the East' (p. 330, note 265); at another, she is instructed at a public gathering to fix her eyes on the 'Lady Governess' indefinitely until acknowledged by her; at still another, she reports breathlessly on the duel between Hastings and Francis. Through commentary pointed and astute, Fay's talent for character portraiture, comedy, and dramatic narrative shows itself in every page of the *Original Letters* as she documents an evolving city and period of transition from Company to Crown rule. Political events are crossed by personal crisis as Anthony Fay's legal career founders and he fathers a child with another woman. Lady Chambers steps in as a protector and patron, taking Fay into her home and sheltering her from inevitable public gossip about her husband's increasingly erratic and anti-governmental behaviour. Successfully suing for legal separation in August of 1781, Fay quietly superintends the return of her modest furniture and effects to their creditors and, with only her clothes left to her, embarks for England.

This, then, is Eliza Fay's first voyage to India (10 April 1779 – 7 February 1783), just one of five. Her second (March 1784 – September 1794) marks the emergence of Eliza Fay the merchant.[8] Setting up a partner, Avis Hicks (later Mrs John Lacey), in a milliner's shop in the former Post Office in the heart of Calcutta, Fay raised sufficient capital to purchase a home of her own and managed her business through a catastrophic economic downturn in the 1780s. Leaving her venture in the hands of her partner's brother-in-law, Benjamin Lacey, Fay returned to Britain via St Helena. But here, too, controversy seemed to dog her, as Fay was called to respond to charges made by a former servant Kate Johnson, who alleged that in 1782 she had been abandoned by Fay and consequently sold into slavery. In addition, she insinuated that she had witnessed some impropriety on the part of Fay with a ship's doctor, a significant threat against a separated woman like Fay since any accusation of infidelity could jeopardize her maintenance. Fay chose to pay the nominated fine of £60 rather than stand trial. At this juncture, Fay was evidently trying to return some part of her Indian capital to Britain but – once again working outside the protection of the East India Company – was prevented from landing her cargo in Ostend for transfer home. Instead she trusted it to an American trader Richard Crowninshield, who arranged the sale of her goods in America, and returned her capital in the shape of a ship – the *Minerva*. A timely inheritance made it possible for her to freight her new ship with goods from London bound for Calcutta, and Fay returned to India on her in August 1795. Loading once again in Bengal with Indian goods for the American market, Fay dispatched the *Minerva* and followed to New York. Here, rather abruptly, her account ends.

The *Original Letters* are organized in two parts, the first and longest of which covers the period from April 1779–September 1782. Comprised of twenty-three letters addressed to Fay's family via her sisters, 'Part First' preserves the recognizable form of a private correspondence. Letters appear written in the moment and betray no knowledge of what might lie ahead, as Fay acknowledges the receipt of packets and news from home even as she details her own movements, state of health, and spirits. Although still epistolary in form, 'Part Second' differs both in its level of detail and in the style of its narration. Composing for a (possibly fictitious) 'Mrs. L— ', Fay provides an 'abstract' or summary of her subsequent voyages (17 March 1784–4 September 1794 and 2 August 1795–1796), one that chronicles her establishment of the millinery business at Calcutta and her growing involvement in speculative trade between Britain, America, and India. Her own logs tally closely with historical records stretching over four continents, meticulously recording ships, ports of call, and relationships of friendship, business, and even patronage. The retrospective mode of her memoir, meanwhile, reveals a further dimension of this genuinely remarkable author and traveller. Marked by an awareness of dangers passed and problems overcome rather than current crises, the Eliza Fay of 'Part Second' is more reflective and sometimes philosophical, but always resourceful and forthright.

Fay was writing the memoir of her later travels to India from Blackheath in 1815. Sometime in that year or perhaps early in the next, she returned to Calcutta – her final voyage – and there began preparing her manuscripts for publication. These were in a forward enough state for the *Calcutta Gazette* (9 May 1816) to give notice of the forthcoming publication of Fay's 'Narrative' and to invite subscriptions. Fay's sudden death clearly disrupted publication plans, and it was not until the following year – largely for the benefit of her creditors – that her writings found their way into print. Featuring a four-page introductory preface and a Calcutta imprint, the edition carried the title *Original Letters from India; Containing a Narrative of a Journey Through Egypt, and the Author's Imprisonment at Calicut by Hyder Ally* (1817). It included a frontispiece showing the author 'Dressed in the Egyptian Costume' that she had purchased at Cairo and carried with her to Calcutta. A rather terse 'Advertisement' to the *Original Letters* marks an important intervention on the part of the anonymous editor:

> The work had been printed thus far when the death of the author took place. The subsequent parts of her journal, not appearing to contain any events of a nature sufficiently interesting to claim publication, no additional extracts have been deemed necessary by the administrator, who

from a view of benefiting the estate has been induced to undertake the present publication.

(p. 304)

Thus it becomes clear that, although Fay had prepared her own writing for publication, the final shape of the printed *Original Letters* was determined not by herself but by the interests and expedience of her executors. And of course, we now have no way of knowing what, from Fay's complete manuscripts, has been lost.

Like each of her voyages to India between 1779 and 1816, Fay's preparation of her India letters for publication was a carefully calculated commercial venture – a cargo as potentially valuable as the linens, muslins, and other commodities she had traded at various stages of her career. Her initial choice of subscription publication – a mode by which readers committed to purchase and partially paid the costs of the publication in advance – represents Fay's attempt to secure a market for her product and to exploit the same networks of commerce, sociability, and patronage she had relied on for nearly four decades. Her title shows her ready to marshal popular genres like the captivity narrative and Gothic romance, and to exploit the notoriety of public figures from Warren Hastings to Hyder Ali. 'At a time when fictitious representations of human life are sought for with so much avidity', she writes, the *Original Letters* will provide something even better: an 'unembellished narrative of simple facts and real sufferings', whose trials and adventures rival even the most improbable of romances (see note 1). As Fay's Preface argues, her residence at Calcutta – and her status as a woman – gave her privileged access to 'important circumstances in the lives of well known . . . individuals' (p. 153). Even as she speculates on the enormous popularity of travel narratives in the late eighteenth and early nineteenth centuries, she trusts that her book's primary value will lie in its lengthy first-hand account of the people and events surrounding Warren Hastings's controversial rule between 1773 and 1785. The *Original Letters* thus invoke several genres at once – captivity narrative, secret memoir, Gothic tale, 'romance of real life', and 'true history' – leveraging travel writing's heterodox qualities to produce a world whose richness and complexity rival the historical fiction of her two celebrated contemporaries, Maria Edgeworth and Walter Scott. In Fay's hands, the results are a shrewd mixture of horror, social critique, and intrigue, all the more powerful because true.

Despite its lively account of people and politics, the *Original Letters* raised only a modest profit of Rs. 220 for Fay's estate. Still, it was successful enough to be reprinted in 1821 at Calcutta with a reset title page but few other alterations. In 1908, Rev. W. K. Firminger oversaw a new edition, published by Thacker, Spink & Co. in conjunction with the Calcutta Historical Society. The next major edition – the first, as its editor E. M. Forster notes, to be produced outside India – was published by Virginia and Leonard Woolf's Hogarth Press in 1925. Forster had encountered Fay in Firminger's 1908 edition while researching the book that would become *A Passage to India* (1924).⁹ Firminger had largely dismissed Fay as a stylist, silently 'correcting' her grammar and expression, and complaining that 'there is something about Mrs Fay which fails to charm, something of a too conscious superiority which alienates sympathy in circumstances in which sympathy would not be grudged'.¹⁰ Later readers were more appreciative: Forster restored the work to the 1817 original, and Francis Bickley – reviewing Forster's edition – considered Fay 'a discovery as valuable as an unrecorded Titian'.¹¹ Despite Fay's resistance to such an identification for her travails, the *Letters'* status as colonial romance has been perhaps inadvertently secured by two further recent editions (both based on the Forster edition), edited and introduced by M. M. Kaye and Simon Winchester respectively.¹²

Harriet Newell

Born in Haverhill, Massachusetts in 1793, Harriet Atwood (later Newell) lived her entire life amidst religious controversy. Attending the First Parish Church at Haverhill as a child, her first pastor was the Harvard-trained Abiel Abbot (1770–1828), Unitarian in his leanings and insufficiently orthodox for many members of his congregation. Newell's tenth birthday would have been marked by Abbot's departure, ostentatiously over a salary dispute, as parishioners declined to increase the salary of a pastor so determinedly Unitarian. (Abbot quickly established himself with a Congregationalist parish in nearby Beverly, which became Unitarian shortly thereafter).

At home and across the river in Bradford, meanwhile, a radical and generational shift was underway: first in the form of Abraham Burnham, a self-taught farmer's son who had joined Bradford Academy as a preceptor in 1805; and next in Joshua Dodge, who became pastor of the First Parish Church of Haverhill in 1808. Both had a profound effect on Harriet Atwood's formative years, Dodge as her family's 'beloved pastor', and Burnham as her 'spiritual father'. Dodge was a man of active spirituality rather than theological minutiae, particularly (as one local historian put it) 'the guidance of each student into a . . . life of Christian service'.¹³ How such ideas of 'service' fed the foreign missionary movement are clear enough; their profound effects on local communities and young women like Harriet Atwood, however, are worth contemplating. Consider, for example, the local dancing school that she attended at the age of eleven and that opens the 'Diary' portion of the *Memoirs*. Torn between her enjoyment of dancing and guilt over its 'vanity' and 'foolishness', she determines 'that, when the school closed, I would immediately become religious' (p. 25). It is a startling passage, and one made more poignant by the fact that the school was made possible by John Hasseltine, the father of Harriet Atwood's close friend Ann. Hasseltine had added a large room to the second story of his house to host assemblies, and the dances that followed caused controversy. In 1805, for example, there appeared in Bradford and Haverhill an anonymous pamphlet attacking a progressive 'parson A[llen]' for being 'corrupted by doctrines of Arians and Socinians', and 'attend[ing] frolicings [sic] and dancings with his young people, not only till nine o'clock, and ten o'clock, and eleven o'clock, and twelve o'clock at night, but even till one o'clock in the morning'.[14] It is hardly surprising, then, to find Harriet Atwood later in the *Memoirs* torn by the prospect of a local ball – as much for how it might divide or endanger the spiritual health of the community, as for the frivolity of its 'frolicings' (see notes 9 and 83).

Within these New England religious communities, one of the closely followed stories of 1810 was a minor sensation created by 'four young gentlemen, members of the Divinity College', who appeared that June in Bradford before the General Association of Congregationalist Ministers.[15] With becoming modesty, they declared to the assembly their serious vocation to do missionary work abroad and petitioned for 'patronage and support' that they might do so.[16] Their testimony had immediate effect: a Board of Commissioners for Foreign Missions was created the next morning, and the four young divinity students – Adoniram Judson, Samuel Nott, Samuel J. Mills, and Samuel Newell – were celebrated within evangelical circles as fundraising began among parishes to finance their mission. *The Panoplist*, *The Advisor*, and *The Connecticut Evangelical* magazines reported that an extraordinary $13,953.48 had been collected from local parishes to finance the missionaries, providing the full ledger of their budget, medical training, supplies, anticipated expenses, and salaries. Over a four-year period, their progress continued to be enthusiastically covered by evangelical journals, who reported on every aspect of their planning, ordination, embarkation, arrival, and progress in India.[17] It was in these same publications that Harriet Newell's journal and correspondence made their first appearance in print.

Such details make clear the attractions of being part of such a movement, particularly for a seriously-minded young woman who had already resolved to dedicate her life to Christian service. Harriet Atwood's correspondence shows her a proponent of missionary work as early as August of 1809. Writing to her friend Fanny Woodbury, she asks why knowledge of the gospel is not 'given to the Heathen, who . . . are perishing for lack of knowledge?' (p. 40). By October of the same year we find her in earnest conversation with 'two servants of Jesus Christ', most likely Rev. Samuel Worcester of Salem and Rev. Joseph Emerson of Beverly, about plans originating in Andover to send missionaries abroad. Her response is among her most fervid:

> Oh, that Jehovah would pour down his Spirit there! Oh, that he would . . . make not only A[ndover] a place of his power, but *Haverhill* also! Arise, blessed Jesus! plead thine own cause, and have mercy upon Zion. Now, when men are making void thy law, arise! build up thy spiritual Jerusalem, and let her no longer mourn, 'because so few come to her solemn feasts'.
>
> (p. 44)

The *American Dictionary of National Biography* informs us that Harriet Atwood and Ann Hasseltine were 'shy and introspective', and that Atwood was not as overtly enthusiastic about missionary service as her friend. From the evidence of her correspondence, it seems more likely that, spending much of her childhood and adolescence in poor health, Harriet Atwood had not yet imagined herself as capable of undertaking such work. Within twelve months, however, much had changed: the petition of the 'four young gentlemen' had created new institutional possibilities within the Congregationalist Church for missionary work; Atwood's friend, Ann Hasseltine, had accepted the marriage proposal of Adoniram Judson; Judson had introduced another of the four, Samuel Newell, to Harriet Atwood; and Harriet Atwood had been impressed enough by Newell's 'account of the dealings of God with his soul' to marry him and accompany him to India. 'If such a man . . . is willing to renounce his earthly happiness for the interest of religion', she argues to herself in her journal, 'what shall I say of *myself*?' (p. 53). For a woman in search of ways to put her faith into practice – who already had begun proselytizing friends – the missionary cause promised a life of meaningful purpose. In many ways, the high risks of death from disease or misadventure posed by missionary work merely strengthened Harriet Atwood's sense of commitment.[18] Within two years of meeting Samuel Newell, the couple had married, landed in British Calcutta, and moved to William Carey's mission in Danish Serampore. Unwilling to return home, they elected to go to the Isle of France (Mauritius) to organize a mission there. Harriet Newell never reached their destination, giving birth prematurely during the voyage, watching her infant daughter die from exposure, and then succumbing herself, likely from complications from childbirth.

Given Newell's status as the first American missionary to die abroad, cultural commentators have generally read the *Memoirs* within the traditions of spiritual biography.[19] Newell thus sits uneasily but suggestively among women travel writers of the early nineteenth century because of her youth, sheltered upbringing, and very brief time on the Indian subcontinent. As Carl Thompson's introduction to this collection notes, Newell's *Memoirs* display at best a 'myopic' view of India, which he describes as amounting to a 'fantasy projection of a benighted, heathen land' (Vol. I, p. xx). What Newell's *Memoirs* do provide, however, is a fascinating glimpse into the literary and cultural sources of such fantasies. Receiving an excellent education at Bradford Academy, Newell supplemented her deficit of lived experience with books and imagination. At the time she meets Samuel Newell, she is, suggestively, the same age as Jane Austen's Catherine Morland of *Northanger Abbey* (1818), another young woman of seventeen who transforms, and is transformed by, the places she encounters. And, like Catherine, what frames Newell's world view is her reading. Of the 212 notes we have provided to Newell's own writing, an astonishing 154 involve literary allusions. As one might expect of a future missionary coming of age during the Second Great Awakening, these bear little resemblance to the Gothic fiction burlesqued in Austen's novel and underpinning Fay's *Original Letters*. Instead, Newell's quotations are comprised largely of passages from the Bible, hymns, and sermons either read or recently heard. In Newell's letters to female friends, allusions serve sometimes as tools for sharing intimacy, and at other times as a means for reflection or solace, as when she loses first an uncle and then her father to illness. Like most young women writing at the turn of the nineteenth century, she makes what she can of the world with the materials she has at hand.

As she gains in both religious conviction and confidence as a writer, the range and patterns of Newell's allusions deepen and change. As she imagines herself into an active role in the global missionary movement, her quotations acquire millennial and evangelical urgency. To her fondness for the hymns of Isaac Watts she adds those of other writers, most notably Susannah Harrison, Elizabeth Singer Rowe, and Anne Steele. Around this time, she begins not just to quote scripture but also periodically to alter it to suit either her situation or emotional state. Though usually compressing sacred source materials, Newell sometimes makes fairly radical alterations, as when, distraught at the seductive power of a local ball on her friend 'E', she draws on Luke 9:62 and Proverbs 29:1 to create her own composition (see note 84). Secular literary sources occasion even greater liberties, such as when Newell taps two minor tales from Ossian to capture the sadness of contemplating the ancient past. Fond of poetry, she finds recourse in Robert Blair's *The Grave* (1743), James Thomson's *The Seasons* (1730), Edward Young's *Night Thoughts* (1742–1745), and William Cowper's *The Task* (1785). Readers of William Blake will find Newell's reading and patterns of quotation particularly suggestive, since they point to a canon and to influences that strikingly resemble Blake's own. One wonders what the two might have made of one another had they met in Regency London, or what path the young Harriet Atwood's brand of radical Protestantism might have taken just twenty years earlier in that city.

We should not be surprised, then, to find Newell, on the eve of her departure to India, finding a literary soulmate in Henry Kirke White (1785–1806), the Romantic poet who had died of consumption at the age of twenty-one and whose *Remains* (1807), edited by Robert Southey, established him among a growing coterie of talented poets cut off by premature death. In Kirke White, Newell found a writer of her own generation committed to the same evangelical causes; she cites him more than any writer save Isaac Watts. Her favourite poems by him – 'The Dance of the Consumptives' from *Fragment of an Eccentric Drama* and the lyric 'Fanny! Upon thy breast I may not lie!' – suggest that she found in him a literary model for facing the possibility of an early death. For Newell's literary executors and publishers, *The Remains of Henry Kirke White* perhaps provided another model, where literary remains take on a monumentalizing function to present a life cut short in all the fullness of its promise. Like the *Remains of Henry Kirke White*, the *Memoirs of Mrs. Harriet Newell* quickly became a bestseller, and it is no accident that the first American publisher of the *Memoirs*, Samuel T. Armstrong of Boston, also brought out an edition of the *Remains* in 1815. Three years after her death, Harriet Newell would have found herself appearing with Kirke White in the same shop window, two evangelical writers who died tragically young.

Conclusion

Comparing these different but strangely complementary texts, we find in them strikingly similar portraits of British India, which functions more as a place of speculation and self-realization than one of cultural discovery or encounter. Placing them side by side also provides a timely corrective to our own ingrained habits of reading, which too often have pigeonholed Fay as colonial adventurer and Newell as dissenting martyr. Framed this way, both Fay and Newell have been strangely disconnected from the generative tradition and genre of travel writing that in fact propels their work. British India was a space of possibility for these two women, and the popular market for travels created the space of possibility for their texts. To reread these very different accounts next to one another is to return both to the powerful tradition of experience, curiosity, and self-representation that is Romantic-era travel writing.

Looking to the reputation of each text, we find both writers again dehistoricized: the *Memoirs* read as exemplary hagiography, the *Original Letters* as creditors' commodity. In the process, their experiences, as recorded in their own voices, become disconnected from the rich contexts each inhabited. These texts are also, it must be remembered, profoundly shaped by editorial intervention: Fay's executor selecting only those parts he considered most appealing to audiences in 1817, and disregarding the rest; Harriet Newell's grieving husband Samuel literally creating the fiction of the 'Memoir' out of her teenage diaries and letters. If we are frustrated by learning of the 'missing' Fay manuscripts, we are – and should be – made doubly uncomfortable about reading the private diaries of the teenage Harriet Newell. We cannot know, after all, whether she gave permission for her writing to be circulated, let alone published. As a result, we must make distinctions between the private journal entries that dominate the early section and the more public, family letters that constitute the latter part. Such considerations remind us that travel writing always comes accompanied by other movements, whether religious or imperial.

Fay and Newell never met, although they might well have in 1812 if Fay had returned a little earlier to Calcutta: Newell just nineteen, alighting for the first time on the banks of the Hooghly; Fay in her late fifties, in a city she had called home at five different periods of her life. But there are remarkable resonances between the two women's lives, and they might have recognized in each other a shared determination and strength in the way each pursued her own journey. Newell and Fay died in India within four years of each other, their letters and memoirs appearing in the same period of rapid global change. Their tales twist around one another personally and historically, both strangely shaped by the same global and regional forces at the turn of the nineteenth century: war between America, Britain, and France; the contraction of the Ottoman and Mughal Empires; the rapid growth of the British in India; and the lucrative patterns of trade that linked people and communities across the world.

Notes

1 D. Hopkins, *The Dangers of British India, from French Invasion and Missionary Establishments* (London: Black, Parry, and Kingsbury, 1809), p. 51.
2 Hopkins, *The Dangers of British India*, p. 51.
3 See P. D. Rasico, 'Calcutta "In These Degenerate Days": The Daniells' Visions of Life, Death and Nabobery in Late Eighteenth-Century British India', *Journal for Eighteenth-Century Studies* 42:1 (2019), pp. 27–47.
4 Rev. W. K. Firminger, 'Introduction', in *Original Letters from India* (Calcutta: Thacker, Spink & Co, 1908), pp. vi–vii.
5 See K. Chancey, 'The Star in the East: The Controversy over Christian Missions to India, 1805–1813', *The Historian* 60:3 (March 1998), pp. 507–22.
6 Chancey, 'The Star in the East', p. 508.
7 See R. Said, 'George Baldwin and British Interests in Egypt 1775 to 1798', Unpublished Doctoral Thesis (University of London, June 1968).
8 See N. Gupta-Casale, 'Intrepid Traveller, "She-Merchant", or Colonialist Historiographer: Reading Eliza Fay's *Original Letters*', in S. Towheed (ed.), *New Readings in the Literature of British India, c. 1780–2014* (Stuttgart: Ibidem, 2007), pp. 65–91.
9 See M. W. Khan, 'Enlightenment Orientalism to Modernist Orientalism: The Archive of Forster's *A Passage to India*', *Modern Fiction Studies* 62 (2016), pp. 217–35.
10 Firminger, 'Introduction', p. 5.
11 F. Bickley, 'Review of [Eliza Fay's] *Original Letters from India*', *Bookman* (September 1925), p. 304.
12 The Kaye and Winchester editions are both based on the 1925 Forster edition, but with new introductions and additional notes. See M. M. Kaye (ed.), *Eliza Fay: Original Letters from India* (London: Hogarth Press, 1986); S. Winchester (ed.), *Eliza Fay: Original Letters from India* (New York: New York Review Books, 2010).
13 J. S. Pond, *Bradford: A New England Academy* (Bradford, MA: Bradford Academy Alumni Association, 1930), p. 71.
14 See Pond, *Bradford*, pp. 7–8.
15 *The Connecticut Evangelical Magazine and Religious Intelligencer* 3 (1810), p. 345.
16 *The Connecticut Evangelical Magazine and Religious Intelligencer* 3 (1810), p. 346.
17 See, among other publications, *The Connecticut Evangelical Magazine and Religious Intelligencer* 3 (1810), pp. 345–6; 4 (1811), pp. 419–27; 5 (1812), pp. 120 and 264; 5 (1812), pp. 461–71; 6 (1813), pp. 110–15, 232–9, and 350–7. See also *The Advisor, or Vermont Evangelical Magazine* 2 (1810), p. 351 and p. 353; 3 (1811), pp. 152–3, 344–5, and 374–5; 5 (1813), pp. 87–92, 147–50, 347–51; *The Evangelical Magazine and Missionary Chronicle* 22 (1814), 198–201 and 221–3; and *The Panoplist and Missionary Magazine United*, new series 4 (1812), pp. 179–83 and 425–31; 5 (1813), pp. 225–43, 372–7, and 515–25.
18 See J. B. Gillespie, '"The Clear Leadings of Providence": Pious Memoirs and the Problems of Self-Realization for Women in the Early Nineteenth Century', *Journal of the Early Republic* 5:2 (Summer 1985), pp. 197–221; and C. Midgley, 'Can Women Be Missionaries? Envisioning Female Agency in the Early Nineteenth-Century British Empire', *Journal of British Studies* 45:2 (2006), pp. 335–58.
19 See M. K. Cayton, 'Harriet Newell's Story: Women, the Evangelical Press, and the Foreign Mission Movement', in R. A. Gross and M. Kelley (eds), *A History of the Book in America, Volume 2: An Extensive Republic: Print, Culture, and Society in the New Nation, 1790–1840*

(Chapel Hill, NC: University of North Carolina Press, 2010), pp. 408–16; and M. K. Cayton, 'Canonizing Harriet Newell: Women, the Evangelical Press, and the Foreign Mission Movement in New England, 1800–1840', in B. Reeves-Ellington, K. K. Sklar, and C. A. Shemo (eds), *Competing Kingdoms: Women, Mission, Nation, and the American Protestant Empire, 1812–1960* (Durham, NC: Duke University Press, 2010), pp. 69–93.

HARRIET NEWELL,
MEMOIRS OF MRS. HARRIET NEWELL (1815)

Born in Haverhill, Massachusetts, Harriet Atwood (1793–1812) was one of nine children of Moses Atwood and Mary Tenney. Thoughtful and well-educated by the standards of her time, she was profoundly shaped by the wave of religious feeling usually called the Second Great Awakening. In Haverhill, this spirit of religious renewal came in the form of Abraham Burnham, a Congregationalist minister appointed as a preceptor at Bradford Academy, just across the river from Haverhill, in 1805. Newell attended Bradford between 1807 and 1810, where she received an education that was not only superior to the vast majority of American women, but that also stressed the importance of religious seriousness, practice, and action.

It was through the romance of her close friend Nancy ('Ann') Hasseltine with a student of Andover Theological Seminary, Adoniram Judson, that Harriet Atwood first began to entertain the idea of missionary service. Judson was part of a group of students and ministers calling themselves 'the Haystack Brethren', several of whom (including Harriet Atwood's future husband, Samuel Newell) appeared in 1810 before the Congregationalists' General Association petitioning for support to do missionary work abroad. They were received enthusiastically, and their testimony contributed to the formation of the American Board of Commissioners for Foreign Missions. By 1812 things had moved quickly: Adoniram Judson had convinced Ann Hasseltine to marry him and join him as a missionary in the East Indies; and Hasseltine's decision had inspired Harriet Atwood to consider, and accept, at the age of nineteen, similar proposals to become the wife of Samuel Newell.

Harriet Atwood Newell set sail in the *Caravan* with her fellow missionaries on 19 February 1812; she sighted land 114 days later on 12 June and reached Calcutta (Kolkata) a few days later. She arrived at the last destination, however, in a particularly fraught political situation. The British East India Company was strongly opposed to missions, fearing that they would interfere with its burgeoning opium trade. There was also the prospect of imminent war between the United States and Britain, which rendered the newly arrived missionaries suspected spies and potential enemy combatants. It is hardly surprising, then, that the Newells quickly accepted an invitation to join William Carey, the official English Baptist missionary, at his home in Serampore (a Danish-controlled settlement). There they remained until mid-July, when they were officially ordered to leave the British territories. Not wishing to return to America, Samuel Newell negotiated a passage to the Isle of France (Mauritius) to organize a mission there. In an advanced state of pregnancy, Harriet became ill during the voyage. She gave birth prematurely to a daughter, who died shortly thereafter of exposure caused by a violent storm. Harriet died two weeks later, perhaps from sepsis brought on by childbirth in difficult conditions.

The first American missionary to die overseas, Harriet Newell could not have foreseen her own posthumous fame or the popularity of her correspondence. While periodicals like *The Advisor* and *The Connecticut Evangelical Magazine and Religious Intelligencer* reported on the mission at every stage, publishing letters by Judson and other members as they were received from India, extracts from Harriet Newell's correspondence and journal did not appear until June 1813, approximately eight months after her death. Whether Harriet Newell gave her permission for the extracts to be published is unclear. Published into the same religious fervour from which she came, their popularity was instantaneous, her premature death transforming her writings into hagiography.

On her death Samuel Newell began editing and arranging her papers, which were published with a commemorative sermon as *A sermon preached at Haverhill (Mass.) in remembrance of Mrs. Harriet Newell, wife of the Rev. Samuel Newell, missionary to India . . . To which are added Memoirs of her life* (Boston: Samuel T. Armstrong, 1814). Over the next three decades at least twelve additional American printings appeared, including separate Andover, New York, Utica, Baltimore, Exeter, Lexington, and Philadelphia editions. Within a year of its initial publication, a London piracy had appeared, British copyright law allowing for any foreign work to be reprinted in the United Kingdom without permission. By 1840 there existed in Britain at least thirty additional printings of the *Memoirs*, including competing London imprints and multiple Edinburgh, Bristol, and Dublin editions.

Our edition takes its copy text from the first London edition, *Memoirs of Mrs. Harriet Newell . . . To which is added A Sermon, on Occasion of her Death, Preached at Haverhill, Massachusetts* (London: Booth and Co., 1815), which corrects several errors of typography in the American edition and reverses the order of the texts, printing the sermon as an appendix.

MEMOIRS

OF

Mrs. Harriet Newell,

WIFE OF THE

Rev. SAMUEL NEWELL,

AMERICAN MISSIONARY TO INDIA.

WHO DIED at the ISLE OF FRANCE, Nov. 30, 1812,

AGED NINETEEN YEARS.

TO WHICH IS ADDED

A SERMON,

ON OCCASION OF HER DEATH,

PREACHED AT HAVERHILL, MASSACHUSETTS.

BY LEONARD WOODS, D. D.

Abbot Professor of Christian Theology in the Theol. Sem. Advover.

" God has permitted her to be the first Martyr to the Missionary cause, from the American world. The publication of her virtues will quicken and edify thousands; and hence-forth, every one who remembers Harriet Newell, will remember the foreign Mission from America."—Vide *Funeral Discourse.*

LONDON:

PUBLISHED BY BOOTH AND CO.

Duke-street, Manchester-square.

And sold by Williams and Son, Stationer's Court; Button, Paternoster-row; Ogle and Co. Holborn and Paternoster-row; Burton and Briggs, Leadenhall-street; Blanshard, City-road; and Nisbet, Castle-street, Oxford-street.

1815.

Printed by Paris and Cowell, 19, Great New-street, Fetter-lane.

PREFACE

TO

THE ENGLISH EDITION.

THE present Work was brought from America before the ratification of the late Treaty of Peace,[1] by a much esteemed friend now in a distant part of the kingdom, and with no view to re-publication. It is not possible, however, to read it, without feeling that it is worthy of extensive circulation; and that the sentiments and events which it narrates are such as must deeply interest every Christian heart. It has, therefore, been put to press; and as the friend to whom I advert, was already employed in writing a work for publication, which engrossed the whole of his leisure, he requested me to undertake the care of preparing it for the eye of the British public. This explanation involves all the interest I have in the present work.

When I was solicited to undertake the charge of editing it, it was under the conviction that in a work printed in America, there might possibly occur some things which would invite explanation; but on perusing the piece now offered to the public, there did not appear any strict necessity for remarks of this kind. Not a few readers will perhaps be of opinion, indeed, that there was room for abridgment; but though I myself coincide in this opinion, with regard to Mrs. Newell's Diary, before she was called to Missionary labours, and with reference to some of her letters, (in which, as she wrote to various friends, there is an occasional repetition of the same facts,) yet I concluded it would be more satisfactory on the whole, to the public at large, to have the work in its unabridged state. It is therefore to be understood, that this impression is an unvarnished transcript of that which was published in America, (with the exception, that here the Memoir takes precedence of the Sermon, which in the New York Edition occupies the *first* pages.) It was proposed to prefix some account of the Society, under whose sanction Mr. and Mrs. Newell went out, as well as any information respecting Mr. Newell, which might have been subsequently received; but the enquiries made respecting these particulars were not successful. They may probably appear in a subsequent Edition, and in the mean time, any communication connected with them will be gratefully received.

The amiable character to whose memory these pages are dedicated, will not be unwept or unlamented by British Christians: every feeling heart must be affected by the recital of her sufferings. The former part of her Diary, which was written before she was summoned to Missionary labours, has indeed little to distinguish it from the experience of believers in general; unless it be in the direction which her mind took towards Missions and the Heathen, before she became acquainted with Mr. Newell. No sooner, however, does she dedicate herself to this arduous employment, but from the affectionate associations formed in a reader's mind, the interesting situation in which we behold her placed, and the feeling and wisdom with which she speaks and acts, her Diary and Letters seem to acquire a new and affecting character. But of this narrative there is no part so deeply touching as the Letter addressed by Mr. Newell to his mother. Hard, indeed, must that heart be, that can remain unmoved when this is perused.

In the former part of this Preface, mention was made of the Friend to whom the British Public are more immediately indebted for the publication of this piece. It was the Reverend Joshua Marsden,[2] who brought it from America. He himself has borne the sacred appellation of *Missionary;* and with the appellation, has deeply participated of those trials and perils which checquer the life of a Missionary in a foreign land. For a period of *eight* years he successfully laboured in that "climate of cold" Nova Scotia. He has preached the Gospel on the Shores of the Gulph of St. Lawrence, on the Bay of Fundy, and on the rivers and lakes of New Brunswick; and when his constitution had received a shock there, and he had requested permission of the British Methodist Conference to return home; he was unexpectedly solicited by the Missionary Committee in London to undertake a very painful Mission to the Bermudas, and to succeed one who had been fined, imprisoned, and eventually banished the island for preaching the Gospel. "Mr. Marsden's prospects here were at first truly distressing; but faith, patience, and prayer, opened a glimmering of better times: a hope, which after a short season, was abundantly realized."[3] He continued there nearly *four* years: when returning home to England by the way of America, he was detained prisoner in the United States, during an additional period of two years.

This statement is not made with a view merely to eulogize his character. If his labours and his sufferings are registered in the archives of Heaven, it is enough for him: he seeks no praise but that which might have "blossomed in the garden of Eden." It however affords me pleasure to add, that amid the fatigues which he endured, he was not an idle spectator of what passed around him; and he is now engaged in writing a *Narrative* of his interesting Mission, accompanied with strictures on the climate, productions, natural curiosities, &c. of those comparatively unknown regions where he laboured; subjects to which his long residence there, as well as the resources of his own mind render him so capable of doing justice. During Mr. Marsden's late stay in London, I was favoured with the perusal of part of the MS. and I feel no doubt that the work will greatly interest the attention of the Christian World.

WILLIAM JAQUES.[4]

ADVERTISEMENT

TO THE

AMERICAN EDITION.

―――

THE following Memoirs of Mrs. NEWELL, are derived almost entirely from her own writings. Nothing has been added but what seemed absolutely necessary, to give the reader a general view of her character, and to explain some particular occurrences, in which she was concerned. These memoirs contain only a part of her letters and journal.[5] The whole would have made a large volume. The labour of the compiler has been to select, and occasionally, especially in her earlier writings, to abridge. The letters and journal of this unambitious, delicate female, would have been kept within the circle of her particular friends, had not the closing scenes of her life, and the Missionary zeal, which has recently been kindled in this country, excited in the public mind a lively interest in her character, and given the christian community a kind of property in the productions of her pen. It was thought best to arrange her writings according to the order of time; so that, in a connected series of letters, and extracts from her Diary, the reader might be under advantages to observe the progress of her mind, the developement of her moral worth, and some of the most important events of her life.

MEMOIRS

OF

MRS. HARRIET NEWELL.

THE subject of these memoirs was a daughter of Mr. MOSES ATWOOD, a merchant of HAVERHILL, MASSACHUSETTS, and was born Oct. 10, 1793. She was naturally cheerful and unreserved; possessed a lively imagination and great sensibility; and early discovered a retentive memory and a taste for reading. Long will she be remembered as a dutiful child and an affectionate sister.

She manifested no peculiar and lasting seriousness before the year 1806. In the summer of that year, while at the Academy in Bradford,[6] a place highly favoured of the Lord, she first became the subject of those deep religious impressions, which laid the foundation of her christian life. With several of her companions in study, she was roused to attend to the one thing needful. They turned off their eyes from beholding vanity, and employed their leisure in searching the Scriptures, and listening to the instructions of those who were able to direct them in the way of life. A few extracts from letters, which she wrote to Miss L. K. of Bradford, will, in some measure, show the state of her mind at that time.

1806.

Dear L. I NEED your kind instructions now as much as ever. I should be willing to leave every thing for God; willing to be called by any name which tongue can utter, and to undergo any sufferings, if it would but make me humble, and be for his glory. Do advise me what I shall do for his glory. I care not for myself. Though he lay ever so much upon me, I would be content. Oh, could I but recal this summer!— But it is past, never to return. I have one constant companion, the BIBLE, from which I derive the greatest comfort. *This* I intend for the future shall guide me.

"—— Did you ever read Doddridge's Sermons to Young People?[7] They are very beautiful sermons. It appears strange to me, why I am not more interested in the cause of Christ, when he has done so much for us! But I *will* form a resolution that I will give myself up entirely to him. Pray for me, that my heart may be changed. I long for the happy hour when we shall be free from all sin, and enjoy God in heaven.

But if it would be for his glory, I should be willing to live my threescore years and ten. My heart bleeds for our companions, who are on the brink of destruction. In what manner shall I speak to them? But perhaps I am in the same way."

In another letter to the same friend, she says,—"What did Paul and Silas say to the jailor?[8] *Believe in the Lord Jesus Christ, and thou shalt be saved.* Let us do the same. Let us improve the accepted time, and make our peace with God. This day, my L. I have formed a resolution, that I will devote the remainder of my life entirely to the service of my God.—Write to me. Tell me my numerous *outward* faults; though you know not the faults of my heart, yet tell me all you know, that I may improve. I shall receive it as a token of love."

THE FOLLOWING SUMMARY ACCOUNT OF HER
RELIGIOUS EXERCISES WAS FOUND AMONG
HER PRIVATE PAPERS.

DIARY.

"A REVIEW of past religious experience I have often found useful and encouraging. On this account I have written down the exercises of my mind, hoping that, by frequently reading them, I may be led to adore the riches of sovereign grace, praise the Lord for his former kindness to me, and feel encouraged to persevere in a holy life.

"The first ten years of my life were spent in vanity. I was entirely ignorant of the depravity of my heart. The summer that I entered my eleventh year, I attended a dancing school.[9] My conscience would sometimes tell me, that my time was foolishly spent; and though I had never heard it intimated that such amusements were criminal, yet I could not rest, until I had solemnly determined that, when the school closed, I would immediately become religious. But these resolutions were not carried into effect. Although I attended every day to secret prayer, and read the Bible with greater attention than before; yet I soon became weary of these exercises, and, by degrees, omitted entirely the duties of the closet. When I entered my thirteenth year, I was sent by my parents to the Academy at Bradford. A revival of religion commenced in the neighbourhood,[10] which, in a short time, spread into the school. A large number of the young ladies were anxiously inquiring, what they should do to inherit eternal life. I began to inquire, what can these things mean? My attention was solemnly called to the concerns of my immortal soul. I was a stranger to hope; and I feared the ridicule of my gay companions. My heart was opposed to the character of God; and I felt that, if I continued an enemy to his government, I must eternally perish. My convictions of sin were not so pungent and distressing, as many have had; but they were of long continuance. It was more than three months, before I was brought to cast my soul on the Saviour of sinners; and rely on him alone for salvation. The ecstacies, which many new-born souls possess, were not mine. But if I was not lost in raptures on reflecting upon what I had escaped; I was filled with a sweet peace, a heavenly calmness, which I never can describe. The honours, applauses, and titles of this vain world, appeared like trifles light as air. The character of Jesus appeared infinitely lovely, and I could say with the Psalmist, *Whom have I in heaven but thee; and there is none on earth I desire besides thee.*[11] The awful gulf, I had escaped, filled me with astonishment. My gay associates were renounced, and the friends of Jesus became *my* dear friends. The destitute, broken state of the church at Haverhill[12] prevented me from openly professing my faith in Jesus; but it was a privilege, which I longed to enjoy. But, alas! these seasons so precious did not long continue. Soon was I led to exclaim,—Oh, that I were as in months past! My zeal for the cause of religion almost entirely abated; while this vain world engrossed my affections, which had been consecrated to my Redeemer. My Bible, once so lovely, was entirely neglected. Novels and romances engaged my thoughts, and hour after hour was foolishly and sinfully spent in the perusal of them. The company of Christians became, by degrees, irksome and unpleasant. I endeavoured to shun them. The voice of conscience would frequently whisper, "all is not right." Many a sleepless night have I passed after a day of vanity and sin. But such conflicts did not bring me home to the fold, from which, like a stray lamb, I had wandered far away. A religion, which was intimately connected with the amusements of the world, and the friendship of those who are at enmity with God, would have suited well my depraved heart. But I knew that the religion of the gospel was vastly different. It exalts the Creator, while it humbles the creature in the dust.

"Such was my awful situation! I lived only to wound the cause of my ever blessed Saviour. Weep, O my soul! when contemplating and recording these sins of my youth. Be astonished at the long suffering of Jehovah![13]—How great a God is our God! The death of a beloved parent, and uncle, had but little effect on my hard heart. Though these afflictions moved my passions, they did not lead me to the Fountain of consolation. But God, who is rich in mercy, did not leave me here. He had prepared my heart to receive his grace; and he glorified the riches of his mercy, by carrying on the work. I was providentially invited to visit a friend in Newburyport. I complied with the invitation. The evening previous to my return home, I heard the Rev. Mr. Mac F. It was the 28th of June, 1809. How did the truths, which he delivered, sink deep into my inmost soul! My past transgressions rose like great mountains before me. The most poignant anguish seized my mind; my carnal security fled; and I felt myself a guilty transgressor, naked before a holy God. Mr. B. returned with me the next day to Haverhill. Never, no never, while memory retains her seat in my breast, shall I forget the affectionate manner, in which he addressed me. His conversation had the desired effect. I then made the solemn resolution, as I trust, in the strength of Jesus, that I would make a sincere dedication of my all to my Creator, both for time and eternity. This resolution produced a calm serenity and composure, to which I had long been a stranger. How lovely the way of salvation then appeared!—Oh, how lovely was the character of the Saviour! The duty of professing publicly on which side I was, now was impressed on my mind. I came forward, and offered myself to the church; was accepted; received into communion; and commemorated, for the first time, the dying love of the blessed Jesus, August 6th, 1809. This was a precious season, long to be remembered!—Oh, the depths of sovereign grace! Eternity will be too short to celebrate the perfections of God.

August 27th, 1809.   HARRIET ATWOOD."

1806.

Sept. 1. A large number of my companions of both sexes, with whom I have associated this summer, are in deep distress for their immortal souls. Many, who were formerly gay and thoughtless, are now in tears, anxiously inquiring, what they shall do to be saved. Oh, how rich is the mercy of Jesus! He dispenses his favours to whom he pleases, without regard to age or sex. Surely it is a wonderful display of the sovereignty of God, to make me a subject of his kingdom, while many of my companions, far more amiable than I am, are left to grovel in the dust, or to mourn their wretched condition, without one gleam of hope.

Sept. 4. I have just parted with my companions, with whom I have spent three months at the academy. I have felt a strong attachment to many of them, particularly to those, who have been hopefully renewed the summer past. But the idea of meeting them in heaven, never more to bid them farewell, silenced every painful thought.

Sept. 10. Been indulged with the privilege of visiting a christian friend this afternoon. Sweet indeed to my heart, is the society of the friends of Immanuel. I never knew true joy until I found it in the exercise of religion.

Sept. 18. How great are the changes which take place in my mind in the course of one short day! I have felt deeply distressed for the depravity of my heart, and have been ready to despair of the mercy of God. But the light of divine truth, has this evening irradiated my soul, and I have enjoyed such composure as I never knew before.

Sept. 20. This has been a happy day to me. When conversing with a Christian friend upon the love of Jesus, I was lost in raptures. My soul rejoiced in the Lord, and joyed in the God of my salvation. A sermon preached by Mr. M. this evening has increased my happiness. This is too much for me, a sinful worm of the dust, deserving only eternal punishment. Lord, it is enough.

Oct. 6. The day on which Christ arose from the dead has again returned. How shall I spend it? Oh, how the recollection of mispent Sabbaths, embitters every present enjoyment. With pain do I remember the holy hours which were sinned away. Frequently did I repair to novels, to shorten the irksome hours as they passed. Why was I not cut off in the midst of *this* my wickedness?

Oct. 10. Oh, how much have I enjoyed of God this day! Such views of his holy character, such a desire to glorify his holy name, I never before experienced. Oh, that this frame might continue through life.

"My willing soul would stay
In such a frame as this,
And sit and sing herself away,
To everlasting bliss."[14]

This is my birth day. Thirteen years of my short life have gone for ever.

Oct. 25. Permitted by my heavenly Father once more to hear the gospel's joyful sound. I have enjoyed greater happiness than tongue can describe. I have indeed been joyful in the house of prayer. Lord let me dwell in thy presence for ever.

Nov. 2. How wonderful is the superabounding grace of God![15] Called at an early age to reflect upon my lost condition, and to accept of the terms of salvation, how great are my obligations to live a holy life.

Nov. 4. Examination at the Academy. The young ladies to be separated, perhaps, for life. Oh, how affecting the scene! I have bid my companious farewell. Though they are endeared to me by the strongest ties of affection, yet I must be separated from them, perhaps never to meet them more, till the resurrection. The season has been remarkable for religious impressions. But the harvest is past, the summer is ended, and there are numbers who can say, *we are not saved.*

Nov. 25. A dear Christian sister called on me this afternoon. Her pious conversation produced a solemn but pleasing effect upon my mind. Shall I ever be so unspeakably happy as to enjoy the society of holy beings in heaven?

"Oh, to grace how great a debtor!"[16]

Dec. 3. I have had great discoveries of the wickedness of my heart these three days past. But this evening, God has graciously revealed himself to me in the beauty and glory of his character. The Saviour provided for fallen man, is just such a one as I need. He is the one altogether lovely.

Dec. 7. With joy we welcome the morning of another Sabbath. Oh, let this holy day be consecrated entirely to God. My Sabbaths on earth will soon be ended; but I look forward with joy unutterable to that holy day, which will never have an end.

Dec. 8. This evening has been very pleasantly spent with my companions, H. and S. B. The attachment which commenced as it were in infancy, has been greatly strengthened since their minds have been religiously impressed. How differently are our evenings spent now, from what they formerly were! How many evenings have I spent with them in thoughtless vanity and giddy mirth. We have been united in the service of Satan; Oh, that we might now be united in the service of God!

Dec. 11. This morning has been devoted to the work of self-examination. Though I find within me an evil heart of unbelief, prone to depart from the living God, yet I have a hope, a strong, unwavering hope, which I would not renounce for worlds. Bless the Lord, Oh my soul, for this blessed assurance of eternal life.

Dec. 15. Grace, free grace is still my song. I am lost in wonder and admiration, when I reflect upon the dealings of God with me. When I meet with my associates, who are involved in nature's darkness, I am constrained to cry with the poet,

"Why was I made to hear thy voice,
  And enter while there's room;
While thousands make a wretched choice,
  And rather starve than come?"[17]

Dec. 31. This day has passed away rapidly and happily. Oh, the real bliss that I have enjoyed; such love to God, such a desire to glorify him, I never possessed before. The hour of sweet release will shortly come; Oh, what joyful tidings.

1807.

Jan. 3. A sweet and abiding sense of divine things, still reigns within. Bad health prevented my attending public worship this day. I have enjoyed an unspeakable calmness of mind and a heart burning with love to my exalted Saviour. Oh, how shall I find words to express the grateful feelings of my heart. Oh, for an angel's tongue to praise and exalt my Jesus.

Jan. 5. I have had exalted thoughts of the character of God this day. I have ardently longed to depart and be with Jesus.

Jan. 9. How large a share of peace and joy has been mine this evening. The society of Christians delights and animates my heart. Oh, how I love those who love my Redeemer.

March 25.[18] Humility has been the subject of my meditations this day. I find I have been greatly deficient in this Christian grace. Oh, for that meek and lowly spirit which Jesus exhibited in the days of his flesh.

March 25. Little E.'s birth day. Reading of those children who cried Hosanna to the Son of David, when he dwelt on earth, I ardently wished that this dear child might be sanctified. She is not too young to be made a subject of Immanuel's kingdom.[19]

May 1. Where is the cross which Christians speak of so frequently? All that I do for Jesus is pleasant. Though, perhaps, I am ridiculed by the gay and thoughtless for my choice of religion, yet the inward comfort which I enjoy, doubly compensates me for all this. I do not wish for the approbation and love of the world, neither for its splendour or riches. For one blest hour at God's right hand, I'll give them all away.

Extracts from a Letter to her sister M. at Byfield.[20]

Haverhill, August 26, 1807.

—"IN what an important station you are placed! The pupils committed to your care will be either adding to your condemnation in the eternal world, or increasing your everlasting happiness. At the awful tribunal of your Judge you will meet them, and there give an account of the manner in which you have instructed them. Have you given them that advice, which they greatly need? Have you instructed them in religion? Oh, my sister! how earnest, how engaged ought you to be, for their immortal welfare. Recollect the hour is drawing near, when you, and the young ladies committed to your care, must appear before God. If you have invited them to come to the Saviour, and make their peace with him, how happy will you then be! But on the other hand, if you have been negligent, awful will be your situation. May the God of peace be with you! May we meet on the right hand of God, and spend an eternity in rejoicing in his favours." –

HARRIET ATWOOD.

When HARRIET ATWOOD was a member of Bradford Academy, it was customary for her companions in study, whose minds were turned to religious subjects, to maintain a familiar correspondence with each other. A few specimens of the letters or billets, which HARRIET wrote to one of her particular friends at that time, will shew the nature of the correspondence.

To Miss F. W.[21] of Bradford Academy.

Bradford Academy, Sept. 1807.

As we are candidates for eternity, how careful ought we to be that religion be our principal concern. Perhaps this night our souls may be required of us—we may end our existence here, and enter the eternal world. Are we prepared to meet our Judge? Do we depend upon Christ's righteousness for acceptance? Are we convinced of our own sinfulness, and inability to help ourselves? Is Christ's love esteemed more by us, than the friendship of this world? Do we feel willing to take up our cross daily and follow Jesus? These questions, my dear Miss W. are important, and if we can answer them in the affirmative, we are prepared for God to require our souls of us when he pleases.

May the Spirit guide you, and an interest in the Saviour be given you! Adieu.

HARRIET.

Wednesday afternoon, 3 o'clock.

To the Same.

Bradford Academy, Sept. 11, 1807.

As heirs of immortality, one would naturally imagine we should strive to enter in at the strait gate, and use all our endeavours to be heirs of future happiness. But, alas! how infinitely short do we fall of the duty we owe to God, and to our own souls! O my friend, could you look into my heart, what could you there find but a sinful stupidity, and rebellion against God? But yet I dare to hope! O how surprising, how astonishing is the redemption which Christ has procured, whereby sinners may be reconciled to him, and through his merits dare to hope! O may his death animate us to a holy obedience.

H. A.

To the Same.

Bradford Academy, Sept. 1807.

How solemn, my dear Miss W. is the idea, that we must soon part! Solemn as it is, yet what is it, when compared with parting at the bar of God, and being separated through all eternity! Religion is worth our attention, and every moment of our lives ought to be devoted to its concerns. Time is short, but eternity is long;

and when we have once plunged into that fathomless abyss, our situation will never be altered. If we have served God here, and prepared for death, glorious will be our reward hereafter. But if we have not, and have hardened our hearts against the Lord, our day of grace will be past, and our souls irrecoverably lost. Oh then, let us press forward, and seek and serve the Lord here, that we may enjoy him hereafter. Favour me with frequent visits while we are together, and when we part, let epistolary visits[22] be constant. Adieu, yours, &c.

HARRIET.

A very frequent and affectionate correspondence was continued between Harriet Atwood and the same friend, after that young lady left the Academy and returned to Beverly, her place of residence.

To the same.

Haverhill, Oct. 12, 1807.

Once more, my dear Miss W. I take my pen and attempt writing a few lines to you. Shall religion be my theme? What other subject can I choose, that will be of any importance to our immortal souls? How little do we realize that we are probationers for eternity? We have entered upon an existence that will never end; and in the future world shall either enjoy happiness unspeakably great, or suffer misery in the extreme, to all eternity. We have every inducement to awake from the sleep of death, and to engage in the cause of Christ. In this time of awful declension,[23] God calls loudly upon us to enlist under his banners, and promote his glory in a sinful, stupid world. If we are brought from a state of darkness into God's marvellous light, and we are turned from Satan to the Redeemer, how thankful ought we to be. Thousands of our age are at this present period going on in thoughtless security; and why are we not left? It is of God's infinite mercy and free unbounded grace. Can we not with our whole hearts bow before the King of kings, and say, "not unto us, not unto us, but to thy name be all the glory?"[24] Oh, my dear Miss W. why are our affections placed one moment upon this world, when the great things of religion are of such vast importance? Oh, that God would rend his heavens and come down, and awaken our stupid, drowsy senses. What great reason have I to complain of my awfully stubborn will, and mourn my unworthy treatment of the Son of God? Thou alone, dear Jesus, canst soften the heart of stone, and bow the will to thy holy sceptre. Display thy power in our hearts, and make us fit subjects for thy kingdom above.

How happy did I feel when I read your affectionate epistle; and that happiness was doubly increased, when you observed that you should, on the sabbath succeeding, be engaged in the solemn transaction of giving yourself to God, publicly in an everlasting covenant.[25] My sincere desire and earnest prayer at the throne of grace shall ever be, that you may adorn the profession which you have made, and become an advocate for the religion of Jesus.

Let us obey the solemn admonitions we daily receive, and prepare to meet our God. May the glorious and and blessed Redeemer, who can reconcile rebellious mortals to himself, make us both holy, that we may be happy. Write soon and often. I am yours affectionately,

HARRIET ATWOOD.

To the Same.

Haverhill, Dec. 2, 1807.

MOST sincerely do I thank you, my dear Miss W. for your kind and affectionate epistle, which you last favoured me with. Are religion and the concerns of futurity still the object of your attention? New scenes daily open to us, and there is the greatest reason to fear that some of us will fall short at last of an interest in Jesus Christ. A few more rising and setting suns, and we shall be called to give an account to our final Judge, of the manner in which we have improved our probationary state; then, then, the religion which we profess,—will it stand the test? Oh, let us with the greatest care, examine ourselves, and see if our religion will cover us from the storms of divine wrath;—whether our chief desire is to glorify God, to honour his cause, and to become entirely devoted to him. What a word is ETERNITY! Let us reflect upon it; although we cannot penetrate into its unsearchable depths; yet, perhaps, it may have an impressive weight upon our minds, and lead us to a constant preparation for that hour, when we shall enter the confines of that state, and be either happy or miserable through an endless duration.

Last evening I attended a conference[26] at Mr. H's. Mr. B. addressed us from these words, "I pray thee have me excused."[27] His design was to shew what excuses the unconverted person will make for not attending to the calls of religion. It was the most solemn conference I ever heard. Oh! my friend, of what infinite importance is it, that we be faithful in the cause of our Master, and use all our endeavours to glorify him, the short space of time we have to live on earth. Oh! may we so live, that when we are called to enter the eternal world, we may with satisfaction give up our accounts, and go where we can behold the King in his glory. We have every thing to engage us in the concerns of our immortal souls. If we will but accept of Christ Jesus as he is freely offered to us in the gospel, committing ourselves unreservedly into his hands, all will be ours; life and death, things present and things to come. We should desire to be holy as God is holy. And in some degree we must be holy, even as he is, or we never can enter that holy habitation where Jesus dwells.

Oh! my dear Miss W. I cannot but hope that you are now engaged for Christ, and are determined not to let this world any longer engross your attention. Be constant in prayer. Pray that your friend Harriet may no longer be so stupid and inattentive to the great concerns of religion. Pray that she may be aroused from this lethargic state and attend to Christ's call. With reluctance I bid you adieu, my dear Miss W. Do favour me with a long epistle; tell me your feelings; how you view the character of God in the atonement for sinners. May we have a part in that purchase! Remember your friend,

HARRIET.

To Miss F. W. of Beverly.

Haverhill, Feb. 13, 1808.

ACCEPT, my dear Miss W. my sincere thanks for your epistle. Your ideas of the necessity of religion in the last extremity of expiring nature, perfectly coincide with mine. Yes, although we may reject the Saviour, and become engaged in the concerns of this vain and wicked world; although while in youth and health, we may live as though this world were our home; yet, when the hour of dissolution shall draw near, when eternity shall be unfolded to our view, what at that trying moment will be our consolation, but an assurance of pardoned guilt, and an interest in the merits of Christ the Redeemer? We are now probationers for a never-ending state of existence, and are forming characters, upon which our future happiness or misery depends. Oh, if we could only have a sense of these all important considerations!—How criminally stupid are we, when we know that these are eternal realities! Why are we not alive to God and our duty, and dead to sin? This world is a state of trials, a vale of tears, it is not our home. But an eternity of happiness or woe hangs on this inch of time. Soon will our state be unalterably fixed. Oh, let this solemn consideration have its proper weight on our minds, and let us now be wise for eternity.

How little are we engaged to promote the interest of religion! At this day, when the love of many waxeth cold,[28] and iniquity increaseth, how ought every faculty of our souls to be alive to God.

Do write often, and perhaps, the blessing of an all-wise God may attend your epistles. In your earnest supplications at the throne of almighty grace, remember your affectionate, though unworthy friend,

HARRIET.

P. S. I long to see you, and unfold to you the inmost recesses of my heart. Do make it convenient to visit H.[29] this spring, and although it may be unpleasing to you to hear the wickedness of your friend Harriet's heart, yet perhaps you, my dear Miss W. can say something which will now make me resolve in earnest, that, let others serve whom they will, I will serve the Lord.

To the Same.

Haverhill, April 20, 1808.

THIS morning, my beloved Miss W. your kind epistle was handed me, in which you express a wish, that it might find me engaged in the cause of God. Oh, that your wish could be gratified! But let me tell you, I am still the same careless, inattentive creature—What in this world can we find capable of satisfying the desires of our immortal souls? Not one of the endowments, which are derived from any thing short of God, will avail us in the solemn and important hour of death. All the vanities, which the world terms accomplishments, will then appear of little value. Yes, my beloved companion, in that moment we shall find that nothing will suffice to hide the real nakedness of the natural mind, but the furnished robe, in which the child of God shines with purest lustre—the Saviour's righteousness. Oh, that we might, by the assistance of God, deck our souls with the all-perfect rule! Our souls are of infinite importance, and an eternity of misery, "where the worm dieth not, and the fire is not quenched,"[30] awaits us, if we do not attend to their concerns. I should be happy, my amiable friend, in visiting you this spring. But with reluctance I must decline your generous offer. A dear and beloved parent is in a declining state[31] of health, and we fear, if indulgent Heaven do not interpose, and stop the course of his sickness, death will deprive us of his society, and the grave open to receive him. Oh, that his life might be spared, and his health once more established, to cheer his family and friends! But in all these afflictive dispensations of God's providence, may it ever be my prayer, "not my will, O Lord! but thine be done."[32]

I do not expect to attend Bradford Academy this summer. We shall have a school in Haverhill, which, with my parents' consent, I expect to attend. Do visit me this spring, my dear Miss W. Your letters are always received with pleasure. My best wishes for your present and eternal happiness attend you.

I am yours, &c.   HARRIET.

To Miss C. P. of Newburyport.[33]

Dear C.   *Haverhill, Feb.* 16, 1808.[34]

SINCE you left us, death has entered our family,[35] and deprived us of an affectionate uncle. After lingering two days after you returned to your friends, he fell asleep, as we trust, in Jesus.

Oh, C. could you but have witnessed his dying struggles! Distress and anguish were his constant companions, till about ten minutes before his spirit winged its way to the eternal world; then he was deprived of speech; he looked upon us, closed his eyes, and expired. He would often say, 'Oh, how I long for the happy hour's approach, when I shall find a sweet release; but "not my will, but thine, O God, be done!"' When we stood weeping around his dying bed, he looked upon us and said, "Mourn not for me, my friends, but mourn for yourselves."[36] Oh my C. let us now be persuaded to lay hold on Jesus, as the only Saviour. If we trust in him for protection, he will preserve us in all the trying scenes of life, and when the hour of dissolution shall come, we shall be enabled to give ourselves to him, and consign our bodies to the tomb with pleasure.

What a world is this! full of anxiety and trouble! My dear father is very feeble; a bad cough attends him, which we fear will prove fatal. What a blessing my friend, are parents! Let us attend to their instructions and reproofs, while we possess them, that, when death shall separate us, we may have no cause for regret that we were undutiful. While we do every thing we can to make them happy, let us remember, that it is God alone can compensate them for their labours of love. Far distant be the hour when either of us shall be called to mourn the loss of our dear parents.

Do, my dear C. write to me; tell me if this world does not appear more and more trifling to you. May the sweet influences of the Holy Spirit be shed abroad in your heart. Oh, may happiness attend you in this vale of tears, and may you be conducted to the haven of eternal rest. Accept the wish of your ever affectionate

HARRIET.

To Miss C. P. of Newburyport.

Haverhill, April 24, 1808.

ACCEPT, my dear C. my kindest acknowledgments for your last affectionate epistle; in the perusal of which, I had the most pleasing sensations. You observed, your contemplations had frequently dwelt on those hours we spent in each others' society, while at Bradford Academy; and that you regretted the mis-improvement of them. Alas! how many hours have we spent in trifling conversation, which will avail us nothing. Let our imaginations often wing their way back to those hours, which can never be recalled.

> "Tis greatly wise, to talk with our past hours,
> And ask them what report they've borne to heaven,
> And how they might have borne more welcome news."[37]

Will the recollection of the moments that are now speeding their flight, afford satisfaction at the last? Oh, that we might improve our time and talents to the glory of God, that the review of them may be pleasing.

You ask me to write to you, and to write something that will awaken you from stupidity. I would, my dear C. but I am still in the same careless state.

My father still remains in a critical situation. Permit me to request an interest in your prayers for him; but be assured, there is none they will be more serviceable to, than your dear friend,

HARRIET.

To Miss F. W. of Beverly.

AFTER THE DEATH OF HER FATHER

Haverhill, May 24, 1808.

IN the late trying and afflictive scenes of God's providence, which I have been called to pass through, I have flattered myself, that the tenderest sympathy has been awakened in the heart of my beloved F. Oh my companion! this is a scene peculiarly trying to me. How much do my circumstances require every divine consolation and direction, to make this death a salutary warning to me. The guardian of my tender years, he who, under God, has been made an instrument in giving me existence, my father, my nearest earthly friend, where is he? The cold clods of the valley cover him, and the worms feed upon his cold and lifeless body. Can it be, that I am left fatherless? Heart-rending reflection! Oh my dear, dear Miss W. may you never be left to mourn the loss which I now experience! Oh, that your parents may be spared to you, and you ever honour them, and be a blessing to them, even in their declining years.

Glance a thought on *nine* fatherless children, and a widowed and afflicted mother. But if we are fatherless, Oh, may we never be friendless! May He who has promised to be the father of the fatherless, and the widow's God,[38] enable us to rely upon him, and receive grace to help in this time of need; and although the present affliction is not joyous, but grievous, Oh that it may be instrumental in working out a far more exceeding and eternal weight of glory.

Do come and see me—I long once more to embrace my friend, and to tell her what I owe her for all her favours. Adieu, my beloved Miss W. receive this as a token of renewed affection from your,

HARRIET.

Respects to your parents and love to sister N.

From some passages in the foregoing papers, and also from what follows, it appears, that during the year 1808, she was in a state of religious declension and darkness.[39] According to the statement of one who was competent to testify— "She appeared gradually to lose her fondness for retirement, and her delight in the Scriptures, and associated more freely with her former gay companions. But nothing was manifested, which afforded any just ground for suspecting her sincerity." What views she entertained of that state of declension, and by what means she was recovered to duty and comfort, will appear from some of the following letters and from her diary.

To Miss C. P. of Newburyport.

My dear C. *Haverhill, Feb.* 27, 1809.

WHAT have you been reading this winter? I presume you have had sufficient time to improve your mind in the study of history, &c. For my part, I know not what to say. A constant round of worldly engagements and occupations have, I fear, engrossed far too much of my time.

I have of late been quite interested in reading Miss Helen Maria Williams's Letters on the French Revolution,[40] and am now reading Rollin's Ancient History.[41] In the morning of life, when no perplexing cares interrupt or vex our minds, we should spend every moment of our time in improving our minds, by reading, or attending to conversation that is beneficial. Our time is short! Perhaps we may be cut off in the morning of our days. Oh that we might improve each moment of our lives, "And make each day a critic on the last."[42]

Adieu, I am, &c.   HARRIET.

1809.

July 1. God has been pleased in infinite mercy, again to call up my attention to eternal realities. After spending more than a year, in the vanities of the world—thoughtless and unconcerned respecting my eternal welfare, he has, as I humbly trust, showed me my awful backslidings from him, and my dependance upon his grace for every blessing.

I do now, in the strength of Jesus, *resolve*, that I will no longer sacrifice my immortal soul for what I have *hitherto* deemed my temporal happiness. Oh, that I might be enabled to come out from the world, and to profess Christ as my Redeemer before multitudes. I now see, that I have enjoyed no happiness in my pursuit of worldly pleasure. Not in the play-room, not in the vain and idle conversation of my companions, not in the bustle of a crowded life, have I found happiness. This heaven-born guest is found only in the bosom of the child of Jesus. How awfully aggravated will be my condemnation, if I do not, after this *second* call, awaken all my drowsy faculties, and become *earnestly* engaged for God.

July 10. How foolishly, how wickedly have I spent this day! What have I done for God? Nothing I fear. Oh, how many mispent days shall I have to answer for, at the tribunal of a holy Judge! Then how does it become me, to set a watch upon my behaviour; as one that must shortly give an account to God. Oh, thou blessed Jesus! grant thy assistance, that I may live as I ought.

July 16. *Sabbath morn*. Solemnly impressed with a sense of my duty to God, I entered his holy courts this morning. What am I, that I should be blessed with the gospel's joyful sound, while so many are now perishing in heathen darkness for lack of the knowledge of Christ.[43]

Sabbath eve. I have now offered myself to the Church of God, and have been assisted by him. Perhaps they will not receive me; but, O God! wilt *thou* accept me through a Mediator?

I have now let my companions see, I am not ashamed of Jesus. Oh, that I might not dishonour the cause I am about professing! In Christ *alone*, will I put my trust, and rely entirely on *his* righteousness for the pardon of my aggravated transgressions.[44]

July 17. Have spent the day at home. I think I have enjoyed something of God's presence. Felt a disposition frequently to call upon him by prayer and supplication.

July 18. At this late hour, when no one beholdeth me but God, how solemnly, how sincerely ought I to be engaged for him?

The family are retired to rest. The darkness and silence of the night, and the reflection, that the night of death will soon overtake me, conspire to solemnize my mind. What have I done this day for God? Have I lived as a stranger and pilgrim on the earth; as one that must soon leave this world, and "go the way from whence no traveller returns?"[45]

Oh that I were more engaged for God—more engaged to promote his cause, in the midst of a perverse generation!

July 20. This evening, I had a most solemn meeting with one of my dear and most intimate companions. I warned her in the most expressive language of my heart, to repent. She appeared affected. I left her; and after returning home, I trust, I was enabled to commend her to the God of infinite mercy, and to wrestle with him for her conviction and conversion.

July 22. Was informed that —— appeared serious and unusually affected. Oh, that God might work a work of grace in his heart, and enable him to resign all earthly vanities, for an interest in the great Redeemer. He has talents, which if abused, will only add to his everlasting condemnation. Oh, thou God of infinite mercy!—thou who hast had pity on *me*, show *him* mercy, and awaken him to a sense of his situation, before the things that concern his peace are hid for ever from his eyes.

July 30. *Sabbath day*. Arose this morning, but little impressed with a sense of the duties before me, upon this holy day. My health obliged me to decline going to the house of God, in the morning. But I think I could say, it was good for me to be afflicted. God was graciously pleased to assist me in calling upon his name, and permitted me to wrestle with him in prayer[46] for the prosperity of Zion,[47] and for the conversion of sinners. I felt a desire that every one of my friends might be brought to a knowledge of the truth. This afternoon I have attended meeting,[48] and heard a most excellent sermon, preached by Mr. W. from Matt. xxvi. 6–13.[49] He passed the Sabbath with us, and gave us excellent instructions. But of what use are advice and religious conversation to me, if I do not improve them as I ought? These instructions will rise up in judgment against me, and condemn me, if I am not, indeed, a child of God. Oh, for a heart to love God more, and live more to his glory! How can I hope to enter that heavenly rest, prepared for the people of Jesus, when I so often transgress his laws!

Aug. 6. *Lord's day morning*. Upon this sacred morning, Oh that the Holy Spirit of God would enliven and animate my cold and stupid affections. Oh, that I might this day enter his earthly courts, worship him in an acceptable manner, profess his name before a scoffing world, sit down at his table, and partake, in faith, of the body and blood of Jesus.

Sabbath eve. And now I have entered into the most solemn engagement to be the Lord's. I have confessed Christ before the world—I have renounced my wicked companions—I have solemnly promised, that denying ungodliness and every worldly lust, I will live soberly, righteously, and godly, in this present world. If I should, after taking these solemn vows and covenant engagements upon me, dishonour the cause of my Redeemer; if I should give the enemies of religion reason to say, there is nothing in religion; if I should again return to my former courses, Oh, how dreadfully aggravated will be my condemnation! What excuse could I render at the tribunal of a just Judge? My mouth would be stopped, and I should plead guilty before him. How then does it become me to watch and pray, lest the devices of Satan, the world, or my own remaining corruptions should lead me into temptation!

In thee, O God, do I put my trust! from thee do I hope to obtain mercy in the day of retribution!

Aug. 10. How stupid, how cold I grow! Where is that fervour, that zeal, that animation, I ought to have, after professing to know and receive Jesus, as my Redeemer? How alluring are the vanities of time! How prone my heart to wander from God! How ready to engage in the trifles of this wicked world! Descend, thou Holy Spirit: breathe into my soul a flame of ardent love; let not my affections wander from the *one* and *only* thing that is needful.

To Miss F. W. of Beverly.

Haverhill, August, 1809—*Sabbath morn.*

A FEW moments this sacred morning shall be devoted to my beloved Miss W. After discontinuing for so long a time our correspondence, I again address you. By the endearing title of a friend, I again attempt to lay open my heart before you. But what shall I say? Shall I tell you, that since I last saw you, I have made great progress in divine grace? To you, my ever dear friend, will I unbosom my heart; to you will I describe my feelings. Yes; I will tell you what GOD has done for my soul. About six weeks since he was pleased, in infinite mercy, again to call up my attention to the concerns of my soul; again to show me the evil of my ways. I have now publicly confessed my faith in him. I have taken the vows of the covenant upon me, and solemnly surrendered myself to him, eternally. Oh! Miss W. should I now be left to dishonour this holy cause, what would be my eternal condemnation? Oh! pray for me. Entreat God to have mercy upon me, and keep me from falling. After I left you at the Academy, I by degrees grew more and more neglectful of serious and eternal realities. When I review the past year of my life; when I reflect upon the wound I have brought upon the blessed religion of Jesus, I am constrained to cry, why has God extended his mercy to the vilest of the race of Adam? Why has he again showed favour to me, after I have so wickedly abused his precious invitations and grieved his Holy Spirit? It is a God, who is rich in mercy, abundant in goodness, and of great compassion, that has done these great things, as I trust, for me. How can I be too much engaged for him, too much conformed to his holy will, after these abundant manifestations of his love and mercy? Oh, that I could spend my few remaining days as I ought, even *entirely* devoted to the delightful service of the dear Redeemer.

Sabbath eve. I have just returned from the house of God, where I have heard two excellent sermons preached by our beloved pastor.[50] What unspeakable privileges we enjoy! The Gospel trump[51] is sounding in our ears; Jesus is proclaimed as "ready and willing to save all those that come unto God by him."[52] And why, my dear Miss W. are not these privileges taken from us, and given to the Heathen, who have never heard of a Saviour, and are perishing for lack of knowledge?[53] God is indulging us with them for wise and holy ends. And if we do not estimate them according to their real value, and improve under the calls and invitations of the Gospel, there will remain for us "no more sacrifice, but a fearful looking for of judgment and fiery indignation."[54] When sitting beneath the Gospel's joyful sound, I think I can never again be careless or inattentive to religious concerns. But how soon does the world intervene between God and my soul! How soon do the trifling vanities of time engross my affections. Oh, my dear friend! did you know the temptations with which I am surrounded, I am confident you would pity me, and intercede for me at the throne of grace. But I have this consolation—Jesus was tempted while on earth; he pities his tempted saints, and will surely enable them to persevere unto the end.

> "He knows what sore temptations mean,
> For he has felt the same."[55]

I long, dear Miss W. to see you. I long to converse with you on the great importance of being really children of God. I long for your assistance while wandering in this wilderness. I think, if I know my heart, I can say, I *do* love God and his children. If I do not love him, if I do not love his image whenever I see it, I know not what I love. Though Providence sees fit to separate us, yet let us be active in our endeavours to assist each other in our journey to the heavenly Canaan, by our letters and our prayers.

I have now opened to you my heart. Do write to me; do instruct me in the important doctrines of the Gospel. May your journey in this vale of tears be sweetened by the presence of the blessed Jesus! May you go on from strength to strength, and when you are released from this burden of clay, appear in the heavenly Jerusalem before God, and spend an eternity at his right hand, where is fulness of joy! Adieu.

I am yours, &c.   HARRIET ATWOOD.

1809.

Aug. 13. Again have I enjoyed sabbath and sanctuary privileges. But my heart—alas! how can I live in such dreadful stupidity! Awaken, O God, my drowsy powers! animate and warm these cold and languid affections! Why are not my privileges taken from me, and given to the Heathen?

Aug. 18. I have been this day in the company of some of my young and gay companions. Oh! why did I neglect, faithfully, to warn them of their danger, and entreat them to repent? How foolish, how trifling is the conversation of the children of this world! Give me but my BIBLE, and my *retirement;* and I would willingly surrender every thing else on earth.

Aug. 26. How fleeting are the days appointed to mortals! Another week has glided away. It becomes me to ask myself, have I lived to the glory of God? What have I done in the service of Him, who has done so much for me, even laid down his precious life, to redeem my soul? What answer does conscience make? Oh, that I could be enabled to come to that fountain[56] which is open for Judah and Jerusalem to wash in, and cleanse my soul from all pollution! The time, which ought to have been spent in the service of a holy God, has been trifled away in the vanities of a wicked world.

Aug. 27. Have again been indulged with sabbath and sanctuary privileges. The gospel trump has again sounded in my ears. Christians have been called to be more engaged in the cause of Jesus; and sinners have been affectionately urged to attend to the concerns of their never-dying souls.

Mr. D. addressed us from these words; "Wickedness proceedeth from the wicked."[57] Afternoon—"As we have therefore opportunity, let us do good unto all men."[58] He explained the various duties incumbent on Christians, whereby they might do good unto their fellow mortals. Let me examine my own heart. Have I done good, according to the ability with which God has blessed me, to the souls of my friends and acquaintance? How much reason have I to complain of my unfruitfulness; of my little engagedness in prayer! Awaken in me, O thou that hearest prayer! a disposition to cry, in earnest, for the salvation of souls. Oh, that I might realize the greatness of the privilege, with which the blessed Jehovah has indulged me, in giving me a throne of grace through the mediation of Jesus.

Aug. 28. I awoke last night, and spent a most delightful hour in contemplating divine truth. The words of David flowed sweetly through my mind, "In the multitude of my thoughts within me, thy comforts delight my soul."[59] Most willingly would I resign all earthly pleasures for *one* such hour in communion with my God.

Sept. 29. Mr. T. preached our preparatory lecture this afternoon. Text, "Jesus answered and said, my kingdom is not of this world."[60] Examined myself strictly by this question; Am I indeed a real member of Christ's kingdom? If I am, why are my affections so languid—my heart so cold—my desires so few for the enlargement of Christ's kingdom? Why is my heart so prone to leave God? Why am I so interested in the concerns of time and sense—and why are the important concerns of my soul so little regarded? Decide, dearest Jesus, the doubtful case! If I never yet have tasted and seen that thou art gracious, oh, let me now, before it be for ever too late!

Attended our conference this evening. I think I enjoyed what the world could neither give, nor take away.

Sept. 30. How inestimable the blessing of a sincere, a pious friend! Drank tea with Mrs. M. In the most friendly manner she spoke of my former conduct, and tenderly reproved me for an incident which occurred the past day. I acknowledged my fault, confessed my obligations to her for her advice, and sensibly felt the importance of watchfulness and prayer, that I might be kept from entering into temptation. May the review of my former life, serve to humble me in the dust before God, and make me more active than ever in his blessed service!

Oct. 1. The vanities of time have engaged too great a share of my affections. The concerns of my soul have been too much neglected. Oh, for the invigorating influences of the Holy Spirit, to animate my drowsy faculties! Time is short—this month, perhaps, may be my last. Have again been permitted to sit down at the table of the Lord. Oh, how unworthy am I of these precious privileges! Why am I suffered to enjoy them?

Have this day heard a most solemn discourse preached by Mr. D. from these words, "Unto you, Oh, men I call, and my voice is unto the sons of men."[61] He mentioned the dying exercises of a Mr. B. whose remains were committed to the tomb the Saturday preceding. His resignation to the Divine will was remarkable. In his dying moments, he warned his young companions of their danger, while out of Christ. May this solemn stroke of Providence be sanctified to the young people in this place! Oh, that God, in infinite mercy, would be pleased to bring it near *my* heart, and make it the means of weaning me from this world, and preparing me for the enjoyment of his celestial kingdom!

Oct. 7. Another week has rolled away, and my probationary existence is still lengthened out. But to what purpose do I live? Why am I supported in this world of *hope*, when I am daily transgressing the laws of a holy God, and grieving his blessed Spirit? Astonishing grace! Wonderful compassion, that still prolongs my days, after such rebellion! Spare me, Oh my God, spare me yet a little longer, and by thy grace enable me to do *some little* work in thy vineyard.

Oct. 12. Attended another of our conferences. But how stupid have I felt this evening! It is perfectly just that I should not have enjoyed the light of God's countenance; for I had no heart to ask him, to make the evening profitable to my *own* soul, or to the souls of *others*.

Prayer is the breath of the Christian; when that is omitted, farewell enjoyment.

To Miss F. W. of Beverly.

Haverhill, Oct. 12, 1809.

The pleasing sensations, dear Miss W. which your letter excited, can better be conceived than described. Your affectionate advice I sincerely thank you for. And Oh! that I might be enabled to follow it. But what shall I write you? Shall I tell you I grow in grace and in conformity to God? *Alas!* I still have reason to lament my awful stupidity, my distance from God, and in the language of the publican, to cry, "God be merciful to me a sinner."[62] "Laden with guilt, a heavy load;"[63] oppressed with the temptations of a subtle adversary, the world ever ready to call my affections, how can I be supported? But here, my friend, I find there is a way provided whereby God can be just and yet justify even me. In the redemption a Saviour has purchased there is an infinite fulness, sufficient to supply all our wants. On the precious mount of Calvary hangs all my hope. In his atoning blood, who suffered and died, my sins can be washed away; and however vile and loathsome in myself, in him I can find cleansing. What wonderful compassion is displayed in the plan of Salvation! That the Maker and Preserver of the universe having all things under his controul, should not spare even his own son, but deliver him up to die on the accursed tree, for mortals who had transgressed his law, and deserved eternal misery! This mystery of mysteries the angels desire to look into. That the *just* should endure the agonies of a painful and ignominious death for the *unjust*, is what we cannot comprehend. But my friend, *what* must be our situation to all eternity, if after such wonderful compassion, we should fall short of an interest in the death of Jesus? How awful must be the sentence that will be passed upon *us* who sit under the Gospel's joyful sound, if we slight the offers of salvation? Oh, may this never be our situation! But by unfeigned repentance and cordial submission to the blessed Redeemer, and by lives spent in his service, Oh, may we be prepared to join the society of the redeemed above!

Yesterday afternoon I attended a Lecture in the Academy at Bradford. The emotions which vibrated in my mind, while sitting in this seminary of learning, I cannot describe. Imagination recalled those scenes which I had witnessed in that place. That season was a precious one to many souls, when the Spirit of God moved among us, and compelled sinners to tremble and earnestly inquire what they should do to inherit eternal life. But those days are past. No more do I hear my companions exclaiming, "Who can dwell with devouring fire? Who can inherit everlasting burnings?"[64] No more do I hear souls, who for years have been under the bondage of sin, exclaim, "Come, and I will tell you what God hath done for me."[65] He has, I hope, "delivered me from the horrible pit and miry clay; has established my goings, and put a new song into my mouth, even praise to his name."[66] But under these general declensions from the truth of the Gospel, still "the Lord doeth all things well."[67] He will revive his work in his own time. He will repair the waste places of Zion, and sinners will again flock unto him as clouds, and as doves to their windows. And blessed be his name he makes his children the honoured instruments in building up his kingdom. Let us then, my dear Miss W. exert all our faculties to promote his cause. Let us warn sinners of their danger, and walk worthy of the vocation wherewith we are called. Wishing you the light of God's countenance, I bid you adieu.

HARRIET.

1809.

Oct. 19. Drank tea with mamma, at Mrs. C.'s. A conference there in the evening. Mr. D. paraphrased the Lord's prayer; and was enabled to wrestle fervently with his divine Master, for the revival of religion in this place. As for myself, I felt stupid,— could easily trace the cause of my feelings: Had no opportunity, this day, of pouring out my soul to God in prayer. My mother insisted on my accompanying her to Mrs. C.'s; I did, though with as great reluctance as I ever obeyed a command of hers.

I know by experience, that no opportunities for improvement do me any good, unless the divine blessing is previously requested.

> "Restraining prayer, we cease to fight,
> Prayer makes the Christian's armour bright:

> And Satan trembles, when he sees
> The weakest saint upon his knees."[68]

Oct. 21. This day, God, in infinite mercy, has seen fit to grant me near access to his mercy seat. I have been enabled to call upon his name, and to plead with him, for his spiritual Jerusalem. Oh, that he would hear and accept my feeble petitions, and answer them for his own name's sake!

Oct. 23. Have just returned from our reading-society;[69] and feel condemned for my gaiety and light conduct, before my companions. Have found nothing this evening to satisfy the desires of my soul. Greatly fear, that I have brought a wound upon the cause of the blessed Immanuel. Oh, that I might be enabled to glorify God, by my future devotedness to him.

Oct. 27. Two servants of Jesus Christ, called upon us this afternoon, Mr. W. and Mr. E.[70] Their conversation was very interesting and instructive. Mr. W. informed us of the serious attention that appeared to be commencing in A.[71] Oh, that Jehovah would pour down his Spirit there! Oh, that he would ride from conquering to conquer, and make, not only A. a place of his power, but *Haverhill* also! Arise, blessed Jesus! plead thine own cause, and have mercy upon Zion. Now when men are making void thy law, arise! build up thy spiritual Jerusalem, and let her no longer mourn, "because so few come to her solemn feasts."

Oct. 30. Have just returned from our reading-society. Have nothing to complain of this evening but my gaiety and lightness. Ramsay's History of Washington was introduced. The meeting very regular and orderly. Sincerely wish it might be the means of improving our minds in the knowledge of our *own*, and *other* countries. And Oh, that from a knowledge of the world which God has made, our minds might be led to the Creator!

Oct. 31. Have spent this day prayerless and stupid. Oh, that I were, "as in months past,"[72] when I felt a spirit of prayer, for the interest of Zion; for the salvation of immortal souls!

Nov. 6. Our reading society met this evening. Have just returned home:—find little or no satisfaction in the review.

Although the company were light and gay, I pitied them, and in my heart commended them to God. But I fear I countenanced them, and gave them reason to say of me, "what do you, more than others?"

Possessed naturally of such a rude and ungovernable disposition, I sometimes find it difficult to keep within proper bounds. Often does my heart condemn me for my trifling conduct; conscience reproaches; and frequently, I am led to the conclusion that I will no more leave the residence of my mother; have no more to do with the world, but seclude myself, and spend my few remaining days, *entirely* devoted to the Best of beings. But this will not be following the example of the blessed Jesus. No, while I am in the world, let it be my constant endeavour, to do all the good I can to my fellow mortals; to rise above its frowns and flatteries; and give no occasion for any reproach to be brought upon the cause of religion.

Nov. 8. My dear friend, and as I humbly trust my spiritual father, Mr. B. called upon us, a few moments.[73] He expects to preach for Mr. D. next Sabbath. On seeing him, I could not but recal the many different scenes that passed while under his instructions. But those scenes remain in remembrance *only*. No more, I hear my companions exclaiming, "What shall I do to inherit eternal life."[74] No more, I hear them telling to all around them, what the Redeemer has done for their souls. That was indeed a precious season to many, and will be remembered with joy to all eternity. But to some, the privileges of that season, will, I fear, be the means of sinking them lower in eternal torments!! Dreadful thought!

Nov. 12. This has indeed been a blessed day to my *soul*, though I have been afflicted with a severe pain in my head. Attended public worship; heard two solemn sermons from our dear friend Mr. B. What a striking instance is it, of the awful hardness of the heart, that when the terrors of the Almighty are set before mortals, and they are told by God's faithful servants, their awful situation, while unreconciled to the divine character, that it has so little effect upon them.

Nov. 13. A severe head-ache still attends me; but I desire to be submissive to the will of God, and bear without murmuring, whatever he sees fit to lay upon me. His ways are best: and he has graciously promised, "that all things shall work together for good to those that love him."[75] But do I love him? Have I that love to him, that will enable me to keep all his commandments? Do I love him with all my heart, having no rival in my affections? "Search me, Oh God, and know me;"[76] try me by thy Spirit, and lead me in the way of eternal life.

Nov. 16. Have just returned from singing school. Surrounded by my gay companions. I have found that I could place no dependance on my *own* strength; without the assistance of Jesus, I shall fall into temptation, and wound his cause.

To Miss C. F. of Boston.

Haverhill. Not dated.

PARDON, dearest C. the long silence of your friend Harriet. Although I have omitted answering your affectionate epistle, my heart has been often with you. Yes, C. often have I fancied seeing you, engaged to promote the cause of the blessed Immanuel, solemnly renouncing the vanities of an alluring world, and taking the decided part of a child of God. Oh, may you be enabled to follow on to know the Lord, and constantly live as a disciple of the meek and lowly Jesus! I sincerely and ardently wish you the aid of the Holy Spirit, and a heart habitually conformed to the holy character of God. Great and precious are the promises, an infinitely merciful Jehovah has made in his Word, to those who persevere in well-doing. But how great the guilt, and how aggravated must be the condemnation of those, who are represented as being often reproved, and yet harden their hearts against God?

While we hear the denunciations of God's wrath to the finally impenitent, let us, my friend, be active to secure an interest in his favour. Then, let what will befal us in this life, our souls will rest safe on the rock of ages; Jesus will be our guide and friend through earth's tedious pilgrimage; he will be our support through the valley of the shadow of death;[77] and when released from this clayey tenement, will admit us to the new and heavenly Jerusalem.

Upon reviewing the scenes of the past, I find but little or no satisfaction. A hard, impenitent heart, an engagedness in the concerns of time and sense, and an awful stupidity respecting eternity I have this day felt. Oh, C. I am astonished when I view the feelings of my heart! But still more am I astonished, when I reflect upon the forbearance of God, who still supports me in existence, still indulges me with the day and means of grace.

Thursday morning. Yesterday I attended a fast at the West parish. Heard one most excellent sermon, and a number of interesting addresses. The exercises were very solemn and instructive. I long to have you with us. Since I last saw you, we have been highly favoured by God. Oh, that he would hasten that happy period, when the whole earth shall be brought to a knowledge of the truth as it is in Jesus. Let us frequently and earnestly intercede at the throne of grace, for the commencement of the Millennium.[78]

Wishing you the light of God's countenance, and a heart to labour aright in his vineyard, I bid you, my friend, an affectionate farewell. Yours, &c. HARRIET.

To Miss F. W. of Beverly.

Haverhill, Sabbath eve, Nov. 26, 1809.

I HAVE this moment received, dear Miss W. your inestimable letter; in which you affectionately congratulate me on the happiness of "tasting that the Lord is gracious."[79]

Assailed by temptations, surrounded with the gay and thoughtless, and with but few of the humble followers of the Lamb to guide me in the path of duty, or to instruct me in the great things of the kingdom, what feelings do I experience, when receiving from my beloved friend, a letter, filled not only with assurances of continued affection, but with encomiums upon the character of the dear Immanuel, as being "the chief among ten thousands and altogether lovely."[80] Often does my heart glow with gratitude to the Parent of mercies, for bestowing on *me* such a favour, as *one* friend to whom I can disclose the secret recesses of my heart, and with whom I can converse upon the important doctrines of the gospel, and an eternal state of felicity prepared for those, whose "robes have been washed and made white in the blood of the Lamb."[81]

Have you not, my friend, often felt, when conversing upon these great truths, a flame of divine love kindle in your heart; and have you not solemnly resolved, that you would live nearer to the blessed Jehovah?

I have this day been permitted to worship God in his earthly courts. How unspeakably great are the privileges with which we are indulged, in this land of gospel light! The Sabbath before last, Mr. B. exchanged with Mr. D. Oh, my beloved Miss W. could you have heard the important truths he preached, the impressive manner in which he held forth the terrors of God to the impenitent, and the necessity of immediate repentance, surely, it must to you have been a blessed season. But it had no visible effect upon the minds of the people here. A dreadful inattention to religion still prevails. The youth are very thoughtless and gay; "iniquity abounds, and the love of many waxes cold."[82] But there are, as I humbly trust, a pious *few*, who are daily making intercession at the throne of grace, for the prosperity of Zion.

What encouragement have we, my dear friend, to wrestle at the throne of mercy, for renewing and sanctifying grace, for ourselves and the whole Israel of God: even in times of the greatest declension. Jehovah hath promised, that he will hear the prayers of his children; and that if offered up in sincerity of heart, he will, in his own time, send gracious answers.

Next Friday evening, it being the evening after Thanksgiving, a *ball*[83] is appointed in this place. I think it probable that E. whom you once saw anxiously inquiring, what she should do to inherit eternal life? will attend. Oh, my beloved friend, you cannot know my feelings. It is dreadful to see mortals bound to eternity, spending their lives with no apparent concern about their never-dying souls. But it is, if possible, more dreadful to see those, who have "put their hands to the plough, look back; or being often reproved, harden their hearts against God."[84]

How unsearchable are the ways of Jehovah! When I look around me, and see so many of my friends and companions, who are by nature endowed with much greater talents than I am, and who would, if partakers of the grace of God, be made the instruments of doing so much more good in the world, left in a state of sin, I am constrained to say,

> "Why was *I* made to hear thy voice,
> And enter while there's room;
> When thousands make a wretched choice,
> And rather starve than come."[85]

I could, my dear Miss W. write you all night: but a violent head-ache has attended me this day, and wearied nature requires repose.

I sincerely thank you, for the affectionate invitation you have given me to visit you. I wish it were possible for me to comply with your request; perhaps I may, this winter; but I shall not place much dependance upon it, as every thing is so uncertain. Do, my friend, visit Haverhill.—I long to see you: but if Providence has determined we shall never meet again in this world, Oh, may we meet in our heavenly Father's kingdom, and never more endure a separation. In haste.

I am, yours, &c. HARRIET.

1809.

Dec. 1. This evening a *ball* is appointed at ———. My dear ——— will probably attend. I have resolved to devote some part of the evening in praying particularly for them. Oh, that God would stop them in the midst of their sinful career, and let them no longer spend their *precious* moments in following the pleasures of this vain world!

Dec. 31. I have now come to the close of another year. How various have been the scenes which I have been called to pass through this year! But what have I done for God? what for the interest of religion? and what for my own soul? I have passed through *one* of the most solemn scenes of my life—I have taken the sacramental covenant upon me—I have solemnly joined myself to the Church of the blessed Jesus.

Oh! that I might now, as in the presence of the great Jehovah, and his holy angels, with penitential sorrow, confess my past ingratitude, and in humble reliance on the strength of Jesus, resolve to devote the ensuing year, and the remaining part of my days to his service.

1810.

Feb. 10. What great reason have I for thankfulness to God, that I am still in the land of the living, and have another opportunity of recording with my pen, his tender mercy and loving kindness! I have been, for almost five weeks, unable to write; and for a week confined to my bed. But JESUS has undertaken to be my Physician; he has graciously restored me to health; and when greatly distressed with pain, he has afforded me the sweet consolations of the Spirit, and brought me willingly to resign my soul into his arms, and wait the event of his Providence, whether life or death.

Oh, that this sickness might be for my eternal good! may it be made the means of weaning me from all terrestrial enjoyments, and of fixing my hope and trust in the merits of Jesus! Then should I have cause to bless God, for his chastening rod, and through eternity, count all these afflictive dispensations as great mercies.

Feb. 18. How easily can God disconcert the plans formed by short-sighted mortals! I had fondly flattered myself, that before this, I should have met with the assembly of the saints, and have sitten under the droppings of the sanctuary;—that I should have joined my Christian friends, in their social conference, and heard the truths of the gospel explained by our dear Pastor. But Jehovah determined otherwise. He has again laid his chastising rod upon me, by afflicting me with sickness and pain. But, "I will bear the indignation of the Lord, because I have sinned against him."[86] I have a renewed opportunity of examining my submission to God; and do now, as in his presence, renewedly resolve to devote myself a living sacrifice to him. I think I can say, that afflictions are good for me. In times of the greatest distress, I have been brought to cry within myself; "It is the Lord, let him do what seemeth him good."[87] I think I am *willing* to bear whatever God sees fit to lay upon me. Let my dear heavenly Father inflict the *keenest* anguish, I will submit; for he is infinitely excellent, and *can* do nothing wrong.

Feb. 25. With the light of this holy morning, I desire to offer to the kind Shepherd of Israel,[88] who never slumbers nor sleeps, a morning tribute of thanksgiving and praise. Oh that my whole soul might be drawn out in love to God; and may all my faculties unite with the inhabitants of the New Jerusalem, in praising the immortal King, for what he *has* done, and still *is doing* for rebellious man! But I fall *infinitely* short of the honour due to his glorious name. When shall I arrive at the destined port of rest, and with the blood-washed millions,[89] praise the Lamb of God for redeeming love? Hasten, blessed Immanuel, that glorious period, when all thy exile children shall arrive at their eternal home! Oh, for a tongue to sound aloud the honours of the dear Jesus!

March 2. Have, this afternoon, been solemnly admonished, by seeing the remains of Mr. E. carried by the house. And can it be that I, who am now so actively engaged in the affairs of *this* world, shall shortly be conveyed, on a bier, to the cold grave? Yes, the righteous Judge has declared to the race of Adam, "dust thou art, and unto dust shalt thou return."[90] Soon this sentence will be executed upon me. Prepare, O my soul, to meet thy God!

March 6. What unspeakable consolation does it afford the children of God, to reflect that the great Jehovah is carrying on his work of grace; that earth and hell *combined*, cannot hinder what he has designed to accomplish.

March 10. How awfully depraved is the natural heart! Every day I can see more and more of *my own* apostasy from God. Break, compassionate Immanuel, oh! *break* this stony heart of mine, and *compel* me to live as an obedient child!

March 13. How engaged am I in the concerns of this world! I cannot but ask myself the question, have I any reason to imagine that I am interested in the covenant of life? If so, why am I thus? Why this awful distance from God? "Search me, O God! and know my heart; try me, and know my thoughts, and see if there be any wicked way in me, and lead me in the way everlasting."[91]

March 22. Have again been permitted to attend a religious conference. Mr. T. preached from these words; "Do thyself no harm."[92] How astonishing that I can be so negligent in duty, when there are so many immortal souls around me, that are doing themselves *eternal* harm! Why do I not *feel* their awful condition, and solemnly warn them, both by precept and example, "to flee from the wrath to come?"[93]

To Miss F. W. of Beverly.

Haverhill, March 31, 1810.

FAVOURED by Divine Providence with an opportunity of expressing my gratitude to my beloved Miss W. for all the testimonies of friendship which she has shewn me, I cordially embrace it. Your last friendly letter was this day received. To assure you how much happiness your letters confer on me, would be but what I have already told you. The one I received when on a bed of sickness, was a *real treasure*. My feeble health alone prevented my answering it before. I have lately been led to dwell much on the doctrine of the Divine Decrees. I should like to have your ideas on the subject. Although God is under no obligations to save *one* of the apostate race of Adam, and it would not derogate from his justice, were he to send all to eternal torments; yet, to display the riches of his grace, he determines to save a few. Why should we say, what doest thou? The children of God are, or ought to be, lights in the world.[94] But I fear that I shall be a stumbling-block to others. I have often thought myself one of those who are "tossed to and fro, and carried about by every wind of doctrine."[95] When I hear arguments on one side, I think I am convinced. When on the other, I think the same. But I leave this subject for the present.

Let me tell you, that I fondly indulge the hope of seeing you before long. Mr. H. and myself have thought considerably of a ride to Beverly. Should not our wishes be frustrated, I shall probably see you in four or five weeks; if not, then I shall relinquish the idea, as I shall commence attending school in May. When I see you, I will relate to you my exercises in my past illness.

Have we not abundant reason to rejoice in the government of God? He is carrying on his work, converting sinners, and making the wrath of man to praise him. Oh, that Haverhill and Beverly might experience the influence of the Holy Spirit! God can work here as easily as in Salem and Manchester. Let us be ardent and constant at the throne of mercy, that the blessed Immanuel would revive his work, and pour out his Spirit on the Churches and people, with which we are connected. Oh! why, my friend, are we so cold and stupid? I earnestly request an interest in your prayers.

Yours sincerely,   HARRIET.

1810.

April 6. This evening had some interesting conversation with a friend, upon the past scenes of my life. Oh, how is my life filled up with folly and sin! Surely, if I am ever pardoned and accepted by the blessed Redeemer, I must ascribe it *wholly* to the mercy of God.

April 29. A sudden death, this week. Mrs. C. was in health and prosperity *one* hour, and the *next*—in the cold embraces of the universal conqueror! May this solemn event, be sanctified to surviving friends! And may it lead *me* to place my affections on the things of eternity!

May 4. Just returned from the house of God. Had a most interesting sermon preached by Mr. A. Text; "Ye are the salt of the earth; but if the salt have lost its savour, wherewith shall it be salted."[96]

Mr. E. called upon us a few moments, and informed us, there was a great revival of religion in his society and town.[97] Oh, how did it rejoice my heart! However cold and stupid, I can *in sincerity* say, that I *love* to hear of the conversion of sinners. Must Haverhill be left destitute of the work of the Spirit? Oh, let me be ardent and constant at the throne of grace, for the outpouring of the Spirit, and a revival of religion amongst us.

May 11. Called upon a friend this morning, who, to human appearance is on the brink of the grave. She was speechless, though not senseless. Her very *countenance* declared the importance of religion.[98] Never shall I forget the affectionate manner in which she pressed my hand to her bosom, and lifted her eyes to heaven, as if calling down a blessing upon me. Oh, that I could rightly improve this affecting dispensation of Providence!

May 24. I have been where heaven and hell, the soul and eternity, appear important subjects! The people in B. are awake. Attended two evening lectures—the meeting-house thronged with solemn and attentive hearers.

May 29. Attended singing school this evening. Though meetings for this purpose be ever so pleasant, yet so great have been my temptations the winter past, that I could not feel sorry that the meetings were concluded. Hope I have not brought dishonour upon the cause of Jesus, by my careless behaviour before my companions.

May 30. Election day. This day recalls many painful events, which occurred last year at this time. How was I then labouring for "the meat that perisheth,"[99]—following the leadings of a trifling heart! It was infinite mercy, that snatched me from the abyss, and, as I humbly trust, made me a monument of redeeming love. "Praise the Lord, Oh my soul!"[100]

June 2. Have had some interesting conversation with Miss W. upon the situation of my dear E. Who knows, thought I, but what she might now have been earnestly engaged in the cause of the Redeemer, if it were not for my unchristian conduct. How can I think of being an enemy to the souls of my dear friends?

June 3. Solemn indeed have been the transactions of this day. Oh, that they might be remembered with joy through eternity! Had some humbling views of my past ingratitude. The aggravated transgressions of my life, the last six months, in particular, have been laid open before me. Have again solemnly resolved to live to God. If I should again become stupid—but no,—I *cannot*—I *will* surrender myself to Jesus. He will keep me from falling, and present me faultless before his Father's throne.

June 4. Have been solemnly impressed with the worth of immortal souls this day. The welfare of my school companions, lies near my heart. In what way can I be serviceable to them? They have souls, as valuable as mine. Oh, then, let me use my best endeavours to bring them to the knowledge of the truth, and save them from the awful punishment, which awaits the finally impenitent.

June 8. Afflicted with a severe pain in my head. A celebrated author observes, that every pain we feel, is a warning to us to be prepared for death. Oh, that it may have this effect upon me!

June 20. How unsatisfying and unstable are all the enjoyments of time. I am daily more convinced that nothing short of the unchangeable Jehovah, can afford real happiness. To day, we may imagine ourselves possessed of a friend, who will not forsake us; to-morrow, that same person may prove a deceiver.[101] May I learn wisdom from the news I have this evening heard! Oh, that *such* things might have a happy tendency to wean me from this world, and prepare me for another!

June 30. Called on my dear friend E. She has lately experienced affliction. She told me that she was resigned to divine Providence, and could rejoice, even in the hour of distress. Happy composure! What joys, Oh, ye deluded followers of unrighteousness, have you to boast, compared with that experienced by a humble follower of Jesus?

July 1. Hail, sacred morning! Once ushered in with the most interesting events, ever registered in the records of time. On this holy morning, the Saviour rose from the grave.[102] Expect this day to commemorate the sufferings of the Lamb of God. Grant me, gracious God, sweet communion with thee. Let me not eat and drink judgment to myself.

July 7. How have I spent this day? What a dreadful sink of wickedness is my heart! Must I resign the idea of ever feeling the *power* of religion? Surely, if I am a child of God, I could not live so stupid.

July 19. Favoured with the privilege of attending a lecture this afternoon. Our dear minister preached from these words: "How long halt ye between two opinions;"[103] a most solemn discourse. In the evening, a meeting at Mr. D.'s for religious conversation. A small number of young people appear unusually solemn. Has not God already begun to shew the riches of his grace? Will he not arise, and have mercy on Haverhill, and make it a place, where he will delight to dwell?

August 6. How soon are my resolutions, to live wholly to God, broken! My conscience daily reproaches me, for my unfaithfulness to my companions, to myself, and to my God. If any one should have told me, when light first shone on my mind, that I should feel such indifference to the salvation of sinners, and so little love to God, as I now feel, I should have exclaimed, *impossible!*

Oct. 10. This day entered upon my eighteenth year. Seventeen years have rolled, almost insensibly, away. I still remain a pilgrim in this barren land. Merciful Jesus, on the commencement of this year, may thy supporting hand be underneath me, and if my life is prolonged, may it be more faithfully devoted to thee, and to thy blessed cause.

Oct. 20. A female friend called upon us this morning. She informed me of her determination to quit her native land, to endure the sufferings of a Christian amongst heathen nations—to spend her days in India's sultry clime.[104] How did this news affect my heart! Is she willing to do all this for God; and shall I refuse to lend my little aid, in a land where divine revelation has shed its clearest rays? I have *felt* more, for the salvation of the Heathen, this day, than I recollect to have felt through my whole past life.

How dreadful their situation! What heart but would bleed at the idea of the sufferings they endure, to obtain the joys of Paradise? What can *I* do, that the light of the gospel may shine upon them? They are perishing for lack of knowledge, while I enjoy the glorious privileges of a Christian land. Great God direct me! Oh, make me in *some* way beneficial to their immortal souls!

Oct. 21. Had a joyful meeting, this day, in the house of God. "When I am weak, then am I strong."[105] Have experienced the truth of this declaration, this day. Went to meeting in the morning afflicted with bodily pain, yet joyful in the God of my salvation. Reflecting on the melancholy state of our church, was distressed, lest the deserved judgments of the Almighty, should be poured out upon us. But the words of the dear Redeemer, "fear not little flock, for it is your Father's good pleasure to give you the kingdom,"[106] sweetly refreshed and animated my desponding spirit. I desire ever to bless the Lord, for the manifestations of his love, this day. He has taught me, that neither Paul nor Apollos,[107] is any thing, without his grace. Ministers may faithfully preach, but the word will not prove successful, if God does not touch the heart.

I have seen the glory of God in his sanctuary. "I had rather be a door-keeper in the house of my God, than to dwell in the tents of wickedness."[108] The Lord is good; may it be my delightful employment on earth, to praise him; and in heaven may I join the enraptured millions, in a song that shall *never* end.

Oct. 23. Mr. M. introduced Mr. N.* to our family,[109] He appears to be an engaged Christian. Expects to spend his life, in preaching a Saviour to the benighted Pagans.

Oct. 31. Mr. N. called on us this morning. He gave me some account of the dealings of God with his soul. If such a man who has devoted himself to the service of the gospel, has determined to labour in the most difficult part of the vineyard, and is willing to renounce his earthly happiness for the interest of religion; if *he* doubts his possessing love to God;—what shall I say of *myself?*

Nov. 4. Have once more commemorated the dying love of Jesus. Have entertained some faint views of the character of God; and mourned for the evil of sin. How condescending is God, to permit hell-deserving rebels to commune with him at his table! What on *earth*, can equal the love of Jehovah? He treats those who are by nature, his *enemies*, like *children*.

Nov. 6. Sleep has fled from me, and my soul is enveloped in a dark cloud of troubles! Oh, that God would direct me! Oh, that he would plainly mark out the path of duty, and let me not depart from it!

Nov. 10. Have this day commenced reading Law's Serious Call to a holy life.[110] How infinitely short do I fall of this holy conformity to my Maker, which he describes as the property of a Christian! I am as much obligated to yield myself a willing soldier to Christ, to fight his battles, and glorify him, in every action of my life, as he who ministers at the altar, and performs the office of a preacher. Why then am I not employed in his service? Why stand I here *idle* all the day?

Extract of a letter to her sister M. at Charlestown.

Nov. 18, 1810.

"How gracious, my dear sister, has God been to us! Uninterrupted health, food, and raiment are ours. But when I enumerate our many mercies, it is with deep humility that I look back on my past life, and discover so *little* gratitude, and so *much* unworthiness. How much has sovereign grace done for me! Though I have solemnly professed to find consolation in Religion, to derive my hopes of happiness only from God; yet how often have I roved in quest of pleasure, and dishonoured the best of Masters, by an unholy life. How ungrateful have I been for the

---

* Mr. Newell, it is presumed.

common mercies of life, and for the still more precious blessings of the Holy Spirit. May every temporal blessing which your heart can wish, be yours. But whatever be the trials through which you are called to pass, oh, may that heaven-born religion attend you, which can sweeten the bitter cup of life, afford you joy in this vale of tears, support you in nature's last extremity, and conduct you to the Heavenly Canaan, where undisturbed happiness will ever reign! Life is but a vapour. Whether we spend it in tranquillity and ease, or in pain and suffering, time will soon land us on the shores of Eternity, our destined home. These things, my dear sister, my heart tells me, are solemn realities. They are not fictions. Though the language of my past life has been, "there is no future state;"[111] yet I *now* feel there is an Eternity, where I shall meet my earthly friends, and stand accountable at the great tribunal for my conduct towards them. I regret the loss of those hours I have lost in vanity, and in wounding the cause of that dear Redeemer, whom I think, if I am not greatly deceived, I can now call *mine*. I think I can say with the Psalmist, "whom have I in Heaven but thee? and there is none upon earth that I desire beside thee."[112]—His religion comforts and supports my drooping spirits; his promises encourage, and his glories warm my heart. But where am I? The striking clock reminds me of the lateness of the hour. These delightful, these heart-consoling subjects have almost made me forget that tired nature requires repose."

To Miss S. H. Andover.

Haverhill, Nov. 20, 1810.

WILL it afford my dear Miss H. the best satisfaction to hear of the health and happiness of her friends at Haverhill? Let me assure you of our perfect health, and of our united wishes for your happiness, both temporal and eternal. While many of our friends are languishing on beds of sickness, sighing for the return of health,—while many have gone the "way of all the earth,"[113] "have heard their sentence, and received their doom;"[114] we are still enjoying the blessings of health, and are not out of the reach of pardoning mercy. Ought not a review of these daily blessings to excite in us the liveliest gratitude? How should our whole lives be a constant series of grateful acknowledgment to the Parent of mercies, for bestowing such great, such unmerited favours on rebels doomed to die!—Is my friend, Miss H. rejoicing in God? Does she find joy and peace in believing? This I sincerely hope is your happy situation. I have infinite reason to confess my obligation to God, for the faint discoveries I have lately entertained of his glorious character. Yes, my dear Miss H. I still find the promises precious, and Jesus unchangeable. Though I am worthless and undeserving, yet the blessed Immanuel is lovely, and worthy of the united praises of saints and angels. Though I am often led to doubt my interest in this *dear* Saviour, yet *sometimes* I can rejoice in his perfections, and exclaim with Thomas, "my Lord and my God."[115]

You have, undoubtedly, heard of the departure of Mrs. S. Her faith and patience endured to the end. What a happy exchange has she made! Who would not wish to die the death of the righteous, who would not wish their last end to be like her's?

Mrs. M. appears to enjoy religion; she wishes much to see you. A general stupidity to the one thing needful still prevails. When will the showers of divine grace be poured out upon this place? Will not this church, this vine of God's planting, rejoice to see the work of the Lord prospering? Your earnest prayers are requested for a revival of pure and undefiled religion in Haverhill. Mr. Newell preached a lecture here last evening. Do we not need such *faithful* preachers here as much as the benighted Pagans in India? Is not the situation of gospel sinners much more desperate, than that of those who have never heard of a Saviour? But still we have reason to rejoice that God has inclined a faithful few to preach Jesus to the Heathen. Oh, may their labours be blessed! May they see the inhabitants of the wilderness embracing the offers of mercy! We shall expect to see you with Mr. W. on Saturday. Do not disappoint us. Accept this from HARRIET.

To Miss M. T. of Newbury.

Boston, Feb. 18, 1811.

WHAT, my dear friend, (if I may enjoy the privilege of corresponding with you) shall be the subject of our letters? Shall the common occurrences of life, and the flattering compliments of the *polite world*, fill our sheets; or that religion, which is the glory of the bright intelligences in heaven, and the consolation of trembling believers on earth? I think I can confidently affirm, that the latter will be *your* choice. As for *myself*, I can say that if I never felt the power of *this* religion, yet it is a theme upon which I love to converse, write, and reflect. It is a duty incumbent on the children of God to reprove, encourage, and animate each other on their journey to the upper world. Every christian has difficulties to overcome, temptations to encounter, and a warfare to accomplish, which the world are strangers to. If pilgrims in the same country can in the least console each other, and sweeten the thorny journey, by familiar intercourse, they ought not to neglect it. We, my dear M. are professedly interested in the same cause. Our home is professedly in heaven; we have temptations, difficulties, trials, and doubts, which, if we are believers, are in unison. I feel that I need the prayers and the advice of all the followers of the Lamb. I have "an evil heart of unbelief," prone to "depart from the living God."[116] Will M. pray for me? Will she bear me in remembrance when supplicating mercy for *other* sinners? You *shall not* be forgotten by H. No.—If the Friend of sinners will lend a listening ear to *my* feeble cries, M. *shall* be strengthened and blessed. By these united cries, we may draw down from heaven favours never to be forgotten. *Painful* recollection often recurs to those weeks that I spent at Bradford. I say *painful*, because I fear that my conduct brought a wound on that religion, that I should wish to honour. While I lament with humility the loss of many precious hours, and the stupidity which I then experienced, I have reason to adore the mercy of Jehovah, that has since granted me refreshing showers of grace. Yes, M. my mind has been greatly exercised since I last saw you. Never before did the promises of the Gospel appear so precious, the character of God so lovely, and immortal souls of so much worth. I tremble at the idea of being again involved in the vanities of a world which can afford no pleasure, and of feeling indifferent about the kingdom of Jesus. But I am a dependant creature; if forsaken of God I shall perish. My hope is on his grace. What, my friend, is the state of *your* mind? Are you enjoying the light of a Saviour's countenance? Are you fast progressing heavenward; and are you possessing joy that is unspeakable and full of glory? This I hope is your situation. "A soul redeemed demands a life of praise."[117] Let our future lives evince our gratitude, and every thought be brought into subjection to the Father of spirits. It is now about three weeks since I left H. Last Sabbath I enjoyed the pleasure of hearing the good Dr. G. preach. This pleasure I hope often to be favoured with while I continue with my sister M. I have been these two days with our friends, the Misses F's. My time has passed very pleasantly with them.

I have more things to *tell* you than I have time to *write*. A number of interesting occurrences have happened since I saw you. Should I again be indulged with an interview with you, I fear I shall tire your patience with a history of my troubles and pleasures. But I must leave you, my M. May you enjoy the influences of the Holy Spirit in life, consolation in death, and a seat in the mansions of blessedness!

HARRIET.

1811.

Feb. 24. For four weeks past, have been visiting my sister at C. The first week, I was remarkably favoured with the presence of Immanuel. Never before did I gain such access to the mercy-seat, and entertain such glorious views of the character of God, and such humiliating ideas of my *own* as a sinner. But I have since experienced a sad reverse. My God why hast thou forsaken me? O for that invigorating grace, which the Saviour dispenses to his followers! But can I hope myself his follower?

Last Sabbath went with Mr. H. and sister M. to hear Dr. G. His language, his very features spoke the emotion of his soul. His text was in Corinthians, "When I was a child, I spake as a child," &c.[118]

As we entered the meeting-house, they were singing my favourite hymn, "Lord, what a wretched land is this,"[119] &c. in a melancholy air. Such were my sensations, that I could hardly refrain from weeping. How lovely are thy tabernacles, O Lord of hosts, where the gospel of Jesus is proclaimed!

Feb. 25. After spending the day in trifling conversation, I was permitted to enjoy the privileges of attending a Christian conference, where the evening was spent in praying, singing, and conversing upon the things of religion.

Feb. 26. Mr. H. and sister M. informed me that my dear mamma wished me to engage in a school, the ensuing summer. Can I think of such a responsible situation as that of instructing little immortals? I know that I ought not to consult my own ease; the question should be, how can I be most useful in the world? I hope I shall be directed by Heaven! Oh that God would use me as an instrument of promoting his glory; whether it be in the domestic circle, or in the arduous employment of "teaching young ideas how to shoot."[120]

Feb. 27. I have spent the greatest part of the day in reading. I find that I am *indeed* ignorant—long to have time to devote myself *wholly* to the improvement of my mind. While endeavouring to obtain useful knowledge, Oh may I never forget, that if at last found a hypocrite, I shall be capable of greater sufferings than if totally ignorant.

Feb. 28. Afflicted with a violent pain in my head. Experience daily evinces, that afflictions will do me no good, unless sanctified. Have had some sense of the presence of Jehovah, and some longing desires to be wholly conformed to him. When shall this vain world lose its power to charm, and the religion of the Gospel influence my heart and life? Oh, when shall I die, when shall I live for ever? How many times this day, have I repeated that Hymn of Dr. Watts; "Lord, what a wretched land is this."

March 1. Father of lights, it is the office of thy Spirit, to create holy exercises in the hearts of thy creatures. O may I enter upon this month with renewed resolutions to devote myself exclusively to thee; that at the close of it, I may not sigh over mispent hours.

March 3. Heard an admirable sermon this morning from Dr. G. Have likewise communed with God at his table. Oh, this cold, stupid heart! I long for wings to fly away from this clod of earth, and participate the holiness and pleasures of the saints within the vail.

March 4. Have this day visited at ——. The entertainment of the evening was splendid and *extravagant*. Query. Is it consistent with the humble religion of the Gospel, for professors, who ought to deny themselves, and take up their cross daily, to expend *that* money, which is God's, and is only lent them for pious uses, in providing dainties to please the palate, and in clothes, to *ornament* their bodies?

Where is the vast difference between the children of God and the children of this world? As far as I have examined the subject, it is my candid opinion, that if Christians would appropriate more of their property to charitable purposes, instead of making such extravagant provision for the flesh; would men imitate the example of the meek and lowly Jesus, feel indifferent to the smiles and frowns of the world; religion would flourish, the kingdom of God would be built up, and happy effects would be visible through the world.

March 9. This is a delightful evening! Not a cloud is in the heavens to intercept the bright rays of the moon. All nature, both animate and inanimate, appears combined in the blessed employment of praising God. The moon shining in her glory, and the planets and stars are monitors that speak loud—more lovely to me, than ten thousand human voices. Awake my slothful soul; nothing in creation has half the work to perform, and Oh, let it not be said, that nothing is half so dull!

March 25. God has not left himself without witness in the earth. No; he is still manifesting the riches of his grace, in bringing home his chosen ones. A young lady of my acquaintance, formerly gay and a stranger to piety, has hopefully become a follower of the Lamb! And has my dear M. chosen Jesus for her friend and portion? I cannot but stand amazed, to see the salvation of God.

March 30. Have found much encouragement and satisfaction of late in reading some of Newton's works.[121] They are *indeed* a treasure. He penetrates my heart; and while he exposes my depravity, he points me to the Lamb of God, who taketh away the sin of the world.

April 1. This is an interesting public day. O that the supreme Ruler of all events, would incline every citizen, to vote for that man who is most worthy of the office of a governor. The aspect of the times is dark; but God can bring good out of evil, and continue to us our national blessings. I often find this reflection a sweet solace in the hour of darkness, that no event, however small, can take place without the permission and direction of the great Jehovah.

April 7. This is a day, on which God usually manifests the glories of his character to his dear children. How exactly calculated are all the means and ordinances of the Gospel, for the comfort and improvement of the saints. What an act of love and wisdom was it in God, to select one day from the week, to be appropriated to his worship. Were it not for this glorious day, I should be in danger of losing all sense of eternal things.

April 9. What shall a stupid Christian do? Stupid Christian did I say! Can a *Christian* ever feel stupid? It is an inconsistent title. But notwithstanding all my death-like stupidity, I *cannot* renounce the hope of being a child of the Most High. What shall I do, a dependant, guilty creature, to gain access to the mercy seat,[122] and derive a supply of grace from the fountain of life? Draw me, thou Saviour of sinners, and I will run after thee. O lead me beside the still waters, and refresh my soul with heavenly food.

April 17. How shall I record the events of this day! How can I tranquillize my disturbed mind enough to engage in the *once* delightful employment of writing? Returned from Boston in the evening, after spending three days very agreeably with my friends C. and N. M. handed me a letter with an appearance which indicated that something unusual was contained in it. I broke the seal, and what were my emotions when I read the name of ——— .[123] This was not a long wished-for letter: no; it was a long dreaded one, which I was conscious would involve me in doubt, anxiety, and distress. Nor were the contents such, as I might answer at a *distant* period; they required an *immediate* answer. And now what shall I say? How shall I decide this *important*, this *interesting* question? Shall I consent to leave for ever the *Parent* of my youth, the *friends* of my life, the dear scenes of my childhood, and my native country, and go to a land of *strangers*, "not knowing the things which shall befal me there?"[124] O for direction from heaven! O for "that wisdom which is profitable to direct!"[125] I will go to God, and with an unprejudiced mind, seek his guidance. I will cast this heavy burden on him, humbly trusting that he will sustain me, and direct me in the path of duty.

April 19. The *important decision* is not *yet* made. I am still wavering. I long to see and converse with my dear mother. So delicate is my situation, that I dare not unbosom my heart to a single person. What shall I do? Could tears direct me in the path of duty, surely I should be directed.—My heart aches.—I know not *what to do!*—"Guide me, O thou great Jehovah!"[126]

April 21. Have now retired to my chamber, once more, to vent in silence, my unavailing sighs, and with an almost *bursting heart*, implore divine relief and direction.

I shall go home on Tuesday.—Never did I so *greatly long* to visit the dear native dwelling.

April 22. Perhaps, my dear Mother will *immediately* say, *Harriet shall never go*. Well, if this should be the case, my duty would be *plain*. I *cannot* act contrary to the advice and express command of a *pious mother*.

The fact was, that her mother made no objection to her accepting the offer of Mr. Newell, but cheerfully left her to act according to her conviction of duty.

To Miss F. W. of Beverly.

Haverhill, April 29, 1811.

It has not been for want of inclination, or from forgetfulness, that I have thus long neglected writing to my dear friend, Miss W.; but every day has brought with it various and new occupations; and though my friends have not been forgotten, yet I confess I have not been so punctual as I ought. I need not assure you, that your letter produced many pleasing sensations. I hope this will find you enjoying the presence of our covenant Saviour, and engaged in the promotion of his glorious cause. Christians are greatly criminal for not living in the constant enjoyment of God. He is ever ready and willing to manifest the glories of his character to their souls; and nothing but their native opposition to holiness, and their love of evil, ever prevents. Are not believes inconsistent creatures? They can speak of a Saviour's love—the happiness resulting from an acquaintance with God, and point out the road to impenitent sinners, which alone will lead to substantial bliss; and yet often wander in forbidden paths, lose all relish for spiritual enjoyments, and rest contented with the low pleasures of sense.

If I am a child of Jesus, this inconsistency has often been mine. And yet I long for a greater sense of my dependance, and more entire conformity to Him who died for me. If any thing here deserves the name of happiness, it does not spring from earth. No; it is of heavenly birth, and comes from the regions of purity. The vast and boundless desires implanted in the human heart, cannot be satisfied with any thing short of God. Nothing in heaven or earth is capable of affording real bliss without him.

I have spent three months this last winter with my sister at C. My religious privileges have been more extensive than usual. I have been favoured with frequent opportunities of hearing Dr. G. preach, and have likewise attended many serious meetings. But I still wanted a heart to improve under the cultivation of Jehovah's hand. Neither afflictions nor enjoyments will do us good, unless sanctified by divine grace.

Since my return to H. I have sometimes enjoyed much consolation in committing myself and all my concerns into the hands of God. Some *circumstances*, which at some future time I may communicate to you, I hope will have a tendency to wean me from this world, and fasten my heart to Heaven. I *do*, my dear friend, find, *this* "a desert world, replete with sin and sorrow."[127] I often long to leave it, and find a sweet release from every woe.

I visited Miss F. at Boston often. H. returned from H. about three weeks since; she observed, she intended writing to your sister N.

I have not read the book, mentioned in your last, but confide in your judgment; think it must be entertaining.

I hope to have the pleasure of a visit from you this summer; I wish much to see you and your sister; hope you are both enjoying the light of the Sun of righteousness. Persevere, my friend, in the Christian life, and pray for your friend Harriet. Our pilgrimage will shortly be ended, and all the trials of life will be over. Oh, may we meet in heaven; and join with the angelic host around the throne, in adoring the matchless perfections of Immanuel, through the ages of eternity! I am, my dear Miss W. affectionately yours.	HARRIET.

To Miss M. S. of Boston.

Haverhill, Sabbath eve, May, 1811.

WHILE agitated with doubts and conflicts, with the gay world in opposition, it has afforded me much consolation to think I have a friend in M. who can feel my sorrows, and sympathize with me in grief. I have passed through many interesting and solemn scenes, since I last saw you. Returning to Haverhill, I found my dear mamma calm and composed. So completely was she filled with a sense of the shortness of time, the uncertainty of life, and the duty of giving up our dearest comforts to the Lord, that she never raised one objection, but wished me to act according as my conscience directed. I felt an unspeakable consolation in committing the disposal of this event to God. I thought I could willingly renounce my own opinion, and sitting at the feet of Jesus, be guided entirely by him. Mr. N. has visited us frequently. He wishes not to influence me; he would not if he could.

And now, my dear M. what will you say to me, when I tell you, that I *do* think, seriously think, of quitting my native land for ever, and of going to a far distant country, "not knowing the things which shall befall me there."[128] Should I refuse to make this sacrifice, refuse to lend my little aid in the promulgation of the Gospel amongst the Heathen, how could I ever expect to enjoy the blessing of God, and peace of conscience, though surrounded with every temporal mercy? It would be pleasant to spend the remaining part of my life with my friends, and to have them surround my dying bed. But no! I must relinquish their society, and follow God to a land of strangers, where millions of my fellow sinners are perishing for lack of vision. I have professed, my friend, for these two years past, to derive comfort only from God. Here then is a consoling reflection; the ever-blessed Jesus is able to support and comfort me, as well in the sultry climes of India, as in my dear native land. I trust that he will make his promise good, that as my day is, so shall my strength be. The wintry storms of life will soon be over, and if I have committed my immortal interest into the hands of God, I shall shortly find a sweet release from every woe. So visibly have I beheld the hand of Providence in removing some obstacles which once I thought almost insurmountable, that I dare not object. *All* my friends with whom I have conversed since my return to Haverhill, advise me to go. Some Christians who were formerly opposed, after obtaining a more extensive knowledge of the subject, think females would be useful. The people of this world probably view this subject as they do others. Those who have never felt the worth of their own souls, account it superstition and hypocritical zeal, for Christians to sacrifice their earthly pleasures, for the sake of telling the Heathen world of a Saviour. But all the ridicule that the gay and thoughtless sinner can invent, will not essentially injure me. If I am actuated by love to the Saviour and his cause, nothing in earth or hell can hurt me. I must ask your prayers for me. We have prayed together; oh, let us now, though separated in person, unite at the throne of grace. Perhaps my views of this subject may be altered; and God may yet prepare a way for me to continue in America. Oh, that I might be submissive and humbly wait on God! He can direct me, at this eventful crisis, and glorify himself. Affectionately yours!

HARRIET.

To Miss S. H——, Newbury.

Haverhill, June 12, 1811.

How shall I sufficiently thank my dear Miss H. for the kind token of affectionate remembrance, which she was kind enough to send me? Your letter really exhilarated my languid spirits. I had spent the evening in private conversation with *our dear* Mr. N. The usual subject of the contemplated Mission was renewedly talked over, and consequently the dangers, the crosses, the manifold trials of such an important undertaking, were themes which engrossed our thoughts. Depressed with anxious apprehensions, and in doubt respecting duty, Mrs. G. handed me a letter, and the well known hand of the writer I soon recognised. The contents dispelled many a heart-rending sigh. This eve, mamma received a letter from dear brother J.; I had previously written to him. Dear boy! he is much distressed for Harriet. He thinks she is doing wrong, and causing her friends needless anxiety. Would to heaven I could prevent distress from ever entering the heart of a widowed, beloved parent, and the dearest brothers and sisters! Oh, Miss H. could these dear friends but go with me to distant India—but alas! that is a fruitless wish; but were it possible that this could be the case, I think I could quit America without reluctance, and even *rejoice* to spend my life among the benighted Heathen. Sometimes I can reflect on this subject with composure, and even long to be on Missionary ground, where superstition and idolatry usurp the sway; think I can bid my dear friends a last farewell with calmness, and follow with delight the leadings of Providence. But at other times, I fear that this is not the situation God has designed for me; and if it is not, I can never lay claim to the promises of the Gospel, or expect the support of an Almighty arm, when dangers stand thick around me. My greatest fear is, that I shall lose all courage and perseverance should I set out to go, and not only be unhappy myself, but make those wretched who are with me. But are not these thoughts criminal when carried to excess? Ought I not to praise the Lord for what I have received, and trust Him for a supply of grace? Ought I not to examine the subject prayerfully, and if on examination I am convinced that Jesus calls me to make these great sacrifices, ought I not to do it voluntarily, and leave the event with the Ruler of the universe?

I find, my dear Miss H. that I am now in great danger of being actuated by a strong attachment. Oh, could I but give the ever blessed God the first place in my affections, I should not be in danger of being misled by earthly objects. Often have I adopted the words of the pious Mr. Newton:

> "The dearest idol I have known,
> Whate'er that idol be;
> Help me to tear it from thy throne,
> And worship only thee."[129]

When shall we hope for a visit from you? Do write me often, your letters will always be acceptable. Although tired and fatigued with the employments of the day, I have improved this late hour in writing.

Do you not admire Mr. Hall?[130] I heard him preach a preparatory sermon at Bradford last week; which was clear, distinguishing, and very excellent. He called here one morning, but I had gone to walk. Mr. Nott likewise called on us last week; we were in the meeting-house and did not see him. Our friend N. is still in Salem; I long to see her.

Can I ask the favour of being remembered in your intercessions at the throne of grace! Oh, that Christians would pray for me. Farewell, my dear Miss H. May the choicest blessings of Heaven be yours. I am affectionately your   HARRIET.

I had forgotten to tell you that our dear Mr. W. called here again, and I did not see him. Do you think I ever shall?

1811.

June 22. I have this day taken my leave of Mr. N. not expecting to see him again for nine months.[131] I can hardly feel reconciled to his departure; but the will of the Lord be done. Taking every circumstance into consideration, I am fully persuaded it will be most for his interest to spend the summer and winter in Philadelphia. Why then should I object?

June 27. It is now almost five years since my mind became seriously impressed with eternal realities. What have I learnt in these five years of myself? and what of God? Weep, Oh my soul, for past transgression, and present unfruitfulness.

To Miss C. F. of Boston.

Haverhill, June 29, 1811.

I THANK you, dear C. for your affectionate letter. My engagements have been such, that I could not conveniently answer it before; hope you will pardon the neglect. The kind interest you have of late taken in my happiness has greatly endeared you to my heart. May you never want a friend to sympathize with you when "adverse fortune frowns,"[132] or to rejoice with you, when "life's vale is strew'd with flowerets fresh."[133] If the remaining days of my short pilgrimage are to be spent in sorrow, O that Heaven would grant C. peace and happiness, and a sure pledge of joys to come. Where my future lot may be cast, time only can determine. If I can but maintain a firm and unshaken confidence in God, a humble reliance on his blessed promises, I shall be safe, though temporal comforts languish and die. I am now calculating upon a life of trials and hardships; but the grace of Jesus is sufficient for me. The Friend of sinners is able and willing to support me amid scenes of danger and distress.

When I bade you a parting adieu, my mind was in a state of agitation which I can never express. Dejected and weary I arrived at the dear mansion, where I have spent so many pleasant hours. My dear mamma met me at the door, with a countenance that bespoke the tranquillity of her mind. The storm of opposition, as she observed, had blown over, and she was brought to say from the heart, "thy will be done." Yes C. she had committed her child to God's parental care; and though her affection was not lessened, yet, with tears in her eyes, she said, "If a conviction of duty and love to the souls of the perishing Heathen lead you to India, as much as I love you, Harriet, I can only say, *Go.*" Here I was left to decide the all important question. Many were the conflicts within my breast. But, at length, from a firm persuasion of duty, and a willingness to comply, after much examination and prayer, I answered in the affirmative.

I wish to tell you all the motives that have actuated me to come to this determination; likewise, how all the difficulties, which applied to me particularly, have been removed. But this I cannot do until I see you. Why cannot you make it convenient to spend three or four weeks with me this summer? To assure you that it would afford me happiness, would be but what you already know. Write to me C. next week, if possible. Let me know when I may expect you, and I will be at home. Perhaps we may go and spend a day or two with our friends in N. I am very lonely. N. H. has been visiting at S. ever since I returned from C. Mr. Newell has gone to Philadelphia, where he expects to continue until a short time before he quits his native country. He is engaged in the study of physic, together with Mr. Hall. How has your mind been exercised of late? Are you living in the enjoyment of religion!

C. we must live nearer to God; we must be more engaged in his cause. We are under the most solemn obligations to be active in the Redeemer's service. Let us not calculate upon a life of idleness and ease; this is not the portion of the followers of the Lamb. They must expect tribulations and crosses in their way to the kingdom of heaven. But let us ever remember, that if we are the believing children of God, a rest awaits us in heaven, which will doubly compensate us for all the troubles of this life.

When interceding at the mercy seat, Oh forget not C. to pray for the salvation of the benighted Heathen, whose souls are as precious as our own. With them, remember your friend HARRIET.

1811.

June 30. Mr. D. preached from this text, "And as he drew nigh to the city, he wept over it, saying,"[134] &c. My whole soul was melted into compassion for impenitent sinners. Can I ever again feel regardless and unconcerned for their immortal souls?

> "Did Christ for sinners weep,
> And shall our cheeks be dry?
> Let floods of penitential grief,
> Burst forth from every eye."[135]

Did Jesus say to sinners, "Oh that thou hadst known in this thy day, the things that belong to thy peace,"[136] &c. and shall I smile upon them, while in the road to ruin?

July 15. The long expected letter has at length arrived. How can I wish for a friend, more worthy of my love, more deserving of my heart? But my heart is already his. A friend, how rich the treasure! If an earthly friend is thus near to my heart, how strong should be my attachment to a holy God, whose friendship to his children is lasting as eternity! How can I love him sufficiently? How can I take too much delight in honouring him before the world, and in promoting his cause?

July 23. I have just read a little passage in Thomson's Seasons, which I thought I could adopt as my own language;

> "Should fate command me to the farthest verge
> Of the green earth, to distant barb'rous climes,
> Rivers unknown to song; where first the sun
> Gilds Indian mountains, or his setting beam
> Flames on the Atlantic Isles; 'tis nought to me,
> Since God is ever present—ever felt,
> In the void waste, as in the city full;
> And where *he* vital breathes, there *must be joy*."[137]

Extracts from a Letter to her Sister M. at Charlestown.

August 1, 1811.

——— "SHOULD I tell you there is a prospect of my spending the remaining part of this short life in a land of strangers; should I tell you I *do* seriously think of leaving my native dwelling, my friends and companions for ever; would you upbraid me? Could you attribute it to want of attachment to the friends of my youth, or to entire ignorance of this great undertaking? You would not, you *could not*, did you know the conflict which almost rends my heart. Never before did my dear mamma, brothers, and sisters, appear so dear to me. But God commands me! In his holy providence he now offers me an opportunity of visiting the Heathen. While many of my female friends, who are far more adequate to the important employment, are permitted to enjoy the society of their earthly relatives through life, I am called to quit the scenes of my childhood, and go to a far distant country. How can I ever pray for the promotion of the Gospel among the Heathen, if I am unwilling to offer my little aid when such an opportunity is given? I know what to expect from a gay and thoughtless world. But I have this consolation, that ridicule cannot injure my soul. In the eternal world, how trifling will it appear! That some professing Christians oppose it, will cause me many unhappy feelings. But I must think, that were they to view the subject impartially, divesting themselves of the love of worldly ease, they would favour it. With my present feelings, I would not oppose it for all this earth can afford; lest I should be found fighting against God, discouraging Missions, and preventing the Gospel's being spread among the Heathen.

I have this consolation, if the motives by which I am actuated are sincere and good, God will accept the inclination to glorify him, even though I should not be made useful. But my dear sister, this is a trying season! It is from God alone that I derive the least sensible comfort. This world has lost its power to charm, and all its applause is a trifle, light as air. My companions are perhaps accusing me of superstition, and the love of novelty. But God alone knows the motives by which I am actuated, and he alone will be my final Judge. Let me but form such a decision as he will approve, and I ask no more. Willingly will I let go my eager grasp of the things of time and sense, and flee to Jesus. Oh, that he would prepare me for the future events of life, and glorify himself in the disposal of my concerns!"

1811.

Aug. 7. I have just laid down Horne on Missions.[138] How did his pious heart glow with benevolence to his fellow creatures! How ardently did he wish for the promulgation of the Gospel, among the benighted Heathen! I think, for a moment,

I partake of his ardour, and long to hear that the standard of the cross is set up in the distant nations of the earth.

> "Yes, christian heroes! go—proclaim
> Salvation through Immanûel's name:
> To India's clime the tidings bear,
> And plant the rose of Sharon there."[139]

Willingly would I sacrifice the dearest earthly friend to engage in this blessed service. Oh, that I had a thousand pious relatives, well calculated for the important station of Missionaries; the tenderest ties, that bind me to them, should be rent. I would say to them, go—and let the destitute millions of Asia and Africa know, there is *compassion* in the hearts of *christians;* tell them of the love of Jesus, and the road to bliss on high. Providence now gives me an opportunity to go myself to the Heathen. Shall I refuse the offer? shall I love the glittering toys of this dying world so well, that I cannot relinquish them for God? Forbid it, Heaven! Yes, I will go—however weak and unqualified I am, there is an all-sufficient Saviour, ready to support me. In God alone is my hope. I will trust his promises, and consider it one of the highest privileges that would be conferred upon me, to be permitted to engage in his glorious service, among the wretched inhabitants of Hindostan.

Aug. 11. How reviving to my disconsolate mind, has been the word of life this day! Oh, this adorable[140] plan of salvation! Have I the least inclination to alter *one single part of it*, if I could? O no! I *would not* be less holy—I would not wish God to exact *less perfect* obedience from his creatures.

Mr. R. drank tea with us. I felt the same backwardness in conversing upon the things of the kingdom, that I usually do. Whence this criminal diffidence? Oh, when will divine grace so absorb my heart, that my stammering tongue shall be loosed, and Jesus and his salvation be my theme! If I cannot unite in conversing with *believers*, in a land where religion flourishes, how can I speak to the benighted Heathen of India, whose minds are involved in Pagan darkness?

To Miss M. S. of Boston.

Haverhill, Sabbath, Aug. 11, 1811.

How great, my dear M. would be the pleasure, could I retreat with you to some lonely corner, far from the busy haunts of this vain world, and unbosom to you the secrets of my heart, instead of writing to you. But this dear privilege is denied me. I must be content with expressing a few unconnected thoughts on paper for the present, and will anticipate a happy meeting with you on earth, and a still happier one in those regions, where the friends of Immanuel will never more be separated. What if our intercourse on earth should cease? If we are the followers of the Lamb, our prayers will unitedly ascend to the same blessed throne while we live; and when our pilgrimage is ended, our friendship will exist and flourish for ever. M. we are pilgrims, we are strangers in a barren land. This world is not our portion; it is incapable of satisfying our desires. The glittering toys of life are not calculated to afford real enjoyment. There is nothing in heaven or earth, but God, that can delight our hearts, and ease us of the heavy load of sin. Let us not be satisfied with the low and grovelling pursuits of time; but let us look to the unchangeable Jehovah, for a supply of his soul-refreshing grace. How much has God done for us individually? He has, as we humbly trust, made us partakers of his grace, and redeemed us from eternal death. What shall we render to him for this abundant mercy? Oh, let our future lives evince our gratitude, and let our praises unceasingly flow to his throne! Dear M. I feel as though I had done nothing for God. Where are the last five years of my wretched life? Can they witness to my exertions in the cause of the Lord? "I think of the days of other years, and my soul is sad."[141] All is a barren waste. A few heartless duties and cold formalities, will never carry me to heaven.

Sabbath eve. This day, my dear M. I have been highly privileged. I have heard three sermons preached by the excellent Mr. R. How sweet is the Gospel to the heart of the believer! How does the pure word of truth animate the desponding sinner, and encourage him to apply to the Lamb of God for pardon and sanctification! But this glorious Gospel, which reveals to mortals the way of salvation, the far greater part of the inhabitants of the earth are deprived of. "Where there is no vision the people perish." Thousands of immortal souls are entering eternity, and peopling the dark realms of woe. If our souls are of greater importance than this world, with all its boasted treasures, how can we calculate the worth of those millions of souls, which are equally as precious as our own? We have had the Bible in our hands from our childhood; we are instructed regularly from this precious volume, every sabbath. We have believing friends to associate with; we enjoy the stated ordinances of the Gospel. But the dear Heathen have no such privileges. They are destitute of Bibles, Sabbaths, and Churches. The inhabitants of Hindostan,[142] to atone for their sins, will submit to the most cruel tortures imaginable. Widows consent to be burned[143] with their deceased husbands; parents sacrifice their infant offspring to appease the anger of their idol gods; they cast them into the river Ganges,[144] where they perish. But this dreadful superstition vanishes before the benignant rays of the Gospel, as the morning dew before the rising sun. We enjoy its meridian splendours. Have we any benevolence? Are we susceptible of feeling for the distresses of our fellow creatures? As we value the salvation which a Saviour offers; as we value his tears, his labours, and his death, let us now seriously ask what we shall do for the salvation of the benighted Heathen? If we are not permitted to visit them ourselves, and declare to them the efficacy of a Saviour's blood, yet we can ardently pray for them. And not only pray for them, but by our vigorous exertions we can awaken a missionary spirit in others, and excite them also to feel for those who are perishing in Pagan darkness. M. the subject is copious indeed. I might easily write till the rising sun, and then not give you a perfect delineation of the wretchedness of many of our fellow creatures. But I must leave these forlorn wretches. Suffice it to say, that when the whole universe shall stand collected at the bar of God, we shall meet them, and there render a solemn account for the manner with which we have conducted ourselves towards them in this world. I hope my dear M. you are living near to God, and enjoying times of refreshing from his presence. Oh pray often, and remember me in your prayers. Should stormy oceans roll between us, yet I shall ever continue to love you. Farewell, my dear M.

Your affectionate   HARRIET.

Extracts of a Letter to her Sister M. at Charlestown.

Aug. 1811.

———— "A FEW moments this morning shall be spent in writing to my dear sister. Accept my hearty congratulations for your returning health. I often think of you, and imagine you possessed of every comfort, which can render life desirable. I have been contrasting your present delightful situation with the trying one that is probably to be mine. Although I could shed floods of tears at the idea of bidding a final farewell to the dear associates of my youth, and the guardian and instructor of my early years; yet a consciousness that this is the path marked out for me by my Heavenly Father, and an assurance that the cause I have engaged in is a blessed one, impart at times an indescribable pleasure. If some unforeseen occurrence should prevent my going to the East Indies,[145] I shall still enjoy the satisfaction of thinking that *this* also is ordered by God. Should I never go, Oh may I never forget the wretched inhabitants of Hindostan, nor cease to pray that they may enjoy the blessings of the Gospel.

HARRIET ATWOOD.

1811.

Aug. 13. How consoling has been the beloved promise, when sinking under the contemplated difficulties of a missionary life, "my *grace* is *sufficient* for thee."[146] Have I any thing but an unfaithful, depraved heart, to discourage me, in this great undertaking? Here the Almighty God, the Maker of all worlds, the infinite Disposer of all events, has pledged his *word* for the safety of his believing children. Sooner will the universe sink into nothing, than God fail of performing his promises. The cause is good, the foundation is sure. If the Saviour has promised a sufficiency of his grace, what have I to fear? Oh that I had a stronger confidence in God—a heart to rely on him for grace to help in every time of need! When I reach my journey's end, how trifling will earthly sorrows appear!

Aug. 14. This is indeed a wretched world. How few the joys! How many and various the sorrows of life! Well, if this world is unsatisfying, "if cares and woes promiscuous grow," how *great* the consolation, that I shall soon leave it!

"Loose, then, from earth, the grasp of fond desire,
Weigh anchor, and the happier climes explore."[147]

In the Paradise of God, every rising wish that swells the heart of the celestial inhabitant, is immediately gratified. Oh for a dismission from this clayey tabernacle! Oh for an entrance into those lovely mansions! My soul pants for the full enjoyment of God. I cannot bear this *little* spirituality—this absurd indifference; I long to be swallowed up in endless fruition!

Aug. 15. A letter from my friend, Mr. Newell. He appears much impressed with eternal concerns. May he enjoy the light of Immanuel's countenance! Have just heard of Mr. J.'s arrival, and that he expects soon to set out for India. This unexpected news solemnized my mind. A consciousness of my unpreparedness for this arduous undertaking makes me tremble. But I will give myself to God; "'tis all that I can do."[148]

Aug. 19. Conscious that the riches and honours of this world will not be mine, my deceitful heart often promises happiness in the society of a dear friend. But how vain this hope! Oh let me from this hour cease from anticipating creature happiness! Oh that I could look to God alone for permanent satisfaction!

> "Dear Saviour, let thy beauties be
> My soul's eternal food;
> And grace command my heart away
> From all created good."[149]

Aug. 20. How strong is Christian friendship! He who enjoined it upon his followers, to love *God*, has likewise commanded them to love *one another*. If I am a stranger to the joys of pardoning mercy; if I am an enemy to holiness; whence arises this *union* with *Christians?* What has produced this love to those who resemble *God? Formerly*, I preferred the friendship and society of those, whose hearts were at enmity with God; who disliked the sublime and humbling doctrines of the Gospel; but now I can say with Ruth, "thy people shall be *my* people."[150] My soul is cemented to them; and if I am not greatly deceived, my affection is the strongest for those who live nearest to God, and are most concerned for his glory. I love the most abject creature in existence, however despised by the wise men of this world, who bears the *image* of the lowly *Jesus*. Yes; how could I rejoice to give the endearing appellation of *brother* or *sister*, to one of the tawny natives of the East, whom grace had subdued.

Aug. 22. Sweet is the name of Immanuel to believers. That name speaks peace and consolation to their troubled minds. In him they find a balm for every woe.

> "Jesus to multitudes unknown,
> Oh name divinely sweet!
> Jesus in thee, in thee alone,
> Wealth, honour, pleasure meet.
> Should both the Indies, at my call,
> Their boasted stores resign;
> With joy, I would renounce them all,
> For leave to call *thee* mine.

> Should earth's vain treasures all depart;
> Of this dear gift possess'd,
> I'd clasp it to my joyful heart,
> And be for ever bless'd."[151]

Is this the language of *my* heart? Am *I* willing to relinquish the pleasures, the honours, the riches, and the applause of the world, for leave to call *Immanuel* mine? If so, I may enjoy exalted happiness, in a land of strangers.

To Miss H. B. of Salem,

Haverhill, Aug. 23, 1811.

INDUCED by the repeated solicitations of your sister S. I have retired to my chamber, determined to devote a leisure hour, in renewing a correspondence, which has for a long time been entirely relinquished. The attachments which I formed in the earlier part of my life, have of late been greatly strengthened. Those companions in whose society, "the longest summer days seemed too much in haste,"[152] have become exceedingly dear to my heart. You, my H. were one of the choicest and most loved members of the dear familiar circle. Did pensive melancholy for a moment assume the place of mirth and gaiety in my mind, you were immediately acquainted with the cause. Did my youthful heart beat with joy, if you were a partner, joy was heightened. But particularly dear did the appellation of friend appear, when we were unitedly depressed with a sense of the divine displeasure, and when our souls, as we then thought, were irradiated with the light of truth, and washed in the peace-speaking blood of Immanuel. Should our lives be spared, very different will probably be our future destinies. Blest with those beloved friends, whose sympathy alleviates every grief, whose society contributes so largely to your happiness, and indulged, not only with a competency, but with affluence and ease, you may glide along through this world, almost a stranger to the ills attendant on mortals. But these joys remain not for me. Destined to a far distant land, my affectionate friends, my pleasant home, my much loved country, I must leave for ever. Instead of the soft delights and elegancies of life, self-denials, hardships, privations, and sorrows will be mine. Instead of the improved and polished society of Haverhill associates, will be substituted the society of the uncivilized Hindoos. Instead of being enlivened by the cheering voice of a believing friend, I shall behold thousands prostrating themselves before dumb idols, while the air will ring with the horrid sounds of idol music. No churches will be found for the refreshment of weary pilgrims; no joyful assemblies where saints can resort to unite in the reviving exercises of social worship. All will be dark, every thing will be dreary, and not a hope of worldly happiness will be for a moment indulged. The prime of life will be spent in an unhealthy country, a burning region, amongst a people of strange language, at a returnless distance from my native land, where I shall never more behold the friends of my youth. Amid these discouragements,

I often find my sinking heart desponding. But this is not all. Even while blest with a habitation in my own country, I hear some of those friends, whom I fondly love, accusing me of the love of novelty, of an invincible attachment to a fellow creature, of superstition and of wanting a great name. Wretched, indeed, will be my future lot, if these motives bear sway in my determination. Surrounded by so many discouragements, I find consolation only in God! "None of these things move me, neither count I my life dear unto me."[153] A consciousness that this is the path, which my Heavenly Father hath selected for me, and an ardent desire for the salvation of the benighted Heathen, constrains me to cry, Here am I, Lord, send me where thou wilt. Daily experience convinces me that the glittering toys of life are not capable of conferring real happiness. With my present feelings, I may enjoy as much happiness in India as in America. But my great consolation is that life is short. However great may be my trials, they will be soon over. H. I feel that *this* is a wretched world. It is nearly six years since, I humbly trust, I committed my *all* to God, willing that he should dispose of me, as he saw best. He has given me friends; he has given me many earthly comforts; but he is now appointing me trials, greater than I yet have known. But I think I can say, "*It is well.*" Give me but humble resignation to thy will, Oh my God, and I ask no more. The presence of Immanuel will make a mud-walled cottage, a foreign land, and savage associates, desirable. What but the light of the Redeemer's countenance can make me happy here? and what but that can delight my soul, in a far distant country?

> "For me remains nor time, nor space,
> My country is in every place;
> I can be calm and free from care
> On any shore,—since God is there."[154]

It seems a long time since we had the pleasure of seeing you at Haverhill. Your time, undoubtedly, passes away very pleasantly in Salem. May your happiness be constantly increasing at the return of each succeeding year. May you have that peace of mind, that heartfelt joy, which is known only by the decided followers of Jesus. This is pleasure that knows no alloy, and which death can never deprive you of. May I meet you with all my dear friends, in that world, where a wide sea can never separate us. I hope to spend many happy hours with you before I bid you a final farewell. I am affectionately yours.　　　　　　　　　　　　　　　HARRIET.

1811.

Aug. 25. With the light of this holy morning I desire to make a solemn surrender of myself to God, humbly requesting him, to accept the worthless offering. I think I can say with Mr. Newton,

> "Day of all the week the best,
> Emblem of eternal rest."[155]

Aug. 26. What word can be more impressive and weighty than ETERNITY? How replete with events, that deeply interest every intelligent creature! How full of ideas too big for utterance! And can ETERNITY be *mine?* If the word of Jehovah be true, I shall surely inhabit *Eternity,* when this short life is ended. Yes; I feel that I have an immortal part, which will continue the same when time and nature fail. And shall it exist in glory? Oh, let me fly to Jesus, and make his arms my resting place. Then shall I rest securely, when the heavens are rolled together as a scroll,[156] and the elements melt with fervent heat.[157]

Sept. 1. Again have I been favoured with the blessed privilege of communing with God, at his table. How sweetly calculated are these Gospel ordinances to enliven the cold hearts of believers, and to prepare them for the marriage supper of the Lamb. I have renewedly given myself away to God, in the presence of the holy angels, of the assembly which convened at the house of prayer, and of that Being whose presence fills immensity; whose smile gives hope, whose frown, despair. How solemn the transaction!—Far from the happy land, where salvation is proclaimed, my thoughts have wandered over stormy seas, to regions, whose inhabitants are sitting in the shadow of death. No light of divine revelation beams on them. No sanctuaries—no communion tables—no bread and wine to remind them that a Saviour shed his blood on Calvary for them! Weep, Oh my soul, for the forlorn Heathen. Be astonished at the stupidity of Christians, be astonished at *thine own.* Oh, thou blessed Redeemer, thou who didst commission thy disciples of old to preach the Gospel to every creature, wilt thou send forth labourers, make the wilderness a fruitful field, and cause the desert to blossom like the rose!

Sept. 3.
"I'm but a stranger and a pilgrim here,
In these wild regions, wandering and forlorn,
Restless and sighing for my native home,
Longing to reach my weary space of life,
And to fulfil my task."[158]

Yes; my Redeemer, I know by experience, that this life is a tiresome round of vanities hourly repeated. All is empty. My thirsty soul longs for the enjoyment of God in heaven, where the weary and heavy laden find rest. How long, Oh my Father, shall I wander in this dreary land? When shall I bid a final adieu to these scenes of guilt!

"Oh, haste the hour of joy, and sweet repose."[159]

How refreshing will heavenly rest be to my soul, after a life of toil and hardship!
Sept. 7. "Bless the Lord, Oh my soul, and forget not all his benefits."[160] Yes; I will bless and praise thy name, my God, my King, my everlasting all. I will bless thee for temporal, I will bless thee for spiritual favours. Thou hast ever been loading me with thy benefits. "The Lord is my light and my salvation; whom shall I fear: The Lord is the strength of my life; of whom shall I be afraid? Lord, by thy

favour thou hast made my mountain to stand strong. I will extol thee, for thou hast lifted me up; and hast not made my foes to rejoice over me. Thou hast brought up my soul from the grave, thou hast kept me alive, that I should not go down to the pit. Sing unto the Lord, Oh ye saints of his; and give thanks at the remembrance of his holiness; for his anger endureth but for a moment; in his favour is life; weeping may endure for a night; but joy cometh in the morning."[161]

Sept. 10. Depressed with guilt, and tired with the vanities of this world, I have retired to my chamber, to seek pleasure within. When blest with a sense of Immanuel's love, I find satisfaction in writing, conversing, and thinking on divine things; but when Jesus frowns, all is midnight darkness. No duties—no domestic employments—no earthly pleasures can charm or delight my mind.

Sept. 12.
> "The time is short, I soon shall rise,
> And bid farewell to weeping eyes,
> And reach the heavenly shore."[162]

I have attempted this morning, to bring India, with the parting scenes between, near at hand. Surely, nothing but the sovereign power of God could have led me to contemplate, with serenity and composure, the painful scenes of a missionary life; and nothing but his grace will support me, when farewells are sounding around me. Oh, how can I *think* of that hour! But it is a glorious work, for which I am making these great sacrifices: it is nothing less than to assist in spreading the triumphs of the cross, in foreign lands. Oh, could I become the instrument of bringing *one* degraded *female* to Jesus, how should I be repaid for *every tear*, and every *pain!* To make a female Indian acquainted with the way of life, Oh what a blessing!—my soul exults at the thought!

Sept. 17. How sweet is this text, "Be careful for nothing, but in every thing, by prayer and supplication let your requests be made known unto God."[163] When the difficulties of my future life depress me, how often am I insensibly relieved, and comforted by *this* and similar invitations. How precious, how exceedingly valuable is the word of God!

Sept. 20. Life like an empty vapour flies. Soon will my mortal state be ended. The objects which now occupy so large a portion of my thoughts, will shortly lose their importance, and vanish as though I saw them not. Vanity is stamped on every earthly enjoyment. But pleasure without the least alloy will be found in heaven.

To a Friend.

Haverhill, Sept. 1811.

FORGIVE, my dear M. the liberty I take in addressing you in this manner. From my first acquaintance with you, I have felt deeply interested for your happiness. Nothing but an affectionate regard for you, would induce me to write to you on a subject which the world will undoubtedly ridicule, but which engages the attention and constitutes the felicity of the holy inhabitants of heaven. This subject is the religion of the Gospel—a subject which is infinitely interesting to us both. You have of late witnessed a scene, trying indeed, and solemn as eternity. You have watched the sick-bed, you have heard the expiring groans of your beloved sister. You fondly hope that she was interested in the covenant of redemption, and is now perfectly happy in the enjoyment of her God in heaven. When standing by the dying bed of this dear sister, say, my friend, did you not ardently wish for piety similar to hers; for *that faith* which could triumph over the horrors of a dying hour? Was the hope then cherished that you should meet her in yonder world, when the trials of this short life are over? and did *this* hope support your sinking spirits in the trying hour of separation? She has gone for ever; but *we* are still prisoners of hope. Could we now draw back the covering of the tomb, and listen to her language, how earnestly would she beseech us to become reconciled to God, and devote our lives wholly to his service. My dear M. these are not idle dreams. If we reflect for a moment, we feel conscious that there is an immortal principle within, which will exist when time and nature dies. This principle is corrupted by sin, and without the sanctifying grace of God, we should be unhappy, even though admitted to Heaven. Do but examine the feelings of your heart one hour, and you cannot for a moment doubt the truth of this assertion. How important then that we should have this work of grace begun in our hearts, before it is too late. "Now is the accepted time, now is the day of salvation."[164] Tomorrow our probation may be closed, and we may be irrecoverably lost. M. my heart is full. What inducements can I offer you to receive Jesus into your heart, and willingly sacrifice your all for him? Oh! think of the worth of the soul, the price paid to redeem it, the love of Immanuel, your obligations to live to him, the joys prepared for the righteous;—and oh, think of the torments in reserve for the finally impenitent, and be induced to flee from the wrath to come. If nothing in Providence prevents, before the return of another Autumn, Harriet will be a stranger in a strange land.[165] I go, my friend, where Heathens dwell, far from the companions of my playful years, far from the dear land of my nativity. My contemplated residence will be, not among the refined and cultivated, but among females degraded and uncivilized, who have never heard of the religion of Jesus. How would it gladden my sad heart, in the trying hour of my departure, could I but leave a dear circle of females of my own age, engaged for God, and eminent for their usefulness in Haverhill. Well, I hope to find a circle of Hindoo sisters in India, interested in *that* religion which many of my companions reject, though blest with innumerable privileges. But my friend M. will not treat with indifference *this* religion. O no! I will cherish the fond hope, that she will renounce the world, become a follower of Immanuel, and be unwearied in her exertions to spread the triumphs of the cross through the world. I must leave you my dear M. with God. May you become a living witness for him! When our journey through this barren wilderness is ended, may we meet in heaven!

HARRIET.

1811.

Oct. 10. I have this day entered upon my nineteenth year. Oh, how great the goodness of God which has followed me, through the last twelve months! And shall I be wholly destitute of gratitude? O no! let me this year, if my life should be spared, become a living witness for the truth, as it is in Jesus. How great a change has the last year made in my views and prospects for life! Another year will probably affect, not merely my *prospects*, but my *situation*. Should my expectations be realized, my dwelling will be far from the dear land of my nativity; and from beloved friends, whose society rendered the morning of my life cheerful and serene. In distant India, every earthly prospect will be dreary.

> "But even *there*, content can spread a charm,
> Redress the clime, and all its rage disarm."[166]

Oct. 13. How important is it, that I should be in a peculiar manner devoted to God, and dead to the world. I shall need a large supply of the graces of the Gospel, and of the consolations of religion, to support me amid the numberless trials of a missionary life. When dangers stand thick around, and the world is utterly incapable of affording me the least solid comfort—what will sustain me, but entire confidence in God, as my shield, my only sure defence? Oh, my Father! let a sense of thy love to my soul, influence me to yield implicit obedience to thy commands; and while this love is constraining me to walk in the path which thou hast *selected* for me, may thy grace be sufficient for me—as my *day* is, so may my *strength* be.

Oct. 20.
> "Soon I hope—I feel, and am assured,
> That I shall lay my head—my weary, aching head,
> On its last rest; and on my lowly bed,
> The grass green sod will flourish sweetly." —

The perusal of the life, letters, and poems of Henry Kirke White, has been productive of much satisfaction. While I have respected him for his learning and superior talents, I have ardently wished for a share of that piety, which shone so conspicuously in his life, and which rendered his character so interesting and lovely. His "weary aching head," is now resting in the silent tomb. Henry sleeps, to wake no more; but his spirit, unconfined, is exploring the unseen world! O that his example may affect my heart![167]

To Miss S. H. Andover.

Haverhill, Oct. 20, 1811.

WILL my dear Miss H. pardon this seeming neglect, when I assure her it has not been intentional? Did you but know how numerous have been my engagements since I left Andover, I feel confident that you would not indulge one hard thought.

I have thought much of you, and have often longed to see you. The kindness you showed me, while with you, greatly endeared you to my heart. I hope I shall ever recollect with gratitude the unmerited favours, which you, Mr. and Mrs. W. and my other friends, conferred upon me while in Andover.

This day has been spent in melancholy dejection and sorrow of heart. The trials of a missionary life, united with my entire unfitness for the undertaking, and the fear of being under the influence of improper motives, have produced distress. But the return of evening has dissipated the gloom, and I have been led to rejoice in God, and willingly to surrender my eternal all to him. O my friend! is there not a balm in Gilead? is there not an all-powerful Physician there?[168] Who can doubt of the abilities and willingness of Jesus, to lead his dear children along the green pastures, and beside the still waters? His sacred presence will cause the sinking heart to rejoice, and diffuse gladness around. Rightly is he styled Immanuel. Let us fly immediately to this hiding-place—this covert from the storm and tempest. In Jesus we are safe, though earth and hell combine against us. What are the trials, what the *agonies* attendant on this pilgrimage state! In Jesus, there is a fulness sufficient to supply our every want, healing for every wound, and a cordial for every fear.

With the deepest interest I have lately read Buchanan's Researches.[169] You have probably read it. Has it not inspired you with an ardent missionary spirit? Can it be possible, that Christians, after perusing this invaluable book, can help feeling a deep concern for the salvation of the Heathen, and a strong desire for the promulgation of the Gospel throughout the world? How precious, how exceedingly valuable, is the word of God! How consolatory to the believer, to hear those who were once prostrating themselves before dumb idols, now exclaim with eagerness, "we want not bread, we want not money, we want the Word of God."[170] A FAMINE FOR BIBLES—how sweet, and yet how painful the expression. Surely *this will* lead us to estimate our glorious privileges in this christian land. Possessed of every means of learning the character of God, and the way of salvation by a Redeemer, how can we complain? If ever the religion of the cross has excited within us holy desires, oh let us not forget the destitute millions of Asia. God will be inquired of by his people to do great things for the Heathen world. How importunate then should we be at the throne of grace; and none ever cried unto God in vain.

Dear Miss H. I could write an hour longer, but other engagements prevent. We long to see you; long to hear from you again. Do write us often. Mamma sends much love; intends writing you soon; thanks you for your last letter. Remember me affectionately to dear Mr. and Mrs. W.; likewise to Mr. L. and Mr. M.

I am, dear Miss H. your affectionate   HARRIET.

1811.

Oct. 25. How strong are the ties of natural affection! Will distance or time ever conquer the attachment, which now unites my heart so closely to my mother, the *dear guardian* of my youth; and to my beloved brothers and sisters? Oh no;

though confined to a foreign country, where a parent's voice will no more gladden my melancholy heart, still shall that love, which is *stronger* than death, dwell within, and often waft a sincere prayer to heaven for blessings unnumbered upon her. Long shall remembrance dwell on scenes, past in the dear circle of Haverhill friends.

Nov. 4. It is midnight. My wavering mind would fain dwell on some mournful subject. I weep; then sing some melancholy air, to pass away the lingering moments. What would my dear mother say, to see her Harriet thus involved in gloom? But why do I indulge these painful feelings? Is it because my *Father* is unkind, and will not hear a suppliant's cries? Is he not not willing to direct my wandering steps; to guide my feet in the paths of peace? Oh yes; his ear is ever open to the prayer of the fatherless. Let me then go to him; tell him all my griefs, and ask of him a calm and clear conviction of duty.

> "Why sinks my weak desponding mind,
> Why heaves my soul, this heavy sigh?
> Can sovereign goodness be unkind,
> Am I not safe, if *God* be nigh?"[171]

Nov. 10. The rising sun witnesses for my heavenly Father, that he is good. Oh yes! his character is infinitely lovely—his attributes are perfect. I behold his goodness in the works of creation and providence. But the beauty of his character shines most *conspicuously* in the plan of salvation. In the Redeemer, beauty and worth are combined; and shall my heart remain unaffected, amidst such an endless variety of witnesses of the glory of God? Shall *I* be silent, for whom the Son of God, on Calvary, bled and died?

Here the diary, from which the foregoing extracts have been made, closes. But amid the various engagements, which occupied the time of Mrs. Newell, and the many interesting subjects of her contemplation, she continued a frequent correspondence with her friends. The number of letters which she wrote, from the age of *thirteen* to her death, was remarkable.

To Miss R. F. of Andover.

Haverhill, Nov. 10, 1811.

How shall I sufficiently thank my dear Miss F. for her affectionate communication, received a short time since by Mr. Judson? This was a favour which I had long wished for, but which I had ever considered an unmerited one.

I have this day visited the sanctuary of the Most High. While listening to the joyful sound of the Gospel, my thoughts were insensibly led to the forlorn and destitute state of the Heathen, who are unacquainted with *Bibles, Churches* and *Sabbaths*. I thought of the glorious privileges, which the inhabitants of *this* my Christian country enjoy; and the thought afforded indescribable pleasure. I reflected on the many millions of Asia and Africa; and the reflection was full of anguish and sympathy. Oh my friend, when will the day dawn, and the day-star arise in Pagan lands, where Moloch reigns, "besmeared with blood of human sacrifice, and parent's tears." Oh! when, will the religion of Jesus, which has irradiated our benighted souls, be promulgated throughout the world? When will Christians feel more concerned for the salvation of the Heathen; and when will the heralds of the Gospel feel willing to sacrifice the soft delights and elegancies of life, and visit the far distant shores, where Heathen strangers dwell? Oh! when will those who have an interest at the mercy seat, intercede for the wretched Heathen!

But my dear Miss F. though I sometimes feel deeply and tenderly interested for the Heathen, and even feel willing to contribute my little aid in the work of a mission; yet the trials of such a life often produce a melancholy dejection, which nothing but divine grace can remove. Often does my imagination paint, in glowing colours, the last sad scene of my departure from the land of my nativity. A widowed mother's heart with anguish wrung, the tears of sorrow flowing from the eyes of brothers and sisters dear, while the last farewell is pronounced—this is a scene affecting indeed. But this is only the commencement of a life replete with trials. Should my life be protracted, my future residence will be far distant from my native country, in a land of strangers, who are unacquainted with the feelings of friendship and humanity.

But I will no longer dwell on these sad subjects. I will look to God; from him is all my aid. He can support his children in the darkest hour, and cause their sinking hearts to rejoice. He has pledged his word, that his grace shall be sufficient for them, and that as their day is, so shall their strength be. How consoling the reflection, that we are in the hands of God! He can do nothing wrong with us: but if we are members of his family, all things will continually work for our good. Trials will wean us from this alluring world, and prepare us for that rest which is reserved for the righteous. And how sweet will that rest be, after a life of toil and suffering. Oh! how does the anticipation of future bliss, sweeten the bitter cup of life. My friend, there is a world, beyond these rolling spheres, where adieus and farewells are unknown. There I hope to meet you with all the ransomed of Israel, and never more experience a painful separation.

> "The thoughts of such amazing bliss,
> Should constant joys create."[172]

H. A.

To Miss F. W. of Beverly.

Haverhill, Dec. 13, 1811.

I HAVE long been wishing for a favourable opportunity to return my thanks to my dear Miss W. for her affectionate letter received last June. A multiplicity of avocations, which could not possibly be dispensed with, have deprived me of this pleasure till now. But though my friends have been neglected, they have not been forgotten. Oh no! dear to my heart, are the friends of Immanuel; particularly those with whom I have walked to the house of God in company, and with whom, I have taken sweet counsel about things which immediately concern Zion, the city of our God. These dear Christian friends, will retain a lasting and affectionate remembrance in my heart, even though stormy oceans should separate me from them. There is a world, my sister, beyond this mortal state, where souls, cemented in one common union, will dwell together, and never more be separated. Does not your heart burn within you, when in humble anticipation of future blessedness, you engage in the delightful service of your covenant Redeemer? When your spirit sinks within you, and all terrestrial objects lose their power to please, can you not say,

> My journey here,
> Though it be darksome, joyless and forlorn,
> Is yet but short; and soon my weary feet,
> Shall greet the peaceful inn of lasting rest:
> The toils of this short life will soon be over.[173]

Yes, my friend, we soon shall bid an eternal farewell to this passing world, and if interested in the covenant, we shall find the rest which remaineth for the people of God. I thank you sincerely for the affectionate interest you have taken in my future prospect in life. I feel encouraged to hope that not only your good wishes, but fervent prayers will attend my contemplated undertaking. I know that the earnest supplications of the faithful will avail with God: plead then, my friend, with Jesus on my behalf. The path of duty is the only way to happiness. I love to tread the path which my Father points out for me, though it is replete with privations and hardships. Who, my dear Miss W. that has felt the love of Jesus, the worth of souls, and the value of the Gospel, would refuse to lend their little aid in propagating the religion of the Cross among the wretched Heathen, when presented with a favourable opportunity? However great the discouragements attending a missionary life, yet Jesus has promised to be with those who enter upon it with a right disposition, even to the end of the world. When will the day dawn, and the day-star arise in Heathen lands? Oh! when will the standard of the Cross be erected, and all nations hear of the glad tidings of Salvation? When will the millennial state commence, and the lands which have long lain in darkness, be irradiated by the calm sunshine of the Gospel? When will the populous regions of Asia and Africa, unite with this our Christian country in one general song of praise to God? Though darkness and error now prevail, faith looks over these mountains, and beholds with transport, the dawning of the Sun of Righteousness, the reign of peace and love.

The clock strikes twelve; I must leave you my friend, for tired nature requires repose. Pray often for me. Write me immediately upon receiving this hasty letter.

Affectionately yours,   HARRIET.

HARRIET NEWELL, *MEMOIRS* (1815)

To Miss R. F. Andover.

Haverhill, Dec. 29, 1811.

An hour this sacred evening, the commencement of another Sabbath, shall be cordially devoted to my dear Miss F. Alone and pensive, how can the moments glide more pleasantly away, than in writing to a friend whose name excites many endearing sensations, and whom, from my first introduction to her, I have sincerely loved. Similarity of sentiment will produce an indissoluble union of hearts. How strong are the ties which unite the members of Christ's family? While dwelling in this the house of their pilgrimage, they are subject to the same trials and privations; and the same hope encourages them to look forward to the happy hour of their release, when their weary souls shall rest sweetly in the bosom of their God. Such I would fondly hope, is the nature of that union which so strongly cements my heart to Miss F. Oh! that when "the long Sabbath of the tomb is past,"[174] our united souls may be safely anchored in the fair haven of eternal security, where friendship will be perfected.

I have thought much of you since the reception of your kind letter. I hope that divine grace has dissipated your doubts, and that you are now enjoying all holy consolation. May you be made eminently holy and useful, live near to God, and be favoured with those rich communications of his love, which he often bestows upon his children.

I have been reading this afternoon, some account of the superstitions of the wretched inhabitants of Asia. How void of compassion must be that heart which feels not for the woes of its fellow mortals! When, my friend, will the day dawn and the day-star arise in those lands, where the prince of darkness has so long dwelt?[175]

The hour is hastening, when I must bid an eternal farewell to all that is dear in the land of my nativity, cross the boisterous ocean, and become an exile in a foreign land. I must relinquish for ever the friends of my bosom, whose society has rendered pleasant the morning of life, and select for my companions the uncivilized Heathen of Hindostan. I shall shortly enter upon a life of privations and hardships. "All the sad variety of grief"[176] will probably be mine to share. Perhaps no cordial, sympathising friend will stand near my dying bed, to administer consolation to my departing spirit, to wipe the falling tear, the cold sweat away, to close my eyes, or to shed a tear upon my worthless ashes. But shall the contemplation of these adverse scenes, tempt me to leave the path selected by my Heavenly Father? Oh no! "I can do all things through Christ, who strengtheneth me."[177] This consideration, exhilarates my sinking soul, and diffuses an ardour within, which I would not relinquish for all the splendours of this world.

You, my dear Miss F. will not forget to intercede with Jesus in my behalf. You will pray for the wretched Heathen of India; this will lead your thoughts to those who have devoted their lives to the work of spreading the Gospel among them. You will feel interested in their exertions; and as often as the sun rises in the East, you will invoke for them the blessing and protection of the universal Parent.

When shall I be favoured with another interview with you? Will you not visit me this winter? I need not assure you, that it would be a source of the highest gratification. Preparations for a long voyage, together with visiting friends, has prevented my answering your letter before. Do write me again soon; recollect that I have a special claim on your indulgence.

Affectionately yours.   HARRIET.

To Miss M. T. of Newbury.

Boston, Jan. 24, 1812.

NEITHER distance nor time has been able to efface from my mind the recollection of that affection, which I once so sincerely professed to feel for you, my beloved M. My pen would not thus long have lain inactive, had inclination been consulted. No, be assured, that nothing less than important, indispensable engagements has prevented me from acknowledging the receipt of your kind letter, which afforded me much pleasure. I hear from my friend N. that you have been indisposed of late. Such, my sister, is the lot of rebel man. Our world is doomed to agonize in pain and sickness, the just desert of sin. Pilgrims and strangers in a dry and thirsty land, where no living waters flow, we, though so young, feel the heavy effects of the first transgression. A composed and tranquil mind, a heart disposed cheerfully to acquiesce in the dispensations of Heaven, however trying, is desirable indeed. But this divine resignation is a gift of the Spirit. May you be favoured with a disposition to rejoice in God, not only when the calm sunshine of prosperity illumines your dwelling, but also when the dreary tempests of affliction beat upon you. The night of sorrow, though dark, is yet but short, if we are the children of the Most High. As Kirke White beautifully expresses the sentiment, "Our weary feet shall ere long greet the peaceful inn of lasting rest."[178] How sweet will be the rest enjoyed in that peaceful inn, after a life of repeated toil and sufferings for Christ! Let this idea stimulate us to a life of exemplary piety.

If ever we are favoured with intimate communion with God, and feel the value of that Gospel which bringeth life and salvation, let us compassionate the forlorn Heathen. Let our souls weep for those who are unacquainted with the glad tidings; who spend their wretched lives in worshipping dumb idols; whose lips have never been vocal with redeeming love. Oh, when will the radiant star in the East direct them to Bethlehem![179] Oh when will the high praises of Immanuel resound from the lips of the Hindoo in Asia, the Hottentot of Africa, and the inhospitable Indian of our dear native America!

The glorious morn of the Millennium hastens.[180] With an eye of faith we pass the mountains, that now obstruct the universal spread of the Gospel, and behold with joy unspeakable, the beginning of a cloudless day, the "reign of peace and love." Shall we, my ever dear M. who fondly hope that we are the lambs of Jesus' flock, be content to live indolent, inactive lives, and not assist in the great revolution about to be effected in this world of sin? Oh no; we will not let it be said, at the great day, that one soul for whom the Son of God became incarnate, for whom he groaned away a dying life, has perished through our neglect. Let worldly ease be sacrificed; let a life of self-denial and hardships be welcome to us, if the cause of God may thereby be most promoted, and sinners most likely to be saved from destruction.

Notwithstanding all the encouragements which the Scriptures afford to those who leave all things for God, and devote their lives to his service, still my heart often recoils at the evils of a missionary life. The idea of taking a last farewell of friends, and country, and all that is dear on earth, (a few friends only excepted) is exceedingly trying. Yes, my friend, Harriet will shortly be an exile in a foreign country, a stranger in a strange land. But it is for God that I sacrifice all the comforts of a civilized life. This comforts me; this is my hope, this my only consolation. Will M. think of me, will she pray for me, when stormy oceans separate us? Will imagination ever waft her to the floating prison or the Indian hut, where she, who was once honoured with the endearing appellation of friend, resides? May we meet in heaven, where friends will no more be called to endure a painful separation! May peace and happiness long be inmates of M.'s breast! May she increase in the enjoyment of her God, as days and years increase! How can I wish her more substantial bliss? Shall I not be favoured with one more undisturbed interview with you? Shall I not give you a parting kiss? Shall I not say, *Farewell?* Why may I not spend the little remnant of my days with you? Must I be separated? But enough—my heart is full; gladly would I fill my sheet with ardent expressions of lasting friendship.

> "But, hush, my fond heart, hush, –
> There is a shore of better promise;
> And I hope at last, we two shall meet
> In Christ to part no more."[181]

A few more letters will probably close our correspondence for ever. Will you write me immediately? M. will gratify me if she loves me. Will you not visit Haverhill this winter? I long to see you. I cannot tell you how much I regretted the loss of your society last summer. I have since been favoured with an introduction to your dear Miss G. A lovely girl.

Affectionately yours,   HARRIET.

To Miss S. H. Andover.

Haverhill, Feb. 3, 1812.

THE long expected hour is at length arrived, and I am called to bid an eternal adieu to the dear land of my nativity, and enter upon a life replete with crosses, privations, and hardships. The conflicting emotions which rend my heart, imagination will point out to my dear Miss H. better than my pen can describe them. But still *peace* reigns many an hour within. Consolations are mine, more valuable than ten thousand worlds. My Saviour, my Sanctifier, my Redeemer, is still lovely; his comforts *will* delight my soul. Think of Harriet, when crossing the stormy ocean—think of her, when wandering over Hindostan's sultry plains. Farewell, my friend, a last, a long farewell.

May *we* meet in yonder world, "where adieus and farewells are a sound unknown!"

Give dear Mrs. W. a parting kiss from Harriet.

Write to and pray often for   HARRIET.

To Miss S. B. of Haverhill.

Haverhill, Feb. 1812.

ACCEPT, my ever dear Sarah, the last tribute of heart-felt affection from your affectionate Harriet, which you will ever receive. The hour of my departure hastens; when another rising sun illumines the Eastern horizon, I shall bid a last farewell to a beloved widowed mother, brothers and sisters dear, and the circle of Haverhill friends. With a scene so replete with sorrow just at hand, how can I be otherwise than solemn as Eternity! The motives which first induced me to determine upon devoting my life to the service of GOD in *distant India*, now console my sinking spirits. Oh, how valuable, how exceedingly precious, are the promises of the Gospel!

Eighteen years of my life have been spent in tranquillity and peace. But those scenes so full of happiness, are departed. They are gone "with the years beyond the flood," no more to return. A painful succession of joyless days will succeed; trials, numberless and severe, will be mine to share. Home, *that dearest, sweetest spot*, friends, whose society has rendered the morn of life pleasant, must be left, for ever! The stormy ocean must be crossed; and an Indian cottage in a sultry clime, must shortly contain all that is Harriet. Perhaps no sympathizing friend will stand near my dying bed, to wipe the falling tear, to administer consolation, or to entomb my worthless ashes when my immortal spirit quits this earthly tabernacle.

But why indulge these melancholy sensations? Is it not for Jesus that I make these sacrifices—and will He not support me by his grace? Oh, yes, my heart replies, he will.

> "The sultry climes of India then I'll choose;
> There will I toil, and sinner's bonds unloose;
> There will I live, and draw my latest breath;
> And, in my Jesus' service, meet a stingless death."[182]

My Friend, there is a rest for the weary pilgrim in yonder world. Shall we meet *there*, "when the long Sabbath of the tomb is past?"[183]

Sarah, my much loved friend, farewell. Farewell, perhaps for ever. Though trackless forests separate, though oceans roll between, Oh, forget not

HARRIET.

These were the last letters written by Mrs. NEWELL, before her departure from America. On the 6th of Feb. 1812. when the Missionaries were ordained, at Salem, Mrs. NEWELL was present. On that interesting occasion, she manifested remarkable tranquillity and resolution. Feb. 19, 1812, with Mr. Newell, and Mr. and Mrs. Judson, she sailed from Salem, and took leave for ever of her native land, amidst the prayers and benedictions of multitudes.

The following diary, written on her passage to India, and addressed to her mother, was lately received.

1812.

March 9. To you, my beloved mother, shall these pages be cheerfully dedicated. If they afford you amusement in a solitary hour, if they are instrumental in dissipating one anxious sensation from your heart, I shall be doubly rewarded for writing. Whatever will gratify a mother, so valuable as mine, shall here be recorded, however uninteresting it might be to a stranger. The first week after our embarkation I was confined to my bed with sea-sickness. This was a gloomy week. But my spirits were not so much depressed, as I once expected they would be. The attendants were obliging, and I had every convenience which I could wish on board a vessel. Feb. 24, the vessel sprung a leak. We were in the greatest danger of sinking during the night. The men laboured almost constantly at the pump. Capt. H. thought it best to alter the course of the Caravan, and make directly for St. Jago. The wind changed in the morning. In a day or two the leak was providentially discovered, and prevented from doing any further injury. Though much fatigued, sleep departed from me. It was indeed an interesting night. Though a sudden exit from life appeared more solemn than ever before, yet I felt a sweet composure in confiding in God, and in leaving the disposal of my life with him.

We have no family worship, which we consider a great affliction. Sabbath forenoon, Mr. N. or brother J. read a sermon and perform the other exercises of worship in the cabin. The captain and officers favour us with their attendance. I have found much enjoyment at these seasons. I often think on my American friends, who are blessed with the privilege of attending statedly on the means of grace. My thoughts were particularly fixed on my brethren and sisters the first sabbath in March. I thought that our dear pastor would not forget to intercede with God for an absent sister, while sitting at the communion table, where I have often had a seat. I shall devote much of my time to reading while on the water. There is but little variety in a sea life. I have noticed with pleasure that many little articles, which I *accidentally* brought with me; have contributed much to my comfort.

The vessel is very damp, and the cabin collects *some dirt*, which renders it necessary that I should frequently change my clothes, in order to appear decent. I think I shall have clothes enough for the voyage, by taking a little care. We have had contrary winds and calms for ten days past, which will make our voyage longer. How can it be that I wish for those winds that waft me farther from my dear mother, and all that I have in a much loved native country. Surely this wish does not originate from want of affection for my friends.

March 10. We have prayers regularly every evening in brother J.'s room, which is larger and more convenient than ours. We have met another brig, bound to America, as we imagine, but on account of contrary winds, which renders it difficult to come near enough to speak with her, she has proceeded on her passage. This is the second vessel which we have seen at a distance, going direct to America; but I have not been favoured with the privilege of sending letters to you. Oh, how ardently do I long to tell you, just how I am at present situated, and that I am happy and contented. We find there is great danger of speaking with any vessel, lest it should prove to be a French privateer. It is very difficult writing to-day, on account of the constant motion of the vessel. The wind is favourable; we go nearly seven miles an hour.

March 12. A heavy sea to-day; the waves have repeatedly broken on deck, and rushed with violence down the gang-way into the cabin. Our room has not yet been wet.

March 14. I have been on deck, and seen the sailors take a turtle. They went out in a boat two or three miles, and took it by surprise, with their hands. It weighs about twenty pounds. We have learned how to make yeast. We have occasionally flour-bread, nuts, apple-puddings, apple-pies, &c. We have baked and stewed beans twice a week, which you know are favourite dishes of mine, also fowls, ham, &c. We drink tamarind-water, porter, cyder, &c. I have been agreeably disappointed respecting our manner of living at sea, though we are not free from inconveniences, by any means.

March 16. Yesterday morning, religious exercises were performed as usual in the cabin. Several pages in Law's Serious Call read. My thoughts dwell on home, and my much-loved country, more intensely on the Sabbath, than on any other day. The sun rises much earlier here than in Haverhill. At one I think you are going to Church. Dined on turtle soup yesterday; do not like it. Saw a flying-fish to-day;[184] breakfasted upon it. Several gales of wind last evening. I do not know why it is that I do not suffer more from fear than I do. Cousin J. will tell you how dreary every thing appears, in a dark evening, when the wind blows hard, and the vessel seems to be on the point of turning over. But we have been highly favoured, the weather has generally been remarkably pleasant.

March 17. I have just seen a third vessel, bound, as we have every reason to think, to dear America. We came so near her as to see the men walking on deck: But Capt. H. received particular orders to speak with no vessel on the passage. I have a great desire to send you, my dear mother, some communication. But this gratification I must give up. Five weeks yesterday since I bid you adieu. Oh that you may never, for one moment, regret that you gave me up, to assist in so great, so glorious a work. I want more faith, more spirituality, more engagedness, in so good a cause. Possessed of these blessings, I shall be happy, while crossing the tempestuous ocean, and when I become an inhabitant of Pagan Asia.

March 18. I am sometimes almost sick for the want of exercise. I walk fast on the deck three times a day, which is the only exercise I take. We have seen a number of flying-fishes to-day, which look very pretty. We are now more than 3000 miles from home. I shall ever find a melancholy pleasure in calling my mother's house in Haverhill, *my home*, though the Atlantic floods roll between. Long may the best of Heaven's blessings rest upon the dwelling, where I have spent my playful years in peace, and where in riper age I have known what tranquillity is, by happy experience: Long may my beloved mother, and dear brothers and sisters, enjoy the blessing of my Heavenly Father, and be strangers to affliction and woe.

March 19. It is excessively warm to-day. We are now in the torrid Zone;[185] while my dear mother, brothers, and sisters are probably shivering over a large fire, I am sitting with the window and door open, covered with perspiration. Brother and sister Judson are asleep on one bed, Mr. N. lounging on another, while I am writing. You know not how much I think of you all, how ardently I desire to hear from you, and see you. My time passes more pleasantly than ever I anticipated. I read, and sew, and converse at intervals; rise early in the morning, retire early at night. I find Mr. Newell to be every thing I could wish for. He not only acts the part of a kind, affectionate friend, but likewise that of a careful, tender *physician*.

March 20. I have been into a bath of salt water this evening, which has refreshed me much. I think I shall bathe regularly every other day. I often think of many ways in which I could have contributed to your comfort and happiness, and that of my other dear friends, while with you. My mother, my dear mother, can you, will you forgive me for causing you so much pain, as I surely have done in the course of my life, and for making you so few returns for the unwearied care and kindness you have ever shown me. I think that if your heart is fixed, trusting in God, you will find consolation, when thinking of my present situation. You will be unspeakably happy in commending me to God, and the word of his grace, and praying for my welfare in Heathen lands.

March 21. A large porpoise was taken yesterday. Cousin J. will describe this curious fish to you. I have had a return of my old complaint, the nervous headache. It has attended me for two or three days very severely. I think it is in some measure owing to the confined air of our lodging room. This is one of the greatest inconveniences to which we are subjected. When I awake these extremely hot mornings, I often think of our large cool chambers. The heat is not all. It is also attended with a disagreeable smell, occasioned by the bilge water which is pumped out of the ship. But this is a light trial.

March 22. I have spent a quarter part of this holy day on deck, reading, singing, conversing, &c. I hope this has been a profitable and joyful Sabbath to my dear mother.

Oh, how ardently do I long again to frequent the courts of my God, and hear from his ambassadors the joyful sound of the glorious Gospel! But though in a humbler manner, yet I trust we find his grace displayed towards us while meeting for his worship. The weather is hot in the extreme; we are within a few days sail of the line. I have not found a stove necessary more than once or twice since I left the harbour. The weather has been much warmer than I anticipated. But we keep pretty comfortable in the air.

March 23. I cannot yet drink coffee or tea without milk. We have water porridge night and morning, and sometimes chocolate which is very good. We have every necessary which is possible on the ocean. I am thankful I feel no disposition to complain. I have for the most part of the time since we sailed, enjoyed a great degree of real happiness. The everlasting God is my refuge.

March 24. Mr. Newell often regrets that he had no more time to spend with you previous to our departure. He often says, "Harriet, how I do long to see your dear mother!" We often look the way where Captain H. tells us Haverhill lies. But alas! a *vast* ocean, and the blue sky are all we can see. But there is a land, my dear mother, where stormy seas cannot divide the friends of Jesus. There I hope to meet you and all my beloved friends, to whom, on earth, I have bid adieu. Oh that, when the followers of the Lamb are collected from the East and West, from the North and South, Harriet, an *exile*, in a distant land, with her mother, father, brothers, and sisters, may be united in the family of the Most High in Heaven!

March 25. The weather is about as warm as the extreme hot weather in America, last summer. Mamma may possibly be called to fit out another daughter for India. If so, I think some improvement might be made upon her plan. We all feel the want of more thin clothes. We are told, we shall not be likely to suffer more from the heat in Bengal, than we do now. We do not go more than a mile an hour. Are within 160 miles of the Equator. This is dear little Emily's birthday. Sweet child, will she ever forget her absent sister, Harriet, whom once she loved? Oh no! I will not for one moment indulge the thought. I cannot bear to think of losing a place in the remembrance of dear friends.

March 26. My attachment to the world has greatly lessened since I left my country, and with it all the honours, pleasures, and riches of life. Yes, mamma, I feel this morning like a pilgrim and a traveller in a dry and thirsty land, where no water is. Heaven is my home; there, I trust, my weary soul will sweetly rest, after a tempestuous voyage across the ocean of life. I love to think of what I shall shortly be, when I have finished my Heavenly Father's work on earth. How sweet the thoughts of glory, while I wander here in this waste wilderness! I still contemplate the path into which I have entered with pleasure, although replete with trials, under which, nothing but sovereign grace can support me. I have at times the most ardent desires to see you, and my other dear friends. These desires, for a moment, are almost insupportable. But when I think seriously of the object of my undertaking, and the motives which first induced me to give up all, and enter upon it, I enjoy a sweet serenity of mind, a satisfaction which the heaviest trials cannot destroy. The sacrifices which I have made are great indeed; but the light of Immanuel's countenance can enliven every dreary scene, and make the path of duty pleasant. Should I at some future period be destitute of *one* sympathizing friend, in a foreign sickly clime, I shall have nothing to fear. When earthly friends forsake me, then "the Lord will take me up."[186] No anticipated trials ought to make me anxious; for I know that I can do and suffer all things, "through Christ, who strengtheneth me."[187] In his hands I leave the direction of every event, knowing that he who is infinitely wise and good, can do no wrong.

March 29. We crossed the Equator last night. The weather still continues excessively hot. Heavy gales of wind, and repeated showers of rain rendering it necessary for the captain and officers to be on deck, we had no religious exercises in the cabin.

March 31. It is six weeks, this evening, since we came on board the Caravan. How rapidly have the weeks glided away. Thus, my dear mamma, will this short life pass. Why then do our thoughts dwell so much upon a short separation, when there is a world, where the friends of Jesus will never part more.

April 1. Three sharks caught to-day. In their frightful appearance they far exceeded the description I have often heard given of them.

April 7. The weather grows colder as we draw nearer the Cape.[188] Some Cape birds are seen flying on the water, called *Albatrosses*. We have had a little piece of the gangway taken into our room, which renders it much more pleasant and cool. We can now sit together and read. Mr. J. and N.'s room is large and convenient.

May 1. Again, my ever dear mother, I devote a few leisure moments to you, and my beloved brothers and sisters. The winds and the waves are bearing us rapidly away from *America*. I care not how soon we reach Calcutta, and are placed in a still room, with a bowl of milk, and a loaf of Indian bread. I can hardly think of this simple fare without exclaiming, oh, what a luxury! I have been so weary of the excessive rocking of the vessel, and the almost intolerable smell after the rain, that I have done little more than lounge on the bed for several days. But I have been blest with excellent spirits, and to-day have been running about the deck, and *dancing* in our room for *exercise*, as well as ever. What do some females do, who have unkind husbands in sickness? Among the many signal favours, I am daily receiving from God, one of the greatest is a most affectionate partner. With him my days pass cheerfully away; happy in the consciousness of loving and of being beloved. With him contented I would live, and contented I would die. This, my mother, is the language of your Harriet's heart.

We are in the latitude of the Cape. The weather is cold, and will probably be so for a month. The last winter we shall have. Ten weeks since we left Salem. I often think and often dream of you. Is mamma happy? Oh yes! blest with the rich consolations of the Gospel, she cannot be unhappy. But, mamma, the Heathen are wretched. For their sake shall not some Christians leave friends and country, cross the Atlantic, and submit to many hardships, to carry them the word of life. I do not repent, nor have I ever repented of my undertaking. My health is as good as I could reasonably expect. When I get to Calcutta, I will tell you more of that.

When in the exercise of right feelings, I rejoice that I am made capable of adding to the happiness of one of Christ's dear missionaries. This is the sphere, in which I expect to be useful, while life is prolonged. This is what *you* calculated upon, and I am now happy in seeing this wish daily accomplished. In Heaven I hope shortly to recount to you the many toils of my pilgrimage. My dear mother, and my dear brothers and sisters, farewell for the present. Lest I should forget, I mention it now, request brother E. W. and all who are interested enough to enquire for me, to write me long letters. Oh how acceptable will American letters be. You *will* think of it.

May 8. My dear Mr. N. has been ill this week past with the dysentery, so ill that he has kept his bed the greater part of the time. Should he fall a victim to this painful disease, and leave me alone in a strange land: But I will not distrust the care of my Heavenly Father. I know he will never leave nor forsake me, though a widowed stranger in a strange country. The weather is rainy, the sea runs high, and our room is often overflowed with water. My health has been remarkably good since Mr. N.'s sickness, and I have been able to attend upon him a little. But think, mamma, how painful it must be to the feeling heart to stand by the sick bed of a beloved friend, see him in want of many necessaries, which you cannot provide.

Four years to-day since my father's death. You, my dear mother, have probably thought of it, and the recollection is painful. Dear cousin C. has probably before this time entered the world of spirits; and perhaps more of my dear Haverhill friends.

"This life's a dream, an empty show."[189]

We find, that we have taken passage in an old leaky vessel, which, perhaps, will not stand the force of the wind and waves, until we get to Calcutta. But if God has any thing for us to do in Heathen Asia, we shall get there and accomplish it. Why then do we fear? It is God,

"Who rides upon the stormy winds,
And manages the seas."[190]

And is not *this* God *our* God?

May 10. Mr. Newell's health is much improved. "I will bless the Lord because he hath heard the voice of my supplications."[191] The weather is still cold and unpleasant. We are tossing about on the stormy waves, and are subjected to the numerous inconveniencies of a sea-faring life. We go at the rate of 160 miles in 24 hours. We hope to reach our destined haven in six or seven weeks.

Scarcely a night passes, but I dream of my dear mother, brothers and sisters. My sleeping hours are pleasant. Doubtless, mamma, sometimes dreams of Harriet. Does she not?

May 11. I have been reading what I have written, and fear that mamma will conclude from some sentences, that I am not so happy in my present situation, as she could wish. It has never been my intention to leave this impression on your mind. Believe me, my mother, in the sincerity of my heart I can say, that with a very few exceptions, I am happy all the day long. Though I am deeply sensible of my want of many qualifications, which would render a female highly useful among those of her own sex in Asia, yet I delight in the thought, that weak and unqualified as I am, a sovereign God may see fit to make me the instrument of doing some good to the Heathen, either directly or indirectly. Recollect, mamma, that happiness is not confined to any particular situation.

The humble cottager may enjoy as much happiness, as the king on his throne. Blest with a competency, what more do we want? *This*, God has hitherto granted me; and more than this, he has often given me the enjoyment of himself, which you know by happy experience is of greater value, than all this earth can afford:

"Give what thou wilt, without thee we are poor,
And with *thee* rich, *take what thou wilt away*."[192]

I think I never enjoyed so much solid peace of mind—never was so free from discontent and melancholy, as since I have been here; though I still retain a sinful heart, and often am led to doubt the reality of my being personally interested in the covenant.

May 14. You will not doubt but what my health is excellent, when I tell you, that I eat meat three times a day with a very good relish. I generally drink water-gruel morning and evening, instead of coffee and tea. The gingerbread, which the ladies in Salem made for us, is still good. But we find, that the crackers, which Captain Pearson put up for us, have been, and still are, more acceptable than any thing else, which we have. The preserves, which I brought from home, were almost useless; for in a week or two after we sailed they grew mouldy, and I gave them to the sailors. Those which Mrs. B. gave me, kept very well. Mr. N. relished them much in his sickness. I wish to thank her.

May 17. *Sabbath eve*. This has been a pleasant day. We assembled in the cabin as usual, and joined in the worship of God. I have enjoyed as much this day, as I ever did in an American church. The presence of Jesus is not confined to a temple made with hands. Many hundreds flock to his house every Sabbath. The word preached does not profit them. They go, and return without a blessing; while the believing two or three, who are gathered together in his name are favoured with his presence. This thought often gives me great encouragement, when lamenting my long absence from the courts of the Lord. "I have loved the place where thine honour dwelleth."[193]

Two albatrosses caught to-day. They are very pretty birds, about the size of a goose. We shall have what we call a sea pie made of them. We all long to see land again.

May 20. This is probably a delightful month with you. "The winter is past, and the time of the singing of birds is come."[194] May health, peace, and joy, reside in my dear-loved native dwelling. Oh! may my mother dear and all her children be favoured with those joys, which the Gospel of Jesus affords. Pray that Harriet may possess them too, though far away from friends and home.

May 21. How does our dear Church flourish? Is the little flock which our dear pastor is attempting to direct to glory, increasing in strength, piety and numbers? And how is it with the pious few, whom I left walking closely with God, like pilgrims and strangers, and daily expectants of rest? Oh! that I were with them, to speak a word to our dear sisters, and exhort them to be faithful unto the end. But no, mamma, do not regard the opposition of the world, or Satan; but oh! be active, be engaged in promoting piety around you. Oh! that I had done more for Jesus, when with you. Oh! that those evenings which were spent in vanity, had been sacred to prayer! Tell cousin J. to exert every faculty of his soul for God.

May 22. How does dear little A. do? I should love to see the sweet child. May he long live to comfort his parents, and do good in the world! Our dear Mr. W. is probably now at Haverhill. It would have been pleasant to see him once more. Do give my love to him. Will he write me *one* letter? M. I hope, has become very good, and is affording you much assistance and comfort. C. likewise, and little E. I hope are great blessings to their dear mother. Do kiss all the children for me. I shall expect letters from every one. I shall not ask for them; for mamma knows what I want. I cannot yet give up the idea of having a visit from you, when I get settled in my little Indian hut. Perhaps E. S. or C. may accompany some Missionary to Asia. If the mission-ship should be sent—but let me stop. I have thought more than ever, since I left home, that I shall return to America again, if deprived by death of my dear, dear Mr. N. Oh! that such an event might never happen. But life is uncertain, particularly in burning India. I am trying to familiarize my mind to every affliction. We often converse of a separation. It is his wish, that I should return to you immediately, should such an event take place; unless I am positive of being more extensively useful among the Heathen.

May 24. Hope my Haverhill friends have enjoyed as much comfort as I have, this holy sabbath.

May 29. Do you not think, mamma, I have acquired a little courage since I left home? I have had *two teeth* extracted to-day; they came very hard; but I think I shall have all my defective ones taken out.

May 31. We have, this evening, been reading some account of Birmah.[195] Never before did I so much feel my dependence on God. We are going among a savage people, without the protection of a religious government. We may possibly, one day, die martyrs to the cause, which we have espoused. But trusting in God, we may yet be happy, *infinitely* more happy, than all the riches and honours of this world can make us. I hope you will never indulge an anxious thought about us. Pray often, and pray earnestly for us. Oh! how does the hope of *heaven* reconcile me to a life of trials. When my friends in America hear of my departure from this vale of tears, let the thought, that I am at rest in Jesus, influence them to rejoice rather than to weep.

June 7. The weather grows warmer, and the heat will probably continue to increase, until we reach Calcutta. But we have fine winds, which render the weather *comfortable*. Worship as usual in the cabin to-day. We have commenced and ended this Sabbath, nearly at the same time with the Christians in India. If mamma and our other friends were now to look on the map, they would see us in the torrid zone, passing near the fertile island of Ceylon. The idea of being within some hundred miles of land is really pleasant. We have had strong gales of wind, and heavy rains, attended with thunder and lightning of late; which might terrify a heart, more susceptible of feeling than mine. I know not how it is, but I hear the thunder roll, see the lightning flash, and the waves threatening to swallow up the vessel, and yet remain unmoved.

June 9. We are now looking forward in expectation of shortly seeing the shores of Calcutta. The idea of again walking on the earth, and conversing with its inhabitants, is pleasing. Though, as we often remark to each other, *this* may be the pleasantest part of our lives. We do not calculate upon a life of ease.

June 10. We have been packing some of our things to-day. Hope to reach port Sabbath-day, if the winds prove favourable.

June 11. Some visitors from land to-day,—two *birds* and a *butterfly*. We suppose, that we are about one hundred miles from land. The weather unpleasant and rainy last night and to-day. I dread rainy weather very much at sea. How does dear E. do? Is she a very good child? Do, dear mother, talk often to the children about their sister Harriet. Do not let them forget me. I think much of dear sister E. How happy should I feel, if she were with me. Dear girl! with what sensations do I recal the scenes of other years! I hope that E. is happy. Perhaps ere this, she has given herself to God, and commenced a serious and devout life. If this is the case, my heart congratulates her. My mother, shall so much loveliness be lost?

June 12. Rejoice with us, my *dear, dear mother*, in the goodness of our covenant God. After seeing nothing but sky and water for *one hundred and fourteen days*, we this morning heard the joyful exclamation of *"land, land!"* It is the coast of Orissa, about twenty miles from us. Should the wind be favourable, we shall not lose sight of land again until we get to Calcutta. We hope to see the *pagoda* which contains the *Idol Juggernaut*,[196] before sunset. The view of the Orissa coast, though at a distance, excites within me a variety of sensations unknown before. For it is the land of Pagan darkness,[197] which *Buchanan* so feelingly describes.

June 13. A calm. Passed the temple of Juggernaut, and the Black Pagoda; but the weather being hazy, we could not see them. In the afternoon for the first time, spoke a vessel. An American ship from the Cape of Good Hope. It seemed good to hear the voice of a human being not belonging to our number. Agreed to keep company during the night.

June 14. No public worship to-day. The last night, a *sleepless, tedious one*. Sounded every half hour all night. The water shallow, and of a dirty light green. Surrounded by shoals, in perpetual danger of running upon them. Many vessels have been shipwrecked here, and in the Hoogly river. May that God, who has hitherto been our protector, still stand by us. Anxiously looking for a pilot, but no vessel in sight. The ship and brig close by us. Pleasant having company. Spoke with the brig to-day, owned by some one in Calcutta, and manned by *Bengalees*. I could see them distinctly with a spy glass. Lost sight of land. No sun for three days.

June 15. We anchored last night. Dangerous sailing in this place in the dark; providentially discovered a pilot's schooner this morning. Vessels are sometimes kept waiting ten days or more for a pilot. The pilot, an English lad, called the leadsman, and the pilot's Hindoo servant, came on board, bag and baggage. I should like to describe this Hindoo to you. He is small in stature, about twenty years of age, of a dark copper colour. His countenance is mild, and indicates the most perfect apathy and indolence. He is dressed in calico trowsers, and a white cotton short gown. He is a Mahometan. I should not imagine that he had force enough to engage in any employment.

June 16. Last night by sunset the anchor was thrown again. A heavy sea; the vessel rocked violently all the evening. The water rushing in at the cabin windows, overflowed our rooms. The birth is our only place of refuge at such times.

About eleven the cable broke, and we were dashed about all night in continual danger of running upon some shoal. The anchor was lost, yet we were miraculously preserved from a sudden and awful death, by that God who rules the seas, and whom the winds obey. I slept the greater part of the night *sweetly;* though the dead lights were in, which made our room excessively hot, and much confusion was on deck; all hands hard at work the most of the night. What a blessing, oh, my mother, is health. Were I on land, I think no one would be so free from complaints as I. Even here, notwithstanding all the fatigue to which I am unavoidably subjected, I get along surprisingly. Saugor Island about two miles from us. This is the island where so many innocent children have been sacrificed by their parents, to sharks and alligators.[198] Cruel, cruel! While I am now writing, we are fast entering the river Hoogly. For several days past, we have had frequent showers of rain. This is the time at which the rainy season commences in Bengal. It is the most unhealthy part of the year. The weather is not uncomfortably warm.

12 o'Clock. A boat filled with Hindoos from *Cudjeree*,[199] has just left our vessel. It is called a port-boat. They have taken letters, which will be sent post haste before us, to Calcutta. These Hindoos were *naked*, except a piece of cotton cloth wrapped about their middle. They are of a dark copper colour, and with much more interesting countenances, than the Hindoo we have now on board. They appeared active, talkative, and as though they were capable of acquiring a knowledge of the Christian religion, if instructed. Their hair is black; some had it shaved off the fore part of the head, and tied in a bunch behind; that of the others, was all turned back. I long to become acquainted with the Hindoo language.

1 o'Clock. We are now so near land as to see the green bushes and trees on the banks of the river. The smell of the land air is reviving. We hear the birds singing sweetly in the bushes.

5 o'Clock. I wish my ever dear mother could be a partaker of our pleasures. Were it in my power, how gladly would I describe to you, the beauties of the scenery around us. After passing hundreds of the Hindoo cottages, which resemble

hay-stacks in their form and colour, in the midst of *cocoa-nut, banana* and *date* trees, a large English stone house will appear to vary the scene. *Here* will be seen a large white Pagoda through the trees, the place where the idol gods are worshipped; *there* a large ancient building in ruins. Some Hindoos are seen bathing in the water of the Ganges; others fishing; others sitting at their ease on their banks; others driving home their cattle, which are very numerous; and others, walking with fruit and umbrellas in their hands, with the little tawny children around them. The boats frequently come to our vessel, and the Hindoos chatter, but it is thought best to take no notice of them. This is the most delightful *trial* I ever had. We anchor in the river to night, twenty-five miles from Calcutta. Farewell.

June 17. After a tedious voyage, we have, my dear mother, arrived at Calcutta. We reached here yesterday, at three o'clock in the afternoon. Mr. N. and brother J. went on shore immediately, and returned in the evening. They called at the Police office, entered their names, called upon Dr. Carey[200] at his dwelling-house at Calcutta, were cordially received, and by him invited to go immediately to Serampore. They likewise saw Dr. Marshman and Mr. Ward. I cannot say that our future prospects are at present flattering, but hope before I send you *this*, they will wear a different aspect.

Mr. N. and J. will go on shore again this morning; we hope to be *permitted to land and reside here for a season*, but know not how it will be.

The English East India Company are *violently* opposed to missions; but I will tell you *more* at some future time. Oh that their hearts might be opened to receive the blessings of the Gospel. Oh my mother, my heart is pained within me at what I have already seen of these wretched Pagans. Here we are, surrounded by hundreds of them, whose only object is to get their rice, eat, drink, and sleep. One of the *writer cast*, dressed in a muslin Cuprash and white turban (which is the common habit of *that cast*) who can talk *English*, has just left the cabin. His name is Ram-Joy-Gos. Your pious heart, my dear mother, would melt with compassion to hear him talk. Oh the superstition that prevails through this country! I am sure, if we gain admittance into Asia, I shall plead harder with American Christians to send missionaries to these Bengal heathen, than ever a missionary did before.

Three miles from Calcutta, a native came with a basket of pine-apples, plantains, (which taste like a rich pear) a pot of fresh butter, and several loaves of good bread—a present from one of Capt. H.'s friends. At night, I made a *delicious* meal on bread and milk. The milk, though thin, was a luxury. Yesterday and last night we were not uncomfortably warm, as the day was cloudy, attended with a little rain. But to-day it is *excessively hot*. I dare not go on deck, for I burned my face so yesterday, that it is almost ready to blister; owing to my going on deck without a bonnet. You have heard of the natives dying by being sun-struck.

I think I can say, I never felt better in America, than I do here. Calcutta harbour is a delightful place. But we are quite tired of the noise. The natives are as thick as bees; they keep a continual chattering. I like the sound of the Bengalee much.

June 18. Yesterday afternoon we left the vessel, and were conveyed in a Palanquin[201] through crowds of Hindoos to Dr. Carey's.

No English lady is here seen walking the streets. This I do not now wonder at. The natives are so numerous and noisy, that a walk would be extremely unpleasant. Calcutta houses are built almost entirely of stone. They are very large and airy. Dr. C.'s house appeared like a palace to us, after residing so long in our little room. He keeps a large number of Hindoo servants. Mrs. Carey is very ill at Serampore. The Doctor is a small man and very pleasant. He received us very cordially. This morning we saw some of the native Christians. Ram-Mo-Lund was one. They cannot talk English. A son of Dr. C.'s is studying law at Calcutta. He is an amiable young man. An invitation to go to Serampore to-morrow.

June 20. At Serampore. We came here last evening by water. The dear Missionaries received us with the same cordiality, as they would, if we had been own brothers and sisters. This is the most delightful place I ever saw. Here the Missionaries enjoy *all* the comforts of life, and are actively engaged in the Redeemer's service. After a tedious voyage of four months at sea, think, my dear mother, how grateful to us is this retired and delightful spot. The mission-house consists of four large commodious stone buildings. Dr. Carey's, Dr. Marshman's, Mr. Ward's, and the common house. In the last we are accommodated, with two large spacious rooms, with every convenience we could wish. It has eight rooms on the floor, no chambers; viz. the two rooms above-mentioned, with two other lodging rooms, the dining hall, where a hundred or more eat, a large elegant chapel, and two large libraries. The buildings stand close to the river. The view of the other side is delightful.

The garden is larger and much more elegant, than any I ever saw in America. A few months since, the printing-office was destroyed by fire. This was a heavy stroke; but the printing is now carried on very extensively. There is a large number of out buildings also; the cook-house, one for making paper, &c. &c.

June 21. Mr. N. preached this morning in the Mission chapel. Mr. W. in the afternoon in the Bengalee language to about fifty Hindoos and Mussulmen. This afternoon, I shall ever recollect with peculiar sensations. The appearance of the Christian Hindoos when listening to the word of life, would have reproved many an American Christian. Had you been present I am sure you could not have refrained from weeping. Had an opposer of missions been present, his objections must have vanished. He would have exclaimed, what hath God wrought! To hear the praises of Jesus sung by a people of strange language; to see them kneel before the throne of grace; to behold them eagerly catching every word which proceeded from the mouth of their minister, was a joyful, affecting scene. Rejoice, my mother; the standard of the blessed *Immanuel* is erected in this distant Pagan land; and here the Gospel will undoubtedly continue, till the commencement of the bright millennial day. In the evening, brother J. preached. How precious the privileges I now enjoy!

June 22. I have every thing here which heart could wish, but American friends. We are treated with the *greatest possible* kindness. Every thing tends to make us happy and excite our gratitude. You would love these dear Missionaries, could you see them.

June 24. I have just returned from a scene, calculated to awaken every compassionate feeling. At nine in the morning we took a *budgerow*,[202] and went three or four miles up the river to see the worship of Juggernaut. The log of wood was taken from his pagoda and bathed in the sacred waters of the Ganges. The assembled worshippers followed the example; and thousands flocked to the river, where, with prayers and many superstitious rites, they bathed. Miserable wretches! Oh that American Christians would but form an adequate idea of the gross darkness which covers this people!

July 14. A letter from Calcutta informs us that the Frances will sail for *America* in a day or two. With this information I must be expeditious in writing. As the *Caravan* will sail in a short time, I shall neglect writing now to many of my *dear friends*, to whom I shall then be very particular. I hope the contents of this little book will be gratifying to my dear mother. She will remember that they were written while the events were *passing*, and that they were the *feelings* of the moment. You will therefore feel disposed to pass over all errors, and think it like the private conversation of one of your daughters.

I am sure I love my *dear, dear mother*, and my beloved *brothers* and *sisters;* and all my dear *American Friends*, as well now, as I did on the morning when I took my last farewell of home. I long to *hear* from you all. Whenever you think of me, think, I am happy and contented; that I do not regret coming *here*. But life is *uncertain*, especially in this country. Should God in judgment, remove far from me *lover*,[203] and the *best* of *friends*, and leave your Harriet a lonely widow in this laud of strangers, say *my* mother, ever dear, shall I be a welcome child in your house? I know not what would be my feelings, should such unknown trials be mine. Perhaps I might feel that here I ought to stay. But I want to feel, that a mother's *house* and a mother's *arms*, are open to receive me, should my *all* be removed before me into the land of darkness. Assurance of this gives me joy.

My dear mother, unite with me in praising God for one of the best of *husbands*. Oh what would have been my wretchedness, had I found Mr. N. a cold inattentive partner. But he is *all* that I could wish him to be. Do give much love to all my friends in Haverhill. I cannot stop to particularize them. They are all dear to me, and I shall write to many of them by the *Caravan. Dear mother*, if I supposed you had one anxious thought about me, I should not feel happy. I think I see you surrounded by your dear family, taking comfort in their society, and blessing *God* for one child to consecrate to the work of a mission. Oh that you might find the grace of Jesus sufficient for you! As your day is, so may your strength be! Trust in *God*, he will support you under every trial. I hope to meet my dear mother, and brothers, and sisters, in Heaven, where we shall never be separated.

Farewell, my *dear, dear* mother. May you enjoy as large a share of earthly bliss, as your God shall see best to give you; and oh, that the joys of *that Gospel*, of which the *Heathen* are ignorant, may be yours, in life, and in the solemn hour of dissolution. *Farewell*. A letter to our dear Miss H. almost finished, lies by me; will be sent by the Caravan. One to Mr. Dodge likewise. Love to both.

HARRIET NEWELL.

The first of the following letters was begun at sea, and finished after her arrival in India.

On board the Caravan, at Sea.

My dear Mrs. K. *April* 14, 1812.

MOST sensibly do I feel the loss of the society of my Christian friends in Haverhill, with whom I often took sweet counsel. How repeatedly have I commemorated the death of the blessed Jesus at his table, with my sister and friend, my ever dear Mrs. K. The ties are still strong which attach my heart to her; and though I no more anticipate another meeting with her on earth, yet I hope to sit with her at the Gospel feast in Heaven, where all parting tears will be wiped away. Two months this day since I left my native shores and became a resident of this floating prison. The change has been great indeed which the last months have effected in my situation. Many have been the inconveniences and privations, to which I have been subjected. I have relinquished a life of ease and tranquillity, in the bosom of my relatives and friends, for the hardships of a voyage across the Atlantic, and a habitation in an unhealthy clime among the Heathens. But I am far from being unhappy. I have found many valuable sources of enjoyment, and I believe I can say in the sincerity of my heart, that notwithstanding my separation from every object which once I loved, yet I never was happier, or more contented in my life. In one bosom friend I find the endearing qualities of a parent, a brother, and a husband, all united. This sympathy alleviates every sorrow; his prayers diffuse joy and consolation through my heart; and while he lessens my earthly griefs, he points me to that world, where the weary are at rest.

June 9, lat. 10°, long. 36°.

We are rapidly advancing to the place of our destination. A few days more will probably land us on the shores of Asia. I feel, my dear Mrs. K. a mixture of pleasing and melancholy sensations, as I approach nearer Calcutta. Melancholy, because I can see none of my friends there, and it is an unhealthy, sultry region, which the Gospel has never illuminated; pleasing, because a hope is indulged that ere long the darkness of Paganism will be scattered, and the news of salvation be diffused far and wide.

My health has been remarkably good, since we crossed the equator the last time. This I consider a very great blessing, and some encouragement that I shall enjoy the same favour in India. The weather is excessively hot; the nights are very uncomfortable, owing to the confined air of our rooms. But what is this compared with India? The recollection of departed pleasures often casts a gloom over my present enjoyments. "I think of the days of other years, and my soul is sad." How does dear Haverhill, my much loved native town, appear. How are its dear inhabitants? How is the little flock of Jesus, of which you are a member? How flourishes that dear society of praying females? How is our dear pastor? Are the weekly conferences continued? Are there many who attend them? Are there many enquiring the way to Zion? Are there any new converts to the power of Truth? Are there numbers daily added to the Church of such as shall be saved? Were I with my dear Mrs. K. how gladly would I particularize. But I must stop. In one or two years I may have an answer to these questions. Oh that it might be such an answer, as will gladden my heart, and cause our little Mission band to rejoice. I hope that it will not be long before glad tidings from the East, will give you joy.

Oh that this infant Mission might ever live before God. May that quarter of the globe, where so many wonderful transactions have been performed, be filled with the glory of God. Oh that the standard of Immanuel's cross were already erected in Heathen Asia, and that Mahometans and Pagans were prostrated before it. I cannot but hope that the labours of our missionary brethren will be abundantly successful in winning souls to Christ, and that we shall afford them some comfort and assistance in the arduous, but glorious work.

June 16.

My dear Mrs. K. I think will congratulate us on again seeing land. I have been walking on deck, and have seen a boat filled with Hindoos approach our vessel. I like their appearance much, and feel more reconciled to the idea of living among them than ever before. My heart burns within me while I write. O my friend, will these degraded Pagans ever be brought to Jesus?

Serampore, July 14.

I have not time to review what I wrote to you, my dear Mrs. K. on board the Caravan, but send it you full of errors, with a promise to write you shortly again by vessels which will soon go to America. Do let me hear from you: I long to have letters from Haverhill. You will be kind enough to visit my dear mother often, and console her with your pious conversation. I think much of her. Oh that Jesus would support her under all her trials. Dear woman!—Mrs. K. do not forget me, though I am far away. Let me have your prayers, and the prayers of all my Christian friends in America. A short farewell. Affectionately yours,

HARRIET.

Respects and love to your dear mother and sister, and all other dear friends.

To her Brother J. Member of Yale College.

Mission House, Serampore, June 27, 1812.

I HAVE just received the welcome intelligence that a vessel bound to America will sail in a few days. With sensations of pleasure unknown before, I have taken my pen to address a brother, who, though far distant, is unspeakably dear to my heart. I cannot tell you how I long to see you; nor how much joy a letter from you would give me. Neither distance, nor a long absence, has in the least diminished my affection for you. No, my brother; although the pathless ocean rolls between, and I no more anticipate another interview with you on earth; yet I love you, ardently and sincerely love you. Your happiness will ever make me happy. I sometimes indulge the fond hope that Almighty grace *will* incline your heart to visit this distant Heathen clime, and here proclaim the joyful news of salvation to multitudes of dying Pagans, immersed in superstition and wretchedness. But if this laborious part of the vineyard should not be assigned you, oh that your days might be spent in winning souls to Jesus, in happy America, where you can enjoy ease and security, in the bosom of your friends. I feel assured that my dear brother will be gratified by a recital of the various scenes through which I have passed, since I bid a last farewell to our dear maternal abode, and left my country. I suffered all the horrors of sea-sickness the first week after I left Salem harbour. At the conclusion of the week we were, one dark and stormy night, alarmed by the intelligence, that our vessel had sprung a leak, and that, unless Providence interposed, we should sink in twenty-four hours. In this trying hour I thought of death, and the thought was sweet. Nothing, but anticipating the long-continued anxiety and distress of my dear American friends, made *such* a sudden exit from life, in *such* an awful manner, melancholy and painful. But God, who is rich in mercy, interposed in our behalf the following day, by sending a favourable wind, which enabled the mariners to repair the vessel, when their strength was nearly exhausted by long pumping. We proceeded on our passage with pleasant weather, favourable winds, few heavy gales, until we reached the Cape of Good Hope. The weather was then cold and boisterous, the sea rough, and our room was repeatedly overflowed with water. The newly discovered shoals round the Cape rendered this part of the voyage extremely dangerous. The first land we saw was the Orissa coast, 114 days after sailing. The sight of the adjacent country, after we entered the river Hoogly, was beautiful beyond description. Leaving America in the winter, and for a length of time seeing nothing but sky and water, think what must have been our delight to gaze upon the trees, the green grass, the little thatched cottages of the Hindoos, resembling a stack of hay, the elegant buildings of the English, the animals feeding, and the Hindoos themselves rambling near the shore. My friend Nancy and I were detained two days on board the Caravan, after our arrival at Calcutta. This was a time of great confusion. The Hindoos, of every class, flocked around our vessel like bees round a hive. We were carried in palanquins to the house of Dr. Carey, Professor at the College at Fort William of the Oriental Languages. No white female is seen walking in the streets, and but few gentlemen. English coaches, chaises, chairs, and palanquins are numerous. Every street is thronged with the natives. If you ride in a chaise, it is necessary for a Hindoo to run before to clear the way. The houses in Calcutta, and indeed all the buildings, the Hindoo huts excepted, are built with stone, or brick white-washed. These are lofty, and have an ancient appearance. Some of them are very elegant. There are many half English children in Calcutta. There is a charity school[204] close by Dr. Carey's, supported by subscription, managed by the Baptist missionaries, consisting of about 100 Portuguese children. Here they enjoy the benefit of religious instruction. We attended the English church one evening. This is an elegant building. The Friday after our arrival, we took a boat, and came to Serampore, 15 miles from Calcutta. This is a delightful place, situated on the river Ganges. It is inhabited chiefly by Danes. This retired spot is best calculated to prepare us for our future trials, and our arduous work. There are five large buildings belonging to the Mission; viz. the printing-office, the common house, Dr. Carey's, Dr. Marshman's, and Mr. Ward's dwelling houses, besides several convenient out-houses, one for making paper, one for cooking, &c. &c. There is one of the most delightful gardens here I ever saw. It contains a large number of fruit trees, plants, flowers, &c. The fruit is not as good as ours. Mangoes, plantains, pine-apples, cocoa-nuts, are very plentiful now. Dr. Carey spends most of his time at Calcutta. Dr. and Mrs. Marshman have large schools of English and half English children, about eighty in both schools. The boys are instructed in Chinese and other languages. These children all eat with us in the hall, and attend prayers morning and evening in the Mission chapel. Many of them are sweet singers. Mr. Ward superintends the printing. Here a large number of Hindoos are employed. Mr. Ward has the care of providing for the whole Mission family. Servants are numerous. This is necessary, for their religion will not permit them to do but one kind of work: for instance, one servant will sweep a room; but no persuasion will be sufficient to make him dust the things. The church of Christian natives is large. It is a delightful sight to see them meet together for the worship of God. The missionaries preach to them in Bengalee. They sing charmingly in their language. We went in a budgerow, (a boat with a little room in it, cushions on each side, and Venetian blinds) the 24th of this month, to see the worship of the Hindoo god, Juggernaut, a few miles from Serampore. They took the idol, a frightful object, out of the Pagoda, and bathed him in the water of the Ganges, which they consider sacred. They bathed themselves in the river, repeated long forms of prayer, counted their fingers, poured muddy water down their children's throats, and such like foolish, superstitious ceremonies, in honour of their god. Thousands on thousands were assembled to perform these idolatrous rites. In witnessing these scenes, I felt more than ever the blessedness, the superior excellence of the Christian religion. The Hindoos are very well formed, straight black hair, small, near a copper colour. Their dress is cool and becoming. It consists of white muslin, or cotton cloth wrapped about them. Some wear white muslin turbans. I shall write you again, my dear brother, by the Caravan, and other vessels, which will shortly sail to America. I can then give you a more correct history of the Hindoos, the manners and customs of this country, &c. You will wish to know whether I regret coming to this distant land. *I do not;* but feel an increasing satisfaction, in thinking of my arduous undertaking. Since I have been an eye witness of the idolatry, and wretchedness of the Asiatics; and find it confirmed by the long experience of the Baptist missionaries, whose names will be remembered with honour, by the latest generations, that females greatly promote the happiness and usefulness of missionaries, I am inclined to bless God for bringing me here. I have not as yet had sufficient trials to shake my faith. Providence has smiled upon us, and we know but little of the hardships of a mission. But we shall shortly leave these abodes of peace and security, and enter upon *that* self-denying life, among a savage people, upon which we calculated when we left our native country. It is not determined where our future lot will be cast. With respect to my connection with Mr. Newell, let me tell you that I am, and ever have been, perfectly satisfied with my choice. He is all that I could wish; affectionate, obliging, attentive, and in one word, every way deserving of my strongest attachment. It shall be my study through life, to render him happy and useful in the fatiguing path which he has selected. Oh that God would grant me the accomplishment of my wishes, in this respect! I have enjoyed far better health than I expected, when I left home. I have been miraculously supported through the fatigues of our tedious voyage. This is the rainy, hot season, and the most unhealthy in the year; but I think I never felt better in America; though many around us are suddenly dropping into eternity. There has been ten deaths in the mission family the last year. This is a sickly, dying clime. You are probably still at New Haven, I hope making great proficiency in your studies, and preparing for eminent usefulness in the world. Oh, my brother, shall we meet in Heaven, or shall we be separated *for ever?* Let us be solicitous to obtain an interest in Jesus, whatever else we lose. When the glad tidings reach this distant land, that a brother of mine, dear to my heart, has been redeemed from eternal woe, and become a disciple of the blessed Immanuel; oh how will this delightful intelligence make me rejoice! how will it gladden the days of separation! I long to see our dear mother. Do your utmost, my dear John, to make her happy. The thought of meeting her, in a world where there will be no parting, is sweet. All my beloved brothers and sisters will ever be dear to me. I cannot tell you how much I think of you all. I feel much happier than ever I expected to feel, in this Heathen land. I am glad I came here; I am glad that our dear mamma was so willing to part with me, and that no opposition prevailed with me to relinquish the undertaking. Let me hear from you, my dear, by every vessel bound to Asia. You know not how large a part of my happiness will consist in receiving letters from my American friends. Every particular will be interesting. For the present I must bid you farewell. May you be distinguished for your attachment to the cause of Jesus, and be made an eminent blessing to your dear friends, and to the world. Oh that by sanctifying grace you might shine as a star of the first magnitude in Heaven, when dismissed from this life of toil and pain. Farewell, my dear, ever dear brother, a short Farewell. While I live I shall ever find pleasure, in subscribing myself your affectionate sister,

HARRIET NEWELL.

Extract from a Letter to her Sister M. at Charlestown.

Serampore, June, 1812.

I have found, my dear sister, that the trifling afflictions I have already had, have been more sanctified to me, than all the prosperity of my former life. They have taught me that this is a state of discipline, that permanent bliss must proceed from God alone, and that heaven is the only rest that remains for the children of God.

While I write, I hear the dear christian natives singing one of Zion's songs in the mission chapel. The sounds are melodious; they remind me of that glorious day, when the children of Jesus, collected from Christian and Heathen lands, will sing the song of Moses and the Lamb, on the blest plains of the new Jerusalem.[205]

Letter to Mrs. C. of Boston.

Calcutta, June, 1812.

THE last request of my dear Mrs. C. (when quitting the beloved land of my nativity), and the sincere affection which I feel for her, are my principal inducements for ranking her among the number of my American correspondents.

I have witnessed scenes this morning calculated to excite the most lively sensations of compassion in the feeling mind. My heart, though so often a stranger to pity, has been pained within me. Weep, O my soul, over the forlorn state of the benighted Heathen; and, O that the friends of Immanuel in my Christian country would shake off their criminal slothfulness, and arise for the help of the Lord against the mighty, in lands where the prince of darkness has long been adored. The worship of the great god of the Hindoos has this day been celebrated. We were apprised yesterday at sunset of its near commencement, by the universal rejoicing of the natives, which lasted through the night. This morning we went in a budge-row to see the worship. Between fifteen and twenty thousand worshippers were assembled. The idol Juggernaut was taken from his pagoda, or temple, and bathed in some water taken from the river Ganges,[206] and then replaced in his former situation with shouts of joy and praise. *This* I did not see, the crowd was so great. After this, the people repaired to the river side, where they bathed in the *sacred* waters, said their prayers, counted their fingers, poured the muddy water down their infants' throats, and performed many other superstitious ceremonies with the utmost solemnity, and with countenances indicative of the sincerity of their hearts. Many of the females were decked with garlands of flowers, nose jewels, large rings round their wrists, &c. Some deformed wretches and cripples attracted our attention, and excited our compassion. One man, bent almost to the ground, was supported by two of his companions, to the holy Ganges. There he doubtless hoped to wash away the pollution of his heart, ignorant of the blood of Jesus which does indeed cleanse from all sin. Oh! that an abler pen than mine would delineate to my dear Mrs. C. this idol worship. Surely her pious heart would be filled with tender sympathy for these benighted Asiatics, and her prayers would become more constant more fervent, for the introduction and spread of the blessed Gospel among them. Gladly would American believers leave the healthy civilized land of their birth, and spend their lives in preaching Jesus to the natives of India, did they but know how wretched, how ignorant, they are, and how greatly they need the Gospel. Do Christians *feel* the value of *that* Gospel which bringeth salvation.

Let us leave the melancholy subject, and turn to one calculated to fill our minds with holy joy and devout thanksgivings to God. In this land of darkness, where the enemy of souls reigns triumphant, I see the blessedness of the Christian religion. Yes, my friend, there is in Heathen Asia a favoured spot, where the darkness of Heathenism is scattered, and the benign influences of the Holy Spirit are felt. Here Jesus has a people formed for his praise, redeemed by his precious blood from eternal woe, and made heirs of bliss everlasting. *Bless the Lord, O our souls, and all that is within us, bless and praise his holy name.*[207] Last Sabbath afternoon, I shall ever remember with peculiar emotions. Mr. Ward, a missionary blessed and beloved of our God, preached in Bengalee to a large collection of Hindoos and Mahometans. The dear converted natives appeared to enjoy the precious season greatly. To hear them join in singing one of Zion's songs; to see them kneel before the throne of almighty grace, and listen with eagerness to the word of life, was sufficient to draw tears of joy from eyes which never wept before. After service each dear Christian Hindoo of both sexes came to us with looks expressive of their joy to see new missionaries; and, offering us their hands, they seemed to bid us a hearty welcome. I said to myself, such a sight as this would eternally silence the scruples, and the criminal opposition to missions, of every real believer. While such persons would intercede for the success of Missionaries, and praise the Lord for what he has already done for these once degraded wretches, they would weep and repent in dust and ashes for their former criminality. Oh! that every American might be prevented by sovereign grace from opposing or discouraging those who feel willing to engage in this work, lest the blood of the Heathen, at the last day, should be required at their guilty hands.

Last evening, while thousands were preparing for the impure and idolatrous worship of Juggernaut, the native Christians assembled at the Missionary Chapel for prayer. Their engagedness in prayer, though I could not understand a word they said, made a deep impression on my mind.

To Miss S. H. of Andover.

Serampore, June 27, 1812.

I HAVE taken my pen with an intention of writing my dear Miss H. a very long letter. I know she will not expect the *wife* of a *Missionary* to study correctness of style, or to make her hand writing appear beautiful; the easy, unreserved, unstudied style of a friend will better suit her. "They that cross the ocean change their *climate*, but not their *minds*."[208] This is confirmed by my own experience. In this distant Heathen land, far from the dear spot of my birth, my attachment to my American friends is as strong as ever. Those whom I once loved, I now sincerely, strongly love, though the anticipation of meeting them again in this world is totally relinquished. But would you infer from *this*, that a separation from the friends I love so dearly, renders me unhappy? Far otherwise, my dear

Miss H. Let me assure *you* (and do you remember it for the encouragement of those females who anticipate walking in the same path), that I never enjoyed more solid happiness, never was so free from discontent and anxiety, as since I left my native country. It is true I have suffered *many* privations and inconveniences, and some hardships. But I have likewise had many blessings, and found valuable sources of pleasure, which I did not expect. Since I have been in India, every wish of my heart, as it respects temporal things, has been gratified. The voyage was tedious, but remarkably short. We were blest with a commander, who treated us with uniform respect, kindness, and attention. Our accommodations were good, and we spent many happy hours in our little rooms. The sight of land was very pleasant, as you will imagine. Sailing up the river Hoogly, we were delighted with the variegated charming scenes around us. When we reached Calcutta, we were surrounded by the tawny natives, and half stunned with their perpetual chattering. We had some interesting conversation with the Circars,[209] who could talk English, on board the vessel. While our astonishment was excited at hearing their superstitions, how could our hearts remain unaffected about their wretched state! We were affectionately received by the good Dr. Carey, at his mansion at Calcutta, and treated with the greatest hospitality. Imagine to yourself a large stone house, with six lofty, spacious keeping and lodging rooms, with the same number of unimproved rooms below: such is the building. Imagine a small bald-headed man, of sixty; *such is the one whose name will be remembered to the latest generation.*[210] He is now advanced to a state of honour, with six thousand dollars a year. We accepted his invitation to visit the mission family at Serampore; took a boat, and at eleven the next evening reached the happy dwelling of these friends of Immanuel. Here, peace and plenty dwell, and we almost forget that we are in a land of Pagan darkness. Dr. Carey's wife is ill; he has only one son residing with him, who has lately commenced preaching—aged sixteen. Felix is stationed at Rangoon, where he has lately married a native; William is at Cutwa; Jabes is studying law at Calcutta. Mr. Ward superintends the printing. Mrs. Ward has the care of providing for the whole mission family. Dr. and Mrs. Marshman are engaged in schools. Mrs. Marshman has had twelve children; six are dead. She has now *thirteen*, six of her own, and *seven adopted* ones. These schools are productive of much good.

We attended the worship of the great god of the Hindoos a fortnight since. The idol was taken from his temple, and bathed in the sacred waters of the Ganges. Here were thousands of our fellow creatures, washing in the river, expecting to wash away their sins. A sight which will not admit of description. My heart, if insensible as steel before, was pained within me, when witnessing such a scene. Oh, the beauty of the Gospel of Jesus! Shall a Christian be found in America, who is opposed to missions? Forbid it heaven! To day the great Juggernaut is removed from his temple, placed on his car, and drawn in triumph through the assembled mass of worshippers. Some will probably sacrifice their lives,[211] and this only three miles distant from Serampore. While writing, I hear the drum, and the instruments of idol music.

July 31. I have only time to tell my dear Miss H. that I shall this day leave Calcutta for the Isle of France.[212] I have not time to read the above, but send it full of errors. Do write me; do let me hear soon from all my American friends.

In the greatest haste, your's,

Love to dear Mr. and Mrs. W.   H. NEWELL.

To her Sister E.

Mission-house, Serampore, July 14, 1812.

How is my dear, ever dear Elizabeth? Happy, I would hope, in the possession of every temporal blessing heart can wish, and in the still richer blessings of the Gospel. To tell you that I long ardently to see you, would be only saying what you already know. Though at a great distance from you, the ties are still strong which unite me to you. Never shall I cease to love you. I have given our dear mother many particulars, respecting my past and present situation and prospects. Such is our unsettled state at present, that I can say little or nothing to any one. The Harmony has not yet arrived, we are daily expecting her. No determination can be made without the other brethren. The East India Company have ordered us to return to America. We have relinquished the idea of stationing a Mission at Burmah entirely. Several other places have been thought of, but it is still uncertain where we shall go. You will, perhaps, hardly credit me, when I tell you, that it is fully as expensive living here, as in America. I am disappointed greatly in this respect. Some things are cheap; others very dear. As soon as we fix upon a station, I am positive I shall write you to send me a box of necessaries from America. Tell mamma that my bed-quilt I shall value very highly. India calico bears the same price here as in America. English calicoes, an enormous price. Common English stockings between 3 and 4 rupees. The country stockings 1 rupee, and they are not worth half that. Some articles of provision are very high, and likewise house rent; and yet we are told that no where in Asia can we live so cheap as here. We have excellent accommodations at the Mission-house;—indeed we have every thing at present to make us happy. We shall remove to some rooms in the Garden, when the Harmony arrives, where all our brethren will be invited to stay till we leave Bengal. I love these dear Missionaries very much. I never expected so many kindnesses from them. Mrs. Marshman has a lovely school of English young ladies, where they are instructed in embroidery, working muslin, and various other things. Miss Susan Marshman of 14, is studying Latin, Greek, and Hebrew.[213] Mrs. Ward is a motherly woman, very active and kind. Miss Hobson, a niece of Dr. C. from England, is here, a very pretty girl. Col. Moxen from the Mahratta country is likewise at the Mission-house. Mr. Carapeit Aratoon, the Armenian and wife, are residing here. These, with Drs. Carey, Marshman, and Mr. Ward's families, and all the scholars, make the Mission Family immensely large. Serampore is a charming place. We frequently walk out to admire its beauty. About a week since I went to Gundle Parry, with Mrs. Ward and family, to visit Mrs. Kemp, a charming woman, much like our dear Mrs. B. There I saw something of

Eastern luxury, so much celebrated. We spent the day, returned home in the evening in the budgerow, saw two dead bodies burning on the shore, and a Bengalee wedding. Yesterday we crossed the river at Barry-pore, and walked over the Governor General's park;[214] saw the wild beasts, variety of birds, &c. One of the most delightful places I ever saw. Artificial hills and dales supplied the want of real ones.

This is the rainy season, but very pleasant. It is sometimes excessively hot; but a shower of rain cools the air. The jackalls make a tremendous yell every night under our windows; the noise is like a young child in great distress. I find the musquetoes very troublesome, though not so large and numerous as I expected. I have not seen one snake yet. I bathe every day, which is very refreshing. I have not yet suffered half so much from the heat as I calculated. I can sew or read all day, except an hour or two at noon, very comfortably. I have often thought that you would like the climate of Bengal. I think I shall enjoy at least as good health here, as in America. When I first came here, I disliked all the fruit of the country but pineapples, and those made me ill. The mangoes, plaintains, guaves, &c. were all alike disagreeable. But I love them all now.

We were obliged to submit to a great many inconveniences on our passage, and were exposed to many dangers. But on the whole, I think no missionaries ever had a pleasanter voyage to the East Indies. I used to think, when on the water, that I never should return to America again, let my circumstances in Asia be as bad as they could be. But I think now, that the long tedious voyage would not prevent my returning, if nothing else prevented.

Mr. Robinson, one of the Baptist missionaries, married a lady from Calcutta, about 15 years of age, and set sail for Java. They slept in the open air for a fortnight on deck; were out in a violent storm, and returned to Calcutta again. How different this from our comfortable passage. Oh, that we might be ever grateful to God for past favours, and learn to trust Him for the time to come. Surely we, above most others, have reason to say, "Hitherto hath the Lord helped us."[215]

I regret that time obliges me to be so short. But you shall have letters by the Caravan sufficiently long to make up for this short one. I will begin a journal on the morrow, and write in it every day, till I can send it you. I will not be so negligent again. I have many letters partly written to friends, but must leave them now. My time has been so much occupied since our arrival, that I have scarcely found leisure to write a line. I hope soon to be more at liberty.

Do give love to Sarah, Caroline, Moses, Charles, and Emily. I shall write them all by the Caravan, and shall expect letters from every one of them. Kiss them all for me. Dear, dear Elizabeth, must I leave you? But I shall talk with you again in a week or two. Till then, and ever, I shall love to call you my dear sister, and subscribe myself your HARRIET.

To a Female Friend.

MANY have been the changes through which I have passed, since I left my beloved country. I have found many precious sources of enjoyment, and have had some *light* afflictions. Our voyage was *comparatively* short, but very tedious.

But one week after we left the harbour, the vessel sprung a leak, and we were for some time under the apprehension of perishing. Many gales of wind threatened our vessel with instant destruction; but our gracious God preserved us from every danger, and brought us in safety to these sultry shores, where hundreds of missionaries are needed.

Though a mission among the Heathen is attended with many difficulties and discouragements, yet I do not feel sorry that I have joined the little company engaged in one. Since I have been here, I have been more decidedly positive than ever before, that a pious female, deeply interested for the Heathen, can greatly increase the usefulness of a missionary, and promote the good of the mission. Let me give you one instance of this truth. Mrs. Marshman has had twelve children; (6 are dead, and 7 adopted ones fill their places.) With this numerous family, she has been engaged in a school for 13 years, consisting of 20, 30, 40, and sometimes 50 children. These children are mostly half-cast, i. e. their fathers are Europeans, their mothers natives. The good done in this school is incalculable. The children are not only instructed in all the branches of education taught in our American Academies, but are particularly instructed in the religion of the blessed Gospel. I drank tea with her and her little family a day or two since, under a large tree.

Extracts from her Diary.

I feel more and more willing to be any thing, or to do any thing, that the cause of Jesus might be prospered. I am not discouraged by the trials of a missionary life.

July 15. Spent the greater part of this day in my room alone. Mr. N. went to Calcutta this morning to carry letters to the captain of the ship Francis—Went with Mrs. Ward to one of the mission buildings in the garden, to see the rooms intended for us. There are four convenient pretty rooms, with bathing apartments, which they have kindly offered us and our missionary company. In the afternoon called upon Mrs. M.*—The good woman, as usual, busily engaged in her school. How firm a constitution must she have, to occupy a station attended with so many cares. At four P. M. another message from government was received. Mr. N. and Mr. J. *ordered* to appear before the police again, to receive further *commands*. Mr. J. immediately took the *Buggy* [chaise][216] and set out for Calcutta. In the evening went with Nancy,† and Mrs. W.'s family, to the car of Juggernaut, which stands in the road. A huge building five stories high; images painted all over it; two large horses, with a charioteer made of wood in

---

* Mrs. Marshman, we presume.
† Mrs. Judson

front; with many wheels, drawn by the natives with large cables. From the car we walked through the *Bazar* [market] to the temple, where the great god of the Hindoos is now residing—a horrid object indeed! Not allowed to enter the temple; but could see him plainly—a log of wood, painted red, with large hideous eyes. Little images were kept for sale in the Bazar. We walked through an immense crowd of Hindoos home. I was confused with the noise and bustle of the place, and excessively wearied with my long walk.

July 16. Called with Mrs. W. upon Mrs. Carapeit, the Armenian. Mr. Carapeit, has gone with *brother* Kristno on a mission to Jessore—will be absent four weeks. Mrs. C. very ill; can only talk Hindostanee. Brother J. returned about sunset. A letter from Mr. Newell. He states that a collection has been made for us among the friends of missions in Calcutta. Mr. Thomason presented 500 rupees already collected.

How dark and intricate are the ways of Providence! We are ordered by government to leave the British territories, and return to America immediately. Captain H. will be ready to sail in three weeks. He has requested a clearance, but it has been absolutely refused him, unless we engage to leave India with him. Thus is our way hedged up; thus are all our prospects blasted. We cannot feel that we are called in Providence to go to Birmah. Every account we have from that savage, barbarous nation, confirms us in our opinion, that the way is not prepared for the spread of the Gospel there. The viceroy would not hesitate to take away our lives for the smallest offence. The situation of a female is peculiarly hazardous. But where else can we go? Must we leave these Heathen shores? Must we be the instruments of discouraging all the attempts of American Christians, to give these nations the word of life? My spirit faints within me. These are trials great and unexpected.

9 o'Clock. Just returned from family worship in the chapel. My depressed spirits are a little revived. The good Dr. Marshman felt deeply interested for us, and has been interceding in our behalf. Not mine, O Lord, but thy will be done. I know that the gracious Redeemer will take care of his own cause, and provide for the wants of his little flock. How consoling this; I will trust him, and doubt no more.

July 17. I find that writing has become quite pleasant now I am alone. My natural cheerfulness has returned, and I hope I shall never again make myself unhappy by anticipating future evils, and distrusting the care of my heavenly Father. I have been taking a solitary walk in the mission garden; a charming retreat from the bustle of the world. How happy would a walk with my dear absent mother, or dear brothers and sisters, make me: and yet much as I long for their society, I am not willing to return to them. Yes, I am positively unwilling to go to America, unless I am confident that God has no work for me to do here. How far preferable to me would be an obscure corner of this Pagan land, where the wretched idolaters would listen to the Gospel of Jesus, to all the glittering splendour of a civilized land.

July 18. My dear Mr. N. returned last evening fatigued in body and depressed in mind. There is now no alternative left but a return to America, or a settlement among some savage tribe, where our lives would be in constant danger. Lord we are oppressed; graciously undertake for us. We know not which way to direct our steps. O that the Harmony would arrive. Insurmountable obstacles attend us on every side. Pity us, O ye friends of Immanuel; pity our perplexed situation, and intercede with the prayer hearing Redeemer for direction in the path of duty.

A prayer-meeting in the mission chapel on our account—the dear Baptist brethren deeply interested for us. Fervent were their prayers that God would direct our steps! Four prayers offered, three hymns sung, one chapter read. The exercises were all calculated to comfort our hearts.

I hear the distant sound of Heathen voices. These miserable wretches are probably engaged in some act of idol worship; perhaps in conveying the log of wood, which they call Juggernaut, to his former place of residence. A conference in the chapel this evening. The bell calls us to breakfast at eight in the morning. Immediately after, we have worship in the chapel. At half past one we dine, at seven drink tea, go directly to the chapel again. Sabbath morning and evening service in English; afternoon in Bengalee. Monthly prayer-meeting, Monday morning. Weekly prayer-meeting, Tuesday evening. A lecture for the children, Wednesday evening. A conference, Saturday evening.

With respect to the climate, manners of the people, &c. we have selected from Mrs. Newell's journal the following particulars:

July 18. Excessively warm weather; but not so hot as the last July in America. The Bengal houses are made so as to admit all the air stirring. In the room where I now keep there are four large windows, the size of American doors, with Venetian blinds, and three folding doors. There are no glass windows. A bathing house is commonly connected with each lodging-room, and verandas to walk in, in the cool of the day. The floors of the houses are made of stone; the partitions and walls white washed.

20. From nine to eleven last evening I spent in walking in the garden with Mr. Newell. I do not suffer the least inconvenience from the evening air in this country. When on the ocean we were very cautious of the least exposure. But here, physicians, and every one else, advise walking in the evening. The jackalls are all that I am afraid of here.

Mr. Judson preached yesterday morning; Mr. Ward in the Bengalee, afternoon; Mr. Newell in the evening. Some good people from Calcutta present at worship, a large collection of hearers, all very attentive. Dr. Marshman returned to day from Calcutta. Brought us some intelligence which has revived our spirits a *little*. He has had some conversation with Mr. Rickets, the secretary, about us. He said the Caravan should have leave to depart, if we would engage to leave the British territories, and that possibly we might have leave to go to the Isle of France or Madagascar. So, then, we shall not go to America in the Caravan, but wait the arrival of our dear brethren in the Harmony, and then conclude which way to direct our steps. The Lord is merciful, and full of compassion.

21. Intend going to Calcutta to-morrow, should the weather permit. I like the climate of Bengal much. I do not long for a seat by an American fire-side, nor for pleasant winter-evenings, as I once thought I should; but feel perfectly contented and satisfied with this hot, sultry weather. I am obliged to guard against heating my blood by walking in the sun, or by using too violent exercise. Fevers, and the prickly heat,[217] are in consequence of this imprudence. Rosy cheeks are never seen in India, except where a lady uses paint.

24. Went early on Wednesday morning in the mission budgerow to Calcutta, in company with brother and sister Judson, Colonel Moxen, Miss Hobson, and Mr. Newell. Spent the day and night at Dr. Carey's house. The air of this confined place does not agree with me; a severe head-ache kept me all day within doors. Wednesday morning, breakfasted with Captain Heard at his house. I hope my dear mother and other friends will have an opportunity of seeing and thanking him on his return for his kindness to us. Heard of Mr. Thomason's death of Madras. He had received positive orders from government to return to England, chargeable with no other crime than that of *preaching the Gospel*. He has now gone to his everlasting home, and will trouble his opposers no more. Tired of the confusion and noise of Calcutta, I reached Serampore last evening. Found friends to welcome our return. Why these great favours? Mr. and Mrs. Robinson, Mr. and Mrs. More and family at the mission house. Mrs. R. the second wife of Mr. R. is about 15 years of age, country-born; *i. e.* has an English father and native mother. Mr. and Mrs. M. a charming couple, are stationed at Patna; have come hither on account of their health.

25. I have become a little familiarized to the sound of the Bengalee language. It has become quite natural to say *chene* for sugar, *tony* for water, &c. &c. One servant's name is *Bozu*, another *Lol*,[218] another *Golove*, another *Ram Done*. Ram is the name of one of their gods, and is therefore often added to their own name.

26. I am happy in finding, that the expectations of my American friends, respecting my health in India, will not be disappointed. I think I can say, that I never felt so strong in the summer season, nor ever had such an excellent appetite, as since I have been here. The weather is sometimes excessively hot and sultry, but to me not uncomfortable.

July 27. Moved last Friday to a retired, pretty room in the garden. Letters from the brethren at the Isle of France. Rejoice to hear of their safe arrival there. Long to see them. They will undoubtedly be here in a few days. How welcome will their arrival be to us. Mr. Newell, Mr. Judson, and Nancy [Mrs. Judson] went to Calcutta this morning. Another order from government received last Saturday; and now our fate will be decided. I long to know the result. I do not intend to have one anxious feeling about our future destiny. I know that the cause of Zion is precious to the blessed Jesus, and that he will provide graciously for those who trust in him. I have spent the day alone.

July 28. I love dear Mrs. Ward more and more every day. She is remarkably obliging and kind to us. I go constantly to her for advice. Mr. Newell returned this afternoon from Calcutta. We have obtained liberty from the East India Company to go to the Isle of France. A vessel will sail for that place next Saturday, commanded by Captain Chimminant, a serious man. But he cannot accommodate us with a passage. No other vessel is expected to sail at present. We hear that the English Governor favours missions; that a large field for usefulness is there opened; 18,000 inhabitants ignorant of Jesus. Is not this the station that Providence has designed for us? A door is open wide, shall we not enter and begin the glorious work? This must be a subject for fervent prayer.

July 29. A world of changes this! Early this morning brother Judson called at our room, unexpectedly from Calcutta. Captain Chimminant has agreed to carry two of us in his vessel, to the Isle of France, for 600 rupees. Sail next Saturday. How can such a favourable opportunity be neglected? Halted long between two opinions. If we go we shall relinquish the pleasure of meeting the dear brethren, and sister Roxana [Mrs. Nott.] Perhaps we shall never see them more. They may conclude to labour in some distant part of the Lord's vineyard, and we be separated from them through life. I shall go far away, without *one single* female acquaintance; the dangers of a long voyage must be hazarded at a critical period. But here let me stop, and review all the way in which God has led me, since I left my mother's house, and the land of my birth. How have I been surrounded with mercies! What precious favours have I received! And shall I doubt? Oh, no; my heart gladdens at the thought of commencing with my ever dear companion the missionary work, and of entering upon missionary trials and arduous engagements. So plain have been the leadings of Providence thus far, that I cannot doubt its intimations. I will go, leaning on the Lord, and depending on him for direction, support, and happiness. We shall leave the dear mission family at Serampore, when another rising sun dispels the darkness of the night. Have packed all our things to-day; fatigued much, and very sleepy. The wanderer and the stranger will, ere long, repose sweetly on the bosom of Jesus. It is sweet to be a stranger and a wanderer for such a friend as this. A valuable present from my dear Mrs. Marshman. Thus are all my wants supplied. O for more thankfulness! When will this heart of adamant be susceptible of stronger emotions of gratitude? Bless the Lord, O my dear American friends, for his kindness to me a stranger in a strange land. O pray that these abundant mercies may melt me into deep contrition.

July 30. I have this morning taken my leave of my dear Serampore friends. After a visit of six weeks, I regret parting with them exceedingly. But such are the changes of this changing world. Friends must be separated; the parting tear will often flow. How consoling the hope, that there is a world where separation will be for ever unknown. A pleasant time in going from Serampore to Calcutta in the budgerow, with brother Judson and Mr. Newell. Went on board the ship; much pleased with the accommodations. Our birth is on deck, a cool, pretty place. Dined at Dr. Carey's; spent the afternoon at Mr. Myers's, a charming family, willing to assist us in every thing. Mr. and Mrs. More now residing with them. Drank tea with Mrs. Thomason, one of the kindest, best of women. More money collected for us. Mrs. T. has provided me with many necessaries. Went to church with Mr. and Mrs. T. in the evening; a most elegant church; heard Mr. T. preach.

To her Sister C.

Serampore, July, 1812.

My ever dear sister C.

I CANNOT forget you among the numerous friends I have in America, but must say a few words to you, though in great haste. Can it be possible that I shall never see you again in this world? Have we then parted to meet no more this side eternity? We probably have. But what is this short separation? Nothing, when compared to eternal separation, which will take place at the last day, between the friends and enemies of Jesus. My dear C. listen, I entreat you, to a sister who loves you, who ardently wishes for your everlasting happiness. Make the Friend of Sinners your friend, now while an opportunity is presented. Oh, let not the adversary of souls cheat you out of an interest in the Saviour! Gladden the heart of your dear widowed mother, of saints and angels, by becoming a devout and holy follower of Jesus. Mamma has no child now to go with her to the sacramental supper; will not our dear C. renounce the world and all its vanities, embrace religion, and in the morning of her life openly consecrate herself to God? Think how much good you might do among your dear brothers and sisters. Perhaps you might be made the instrument of rescuing them from endless death. It may possibly be that I may never write you again; will you not then, my dear girl, seriously think of these things? I hope we shall meet in Heaven after death, no more to part. But we never shall, unless our hearts are renewed, and we are made the friends of Immanuel in the present life.

Farewell my dear girl; comfort the heart of your mother, and make her declining days as happy as possible. Do write me.

From your sister   HARRIET.

Extracts from a Letter to her Mother.

Calcutta, July 31, 1812.

Dear Mother,

WITH a week's employment before me this day, I take my pen to write you a few lines. By reading my enclosed journal you will become acquainted with our reasons for leaving Bengal and going to the Isle of France. We sail early to-morrow morning; have furniture and a thousand little necessaries to get to-day.

I go without one female companion; but I go with renewed courage, rejoicing that the Lord has opened us a way to work for him. I have received favours unmerited, unexpected, and great.

My health is really excellent; I never felt so well in America.

After stating that the inhabitants of the Isle of France are chiefly French, she observes, "I long to engage in the great object for which I left my home. I shall begin to study the French language with Mr. N. on the passage. Capt. Chimminant talks French.

"Oh, for more ardent piety!"

The following letter from Mr. Newell to Mrs. Atwood, completes the affecting history of Mrs. Newell:

"*Port Louis, (Isle of France) Dec.* 10, 1812.

"ON account of the unhappy war between us and England,[219] it is probable I shall have no opportunity for a long time of sending directly to America. I enclose this letter to Joseph Hardcastle, Esq. of London,[220] depending on his benevolence to pay the postage at the General Post Office there, without which it would not be forwarded. I beg your particular attention to this circumstance, because it is the reason why my letter is not longer, and also the reason why I do not write to my other friends. You will oblige me by informing my friends of this; particularly Drs. Woods, Griffin, and Worcester.

"When I sit down to address you, my dear mother, from this distant land, to me a land of strangers and a place of exile, a thousand tender thoughts arise in my mind, and naturally suggest such inquiries as these. How is it now with that dear woman to whom I am indebted for my greatest earthly blessing—the mother of my dear Harriet? And mine too; (for I must claim the privilege of considering you as my own dear mother). Does the candle of the Lord still shine on her tabernacle, and is the voice of joy and praise yet heard in her dwelling? Or, what is not improbable in this world of disappointment, has some new affliction, the death perhaps of a dear child, or of some other beloved friend, caused her heart again to bleed and her tears to flow? Ah! my mother, though we may live many years, and see good in them all, yet let us remember the days of darkness, for they too will be many. It is decreed by Infinite Wisdom alone, that through much tribulation we must enter into the kingdom of heaven. You, my dear mother, have had your share of adversity; and I too have had mine. But we will not complain. Sanctified afflictions are the choicest favours of heaven. They cure us of our vain and foolish expectations from the world, and teach our thoughts and affections to ascend and fix on joys that never die. I never longed so much to see you as I have these several days past. What would I now give to sit one hour by that dear fire side, where I have tasted the most unalloyed pleasure that earth affords, and recount to you and the dear children, the perils, the toils, and the sufferings, through which I have passed since I left my native land. In this happy circle I should for a moment forget ———

"Yes, my dear friends, I would tell you how God has disappointed our favourite schemes, and blasted our hopes of preaching Christ in India, and has sent us all away from that extensive field of usefulness, with an intimation that He has nothing for us to do there, while He has suffered others to enter in and reap the harvest. I would tell you how He has visited *us all with sickness*, and how He has afflicted me in particular by taking away the dear little babe which He gave us, the child of our prayers, of our hopes, of our tears. I would tell you—but, oh! shall I tell it or forbear?

"Have courage, my mother, God will support you under this trial; though it may, for a time, cause your very heart to bleed. Come then, let us mingle our griefs, and weep together; for she was dear to us both; and she too is gone. Yes, Harriet, your lovely daughter is gone, and you will see her face no more! Harriet, my own dear Harriet, the wife of my youth, and the desire of my eyes, has bid me a last farewell, and left me to mourn and weep! Yes, she is gone. I wiped the cold sweat of death from her pale, emaciated face, while we travelled together down to the entrance of the dark valley. There she took her upward flight, and I saw her ascend to the mansions of the blessed! O Harriet! Harriet! for thou wast very dear to me. Thy last sigh tore my heart asunder, and dissolved the charm which tied me to earth.

"But I must hasten to give you a more particular account of the repeated afflictions with which God has visited me.

"Harriet enjoyed good health from the time we left you, until we embarked on our voyage from Calcutta to the Isle of France; (excepting those slight complaints which are common to females in her situation.) During the week previous to our sailing for this place, she went through much fatigue in making numerous calls on those dear friends in Calcutta, who were anxious to see her, and who kindly furnished her with a large supply of those little things which she was soon expected to want, and which on account of her succeeding illness, she would not have been able to prepare on the voyage. The fatigue of riding in a palanquin, in that unhealthy place, threw her into a fever, which commenced the day after we were on board. She was confined about a week to her couch, but afterward recovered, and enjoyed pretty good health. We left Calcutta on the 4th of August, but on account of contrary winds and bad weather, we were driven about in the Bay of Bengal without making much progress during the whole of that month. On or about the 27th, it was discovered that the vessel had sprung a leak; and on the 30th, the leak had increased to such an alarming degree, as to render our situation extremely perilous. A consultation of the officers was called, and it was determined to put about immediately, and make the nearest port, which was Coringa, a small town on the Coromandel coast, about 60 miles south of Vizigapatam. We got safe into port on Saturday, Sept. 5th. The vessel was found to be in a very bad case."

[Four days before the arrival of the vessel in port, Mrs. Newell was seized with severe pain in the stomach and bowels, the disease of the country; but in three days, after going on shore, she was so far recovered as to write thus in her journal: "Have been able to sit up most of the day. Begin to look around me a little; find myself again surrounded with Hindoo cottages, and the tawny natives as thick as bees." On the 19th of September they re-embarked, and Mrs. N. enjoyed comfortable health till nearly three weeks after leaving Coringa, and about three weeks before reaching the Isle of France, when she became the joyful mother of a fine healthy daughter. Four days after, in consequence of a severe storm of wind and rain, the child took cold, and died on the evening of the next day, after having been devoted to God in baptism.

On the 14th of October, Mr. N. writes thus in his journal: "About eight o'clock last evening, our dear little Harriet expired in her mother's arms. A sweet child. Though she had been but five days with us, it was painful, inexpressibly painful, especially to the mother, to part with her. To-day, with many tears, we committed her to a watery grave. 'So fades the lovely blooming flower,' &c. May God sanctify this bereavement to us, and oh, may he spare my dear wife!"

About a week after Mrs. N.'s confinement, the symptoms of a consumption appeared. Though Mr. N. feared the worst, he did not consider her case as fatal, till the last fortnight of her life, which commenced about ten days after their arrival at the Isle of France. Mr. N. immediately on their arrival, called in the aid of Dr. Burke, the chief surgeon of the British army in that island, and of Dr. Walluz, a Danish physician, a friend with whom they had become acquainted at Serampore, who had lately buried his wife in Bengal, and had come to the Isle of France for his health. There was but little alteration in Mrs. N.'s health, (excepting that she gradually lost strength) till about a fortnight before her death, when she declined more rapidly, and all hope of her recovery was extinguished. About four o'clock P. M. on Monday, the 30th of November, her eyesight failed her, soon after which she calmly, and with apparent ease, expired, seven weeks and four days after her confinement. These events, with all the attending circumstances, are related by Mr. N. with great tenderness and particularity. He then proceeds as follows:

"There, my dear mother, I have finished the story of Harriet's sufferings. Let us turn from the tale of woe to a brighter scene; one that will gladden your heart, as I am sure it does mine. During this long series of sufferings, the bare recital of which must affect every feeling heart, she meekly yielded to the will of her Heavenly Father, without one murmuring word. 'My wicked heart,' she writes, 'is *inclined* to think it hard, that I should suffer such fatigue and hardship. I sinfully envy those whose lot it is to live in tranquillity on land. Happy people! Ye know not the toils and trials of voyagers across the rough and stormy deep. Oh, for a little Indian hut on land! But hush my warring passions; it is for Jesus who sacrificed the joys of his Father's kingdom, and expired on a cross to redeem a fallen world, that thus I wander from place to place and feel no where at home. How reviving the thought! How great the consolation it yields to my sinking heart! I will cherish it, and yet be happy.'

"In view of those sufferings which she afterwards experienced, she writes thus: 'I hope to reach the place of our destination in good health. But I feel no anxiety about that. I know that God orders every thing in the best possible manner. If He so orders events, that I should suffer pain and sickness on the stormy ocean, without a female friend, exposed to the greatest inconveniences, shall I repine, and think he deals hardly with me? Oh no! Let the *severest trials and disappointments* fall to my lot, guilty and weak as I am, yet I think I can rejoice in the Lord, and joy in the God of my salvation.

"In the first part of the sickness which succeeded the birth of our babe, she had some doubts, which occasionally interrupted her spiritual comfort; but they were soon removed, and her mind was filled with that peace of God which passeth all understanding. When I asked her, a few days before she died, if she had any remaining doubts respecting her spiritual state, she answered with an emphasis, that she had none. During the whole of her sickness she talked in the most familiar manner, and with great delight, of death and the glory that was to follow. When Dr. Burke one day told her, those were gloomy thoughts, she had better get rid of them; she replied, that on the contrary they were to her cheering and joyful beyond what she could express. When I attempted to persuade her that she would recover, (which I fondly hoped) it seemed to strike her like a disappointment. She would say, 'You ought rather to pray that I may depart, that I may be perfectly free from sin, and be where God is.'

"Her mind was from day to day filled with the most comforting and delightful views of the character of God and Christ. She often requested me to talk to her on these interesting subjects. She told me that her thoughts were so much confused, and her mind so much weakened, by the distress of body she had suffered, that she found it difficult steadily to pursue a train of thought on divine things, but that she continually looked to God and passively rested on him. She often spoke of meeting her friends in Heaven. 'Perhaps,' said she, 'my dear mother has gone before me to Heaven, and as soon as I leave this body I shall find myself with her.' At another time she said, 'We often talk of meeting our friends in Heaven; but what would Heaven be with all our friends, if God were not there?'

"She longed exceedingly for the brethren to arrive from India, that we might form ourselves into a church, and celebrate the dying love of Jesus once more before she died. Her desires to enjoy the benefit of this ordinance were so strong and our situation so peculiar, that I thought a deviation from the usage of our churches in this instance would be justifiable, and accordingly on the last Sabbath in November, the day before she died, I gave her the symbols of the body and blood of our Lord; and I trust it was a comfortable season to us both.

"A few days before she died, after one of those distressing turns of coughing and raising phlegm, which so rapidly wasted her strength, she called me to come and sit on the bed beside her, and receive her dying message to her friends. She observed, that her strength was quite exhausted, and she could say only a few words; but feared she should not have another opportunity. 'Tell my dear mother,' said she, 'how much Harriet loved her. Tell her to look to God and keep near to Him, and He will support and comfort her in all her trials. I shall meet her in heaven, for surely she is one of the dear children of God.' She then turned to her brothers and sisters. 'Tell them,' said she, 'from the lips of their dying sister, that there is nothing but religion worth living for. Oh! exhort them to attend immediately to the care of their precious, immortal souls. Tell them not to delay repentance. The eldest of them will be anxious to know how I now feel with respect to missions. Tell them, and also my dear mother, that I have never regretted leaving my native land for the cause of Christ. Let my dear brothers and sisters know, that I love them to the last. I hope to meet them in heaven; but oh, if I should not'—Here the tears burst from her eyes, and her sobs of grief at the thought of an eternal separation, expressed the feelings that were too big for utterance. After she had recovered a little from the shock, which these strong emotions had given to her whole frame, she attempted to speak of several other friends, but was obliged to sum up all she had to say in 'Love and an affectionate farewell to them all.' Within a day or two of her death, such conversation as the following passed between us.

"Should you not be willing to recover, and live a while longer here?

"On some accounts it would be desirable. I wish to do something for God before I die. But the experience I have had of the deceitfulness of my heart leads me to expect, that if I should recover, my future life would be much the same as my past has been, and I long to be perfectly free from sin. God has called me away before we have entered on the work of the mission, but the case of David affords me comfort; I have had it in my heart to do what I can for the Heathen, and I hope God will accept me.

"But what shall I do, when you are gone? How can I bear the separation?

"Jesus will be your best friend, and our separation will be short. We shall soon, very soon, meet in a better world; if I thought we should not, it would be painful indeed to part with you.

"How does your past life appear to you now?

"Bad enough; but that only makes the grace of Christ appear the more glorious.

> "Jesus, thy blood and righteousness
> My beauty are, my heavenly dress;
> Midst flaming worlds in these array'd,
> With joy shalt I lift up my head."[221]

"When I told her that she could not live through the next day, she replied, 'Oh, joyful news; I long to depart.' Sometime after, I asked her, 'How does death appear to you now?' She replied, 'Glorious; truly welcome.' During Sabbath-night she seemed to be a little wandering; but the next morning she had her recollection perfectly. As I stood by her, I asked repented of any sacrifice she had made for Christ; that on her dying bed "she was comforted with the thought of having had it in her heart to do something for the Heathen, though God had seen fit to take her away before we entered on our work." Tell that dear woman, that *Harriet's bones have taken possession of the promised land, and rest in glorious hope of the final and universal triumph of Jesus over the gods of this world.*

"Give my love to all our friends. How glad should I be to see you all! Tell little Aaron about my dear babe; we called her *Harriet Atwood* in her baptism. Poor thing, she found a watery grave. Mary, my dear sister, do not grieve too much for Harriet; she is well now. O may we be counted worthy to meet her in the mansions of the blessed! Dear creature, she comforted me with this hope on her dying bed; and this blissful hope is worth more to me than all the wealth of India.

Farewell,   SAMUEL NEWELL."

THE END.

FUNERAL SERMON.

A SERMON

DELIVERED ON OCCASION OF THE

LAMENTED DEATH OF

MRS. HARRIET NEWELL,

BY LEONARD WOODS, D. D.[222]

MATTHEW XIX. 29

And every one that hath forsaken houses, or brethren, or sisters, or father, or mother, or wife, or children, or lands, for my name's sake, shall receive an hundred fold; and shall inherit everlasting life.

THE Scripture sums up all that is in the world under three heads; "the lust of the flesh, the lust of the eye, and the pride of life." According to this, it has been common to make a threefold division of natural men; the *sensual*, the *covetous*, and the *ambitious*. But our blessed Lord, in the text, exhibits a character widely different; a character formed on another principle; a character altogether superior to any thing, which can result from man's unrenewed nature. The devoted Christian *is born of the Spirit*. All his moral beauty, his usefulness, and enjoyment, are the work of divine grace.

But where shall we find the singular character exhibited in the text? I answer, *in every place*, and *in every condition of life*, where we find true religion.

The *poor cottager*, far removed from public notice, and destined to the meanest employment, possesses this character. He gives himself and all that he has to the Lord. He loves Christ above his cottage, his food, and his rest, and is ready to part with them all for *his sake*. In the sight of God, that same poor man forsakes all for Christ. He who can forsake his sins, and resist the claims of corrupt passion, performs, to say the least, as difficult a service, as to forsake houses, brethren, and lands. The *poor* man, who has little to *give*, and much to *bear*, frequently shows the self-denying spirit of religion to the greatest advantage. In his heart often burns as pure a flame of love and zeal, as in the heart of an Apostle. It may not be visible to the world; but it is visible to Him, who seeth in secret. His prayers are animated by fervent affection for God and man. And when he contributes his *mite* for the advancement of the Redeemer's kingdom, he does it with a heart large enough to part with millions.

The character here exhibited belongs to the devoted Christian, who is possessed of *opulence*. Though he does not *literally forsake* houses and lands, he *uses* them for the glory of Christ. And as he supremely regards the divine glory, and uses the things of this world in subserviency to it, he is ready, when duty calls, to surrender them for the same object. To *use* riches for Christ, and to *forsake* them for Christ, evince the same elevation above self-interest, and the same devotedness to the cause of God. He, then, who values his estate for Christ's sake, and uses it for the advancement of his cause, has the same disposition and character with those, who for the same object actually suffer the loss of all things. In heart he gives his earthly all to Christ; saying with sincerity, *here Lord, I am; and here are my possessions. I yield them all to thee. I will either use them, or part with them, for thy sake, as thou wilt.* Animated with such sentiments, he esteems it comparatively loss, to do any thing with his property, which tends merely to secure his private advantage; while he esteems *that*, as the best use of his property, which tends most to advance the kingdom of Christ. It is for the sake of that kingdom that he values his earthly possessions. Take away that kingdom, and his possessions lose their highest worth.

The character presented in the text clearly belongs to *every faithful minister of the Gospel,* even in the most peaceful days. Whatever may be his earthly prospects, he cheerfully resigns them for Christ's sake. The love of Christ bears him on. He declines no labour, no sacrifice, no suffering. He foregoes indulgence and ease. In private, he gives himself to reading, meditation, and prayer. In public, he preaches the word, and is instant in season, and out of season. Worldly pursuits he totally abandons, and sets his affections on the kingdom of Christ. "If I forget thee," he says, "O Jerusalem, let my right hand forget her cunning."[223]

This character is strikingly exhibited by *a devoted Christian in times of persecution.* He feels as Paul did, when his friends, anxious for his safety, besought him not to go to Jerusalem. "What mean ye," he said, "to weep, and to break mine heart?[224] For I am ready not to be bound only, but also to die at Jerusalem for the name of the Lord Jesus." Times of persecution and distress, have a favourable influence upon Christian character. In such seasons, as the prospect of earthly happiness is overcast, the followers of Christ are led to a more serious contemplation of the heavenly inheritance, and naturally form a stronger and more operative attachment to that kingdom, in which their all is contained. They are reduced to the necessity of feeling that they have no other interest, and no hope of enjoyment from any other quarter. Accordingly, they make a more unreserved surrender of every thing for Christ, and become more consistent and more decided in their religious character. In the discharge of difficult duties they have less hesitation. They are less ensnared by the friendship of the world, and less awed by its frowns. The prospect of suffering, as it becomes familiar to their minds, ceases to move them. To give up the interests and pleasures of the world for the sake of Christ, becomes habitual and easy. It costs them no struggle, and no sigh. They are prepared to encounter any trial, even a violent death, without fear or reluctance. Yea, *they rejoice in their sufferings, and gladly fill up what is wanting of the afflictions of Christ in their flesh, for his body's sake, which is the Church.*[225]

The *Christian Missionary*, whose motives are as sublime as his office, forsakes all for Christ in a *remarkable* sense. The proof which he gives of devotion to Christ, is indeed of the same nature with that which other Christians give; but it is higher in *degree*. Others forsake the world in *affection*, but enjoy it still. *He* renounces the *enjoyment*, as well as the *attachment*. Other Christians esteem Christ above friends and possessions, and yet retain them far enough for the gratification of their natural affections. The Missionary, who has a right spirit, counteracts and mortifies natural affection, by actually abandoning its dearest objects. The distinction in short is this; other Christians have a *willingness* to forsake all for Christ; the Missionary *actually forsakes* all. The cause of Christ among the Heathen possesses attractions above all other objects. It has the absolute controul of his heart. He forsakes father and mother, house and land, not because he is wanting in affection for *them*, but because he loves Christ *more*. He forsakes them, because his heart burns with the holy desire, that Christ may have the Heathen for his inheritance, and the uttermost parts of the earth for his possession.

The *wife of a Missionary*, when influenced by the Spirit of Christ, gives still more remarkable evidence of self-denial and devotion;—evidence, I say, *more remarkable*, because for *her* to forsake friends and country, is an instance of *greater self-denial*. The tie, which binds her to her relatives and her home, is stronger. Her mind is more delicate in its construction; more sensible to the tenderness of natural relations, and to the delights of domestic life. When, therefore, she forsakes *all*, for the name of Christ, she makes a higher effort; she offers a more costly sacrifice; and thus furnishes a more conspicuous proof, that her love of Christ transcends all earthly affection.

My friends, have I been entertaining you with visions and dreams? Or have I been teaching realities? If you admit the truth of the Bible, you must admit that men of the character above described, have existed in all ages of christianity. Indeed, no other can be acknowledged, as disciples of Christ. For he himself has declared, that *whosoever forsaketh not all that he hath, cannot be his disciple.*[226] And again, to teach us in the most forcible manner, that our affection for all other objects must fall below our affection for him, he says;—*If any one come to me, and hate not his father, and mother, and wife, and children, and brethren, and sisters, yea, and his own life also, he cannot be my disciple.*[227] However severe and impossible these conditions of discipleship may seem, they have often been performed. Yea, there are multitudes who daily perform them, and to whom the performance appears not only *just*, but *pleasant*. Multitudes, now on earth, have that supreme love for the Lord Jesus, which leaves little of the heart for any thing else. When they enlisted into the service of Christ, they engaged to follow him, though at the expense of every earthly interest. In the very act of *faith*, there is an *implicit* forsaking of all things for Christ. So that when the trial comes, and they really forsake all things on his account, they only do in open *act*, what they did in *heart* before. When they are called to surrender all things, even life itself, for Christ's sake, they are not called to perform a new condition, to which they did not consent in the first exercise of faith. They made choice of Christ and his ways, Christ and his cross. Had they certainly known, when they first received Christ, that they did it at the expense of every earthly good, they would not have received him with any the less cordiality and joy. Paul knew from the first, that he must sacrifice every thing for Christ;—which, in his view, was only parting with trifles to purchase a pearl of great price. "What things were gain to me, those I counted loss for Christ. Yea, doubtless, and I count all things loss for the excellency of the knowledge of Christ Jesus my Lord; for whom I have suffered the loss of all things, and do count them but dung, that I may win Christ."[228] Such was the spirit and practice of the first Christians. They rejoiced that they were counted worthy to suffer for Christ. To honour him, they gladly took the spoiling of their goods, resigned their dearest friends, and endured persecution and death. There are those at the present day, who possess the same spirit; who willingly give up their worldly interest, and subject themselves to the hatred of men, for the sake of their Lord; who willingly suffer reproach, and expose their name to be trampled under foot, that Christ may be magnified; who hold nothing so dear, that they will not cast it away for Christ's sake.

Do you still ask, where such characters are to be found? I answer again, *wherever there are* CHRISTIANS. You may fix your eye upon ministers of the Gospel, upon ambassadors of Christ in Pagan lands, and upon good men in the various walks of life, who give, I say not, the same *degree*, but the same *kind* of evidence of devotion to Christ, with that which was given by the holy Apostles. And he who slights the evidence of supreme love to Christ, which these exhibit, would equally slight the evidence, which should be exhibited by a new race of APOSTLES and MARTYRS.

The *reward* of Christians is as *certain*, as their devotion to Christ is *sincere*. They *receive an hundred fold in this present life*. Great peace have they, who love God's law. *The wicked*, from the very nature of their affections, *are like the troubled sea when it cannot rest, whose waters cast up mire and dirt*.[229] But cordial devotion to Christ, imparts serenity and peace to the soul. How happy are they, who have cast off the slavery of passion, who have given up the vain cares and pursuits, which distract the minds of worldlings, and yielded themselves wholly to God, resting in him as their *all in all*.

To them belong the pleasures of *benevolence*. As this is their ruling affection, they must be happy in proportion as its object is promoted. That object, which is primarily the prosperity and happiness of the kingdom of Christ, is absolutely secure. Christians know it to be so, and therefore enjoy a peace, which no adversity can destroy. In all that they do; and in all that others do, to advance the welfare of the Redeemer's kingdom, they partake the purest pleasure. Let them see the glory of God displayed in the salvation of sinners; let them see the Church look forth as the morning; let them enjoy communion with Christ; and they have enough. This is their object, their treasure, the heritage which they have chosen.

The eternal glory of God, and the boundless good of his kingdom, is an object infinitely excellent, and worthy of supreme regard. The pleasure of those who are devoted to this glorious object, and see that it is perfectly secure, is a kind of *divine* pleasure, partaking of the nature of its divine and infinite object.

I am well aware, that these are unintelligible things to those who are destitute of religion. What does a man, without taste, know of the sweetness of the honey-comb? How can blindness perceive the pleasantness of light, or deafness the charms of music? But inquire of those who are entitled to speak on the subject,—inquire of *fervent Christians*, what the rewards of self-denial are. With one voice they answer, that those who forsake all for Christ, *receive an hundred fold, even in this life.*[230]

It is the uniform method of divine grace, to give spiritual comfort to those who are freed from earthly affection. The more the world is excluded from the hearts of believers, the more they are filled with all the fulness of God. Blessed exchange! What tongue can describe the happiness of the saints, when they part with all that they have for the name of Christ, and He, their all-gracious Saviour and Friend, takes up his dwelling in their hearts! O what peace! What quietness! What a beginning of Heaven! Ask the Apostles, in the midst of their labours, privations, and sufferings, whether they are losers on Christ's account? You hear them speaking of perpetual triumph, of comfort in tribulation, of joy unspeakable and full of glory. The lonely desert, through which, with weary steps, they travel, witnesses their joy. The dungeon, where they are chained, witnesses their holy transports, and hears their midnight praises. Perils innumerable by land and sea, weariness and painfulness, cold and hunger, prisons, stripes, and tortures, cannot deprive them of their joy.

But all the enjoyment of Christians in this life, is only the beginning of their blessedness. The consummation of it, is the *everlasting life*, which they will inherit in the world to come. It will be a life of perfect holiness, and perfect endless joy. They will live in the society of holy Angels, and dwell in the presence of their blessed Lord, who loved them, and gave himself for them. While they behold his glory, and enjoy his love, they will perfectly possess the object of all their desires. They wish for no higher happiness, than *to enjoy God for ever. This* is everlasting life. Give them *this*, and they ask no more.

I have been led to this train of reflections, by an event which has lately arrested the attention of the public, and caused sensations of unusual tenderness in the friends of Zion. You are aware, that I refer to the lamented death of Mrs. HARRIET NEWELL. I rejoice that, after the most intimate acquaintance with that excellent woman, I am able to say, that she happily exemplified the character which I have drawn. From the uniform tenour of her conduct for several years, we are fully persuaded that she was one *who forsook all for Christ*, and *who received an hundred fold in this present life*. And on the ground of God's immutable promise, we are equally persuaded, that she now *inherits everlasting life* in heaven.

But let God, our Saviour, have the glory of all the moral beauty which adorned her character. The temper of mind which she manifested, was contrary to every principle of human nature, while unrenewed. If she was indeed, what she appeared to be, it was by the washing of regeneration, and the renewing of the Holy Ghost.

Before she indulged a hope that she was a subject of spiritual renovation, she had a long season of distressing conviction, careful self-examination, and earnest prayer. She could not admit the comfortable conclusion, that she was *born again*, before she was conscious that she had given herself to the Lord, and yielded sincere obedience to his holy commands.

Long before she thought her own salvation secure, she began to exercise an enlarged affection for the kingdom of Christ, and to be fervent in her prayers for the building up of Zion, and the salvation of the Heathen. This became the prominent feature of her religion—the supreme object of her pursuit. A considerable time before a Foreign Mission from this country was contemplated, the universal diffusion of the Christian Religion was the favourite subject of her meditations and prayers.

When, in the course of Divine Providence, one of those, who had devoted themselves to the Foreign Mission, sought her as the companion of his labours and sufferings, her great concern was to discover *the will of God*. When she became satisfied respecting her duty, her determination was fixed. Here you come to the point where her character began to assume a lustre, which excited the admiration of all who shared her friendship. Through the grace of God, she entirely consecrated herself to *the establishment of the kingdom of Christ in Pagan lands*. To this great and glorious object, all her thoughts and studies, her desires and prayers tended. It was with a view to *this*, that she considered her talents and acquirements of any special importance. Even her health and life seemed of little consequence to her, except in relation to this grand object.

But this entire self-devotion had no more tendency to blunt the sensibilities of her heart, or to extinguish her natural affections, than the supreme love of God has in any case whatever. Every Christian is the subject of an affection, which holds an entire superiority over the natural affections, and makes them subservient to its purposes. Had our natural affections been designed, as the highest principles of action, the Lord Jesus would never have set up another principle above them. Our dear departed friend, did not more truly rise above the natural principles of action, than every Christian does, when he seeks the glory of God in the common business of life. The nature of her affections was the same with that of Christians generally. If there was a difference, it consisted in this, that she was more earnest and undivided in her attachment. It is to this circumstance, that we must trace her peculiar magnanimity, and elevation of spirit. As all the powers of her soul were united in one grand object, she rose to an uncommon pitch of energy, and things, seemingly impossible to others, became practicable and easy to her.

In acquiring the force and decision of character, which she finally exhibited, it was of great importance, that the question of *duty* was fully settled in her own mind. Had not this been done, she must have been often turned aside from her object by secret misgivings of conscience. Her attachment to the object must have been weakened; and every step must have been taken haltingly and tremblingly.

But by much deliberation, and many prayers to God for direction, the question of duty was at length settled; after which she proceeded without wavering. Devoted, as she was, to the cause of Christ, and borne on with a strong desire of advancing it in Heathen lands, she was prepared for trials. The hardships and sufferings, peculiar to the missionary life, became perfectly familiar. They were so closely associated in her mind with the glory of God, and the conversion of the Heathen, and so continually mingled with her purest affections and joys, that, instead of aversion and dread, they excited sensations of delight.

Is it possible that a character so elevated, should not be universally admired? Is it possible that any should be found capable of admitting the thought, that conduct so noble, so Christ-like, was owing to a weak or misguided zeal? Shall I stoop to notice so unworthy a surmise? If compassion to those who indulge it require, I will. Look, then, upon the Apostles, and primitive Christians, who were so united and consecrated to the Saviour, that they were willing to endure the greatest evils for his sake; whose ardent love to him rendered every affliction light, and reconciled them to the agonies of a violent death. Will you urge the charge of misguided zeal against the holy Apostles?

The character of Mrs. NEWELL, instead of being exposed to any dishonourable imputation, had an excellence above the reach of mere human nature. Behold a tender female, when all the sensibilities of the heart are most lively, united to friends and country by a thousand ties; a female of refined education, with delightful prospects in her own country; behold her voluntarily resigning so many dear earthly objects, for a distant Pagan land. But this fact becomes still more remarkable, when we consider the circumstances attending it. She made these sacrifices *calmly;* with a *sober deliberation;* in the exercise of those *sensibilities* which would be overwhelming to mankind in general, and yet with *steady, unyielding firmness;* and all this, not for wealth, or fame, or any earthly object, but *to make known among the Heathen the unsearchable riches of Christ.*

I should blush to offer a vindication of a character so fair and exalted, as that of HARRIET NEWELL, a lovely saint, who has finished her course, and gone to receive an unfading crown. But if there be any one base enough to envy such excellence, or rash enough to impute extravagance, and folly; I would refer him to a case not wholly unlike the present. On a certain occasion, Mary came to Jesus, as he sat at meat, having an alabaster box of very precious ointment, and poured it on his head. Judas, and some others, instigated by him, charged her with extravagance and waste. But Jesus approved her conduct, declared that she had wrought a *good work,* and that it should be known for a memorial of her, wherever the Gospel should be preached in the whole world.

Do I still hear it said by some selfish calculator, that *"she threw herself away?"* But do you not applaud the conduct of a man, who goes to the earth's end to gratify a worldly passion? And can you think it reasonable to make greater sacrifices for *self-interest,* than for the *kingdom of Christ?*—*"Threw herself away!* What! Does a devoted Christian, who, for the love of Jesus, forsakes all that she has, to receive an hundred fold here, and life everlasting in Heaven, *throw herself away?*

Should any ask, what that *hundred fold reward* was, our appeal would be to herself, to her peace, and quietness, and joy in God. For several of the last months that she spent at home, and from the time of her leaving America till her death, her religious enjoyment was almost constant, and at times elevated.

In her last interviews with her beloved friends in America, and in the scene of final separation, the consolations of the Spirit supported her, and produced not only a tender meekness and calmness of mind, but astonishing resolution. Her happy serenity continued through the dangers of a long voyage, and amid all the difficulties which befel her, after arriving in India. Her spiritual enjoyment was not materially interrupted by the various distresses, which prevented the establishment of the mission; nor by the sufferings she was subsequently called to endure; no, not even by the pangs which rent her heart, over a dear infant child, wasting away with sickness, and soon committed to a watery grave. Through all this sorrow and suffering, the Lord was with her, and gave her rest. During her last long and perilous voyage, separated by half the globe from the presence of a mother, whose presence was more than ever needed, and without a single female companion, she could thus write: "It is for Jesus, who sacrificed the joys of his Father's kingdom, and expired on the cross to redeem a fallen world, that thus I wander from place to place, and feel no where at home. How reviving the thought! How great the consolation it yields to my sinking heart!—Let the severest trials and disappointments fall to my lot, guilty and weak as I am, yet I think I can rejoice in the Lord, and joy in the God of my salvation."

In her last illness, which was attended with many distressing circumstances, she possessed her soul in patience and peace. God was pleased to manifest himself to her, as he does not to the world. "During her whole sickness, she talked in the most familiar manner, and with great delight, of death and the glory that was to follow." At a certain time, being advised by a physician to cast off such gloomy thoughts, "she replied, that those thoughts were cheering and joyful beyond what words could express." When it was intimated to her, that she could not live through another day; "*Oh joyful news!* she replied, *I long to depart;*" and added soon after, "that death appeared to her *truly welcome and glorious*."

But the simple narrative of her afflicted husband shows, better than any thing which I can say, that amid all the pain and languishment of sickness, and in the near view of death, she had that enjoyment of God her Saviour, and that hope of a blessed immortality, which was an hundred fold better than all she had forsaken.

To her widowed Mother, this is an affecting scene. But in the midst of your sorrows, dear Madam, forget not what reason you have to be comforted. Remember the grace of God, which was manifested to your dear Harriet, which, we trust, effectually sanctified her heart, and brought her to love the Lord Jesus Christ in sincerity. While you mourn for her early death, bless God that you do not mourn over a child, who lived without God, and died without hope. Call to remembrance her dutiful and pious temper; her resolved and peaceful mind in the parting hour; and the fortitude and resignation, which she afterwards exercised under her various afflictions. Give thanks to God for the consolations which were afforded her through a languishing sickness. Her amiable and elevated conduct reflected honour upon the grace of God. Through all her sufferings, especially when her dissolution drew near, she displayed a character that was ripe for Heaven.

It must afford you peculiar satisfaction to contemplate *the usefulness of her life.* "That life is long, which answers life's great end."[231] This was eminently the case with your beloved daughter. Had she lived in retirement, or moved in a small circle, her influence, though highly useful, must have been circumscribed. But now, her character has, by Divine Providence, been exhibited upon the most extensive theatre, and excited the attention and love of Christian nations. Yea, may we not hope, that her name will be remembered by the millions of Asia, whose salvation she so ardently desired, and that the savour of her piety will, through Divine grace, be salutary to Pagan tribes yet unborn? Madam, what comforts are these? comforts, which many mourning parents would gladly purchase with their lives. Let your sorrow then be mingled with praise. Render thanks to God, and magnify his name, that he has given you a daughter, so lovely in her character, so useful in her life, so resigned in her sufferings, so tranquil and happy in her death. It is better to be the parent of such a daughter, than to have brought forth a child to bear the sceptre of the earth. Nor is she the less precious, or the less *yours*, because she is absent from the body and present with the Lord. Dwell upon these cheering thoughts, and enjoy these comforts; and may all your surviving children enjoy them too. In her example, in her diary and letters, and in her dying counsels, she has left them a legacy, which cannot be too highly prized. Let me affectionately entreat you, my beloved friends, to attend seriously to the weighty counsels, which you have received from the dying lips of a dear sister. In her name, in the name of her bereaved husband, by whose request I now address you, and in the name of her God and Saviour, I do now, from this sacred place, repeat that solemn counsel. God Almighty open your hearts to receive the message. "*Tell them*, she said, *tell them from the lips of their dying sister, that there is nothing but religion worth living for. Oh exhort them to attend immediately to the care of their immortal souls; and not to delay repentance. Let my brothers and sisters know that I love them to the end. I hope to meet them in Heaven. But oh, if I should not*"——No wonder that tears bursting from her eyes, and her sobs of grief at the thought of an eternal separation from you, prevented her saying more. "May the Spirit of Truth carry her dying entreaties, and tears, and sighs to your hearts," and engage you to follow her, as she followed Christ. This dear departed friend wished you to partake with her the joys of salvation. She never repented of her undertaking; never regretted leaving her native land for the cause of Christ. And could she return and live on earth again, instead of retracting her labours and sacrifices for the advancement of the Redeemer's cause, she would repair to him earlier, give up all for him more cheerfully, and serve him with greater zeal. Imitate her humility, self-denial, and faith, that you may again enjoy her society, and dwell with her for ever, where sorrow and death shall never enter.

In the death of Mrs. Newell, her husband sustains a loss, which no language can adequately describe, and no earthly good compensate. God, whose ways are unsearchable, has taken from him the wife of his youth; a companion eminently qualified to aid him in all his labours, to soothe him in all his sorrows, and to further the great work in which he is engaged. Had he nothing but earthly good to comfort him, a mind so quick to feel, would be overwhelmed with grief. But he will not forget the God of all comfort. He will remember that gracious Redeemer, who took him out of the horrible pit and miry clay; who shed upon the darkness that once enveloped him, a cheering light; who inspired him with hope, and put it into his heart to preach salvation to those who were perishing for lack of vision. This mighty Redeemer will be the rock of his confidence, and a very present help in trouble. It must be a subject of delightful recollection to our afflicted brother, that he has enjoyed the privilege of being united, in the dearest of all relations, with one of so amiable a temper, of an understanding so highly improved, of *benevolence and piety* so eminent, and so entirely devoted to the best of causes. He will also love to remember the favour which God has conferred upon his beloved partner, in enabling her to do and suffer so much, and permitting her to die thus early for the name of Jesus; in permitting her to be the *first martyr* to the missionary cause from the American world; in removing her after so short a warfare, from a world of sin and sorrow, and carrying her so quickly through a course of discipline, which prepared her for a crown of distinguished glory. The God of Jacob bless and comfort our dear brother, and give him strength according to his day. And may this severe trial be turned to the furtherance of the Gospel among the Heathen.

FRIENDS OF THE MISSIONARY CAUSE!

Let not your hearts be troubled by the adverse circumstances which have attended the commencement of our FOREIGN MISSION. Recollect the various hindrances, disappointments, and sufferings, encountered by the APOSTLES, THE FIRST MISSIONARIES OF CHRIST; who yet were destined to spread the triumphs of his cross through the world. The experience of ages leads us to expect that designs of great moment, especially those which relate to the advancement of Christ's kingdom, will be opposed by mighty obstacles. The adverse circumstances, therefore, which have attended the outset of our Foreign Mission, are far from presenting any discouragement. They rather afford new evidence, that this Mission is to be numbered with all other enterprises, calculated to promote the honour of God and the welfare of men. These various trials, Brethren, are doubtless intended not only to qualify *Missionaries* for greater usefulness, but also to humble and purify all, who are labouring and praying for the conversion of the Heathen. How effectually do these events teach us, that no human efforts can ensure success; that the best qualifications of missionaries abroad, with the largest liberality and most glowing zeal of thousands at home, will be of no efficacy, without the blessing of God. When, by salutary discipline, he shall have brought his servants to exercise suitable humility and dependence, and in other respects prepared the way, no doubt he will give glorious success. The cause is *his;* and it is vain to depend for its prosperity on human exertions. The death of Mrs. NEWELL instead of overcasting our prospects, will certainly turn to the advantage of missions. It will correct and instruct those who are labouring for the spread of the Gospel. The publication of her virtues will quicken and edify thousands. It will also make it apparent, that the missionary cause has irresistible attractions for the most excellent characters. *Her* character will be *identified* with that holy cause. Henceforth, every one who remembers HARRIET NEWELL, will remember THE FOREIGN MISSION FROM AMERICA. And every one, who reads the history of *this* Mission, will be sure to read the faithful record of her exemplary life and triumphant death. Thus, all her talents, the advantages of her education, the beauties of her mind, and the amiableness of her manners, her refined taste, her willingness to give up all that was dear to her in her native land; her fervent love to Christ, her desires and prayers for the advancement of his kingdom; her patience and fortitude in suffering, and the divine consolations which she enjoyed, will all redound to the honour of that sacred cause, to which all she had was devoted. Her life, measured by months and years was *short;* but far otherwise, when measured by what she atchieved. She was the happy instrument of much good to the holy kingdom of Christ, which deserved all her affections and all her labours. She died in a glorious cause. Nor did she pray, and weep, and die in vain. Other causes may miscarry; but this will certainly triumph. The LORD GOD of Israel has pledged his perfections for its success. The time is at hand, when the various tribes of India, and all the nations and kindreds of the earth shall fall down before the KING OF ZION, and submit cheerfully to his reign. A glorious work is to be done among the nations. Christ is to see the travail of his soul, and all his benevolent desires are to be satisfied. The infinite value of his atoning blood is to be completely and universally illustrated; and the full orbed splendour of redeeming love is every where to shine forth. The power of God will soon accomplish a work, which, seen in distant prospect, has made thousands, now sleeping in Jesus, before leap for joy. Blessed are they who are destined to live, when the earth shall be filled with the glory of the Lord. And blessed are *we*, who live so near that day, and even begin to see its bright and glorious dawn. O SUN OF RIGHTEOUSNESS arise. Shine upon the dark places of the earth; illuminate all the world. AMEN.

Editorial notes

Abbreviations

EIC	East India Company
Hobson-Jobson	H. Yule and A. C. Burnell, *Hobson-Jobson: The Anglo-Indian Dictionary* (Cambridge: Cambridge University Press, 2011)
OED	*Oxford English Dictionary*

Notes

1 *late Treaty of Peace*: Signed 24 December 1812, the Treaty of Ghent ended the War of 1812.
2 *Reverend Joshua Marsden*: (1777–1837): Wesleyan minister and missionary worker in Bermuda, New Brunswick, and Nova Scotia, after which (in 1815) he emigrated to England.

In 1816 he published *The Narrative of a Mission to Nova Scotia, New Brunswick, and the Somers Islands* (Plymouth-Dock: J. Johns, 1816). He died in 1837 at Hoxton, near London.

3 *"Mr. Marsden's prospects . . . abundantly realized"*: Untraced.

4 *WILLIAM JAQUES*: Little is known about William Jaques other than his publications. In the same year as the London edition of *Memoirs of Harriet Newell* (1815), Jaques also published an abridgment of John Arndt's *True Christianity* (1605–1610) as *The True Christianity of the Venerable John Arndt*, 2 vols (London: Hatchard, 1815). Announcing the book in their 'Literary Intelligence', *Gentleman's Magazine* for March 1815 calls Jaques a 'Private Tutor' (85, p. 256). Jaques is also author of *A Practical Essay on Intellectual Education* (London: Hatchard, 1817) and translator of August Hermann Francke's *Guide to the Reading and Study of the Holy Scriptures* (London: Hatchard, 1819).

5 *these Memoirs contain only a part of her letters and journal*: An expanded edition of the Newell's letters and journals appeared in 1831 under the title *The Life and Writings of Mrs. Harriet Newell* (Philadelphia, PA: American Sunday School Union, 1831). It saw a second printing in 1832.

6 *Academy of Bradford*: Bradford Academy was founded in 1803; originally it was one of New England's first coeducational institutions, and many of its early graduates became Christian missionaries. In 1836 it changed to an academy for women only, and over the next 140 years evolved from a secondary school to a college granting bachelor's degrees. It closed in May 2000.

7 *Doddridge's Sermons to Young People*: Most likely Philip Doddridge, *Sermons to Young Persons, on the Following Subjects* (London: Fowler, Batley, and Wood, 1735), a popular work in its fifth London edition by 1790, and reprinted by at least two Philadelphia booksellers, Joseph Cruikshank and William Young, by 1794.

8 *Paul and Silas say to the jailor*: Referring to Acts 16:25–40, which relates Paul and Silas's imprisonment in Philippi. While the two pray with their fellow prisoners, an earthquake occurs, opening the prison doors and breaking the prisoners' bonds. In suicidal despair, the Philippian jailer next enters, expecting to find his prisoners escaped. When he finds them still there, in gratitude he leads them out of the prison, asks what he must do for his soul to be saved, and, on hearing the gospel, is converted.

9 *dancing school*: Dance was considered an important part of a liberal education, and dancing schools were popular in Massachusetts. As her diary suggests, though not 'criminal', dancing was criticized as a frivolous, expensive, and even irreligious pursuit. While no academies are advertised in Bradford's local weekly newspaper, the *Haverhill Museum* (1804–1806), the *Boston Gazette* and the *Washingtonian* newspapers from these years mention several, the most prominent run by a Mr. Turner and a Mrs. Ruggles, both charging tuition of $5 per quarter for two lessons per week. Curiously, the possibility of dancing for Newell was probably created by John Hasseltine, a founder of the Bradford Academy and father to one of Newell's closest friends, Nancy ('Ann') Hasseltine. John Hasseltine had recently added a large room or dance hall to the second story of his house to host assemblies. Controversially, the dances that followed were not only approved, but also attended, by the progressive minister at West Bradford, Parson Allen. An anonymously published pamphlet of 1805, 'A Letter from Fidelis to His Friend, Exhibiting some Leading Traits of the Character and Conduct of Modern Liberal, Frolicing Ministers', accuses Parson 'A' of being 'corrupted by doctrines of Arians and Socinians, which are infinitely below the true standard of gospel and morality . . . He pretends to be a Calvinist, yet he can be (on occasion) a thorough Arminian. But that is not the worst. At a meeting of ministers, Mr. A. and Mr. E[aton of Boxford] zealously advocated the cause of frolicing and dancing . . . They said that they themselves did attend the frolics with their young people . . . . In seasons past Mr. A. has attended frolicings and dancings with his young people, not only till nine o'clock, and ten o'clock, and eleven o'clock, and twelve o'clock at night, but even till one o'clock in the morning' (See Pond, *Bradford*, pp. 7–8).

John Hasseltine, together with his wife and daughters, later became a central figure in the religious revival of the community brought about by the appointment of a new teacher at the Bradford Academy, Abraham Burnham (see note 10).

10 *A revival of religion commenced in the neighbourhood*: Abraham Burnham was a key figure in the Protestant religious revival (now called the 'Second Great Awakening') experienced in Bradford and Haverhill after 1805. The self-taught son of a New Hampshire famer, Burnham graduated from Dartmouth in 1804 and was appointed as preceptor at Bradford Academy the following year. According to one historian of the Academy, Burnham 'looked upon his office as an opportunity for the personal guidance of each student into a religious experience as a preparation for a life of Christian service. His fervor soon kindled a revival of religion which spread from the school into the church and the town' (Pond, *Bradford*, p. 71). Studying theology with a minister in neighbouring Byfield, Burnham later left the Academy to become pastor of a church in Pembroke, New Hampshire. He married one of his former students, Mary White of Haverhill.

11 *with the Psalmist,* Whom . . . besides thee: Referring to Psalms 73:25.

12 *The destitute broken state of the church at Haverhill*: The Atwoods attended the First Parish Church at Haverhill, established in 1641 and the oldest in the city. Its first pastor was John Ward, son of founder and English Non-Conformist minister Rev. Nathanial Ward, who took charge of the Church in 1645. During Newell's early life (1795–1803) the church became a centre of Unitarian controversy because its pastor, the Harvard-trained Abiel Abbot (1770–1828), was not sufficiently orthodox for many members of his congregation (Abbot left the congregation and moved to nearby Beverly, Massachusetts after 1803 when his request for an increase to his salary was refused). He was appointed once again to a Congregationalist parish; within a short time, and apparently with the support of his parishioners, the Church became Unitarian.

Haverhill had no settled pastor until the Reverend Joshua Dodge arrived in 1808, and must have presented a stark contrast with the religious revival underway at Bradford with Burnham at its centre. See F. A. Gilmore, *Historical Sketch of First Parish Haverhill, Mass.* (Haverhill, MA: C. C. Morse and Sons, 1895); and J. H. Moore, 'The Abiel Abbot Journals: A Yankee Preacher in Charleston Society, 1818–1827 (Continued)', *South Carolina Historical Magazine* 68:2 (1967), pp. 51–73.

13 *Jehovah*: One of the many names of the god of the ancient kingdoms of Israel and Judah, 'Jehovah' is a late medieval translation of the Tetragrammaton, the four Hebrew characters (יהוה) also pronounced *Yahweh*.

14 *"My willing soul . . . everlasting bliss"*: Quoting Isaac Watts, 'Welcome, Sweet Day of Rest', ll. 13–16.

15 *superabounding grace of God*: Although not a direct Biblical quotation, the phrase refers to Romans 5:20 ('Moreover the law entered, that the offence might abound. But where sin abounded, grace did much more abound') and was popular in sermons of the time.

16 *"Oh, to grace how great a debtor!"*: Newell here quotes from line 25 of the hymn, 'Come Thou Fount of Every Blessing', by Robert Robinson. Itself an expansion of Samuel 7:12, the hymn expands on the idea of divine grace.

17 *"Why was . . . than come?"*: Quoting Isaac Watts, 'How sweet and awful is the place', ll. 13–16.

18 *March 25*: This date is corrected in *The Life and Writings of Mrs. Harriet Newell* (Philadelphia, PA: American Sunday School Union, 1831), to 'March 10', and new entries are added from February 2, 3, and 10.

19 *Immanuel's kingdom*: Referring to Isaiah 7:14, where Ahaz is promised that God will protect the house of David and will send a sign: 'Behold, a virgin shall conceive, and

bear a son, and shall call his name Immanuel'. In Hebrew, *Immanuel* (לְאִמָּנֻעֵל) literally means 'God with us'.
20 *her sister M. at Byfield*: Newell's sister Mary Atwood (1789–1833).
21 *Miss F. W.*: Fanny Woodbury (1791–1814), author of *Journals and Writings of Miss F. W., Including Some Interesting Correspondence between Her and Mrs. Newell* (Edinburgh: James Taylor Smith, 1818; London: Longman, 1818), which appeared after her death.
22 *epistolary visits*: Letters and correspondence.
23 *this time of awful declension*: Here, 'awful' denotes 'awe-inspiring', i.e., inspiring dread and reverential fear. In telling her friend that the present moment is a 'time of awful declension', therefore, Newell means that they live in a time of fearful decay, decline, and apostasy.
24 *"Not unto us . . . the glory?"*: A slight truncation and misquoting of Psalms 115:1: 'Not unto us, O Lord, not unto us, but unto thy name give glory, for thy mercy, and for thy truth's sake'.
25 *everlasting covenant*: Here, Newell echoes Jeremiah 32:40: 'And I will make an everlasting covenant with them, that I will not turn away from them, to do them good; but I will put my fear in their hearts, that they shall not depart from me'.
26 *conference*: Here, a meeting for spiritual lectures and conversation on serious subjects; for conferring or taking counsel.
27 *"I pray thee have me excused"*: From Luke 14:18.
28 *love of many waxeth cold*: Slightly altered from Matthew 24:12: 'And because iniquity shall abound, the love of many shall wax cold'.
29 *H.*: Haverhill.
30 *"where the worm . . . is not quenched"*: Quoting Mark 9:44.
31 *A dear and beloved parent is in a declining state*: Referring to Newell's father, Moses Atwood (1761–1808), who died of consumption later that year (May 1808).
32 *"not my will, O Lord! but thine be done"*: Paraphrased from Luke 22:42: 'Saying, "Father, if thou be willing, remove this cup from me: nevertheless not my will, but thine, be done"'.
33 *I do not expect to attend Bradford Academy this summer . . . I expect to attend*: Established as a co-educational school in 1803, Bradford Academy took boys in winter and summer terms, and girls only in the summer; the 'Female Apartment' was open from the first week of May. For this reason, Harriet returns home for half the year. Such limitations – in addition to the costs of boarding their daughters at Bradford – likely contributed to the founding of the Female Seminary at Haverhill under Deacon Ben Colman at Byfield 1806. Harriet's older sister Mary was made headteacher at Byfield, and, instead of attending Bradford, Harriet accompanied her together with her former schoolfellow from Bradford, Ann Hasseltine, in the autumn of 1810.
34 *To Miss C. P. of Newburyport*: As the next letter makes clear, Miss Catherine Pearson is a friend from the Bradford Academy, a young woman perhaps undergoing the same spiritual trials as Newell. Their shared carelessness of their spiritual 'improvement' in favour of 'trifling conversation' while at school together, and now again once returned to their families, is a repeated topic of their correspondence. See Pond, *Bradford*, pp. 78–9.
35 *Feb. 16, 1808 . . . death has entered our family*: This letter appears out of chronological order to provide a dramatic culmination to the fears of the previous letter. The uncle is likely Joshua Atwood, brother of Moses Atwood, Newell's father. The revised and expanded *Life and Writings of Mrs. Newell* (1831) retains this temporal anomaly.
36 *"Mourn not for me, my friends, but mourn for yourselves"*: Altered slightly from Luke 23:28: 'But Jesus turning unto them said, Daughters of Jerusalem, weep not for me, but weep for yourselves, and for your children'.
37 *"Tis greatly . . . welcome news"*: Quoting lines 376–9 of 'Night the Second' of Edward Young's *The Complaint: or, Night-Thoughts on Life, Death, and Immortality*, published in nine parts between 1742 and 1745.
38 *promised to be the father of the fatherless, and the widow's God*: Paraphrasing Psalms 68:5: 'A father of the fatherless, and a judge of the widows, is God in his holy habitation'.

39 *From some passages . . . religious declension and darkness*: Here, the editor interrupts Newell's own testimony of letters to comment on her 'state of religious declension' during the year 1808, supporting this interpretation of her spiritual state by further evidence from another observer, unnamed, but 'competent to testify'. Here the power of the editor – her husband? – in selecting, arranging, and framing interpretation of Newell's narrative, becomes apparent, as 1808–9 is presented as a period wasted 'in the vanities of the world – thoughtless and unconcerned', before she is returned to spiritual resolution.

40 *Miss Helen Maria Williams' Letters on the French Revolution*: Helen Maria Williams's chronicle of the French Revolution was originally published as *Letters Written in France, in the Summer of 1790, to a Friend in England* (London: T. Cadell, 1790). Over the next six years she published further installments narrating the rise of Robespierre, the Terror, and its aftermath. Popular and controversial, she was praised as a 'friend of liberty' (*Critical Review* (1796), p. 210) by progressives and criticized as 'a misguided female' (*British Critic* (1796), p. 7) by conservatives. That Newell is depicted reading Williams during a period of 'declension and darkness' serves as a telling register of her editors' political and religious views.

41 *Rollin's Ancient History*: Born in Paris, Charles Rollin was a distinguished scholar of ancient languages and educational reformer whose works were extremely popular in France, Great Britain, and the United States. The first English translation of his monumental *Histoire ancienne des Égyptiens, des Carthaginois, des Assyriens, des Babyloniens, des Mèdes et des Perses, des Macédoniens, des Grecs*, 14 vols (Paris, 1730–1738) appeared as *The Ancient History of the Egyptians, Carthaginians, Assyrians, Babylonians, Medes and Persians, Macedonians, and Grecians*, 10 vols (London: Knapton, 1738–1740), and went through at least 12 editions and abridgments by 1810. A version published by the Religious Tract Society of London appeared in 1841–1842.

42 *"And make each day a critic on the last"*: Quoting Alexander Pope, *An Essay on Criticism* (1711), Part 3, line 12.

43 *What am I . . . knowledge of Christ*: July 1809 seems to represent a turning point or sedimentation of Newell's convictions, introducing a new preoccupation with the duty of bringing the gospel to those 'in heathen darkness'. This passage is revealing for the way it predicates Newell's own salvation on her extending 'the gospel's joyful sound' to others: the first clear statement of a missionary calling provided by the *Memoirs*. Shortly after 20 July, Newell attempts her first 'conversion' of a 'dear and intimate companion'.

44 *aggravated transgressions*: According to Newell's own account in the preceding letters, these transgressions are probably levity, 'vain and idle conversation', and the 'bustle of crowded life'.

45 *"go the way from whence no traveller returns?"*: Here Newell appears to be loosely quoting from ll. 86–7 of Act 3, scene 1 of *Hamlet* ('That undiscovered country from whose bourn / No traveller returns'), although the quoted phrase also echoes Job 10:20–1 and Job 16:22.

46 *wrestle with him in prayer*: Recalling Jacob's wrestling with God in Genesis 32:24–8.

47 *Zion*: In Hebrew צִיּוֹן, a name synonymous with either Jerusalem or the biblical Land of Israel as a whole. Its earliest appearances occur in 2 Samuel 5:7 ('Nevertheless David took the strong hold of Zion: the same is the city of David') and 1 Kings 8:1 ('Then Solomon assembled the elders of Israel, and all the heads of the tribes, the chief of the fathers of the children of Israel, unto king Solomon in Jerusalem, that they might bring up the ark of the covenant of the Lord out of the city of David, which is Zion').

48 *This afternoon I attended meeting . . . Mr W.*: This would have been a service at the First Parish Church at Haverhill now under the leadership of Rev. Joshua Dodge. The 'Mr. W.' is possibly the Rev. Mr Samuel Worcester of Salem, part of the growing network of pastors preaching in the region.

49 *Matt. xxvi. 6–13*: Matthew 26:6–13 tells the story of the woman who comes to the house of Simon to anoint Jesus with precious ointment. When his disciples object to

the act as an extravagant waste, Jesus replies, 'For ye have the poor always with you; but me ye have not always. For in that she hath poured this ointment on my body, she did it for my burial' (11–12).

50 *our beloved pastor*: Reverend Joshua Dodge (1779–1861). Born in Hamilton, Massachusetts, Dodge attended Atkinson Academy and then Dartmouth College, graduating in 1806. He then entered on a course of study with Rev. Abiel Abbot, who had recently left Haverhill in 1803 and moved to Beverly, before become pastor of the First Parish Church in Haverhill in 1808. See G. W. Chase, *The History of Haverhill* (Haverhill, MA: published by the author, 1861), p. 559.

51 *Gospel trump*: Likely echoing, 'Hark! How the gospel trumpet sounds', a popular hymn written by Samuel Medley (1732–1799).

52 *"ready and willing . . . by him"*: Likely a paraphrase of Hebrews 7:25.

53 *And why . . . lack of knowledge?*: This is the first time Newell explicitly speaks of the attractions of missionary work abroad, and of converting 'the Heathen'.

54 *"no more sacrifice . . . fiery indignation"*: Quoting Hebrews 10:26–7.

55 *"He knows . . . the same"*: Quoting lines 7–8 of 'With Joy We Meditate the Grace' by Isaac Watts, itself a rumination on Hebrews 2:18 ('For in that he himself hath suffered being tempted, he is able to succour them that are tempted').

56 *that fountain*: Referring to Joel 3:11–21, which prophesies the desolation of Egypt and Edom and a new Jerusalem: 'And it shall come to pass in that day, that the mountains shall drop down new wine, and the hills shall flow with milk, and all the rivers of Judah shall flow with waters, and a fountain shall come forth of the house of the LORD, and shall water the valley of Shittim' (18).

57 *"Wickedness proceedeth from the wicked"*: Quoting 1 Samuel 24:13.

58 *"As we have . . . all men"*: Quoting Galatians 6:10.

59 *"In the multitude . . . my soul"*: Quoting Psalms 94:19.

60 *"Jesus answered . . . this world"*: Quoting John 18:36.

61 *"Unto you . . . of men"*: Quoting Proverbs 8:4.

62 *"God be merciful to me a sinner"*: Quoting Luke 18:13.

63 *"Laden with guilt, a heavy load"*: Quoting line 37 of Isaac Watts, 'Remember your Creator', an adaptation of Ecclesiastes 12.

64 *Who can dwell . . . everlasting burnings?*: Quoting Isaiah 33:14.

65 *Come and . . . done for me*: Paraphrasing Psalms 66:16.

66 *delivered me . . . to his name*: Quoting Psalms 40:2–3.

67 *the Lord doeth all things well*: Paraphrasing Mark 7:37.

68 *Restraining prayer . . . his knees*: Quoting William Cowper, 'Olney Hymn 29: Exhortation To Prayer', ll. 9–12.

69 *Have just returned from our reading society*: Here, and a week later, Newell describes her feelings after the meeting of a regular reading group. After both meetings, she condemns herself for her 'gaiety and lightness' and expresses frustration with the company assembled. It is not immediately clear whether this is a religious or secular gathering; in the second meeting of 30 October, the group are introduced to David Ramsay's *Life of Washington* (New York: Hopkins, 1807), which suggests the latter and shows how quickly new books were taken up even in regional areas.

Part of the popularity of reading societies arose from the high cost of books in the eighteenth and early nineteenth centuries, which led to the rapid growth of for-profit libraries and other institutions by which members might pool their resources to purchase worthwhile books so that, over time, a working library might be formed. Usually democratic in nature, reading societies were created by and for their members, who customarily paid a weekly or monthly subscription; books to be purchased were either chosen by the membership or by a subcommittee.

70 *Mr W. and Mr E.:* Probably Reverend Samuel Worcester of Salem (and the Massachusetts Missionary Society), and Reverend Joseph Emerson, pastor of the Third

Congregational Church at Beverly. Both men were active in the missionary cause, and mentors and supporters of the Williams College and Andover Theological Seminary students (Samuel Mills, James Richards, Luther Rice, Gordon Hall, Samuel Newell, Samuel Nott, and Adoniram Judson) who were dedicated to establishing a society for foreign missionary work. Early in 1810, Emerson married Rebecca Hasseltine, daughter of John Hasseltine and sister of Nancy ('Ann') Hasseltine (later Judson). He is credited with encouraging the female missionaries (Newell and Judson) to accompany their husbands to India in the face of general opposition. See *Life of Rev. Joseph Emerson* (Boston, MA: Crocker and Brewster, 1834), pp. 199–201.

71 *a serious intention . . . commencing in A*: Newell refers here to Andover, where several students (including the newly arrived Samuel Newell) attending Williams College and Andover Theological Seminary began planning to undertake missionary work. Their plans culminated in the presentation by the group to the General Association (27 June 1810) of the proposal to establish an *American Board of Commissioners for Foreign Missions*.

72 *"as in months past"*: Quoting from Job 29:2: 'Oh that I were as in months past, as in the days when God preserved me'.

73 *My dear friend, and as I humbly trust my spiritual father, Mr B. called upon us*: At the invitation of Dodge, Abraham Burnham, a preceptor at the Bradford Academy, preached at Haverhill on 12 November.

74 *"What shall I do to inherit eternal life"*: Quoting Luke 18:18.

75 *"that all things . . . love him"*: Quoted, with a few changes, from Romans 8:28.

76 *Search me, O God, and know me*: Slightly misquoted from Psalms 138:23 ('Search me, O God, and know my heart').

77 *valley of the shadow of death*: Referring to Psalms 23:4 ('Yea, though I walk through the valley of the shadow of death, I will fear no evil: for thou art with me; thy rod and thy staff they comfort me'), and the notion that the world would be a place of darkness and death without the presence of God.

78 *the commencement of the Millenium*: Referring to Revelation 20:1–5, in which an angel comes down from heaven, binds Satan and casts him into a bottomless pit, and the few who comprise the first resurrection sit in thrones and reign with Christ for a thousand years.

79 *tasting that the Lord is gracious*: Referring to Psalms 34:8 ('O taste and see that the Lord is good: blessed is the man that trusteth in him') and to 1 Peter 2:3 ('If so be ye have tasted that the Lord is gracious').

80 *"the chief among ten thousands, and altogether lovely"*: Newell brings together parts of the Song of Solomon 5:10 ('My beloved is white and ruddy, the chiefest among ten thousand') and 5:16 ('His mouth is most sweet: yea, he is altogether lovely. This is my beloved, and this is my friend, O daughters of Jerusalem').

81 *"robes have been washed and made white in the blood of the Lamb"*: Altered from Revelation 7:14 ('And he said to me, These are they which came out of great tribulation, and have washed their robes, and made them white in the blood of the Lamb').

82 *"iniquity abounds, and the love of many waxes cold"*: Slightly altered from Matthew 24:12.

83 *ball*: For Newell's reservations against dancing, see note 9.

84 *"put their hands . . . against God"*: Significantly altered from Luke 9:62 ('And Jesus said unto him, No man, having put his hand to the plough, and looking back, is fit for the kingdom of God') and Proverbs 29:1 ('He, that being often reproved hardeneth his neck, shall suddenly be destroyed, and that without remedy'). The wording of the second half of this passage appears to be entirely Newell's adaptation, and appears in no published Bible or sermon we have been able to discover.

85 *"Why was I . . . starve than come"*: Quoting lines 13–16 of Isaac Watts, 'How Sweet and Awful is this Place'. The italicization of '*I*' is Newell's.

86 *"I will bear . . . sinned against him"*: Quoting Micah 7:9.

87 *"It is the Lord, let him do what seemeth him good"*: Quoting 1 Samuel 3:18.

88 *Shepherd of Israel*: Another term for God, taken from Psalms 80:1.
89 *blood-washed millions*: Popular in later nineteenth-century missionary hymns such as 'Blood-washed Throng' and 'Resurrection Morning', which features separate verses on the conversion of India and China to Christianity, the phrase likely finds its source in Revelation 1:5 ('Unto him that loved us, and washed us from our sins in his own blood') and 7:14 ('These . . . have washed their robes, and made them white in the blood of the Lamb'). The earliest occurrence of 'blood-washed millions' that we have been able to locate occurs in *A Sermon Delivered at the Installation of the Rev. Reuben Emerson, A. M. over the First Church of Christ in Reading, Massachusetts: October 17, 1804* (Salem, MA: Joshua Cushing, 1805), p. 31. Given the sermon's date, location, and place of publication, it is likely that Newell would have encountered the text by 1810.
90 *"Dust thou art, and unto dust thou shalt return"*: Quoting Genesis 3:19.
91 *"Search me . . . way everlasting"*: Quoting Psalms 139:23–4.
92 *"Do thyself no harm"*: Quoting Acts 16:28.
93 *"to flee from the wrath to come"*: Quoting Matthew 3:7.
94 *The children of God . . . lights in the world*: Qdapted from Matthew 5:14.
95 *"tossed to and fro, and carried about by every wind of doctrine"*: Quoting Ephesians 3:14.
96 *"Ye are the salt . . . be salted"*: Quoting Matthew 5:13.
97 *Mr. E. called upon us . . . great revival of religion in his society and town*: Reverend Joseph Emerson (1777–1833), pastor of the Third Congregational Church at Beverly and member of the growing foreign mission movement in the region.
98 *Her very* countenance *declared the importance of religion*: Newell's use of 'countenance' here – italicized in the original text – refers not only to facial appearance, expression, or mien, but encompasses a deeper meaning of conduct and moral comportment. This is emphasised by her allusion to the power of her friend's gestures: she was 'speechless, though not senseless'.
99 *"the meat that perisheth"*: Quoting John 6:27.
100 *Praise the lord oh my soul*: Quoting Psalms 103:1.
101 *To-day we may imagine . . . a deceiver*: Possibly gesturing to Matthew 7:15 ('Beware of false prophets, which come to you in sheep's clothing, but inwardly are ravening wolves').
102 *July 1. Hail sacred morning! . . . rose from the grave*: Easter in 1810 occurred on April 22; by 'sacred morning' Newell here means only 'Sunday'.
103 *"How long halt ye between two opinions?"*: Quoting 1 Kings 18:21.
104 *A female friend . . . India's sultry clime*: Nancy ('Ann') Hasseltine, who was very shortly to marry Adoniram Judson and also become a missionary. The daughter of John Hasseltine, whose dance room had created such pleasure and controversy in Bradford, Ann had come – with her family – under the influence of Abraham Burnham at the Bradford Academy and had joined the Bradford church in September of 1809. Although Ann was four years older than Harriet, the girls had become close friends at Bradford and Byfield; between attending the Academy, Ann taught at small schools in Salem, Haverhill, and Newbury. As this diary entry shows, her missionary vocation has a profound impact on Harriet. See *Memoir of Mrs. Ann H. Judson, Late Missionary to Burmah* (Boston, MA: Lincoln & Edmands, 1829), pp. 32–75; Emerson, *Life of Rev. Joseph Emerson*, pp. 199–201; and C. Anderson, *To the Golden Shore: The Life of Adoniram Judson* (Grand Rapids, MI: Zondervan, 1972), pp. 85–6.
105 *"When I am weak, then am I strong"*: Quoting 2 Corinthians 12:10.
106 *"fear not . . . the kingdom"*: Quoting Luke 12:32.
107 *neither Paul nor Apollos*: Referring to 1 Corinthians 3:4–6

> For while one saith, I am of Paul; and another, I am of Apollos; are ye not carnal? / Who then is Paul, and who is Apollos, but ministers by whom ye believed, even as the Lord gave to every man? / I have planted, Apollos watered; but God gave the increase.

108 *"I had rather . . . tents of wickedness"*: Quoting Psalms 84:10.
109 *Oct 23. Mr M introduced Mr N. to our family*: Harriet's introduction to her future husband, Samuel Newell (1784–1821). The youngest of nine children, Newell lost both parents early, and seems to have become independent at a very young age. He took himself at 14 to study in Boston and, at 19, to Harvard where he was influenced by the Baptist preaching of Dr Stillman before joining the First Congregational Church in Roxbury in 1804. After his 1807 graduation from Harvard, Newell taught at several schools in the Massachusetts area and then entered the Andover Theological Seminary in 1809. Together with Adoniram Judson, Samuel Mills, Gordon Hall, and Samuel Nott, he offered himself to the Congregational Clergy of Massachusetts as a missionary in 1810, prompting the foundation of the American Board of Commissioners for Foreign Missions (ABCFM). In February 1812 he married Harriet Atwood and the couple left (with the Judsons and the Notts, and with Hall and Rice) for India in the same month. After Harriet's death in November of that same year, Newell travelled to Ceylon and Bombay to undertake preaching and mission work. In 1818 he married Philomela Thurston, a fellow missionary; in 1821 he died suddenly of cholera. Newell published *A Sermon Preached at Haverhill (Massachusetts) in Remembrance of Mrs. Harriet Newell* in 1814, and his wife's highly-influential *Memoirs* the following year (1815). With his fellow missionary Gordon Hall he published *The Conversion of the World, or the Claims of the Six Hundred Millions, and the Ability and Duty of the Churches* (Andover, MA, 1818).
110 *Law's Serious Call to a holy life*: William Law, *A Serious Call to a Devout and Holy Life*, originally published in 1729 by William Innys of London. By 1800 it had gone through at least fifteen authorized editions as well as several abridgements. The first decades of the nineteenth century saw Massachusetts printings in Boston (1818, 1821) and Andover (1821).
111 *"there is no future state"*: Likely a reference to 'A Second Letter to the Reverend Dr. Francis Atterbury': 'You say, you suppose Mankind *persuaded* that there is no *Future State*; and yet confess, you represent them, as *uneasie* under the *presages* of one: which you *take to be the case of all who profess to disbelieve a Future State*'. See *The Works of Benjamin Hoadly, DD*, 3 vols (London: W. Bowyer and J. Nichols, 1773), vol. 1, p. 64.
112 *"Whom have I . . . beside thee"*: Quoting Psalms 73:25.
113 *"way of all the earth"*: Quoting 1 Kings 2:2.
114 *"I have heard this sentence, and received their doom"*: Source not identified, though possibly taken from Thomas Wilson, 'The Great Danger of Not Knowing the Day of Visitation', in *Sermons*, 4 vols (8th edition, Bath: R. Crutwell, 1795), vol. 2, p. 339: 'we tread upon the graves of those that have already received their doom'.
115 *"and exclaim with Thomas, 'My Lord and my God!'"*: Quoting John 20:28. Here Newell aligns her only capacity to doubt with that of the apostle Thomas, who, on being told by other apostles of Jesus's return from the dead, states that he will not believe that Jesus has risen from the dead unless 'I shall see in his hands the print of the nails, and put my finger into the print of the nails, and thrust my hand into his side, I will not believe'. When Jesus next appears he invites Thomas to 'reach hither thy hand, and thrust it into my side: and be not faithless, but believing' (John 20:27). The episode is the foundation for the term 'doubting Thomas', denoting a sceptic who refuses to believe except from first-hand experience.
116 *"an evil heart of unbelief" prone to "depart from the living God"*: Both quotations are from Hebrews 3:12.
117 *"A soul redeemed demands a life of praise"*: Quoting line 289 of William Cowper, 'Truth', first published in *Poems* (London: J. Johnson, 1782).
118 *"When I was a child, I spake as a child"*: Quoting 2 Corinthians 13:11.
119 *"Lord, what a wretched land is this"*: Hymn by Isaac Watts.

120 *"teaching young ideas how to shoot"*: Quoting line 1070 of James Thomson, 'Spring', originally published in *Spring: A Poem* (London: A Millar, 1728).
121 *Newton's works*: Likely *The Works of the Right Reverend Thomas Newton, D. D. Late Lord Bishop of Bristol*, originally published in London by the Rivington brothers after Newton's death in 1782. Today Newton is best remembered for his variorum edition of John Milton's *Paradise Lost* (1752) and for his extremely popular *Dissertations on the Prophecies* (1754–1758), which included a systematic analysis of Revelation.
122 *the mercy seat*: Referring to the lid of the ark of the covenant, described in Exodus 25:17 and further referred to in Exodus 30:6 and 31:7, 1 Chronicles 28:11, and Leviticus 16:2. In Hebrews 9:5 and Ephesians 2:6 it is compared to the throne of grace described in Revelation 20:4.
123 *the name of——*: Samuel Newell.
124 *"not knowing the things which shall befall me there"*: Quoting Acts 20:22.
125 *"that wisdom which is profitable to direct"*: Quoting Ecclesiastes 10:10.
126 *"Guide me, O thou great Jehovah"*: Hymn written by William Williams (1717–91).
127 *"a desert world, replete with sin and sorrow"*: Quotation not traced, but possibly combining two lines from different psalms by Isaac Watts: line 23 of 'Psalm 107 Part 1' and line 5 of 'Psalm 90 Part 3'. See *The Psalms of David, Imitated in the Language of the New Testament, and Applied to Christian State and Worship* (London: Rivington, Buckland, Longman, Field, and Dilly, 1776).
128 *"not knowing the things which shall befal me there"*: Quoting Acts 20:22.
129 *Mr Newton . . . "only thee"*: Newell here misattributes ll. 17–20 of 'Walking with God', a poem by William Cowper, to Thomas Newton.
130 *Mr. Hall*: Gordon Hall, an associate of Samuel Newell whose missionary work in Bradford is praised by J. D. Kingsbury in *Memorial History of Bradford, Mass* (Haverhill, MA: C. C. Morse, 1883), p. 117. See also *Memoir of Mrs. Ann H. Judson, Late Missionary to Burmah* (Boston, MA: Lincoln & Edmands, 1829), pp. 32–44.
131 *My leave of Mr. N. . . . nine months*: Samuel Newell left Haverhill for Philadelphia to study medicine, most likely at the College of Philadelphia (founded 1765).
132 *"adverse fortune frowns"*: Quoted from Hannah More, 'Daniel Part VI', in *Sacred Dramas; Chiefly Intended for Young Persons: The Subjects Taken from the Bible* (London: T. Cadell, 1782).
133 *"life's vale is strew'd with flowerets fresh"*: Untraced.
134 *"And as he drew nigh to the city, he wept over it, saying"*: Quoting Luke 19:41.
135 *Did Christ . . . every eye*: Quoting ll. 1–4 of a hymn by S. M. Beddome, the earliest printing of which occurs in J. Rippon (ed.), *A Selection of Hymns from the Best Authors, Intended To Be an Appendix to Dr. Watts's Psalms and Hymns* (London: Thomas Wilkins, 1787), p. 367.
136 *Oh that thou . . . to thy peace*: Slightly altered from Luke 19:42 ('Saying, If thou had'st known, even thou, at least in this thy day, the things which belong unto thy peace! but now they are hid from thine eyes').
137 *Should fate command . . . must be joy*: The original passage is from ll. 107–14 of 'Winter' in James Thomson's *The Seasons* (1730); the final line in Newell's passage is of her own composition.
138 *Horne on Missions*: Melville Horne (c. 1761–1841) was an Anglican clergyman who served as chaplain to the Sierra Leone Company in 1792–1793. On his return he wrote and published *Letters on Missions: Addressed to the Protestant Ministers of the British Churches* (Bristol: Bulgin and Rosser, 1794), which helped to spur the founding of London Missionary Society in 1795. While it is possible that Newell means Horne's 1794 text, she also might be referring to the locally published *A Collection of Letters Relative to Foreign Missions; Containing Several of Melville Horne's 'Letters on Missions,' and Interesting Communications from Foreign Missionaries. Interspersed with Other Extracts* (Andover, MA: Galen Ware, 1810).

139 *Yes, Christian heroes!... rose of Sharon there*: Lines 1–4 of a hymn composed in 1797 by Bourne H. Draper, a student of the Baptist Academy of Bristol. A possible source for Draper's lyrics appears to be *Hhadash Hamishcan: or, the New Chapel, at Halifax, in Yorkshire, a Poem* (Halifax: E. Jacob, 1772), which boast similar lines: 'The everlasting Love of God proclaim, / And free Salvation through Immanuel's Name' (p. 10).
140 *adorable*: Here, meaning 'inspiring adoration'.
141 *"I think of the days of other years, and my soul is sad"*: Newell here likely cobbles together two phrases from 'The War of Caros', a poem by Ossian (James Macpherson). Having recounted the tale of Lamor killing his son ('his soul is sad'), Ossian confesses, 'Darkness comes on my soul . . . let me think on the days of other years'. See *The Poems of Ossian*, 2 vols (Edinburgh: Elder and Brown, 1797), vol. 1, pp. 95, 98.
142 *Hindostan*: Or 'Hindustan', the Persian name for India.
143 *Widows consent to be burned*: Newell refers to the practice of *sati* or *suttee*, the self-immolation of widows on the funeral pyres of their dead husbands. This tradition attracted much attention from European visitors, and became a stock topic for eighteenth- and nineteenth-century travel accounts. The practice was eventually banned by the British in 1829; however, there is considerable scholarly debate as to how common sati actually was in Indian society. For a range of views, see L. Mani, *Contentious Traditions: The Debate on Sati in Colonial India* (Berkeley, CA: University of California Press, 1992); A. Major, *Pious Flames: The European Encounter with Sati, 1500–1830* (Oxford: Oxford University Press, 2006); N. G. Cassels, *Social Legislation of the East India Company: Public Justice versus Public Instruction* (Los Angeles, CA and London: Sage, 2010), pp. 88–112.
144 *parents sacrifice . . . river Ganges*: Ritual sacrifice, whether of animals or of humans in effigy, is very rare in Hinduism, and is mostly associated with Shaktism. As with sati, reports of Hindu human sacrifice were widely circulated among European visitors, and Newell references these stories here.
145 *East Indies*: Referring to the lands of South and Southeast Asia.
146 *"My grace is sufficient for thee"*: Quoting 2 Corinthians 12:9.
147 *Loose, then . . . climes explore*: Quoting ll. 387–8 of 'Night the Second' of Edward Young's *The Complaint; or, Night-Thoughts* (1742–5).
148 *"'tis all that I can do"*: Quoting line 24 of Isaac Watts, 'Alas, and did my Savior bleed?'.
149 *"Dear Saviour . . . created good"*: Quoting ll. 17–20 of Isaac Watts, 'How vain are all things here below'.
150 *"thy people shall be my people"*: Quoting Ruth 1:16.
151 *Jesus to multitudes . . . ever bless'd*: Quoting lines 9–20 of 'Ye glittering toys of earth, adieu' by Anne Steele, printed in *Poems, on Subjects Chiefly Devotional*, 3 vols (Bristol: W. Pine, 1780), vol. 3, pp. 142–3.
152 *"the longest summer days seemed too much in haste"*: Quoting ll. 106–7 of Robert Blair, *The Grave* (1743).
153 *"None of these things move me, neither count I my life dear to me"*: Quoting Acts 20:24.
154 *"For me remains . . . God is there"*: Quoting ll. 9–12 of 'The Soul That Loves God Finds Him Every Where', in *Poems, Translated from the French of Madame de La Mothe Guion by the Late William Cowper* (Newport Pagnell: J. Wakefield, 1801).
155 *"Day of all . . . eternal rest"*: Quoting John Newton, 'Safely through another week'.
156 *when the heavens are rolled together as a scroll*: Drawing from the language of Isaiah 34:4 and Revelation 6:14.
157 *elements melt with fervent heat*: Quoting 2 Peter 3:10.
158 *"I'm but a stranger . . . and sweet repose"*: Quoting Elizabeth Singer Rowe, 'III. Longing after the Enjoyment of God', originally published in *Devout Exercises of the Heart in Meditation and Soliloquy, Prayer and Praise* (London: R. Hett, 1738), p. 11.

159 *"Bless the Lord . . . his benefits"*: Quoting Psalms 103:1–2.
160 *The Lord is my light . . . morning?*: Quoting Psalms 27:1, 30:7, 30:1, and 30:3–5.
161 *"The time is short . . . heavenly shore"*: Quoting lines 49–51 of Susannah Harrison, 'I Think My Table Richly Spread', in *Songs in the Night; by a Young Woman under Deep Afflictions* (London: T. Hawes, 1780), p. 113.
162 *"Be careful for nothing . . . unto God"*: Quoting Philippians 4:6.
163 *prisoners of hope*: Quoting Zechariah 9:12.
164 *"Now is the accepted time, now is the day of salvation"*: Quoting from 2 Corinthians 6:2.
165 *stranger in a strange land*: Quoting Exodus 2:22.
166 *"But even . . . rage disarm"*: Quoting ll. 175–6 of Oliver Goldsmith, *The Traveller* (1765).
167 *"Soon I hope" . . . his example may affect my heart!*: Newell quotes from Henry Kirke White, 'Fragment of an Eccentric Drama: The Dance of the Consumptives', first published in R. Southey (ed.), *The Remains of Henry Kirke White*, (London: Vernor, Hood, and Sharpe, 1807), p. 300. Though largely unread today, Kirke White's *Remains* were extremely popular in the early nineteenth century, seeing ten editions, two of them American, by 1818. His combination of evangelical faith – he found a patron in Charles Simeon of King's College, Cambridge – followed by an early death from consumption in 1806 would have rendered him a fascinating figure to Newell, particularly at this highly anxious time in her life.
168 *is there not a balm in Gilead; is there no physician there?*: Quoting Jeremiah 8:22. Balm of Gilead (also called balm of Mecca) is a resin exuded from the Balsam tree (*Balsamodendron Gileadense*) that was valued in the eighteenth century for its antiseptic qualities and as a cure-all. American Balm of Gilead derives from a different tree, the balsam fir.
169 *Buchanan's Researches*: Reverend Claudius Buchanan, D. D., *Christian Researches in Asia: With Notices of the Translation of the Scriptures into the Oriental Languages* (London: Cadell and Davies; Boston, MA: S. T. Armstrong, 1811), which went through nine editions in two years. A chaplain in Calcutta for the EIC, Buchanan zealously supported missionary operations and laboured to promote Christianity in India, raising money for translations of the scriptures and prize essays and poems. Returning to England in 1810, he wrote against the censorship of Christian works in India and campaigned to force the Company to give missionaries unrestricted access there.
170 *We want not bread . . . FAMINE FOR BIBLES*: Referring to the following passage in Buchanan's *Researches*:

> They were *clamorous* for Bibles. They supplicated for teachers. 'We don't want bread or money from you', said they; 'but we want the word of God' . . . Christianity flourishes; but I found that here, as at other places, there is a 'famine of Bibles'.
>
> (London edition, p. 79)

171 *Why sinks my weak . . . God be nigh?*: Lines 1–4 of a hymn by Anne Steele, published in *The Hartford Selection of Hymns from the Most Approved Authors* (Hartford, CT: John Babcock, 1799).
172 *"The thoughts . . . joys create"*: Quoting ll. 27–8 of Isaac Watts's 'Heavenly Joy on Earth', a standard hymn first published in *Hymns and Spiritual Songs* (London: John Lawrence, 1707), pp. 105–6.
173 *My journey here . . . will soon be over*: Quoting from Henry Kirke White, 'Fragment of an Eccentric Drama: The Dance of the Consumptives', in *Remains* (1807), p. 300.
174 *"the long Sabbath of the tomb is past"*: Quoting line 13 of Henry Kirke White, 'Fanny! Upon Thy Breast I May Not Lie!'
175 *the day dawn . . . so long dwelt?*: Quoting 2 Peter 1:19.
176 *"All the sad variety of grief"*: Quoted from J. Norton, *The Blessedness of Those Who Die in the Lord, Illustrated . . . in a Discourse Delivered at Weymouth, Feb. 3, 1811* (Boston, MA: Lincoln & Edmands, 1811), p. 13.

177 *"I can do all things through Christ, who strengtheneth me"*: Quoting Philippians 4:13.
178 *As Kirke White . . . "everlasting rest"*: Slightly misquoted from 'Fragment of an Eccentric Drama: The Dance of the Consumptives', in *The Remains of Henry Kirke White* (1807), p. 300; the line correctly reads 'Will greet the peaceful inn of lasting rest'.
179 *Oh! when will the radiant star in the East direct them to Bethlehem!*: Referring to Luke 2:1–18 and the story of Christ's nativity, where shepherds are visited by an angel and directed to see a child lying in a manger in Bethlehem. Here Newell uses the story as a metaphor for missionary work, the 'star in the East' in this case leading them to India.
180 *The glorious morn of the Millenium hastens . . . 'reign of peace and love'*: Source not identified, though Newell's reference to the millennium suggests she is thinking of Revelation 20:4–6, which tells of the first resurrection of souls and Christ's reigning for 1,000 years on earth.
181 *"But, hush . . . part no more"*: Adapting ll. 11–14 of Henry Kirke White's sonnet, 'Fanny! Upon thy breast I may not lie!'. The original lines go as follows:

> Yet hush! my fond heart, hush! there is a shore
> Of better promise; and I know at last,
> When the long sabbath of the tomb is past,
> We two shall meet in Christ – to part no more!

182 *The sultry climes . . . stingless death*: Source not identified.
183 *when the long Sabbath of the tomb is past*: Quoting line 13 of Henry Kirke White, 'Fanny! Upon they breast I may not lie!'
184 *flying-fish*: Any one of the many kinds of *exocoetidae*, of which over sixty species exist, called 'flying' because they are capable of leaping out of the water and using their long fins like wings to propel themselves, skimming the top of the water, for significant distances.
185 *the torrid Zone*: Geographically, the area between the Tropic of Cancer (23.5° north latitude) and the Tropic of Capricorn (23.5° south latitude) that includes the Equator.
186 *"the Lord will take me up"*: Quoting Psalms 27:10.
187 *"through Christ, who strengtheneth me"*: Quoting Philippians 4:13.
188 *the Cape*: The Cape of Good Hope, a little more than 50 kilometres south of Cape Town, South Africa.
189 *"This life's a dream, an empty show"*: Quoting line 5 of Isaac Watts, 'The Hope of the Christian'.
190 *"Who rides . . . the seas"*: Quoting ll. 15–16 of Isaac Watts, 'Heavenly Joy on Earth'.
191 *"I will bless the Lord . . . my supplications"*: Loosely quoting and compressing Psalms 31:21–2: 'Blessed be the Lord: for he hath shewed me his marvellous kindness in a strong city. / For I said in my haste, I am cut off from before thine eyes: nevertheless thou heardest the voice of my supplications when I cried unto thee'.
192 *"Give what thou . . . wilt away"*: Slightly misquoting Book V, ll. 905–6 William Cowper, *The Task* (1785): 'Give what thou can'st, without thee we are poor, / And with thee rich, take what thou wilt away'. The italics are Newell's.
193 *"I have loved the place where thine honour dwelleth"*: Contracting Psalms 26:8: 'Lord, I have loved the habitation of thy house, and the place where thine honour dwelleth'.
194 *"The winter is past, and the time of the singing birds is come"*: Quoting and compressing The Song of Solomon 2:11–12: 'For, lo, the winter is past, the rain is over and gone; / The flowers appear on the earth; the time of the singing of birds is come, and the voice of the turtle is heard in our land'.
195 *some account of Birmah*: Untraced, though possibly William Hunter's *A Concise Account of Climate, Produce, Trade, Government, Manners, and Customs of the*

Kingdom of Pegu; Interspersed with Remarks Moral and Political (Calcutta; J. Hay, 1785; London: J. Sewell and J. Debrett, 1789).

196 *Juggernaut*: A deity worshipped in some regional Hindu traditions, Jagannath is generally considered an avatar of Vishnu. In her letter of 27 June 1812 to Miss S. H., Newell describes the annual celebration of the deities Jagannath, Balabhadra, and Subhadra, where colossal representations of the gods are transported to the temple in chariots. This is the origin of the modern English word 'juggernaut'. Early European accounts of this festival described devotees being crushed under the wheels of the chariots, perhaps even as a form of honourable suicide.

197 *the land of Pagan darkness, which* Buchanan *so feelingly describes*: Likely quoted from Rev. Charles Buchanan, L.L.D., *The Star in the East; Containing some Extracts from a Sermon Preached in the Parish-Church of St. James, Bristol, on Sunday, Feb. 26th, 1809, for the Benefit of the 'Society for Missions to Africa and the East'* (Danbury, CT, 1810), p. 31.

198 *Saugor Island . . . sharks and alligators*: Sagar is a large island in the Bay of Bengal, in the mouth of the Hooghly river. Although the details are now unclear, some local Hindu communities seem to have regarded being killed and consumed by sharks in the waters around Sagar Island as a purificatory fate that might lead to 'moksha', or freedom from the cycles of mortal existence. Alternatively, local traditions suggested that sacrificing a child in these waters might lead to greater fertility in the future. Whatever the precise motivation here, an EIC ordinance of 1802 proscribed such sacrifices (although not voluntary suicide in such a manner) and a company of sepoys was posted during religious festivals to prevent them. See H. H. Wilson, *Essays and Lectures Chiefly on the Religion of the Hindus*, 2 vols (London: Trubner, 1862), vol. 2, pp. 166–7; Cassels, *Social Legislation of the East India Company*, pp. 86–88.

199 Cudjeree: Also spelled *Kedgeree*, *Khijiri*, or *Kijari*, located 68 miles south of Calcutta in the lowlands near the mouth of the Hooghly on the West bank. *The Edinburgh Gazetteer, or Geographical Dictionary* (Edinburgh: Constable, 1822) describes it as

> situated near the mouth of the Horgley [sic], where ships frequently stop, either coming out or entering the river. It is esteemed healthier than Diamond Harbour, and has a good bazar. A marine officer is stationed here, who makes a daily report to the master attendant, of the ships that sail and arrive. It is situated on the western bank of the river, and is surrounded by a swampy and unhealthy district.
>
> (vol. 3, p. 567)

200 *Dr. Carey . . . Dr Marshman and Mr Ward*: William Carey (1761–1834), English missionary and translator who arrived in Calcutta in 1793 and, forced by the EIC to leave British territory, founded schools for impoverished children in Serampore. He is now known as the 'father of modern missions'. Joshua Marshman (1768–1837), English missionary, linguist and Oriental scholar, and William Ward (1769–1823), missionary, printer, and translator: both joined Carey at the Baptist mission at Serampore in 1799.

201 *Palanquin*: 'A box-litter for travelling in, with a pole projecting before and behind, which is borne on the shoulders of 4 or 6 men – 4 always in Bengal' (*Hobson-Jobson*, p. 502).

202 *budgerow*: *Hobson-Jobson* is much less impressed with this craft, calling it a 'lumbering keel-less barge' (p. 91).

203 *remove far from me* lover: Quoting Psalms 88:18.

204 *charity school*: Also called 'The Institution for the Instruction of Indigent Christian Children', founded in 1810. Its progress is reported in the 17 December 1810 *Missionary Magazine*, which regularly related activities in Serampore and Calcutta: 'The charity school of Calcutta has 50 scholars in it. Great progress is making in the translations of the scriptures, and in printing there'. See the *Missionary Magazine* XV (1810), p. 576. Newell's is one of the earliest eye-witness accounts provided by

someone other than one of its founders. A detailed though highly ideological description of the school's origins and aims was published in *A Friend to India* (Serampore: At the Mission Press, 1818), pp. 131–7.

205 *christian natives . . . new Jerusalem*: Newell again references the events of Revelation, particularly 21:1–5, in which John envisions 'the holy city, new Jerusalem, coming down from God out of heaven, prepared as a bride adorned for her husband' (21:3). Of interest is her term 'Christian natives', and her desire to imagine the 'children of Jesus' as 'collected from Christian and Heathen lands'.

206 *I have witnessed scenes this morning . . . the holy Ganges*: See note 196 above on 'Juggernaut'. Of interest here is Newell's double critique: not only of what she calls Hindu 'superstition', but also the 'criminal slothfulness' and lack of compassion of Christians back home.

207 *Bless the Lord . . . his holy name*: Slightly altered from Psalms 103:1: 'Bless the Lord, O my soul: and all that is within me, bless his holy name'.

208 *"They that cross the ocean . . . their minds"*: A popular quotation from Horace's *Epistles* I:XI: 'Caelum non animum mutant qui trans mare currunt' [*Those who hurry across the sea change their sky, not their souls or state of mind*]. The italics are Newell's.

209 *Circars*: The term usually refers not to a class of people but to a region. The *OED* defines the *Northern Circars* as 'a large maritime province extending along the west side of the Bay of Bengal . . . granted to the East India Company by the Great Mogul in 1765'. This sense is echoed in *Hobson-Jobson*, which describes the *Circars* as the 'territory to the north of Coromondel Coast . . . obtained by Clive in 1765, confirmed by treaty with the Nizam in 1766' (p. 170). An earlier account defining the 'Circar, or Sircar' as a 'general name for the government, or persons concerned in the administration' occurs in the 'Glossary of Persic and Indian Names' found in R. Owen, *An Account of the War in India, between the English and French, on the Coast of Coromandel, from the Year 1750 to the Year 1760* (London: T. Jefferys, 1761), p. xv.

210 *such is the one . . . generation*: Paraphrasing Psalms 45:17: 'I will make thy name to be remembered in all generations'.

211 *Some will probably sacrifice their lives*: See note 196 on 'Juggernaut'.

212 *Isle of France*: Now Mauritius, conquered by British forces from the French in November, 1810. The surrender eliminated the last French territory in the Indian Ocean. Mauritius was held by Britain until 1968.

213 *Mrs. Marshman has a lovely school . . . Latin, Greek, and Hebrew*: The passage reminds us not just of Newell's high level of education but also the educational ambitions among female missionaries generally. Here the study of languages exceeds that common among even well-to-do American and British women.

214 *Governor General's park*: Located at Barrackpore, the land was placed under the Governor General's control in 1803. At the time the Newells arrived, it already had become a park where colonial elites could enjoy the flora and fauna of the tropics. By 1830 its collection of exotic plants and animals had become famous, as is noted by the *Sporting Magazine* 75 (1830), p. 253:

> The Governor has a good menagerie at his country-residence near Barrackpore. I saw the lions, tigers, bears, gluttons, &c. devouring their mess at night . . . . The Government grounds slope down to the brink of the Hoogly with the beautiful appearance of an English park; the lines and cantonments are very agreeable – the country excellent for jackal-hunting; and, altogether, it is to Calcutta what Windsor or Richmond is to London.

215 *"Hitherto hath the Lord helped us"*: Quoting 1 Samuel 7:12.
216 *Buggy [chaise]*: A light horse-drawn vehicle for one or two people.

217 *prickly heat*: According to the *OED*, 'An itchy or prickly skin eruption consisting of small vesicles or papules at the openings of sweat glands, occurring in very hot weather or climates (a kind of miliaria)'.
218 *Bengalee language . . . tony for water*: Also called Bangla, 'Bengalee' is the language of modern West Bengal, the foremost language of the north-eastern part of India and Bangladesh, and is the language of the writer Rabindranath Tagore (1861–1941). In modern phonetic spellings, sugar is *cini* and water is *pani*.
219 *the unhappy war between us and England*: Referring to the War of 1812, which broke out between Britain and the United States in the summer of that year because of disputes over British trade restrictions to impede neutral trade with France, British impressment of American sailors to maintain that blockade, and a number of small naval skirmishes by each intended to insult the other nation. Napoleon's abdication in 1814 rendered most of these issues irrelevant, and a peace treaty was signed in 1815.
220 *Joseph Hardcastle, Esq. of London*: A merchant and evangelical activist, Joseph Hardcastle (1752–1819) was one of the directors (with William Wilberforce, Henry Thornton, and Thomas Clarkson) of the Sierra Leone Company that established the freed slaves colony in West Africa in 1792; and in 1795 one of the founders of the London Missionary Society, holding the office of Treasurer for over twenty years.
221 *Jesus, thy blood . . . my head*: Lines 1–4 of the hymn composed in 1739 by Count Nicolaus Ludwig and subsequently translated by John Wesley.
222 *LEONARD WOODS, D.D.*: The first professor of Andover Theological Seminary, Woods (1774–1854) helped establish several societies including the American Tract Society, the American Education Society, the Temperance Society, and the American Board of Commissioners for Foreign Missions.
223 *If I forget . . . cunning*: Quoting Psalms 137:5.
224 *"What mean ye . . . to break mine heart?"*: Quoting Acts 21:13.
225 they rejoice . . . is the Church: Quoting Colossians 1:24.
226 whosoever forsaketh . . . be his disciple: Quoting Luke 14:3.
227 If any one come . . . cannot be my disciple: Quoting Luke 14:26.
228 *"What things . . . may win Christ"*: Quoting Philippians 3:7–8.
229 The wicked . . . mire and dirt: Quoting Isaiah 57:20.
230 *those who forsake . . . this present life*: Paraphrasing Mark 10:30.
231 *"That life is long, which answers life's great end"*: Quoting line 773 of 'Night the Fifth' of Edward Young's *The Complaint: Or, Night-Thoughts on Life, Death, and Immortality* (1742–1745).

ELIZA FAY,
ORIGINAL LETTERS
FROM INDIA (1817)

The daughter of a shipwright, Eliza Fay, *née* Clement, was born in 1755 or 1756 and died on 9 September 1816 at Calcutta. The details of her education are unknown, although by 23 she was well-read, fluent in French, and had already travelled to France at least three times. She married Anthony Fay in 1772, and in 1779 embarked with him on the first of a series of voyages to India. A resourceful and entrepreneurial woman, Fay engaged in multiple businesses over the next 35 years, including a millinery shop at Calcutta (Kolkata), a boarding school in Surrey, and trade between Britain, America, and India. At 60 years old she prepared for publication her *Original Letters*, her only known work.

The *Original Letters* describes three voyages to India: the first (1779–83) details the couple's journey overland through Egypt and their imprisonment at Calicut on the west coast of India by Sardar Khan and Hyder Ali in the build-up to the Second Anglo-Mysore War (1780–1784). Escaping in February 1780, the Fays finally arrived in Calcutta a year after their departure. Anthony Fay was formally established in legal practice by June 1780, and her own proximity to the highest administrative circles provided Fay with an insider's perspective on the developing conflicts within the Council and Supreme Court, which culminated in the impeachment trial of Warren Hastings. While at Calcutta, Anthony Fay's conduct led to the breakdown of the already precarious marriage, with a private deed of separation signed in August 1781. Left destitute, Fay departed for Britain in 1782.

Fay's second voyage to India (1784–1794) was her longest residence. With her travelling companion Avis Hicks (who later married local businessman John Lacey), Fay established a milliners shop in the former Post Office, adjacent to St John's Church, Calcutta. Her business failed in the general recession of 1788, but she was allowed to continue to trade and gradually repaid her creditors. Leaving her venture in the hands of Benjamin Lacey (John Lacey's brother), Fay sailed for Britain. On route at St Helena she was called to answer charges that in 1782 she had abandoned – without her consent – her servant Kate Johnson, who was subsequently sold into slavery. Fay paid a fine of £60 for the repatriation and compensation of Johnson, rather than stand trial.

Fay's father died in 1794; her mother had died earlier – between 1780 and 1783 – while Fay was in India. Together with her sister Eleanor, Fay inherited family property in London and Ireland. It was probably this windfall that allowed her to launch her career as a merchant later that same year, and to undertake her third voyage to Calcutta (1795–1796). Arriving in the *Minerva*, the ship in which all her personal capital had been invested, Fay disposed of her British cargo at Calcutta and swiftly loaded new freight bound for America. Seeing her ship off at Calcutta in April 1796, Fay made ready to follow: travelling via Madras (Chennai) and Cape Town, and narrowly avoiding a plague-ridden Philadelphia, she arrived in New York in December 1796.

Fay's narrative stops at this point, but we can trace some of her movements, and at least two further voyages to India. In 1800 'Mrs Elizabeth Fay, of Fenchurch-street, London, Widow', and Benjamin Lacey, 'Merchants, Dealers, Chapmen and Copartners', had a commission of bankruptcy awarded against them.[1] In August 1804 Fay again departed England, arriving in Calcutta in January 1805. Her stay was brief: taking up an earlier suggested project of education, Fay left again for England at the end of 1805 accompanied by fourteen children. On her arrival, and in association with a Marian Cousins, she opened a girls' boarding school at Ashburnum House in Blackheath. In 1814 Fay dissolved the partnership with Cousins, although the school continued to run under other ownership. Fay's fifth journey to India was her final. Departing England in the spring of 1815 she spent only a few months in Calcutta, dying on 9 September 1816 while preparing her letters for publication. Her burial is recorded at St John's Church, a building whose planning and construction she had witnessed over the course of her residence in the city.

The text of the *Original Letters* was composed in two parts: a series of journal letters describing in detail her first voyage, composed for her family and addressed to her sister Eleanor Preston (wife of Thomas Wilkinson Preston of Rotherhithe); and a shorter set of memoirs of her second and third voyages written, by her own account, in 1815 for the perusal of a friend. The *Calcutta Gazette* (9 May 1816) gives notice of the forthcoming publication of Fay's 'Narrative' and invites subscriptions, but Fay's death intervened in the publication of her book. Further documents – whether letters or memoirs – were preserved at the time of Fay's death, but her executors declined to include these in the published volume, as being of insufficient interest. They are now, unfortunately, lost. *Original Letters from India* was published in 1817 at Calcutta, with a Preface by the author, and bearing as a frontispiece an engraved plate of Fay in the Egyptian costume she had purchased at Cairo and carried with her to India on her first voyage. No reviews have been discovered, but the book was evidently successful enough to warrant a second edition in Calcutta, which appeared in 1821. For subsequent twentieth-century editions, see the Introduction to the present volume. Our edition takes its copytext from the first, 1817 publication.

Note

1 *Bell's Weekly Messenger* 211 (11 May 1800), p. 5.

Engraved by I. Alais from a Drawing by
A. W. Devis.
The Author Dressed in the Egyptian Costume

See Letter 7th

ORIGINAL LETTERS

FROM INDIA;

CONTAINING A NARRATIVE OF A

JOURNEY THROUGH EGYPT,

AND

THE AUTHOR'S IMPRISONMENT AT CALICUT

BY HYDER ALLY.

TO WHICH IS ADDED,

AN ABSTRACT OF THREE SUBSEQUENT VOYAGES TO INDIA.

BY MRS. FAY.

PRINTED AT CALCUTTA.

1817

PREFACE

THE volume now submitted to the public, exhibits a faithful account of certain remarkable occurrences[1] in the history of an individual, whose lot has been to make frequent visits to several distant regions of the globe, to mingle in the society of people of different kindreds and tongues, and to experience many vicissitudes of fortune. At a time when fictitious representations of human life are sought for with so much avidity, and constitute one of the principal sources of amusement in the hours of solitude, such a work as the present will, it is presumed, not be unacceptable. Those whose curiosity is attracted by the recital of incidents that never took place, or whose sensibility can be awakened by the description of emotions that were never felt, may perhaps derive a similar gratification from the following unembellished narrative of simple facts and real sufferings.

Five and thirty years ago, it was the fate of the author to undertake a journey over land to India, in company with her husband the late Anthony Fay Esq.[2] who, having been called to the bar by the honorable society of Lincolns Inns,[3] had formed the resolution of practising in the courts of Calcutta. They travelled through France, and over the Alps to Italy, whence embarking at Leghorn they sailed to Alexandria in Egypt. Having visited some of the curiosities in this interesting country, and made a short stay at Grand Cairo, they pursued their journey across the Desert to Suez. After passing down the Red Sea the ship in which they sailed touched at Calicut, where they were seized by the officers of Hyder Ally,[4] and for fifteen weeks endured all the hardships and privations of a rigorous emprisonment.

When, after residing two years in India, the author, on account of circumstances explained in the course of the work, returned to her native country, she was repeatedly urged by several of her friends to publish some account of the events that had befallen her, which, it was supposed would engage the attention of the public, being connected with important circumstances in the lives of well known and respectable individuals,[5] and illustrative of the character of a Potentate whose movements were the subject of serious alarm in India. But, at this period a woman who was not conscious of possessing decided genius or superior knowledge could not easily be induced to leave "the harmless tenor of her way,"[6] and render herself amenable to the "pains and penalties"[7] then, generally, inflicted on female authorships; unless inspired by that enthusiasm that tramples on difficulties, or goaded by misfortune which admits not of alternative. Being utterly uninfluenced by either of these motives, and having all the fear of criticism and aversion to publicity which characterizes the young women of her day, the author at that time declined complying with the wishes of those she yet highly honored, and never enquired farther after the fate of her letters, than to learn that they were duly received by those dear friends, to whom all her peregrinations and the knowledge of her eventual safety could not fail to be highly interesting.

Since then, a considerable change has gradually taken place in public sentiments, and its developement, we have now not only as in former days a number of women who do honour to their sex as literary characters, but many unpretending females, who fearless of the critical perils that once attended the voyage, venture to launch their little barks on the vast ocean through which amusement or instruction is conveyed to a reading public: The wit of Fielding is no longer held over them in terrorem,[8] and the delineations of Smollet would apply to them in vain. The race of learned ladies ridiculed by these gentlemen is extinct. A female author is no longer regarded as an object of derision, nor is she wounded by unkind reproof from the *literary Lords of Creation*. In this indulgent era the author presumes to deliver her letters to the world as they have been preserved by the dear sister to whom they were partly addressed, trusting that as this is, in its nature, the most unassuming of all kinds of writing, and one that claims the most extensive allowances, they will be received with peculiar mercy and forbearance.

Since the period to which these letters refer, the Author has made voyages to India, touching in the course of them at various places in all the quarters of the globe, and has been engaged in commercial and other speculations. Her trials and anxieties, however, have produced only a long train of blasted hopes, and heart rending disappointments.— An account of these subsequent occurrences is therefore subjoined in a series of letters lately drawn from the original Journals and Memorandums, and addressed to a lady,[9] whom the Author has the happiness to rank in the number of her friends.

Shadows, clouds, and darkness still rest on the remainder of her pilgrimage, which calls for the pilotage of kindness and the Day-star of friendship. She has, however, by the blessing of Providence been constantly enabled to rise superior to misfortune, and will not now in the evening of her days, derogate from the unostentatious energy of her character, or seek to solicit the pity of her readers by wearisome retrospect or painful complaints. With feelings acutely alive to kindness and truly grateful for every expression of it, she most thankfully esteems the generous patronage with which she has been honoured, and is rendered the more sensible of its value, because she is conscious, that it was not meanly solicited or unworthily obtained.

To the inhabitants of Calcutta, she begs more particularly to render her thanks. Long acquaintance, high esteem, and unfeigned affection call for this peculiar tribute. Five times has she visited this city, under various circumstances, and with different feelings, yet never had cause to regret the length or the dangers of the voyage, secure of ever meeting here all that could encrease the joys of social life, in its happiest moments, or soothe the hours of languishment in the days of adversity.

CALCUTTA, *Anno.* 1816.

LETTER I.

FROM MRS. F——.

PARIS, 18th April, 1779.

I BELIEVE before I left England it was agreed that, my Letters should not in general be addressed to any one particularly, as they will be something in the style of journals;[10] therefore a contrary method would be rather embarrassing—I suppose you begin to think that I have forgotten you all; but it really has not been in my power to write till now, of which assertion an account of our route will furnish abundant proof.—We reached Dover at about seven in the evening of the (*in my* eyes,) ever memorable 10th of April. The thoughts of what we all suffered on that day, can never be banished one instant from my recollection, till it shall please God to grant us a happy meeting. My constant prayers are that, we may be enabled to support this dreadful separation with fortitude—but I dare not trust myself with the subject; my very heart seems to melt as I write, and tears flow so fast as to compel me to shut one eye while I proceed. It is all in vain, I must leave off. And must weeks, nay months elapse before I can have the satisfaction of even hearing from you? How shall I support the idea! oh my dear Father! my beloved Mother! for your poor girl's sake, take care of your precious health; do not be unhappy. The Almighty will, I doubt not, preserve us to each other; something tells me that we shall meet again; and you have still two excellent children left to be your comfort; they I know will use every effort to keep up your spirits; happy to be so employed! but let me not repine; this trial is not permitted, but for all wise purposes. I will now lay down my pen and endeavour to acquire a calmer set of ideas, for I must either write with more fortitude or not at all. Adieu for a little while; I will try to take some refreshment, and then resume my pen.—Half past four P. M.—In vain I strive, the thoughts of home still prevail, and totally preclude every other consideration. I know no better method of chasing these intruders, than by proceeding with the narrative of our journey; *allons donc.*[11] We embarked at Dover for Calais on the 11th at 5 P. M. and had a most delightful passage of just three hours, from port to port. I wished for a little sea sickness but either the wind was not high enough, or I am become too good a sailor, to expect benefit this way, for I remained perfectly well. I assure you there is a deal of ceremony used here now. On coming within gunshot of the Fort, we hoisted a French flag, and were permitted to sail quite up to the Quay. We met the other packet coming out, which accounts for my not writing by that mail.—I have neglected to mention that Mr. B—— the young gentleman whom Captain Mills recommended[12] as a travelling companion, joined us before we left England. His appearance is by no means prepossessing; he seems a dissipated character and more calculated to shine in convivial parties than to render himself agreeable in the common routine of society; whether this opinion be just or not, time will discover. On landing we were all drawn up together, and ordered to the Custom House, where we gave in our names, occupations, &c. they next marched us about half a mile farther to wait on the Governor, in order that he might put any questions he chose to us; his Lordship not being visible, we were forced to arm ourselves with patience and proceed to his Commissary, where we found it a mere matter of form, they asking but what was known before. However I assure you, we thought more than we dared to express on the occasion. Only imagine how disagreeable to be dragged about in such a manner immediately after a Sea voyage instead of reposing ourselves. After all was settled, we first took places in the Diligence[13] for the next day: then called on Monsr. Pigault de l'Epinoye,[14] to whom you will remember I had been formerly introduced. He received us with his usual kindness and hospitality. This gentleman is descended in a direct line from one of the six brave Citizens of Calais, who so nobly offered themselves as victims to save their beloved country from the barbarous sentence pronounced against it by our third Edward.[15] He is much esteemed by his countrymen on this account.

This being my fourth visit to Calais, I must of course have formerly described every thing worth notice there, so shall merely say we set off from thence on the 12th Inst. at 8th A. M. and reached Boulogne about noon. The sight of this place brought to my mind many pleasant recollections of the social hours passed there. I called on several friends, and was much urged to prolong my stay among them, but that you know was impossible. Indeed far rather would I, had time permitted, have taken *one* turn round the ramparts, to enjoy the melancholy satisfaction of once again beholding the white cliffs of my dear native land, so frequently viewed from thence.

You must expect me to make frequent omissions and mistakes, for two men have just placed themselves under my windows with humstrums;[16] and indeed there is constantly some noise or other through the day and evening; sometimes two or three dancing bears; and a few hours ago they exhibited a poor little Porcupine. I pitied the miserable animal from my heart. What can these unhappy creatures have done to merit being so tormented? (now by way of parenthesis, I could almost wish that a London mob had possession of the two musicians, as possibly the discipline of a horse-pond[17] might be of use in teaching them for the future, better employment on Sunday evenings); but to proceed: We left Boulogne (a place I shall ever admire, and perhaps regret), and about ten at night reached Montreiul, from whence we departed at three on Tuesday morning, dined at Abbeville, and by eight in the evening were set down at the same Inn, where you may remember we stopped when travelling this road before,[18] but were hurried away when we had scarcely tasted a morsel, under pretence of the Diligence being ready, and afterwards detained in the yard an hour; nor did our hostess in any respect deviate from her former character, as you shall hear. As a lady in company and myself were greatly fatigued we chose tea, but none being procurable there, were forced to use our own; the rest sat down to supper, which I had predetermined to avoid doing. Before they had a quarter finished, in came the woman; never did I behold such a horribly looking great creature. "Well" said she "the coach is ready" and on being asked if she wanted to get rid of us, replied that it was equal to her whether we went or staid provided she were paid for our suppers: at last when compelled to relinquish her claim on that score from the lady and me, she insisted on being allowed twenty-four sous for the hot water, this we complied with; to oblige our hospitable countrywoman, (tell it not in Gath[19] I blush to acknowledge the claim) but persisted in remaining till on being summoned by the driver, nearly an hour afterwards, we set off and travelled sixty miles without alighting, to Chantilly, where is a famous palace belonging to the Prince of Condé,[20] but to my great mortification, I was through weariness obliged to remain in the house while the rest of the party went to see it. Well never mind, you can read better descriptions of it, than mine would have been. From thence we proceeded to St Denis, where I was fortunate enough to obtain a cursory view of the ancient abbey; a most magnificent structure, the burying place of the Kings of France.[21] Such scenes naturally induce reflections on the vanity of all human grandeur, and lead to a melancholy, rather soothing than otherwise, to minds wearied by exertion, or irritated by disappointment. Having however little leisure to indulge these reveries, we passed on to the Library, where among other trophies is deposited the sword of our illustrious Talbot;[22] a pang shot across my heart at the exulting manner in which it was exhibited; in short I felt as an Englishwoman, a more severe degree of national mortification than this Memento of an event so long gone by seemed calculated to produce. The sacred relics were next displayed, amongst which are, an eye of St Thomas the apostle,[23] the shoulder blade of I forget what saint, and a small phial of the Virgin Mary's milk; at the sight of these absurdities I silently blessed God, that my religious instruction had not been blended with such cunningly devised Fables.[24] If all the gems they shewed us were genuine, the Treasury must be immensely rich, for many of the shrines were almost covered with them. We arrived at Paris about eight on Wednesday; and most dreadfully fatigued was I; nor will that appear strange when one considers that, for the last sixty miles the carriage went as fast as eight horses could draw it, over a strong rough pavement; never stopping but to change horses, and at St. Denis to repair a wheel. As the post went off next morning, I could not recover myself sufficiently to write by it; but now feel quite strong again, and having brought you to Paris, may venture to take a little repose as it is past eleven. 9th 7 A. M. I have arisen thus early on purpose to finish my letter (which must be in the Office before ten). I find little alteration in this Place; the people behave as politely as if there were no War, or even dispute between us.[25] This you know is not the region of Politics,[26] therefore little can be mentioned under that head. I could communicate some few observations, but as perhaps this may be inspected, judge it more prudent to suppress them. A variety of circumstances has contributed to detain us here much longer than we intended; and I am fearful we shall not leave Paris before Thursday; however this will be the only letter I shall write until I can give you intelligence of our safe arrival at Marseilles, which will be I suppose in about a fortnight. From thence to Leghorn we must coast it in a Feluca. So if you write by the mail of the 29th addressed to me at the Post Office Leghorn, your letter will be sure to meet me there. I have a thousand things more to say, but must reserve them for my next, for if I miss the post it will I am sure, make you very uneasy—God bless you.

Your's affectionately.

LETTER II.

Paris 24th April 1779.

My dear Friends,

Being detained for want of our passports,[27] I find it necessary for my comfort to hold the only communication now in my power with you. Last night we were at the Colissée, a place resembling our Ranelagh;[28] there were some brilliant fire works to be exhibited, and as it is the custom for Ladies to stand upon chairs to see them, a gentleman of our party having placed us with our backs against a box, went to procure some. During his absence the Queen entered the box attended by the Duchess D'Alençon,[29] and several other ladies. I had seen her Majesty before at Verseilles, and thought her at that time very handsome, but had no idea how much better she would look, by candle light. She is delicately fair and has certainly the sweetest blue eyes that ever were seen; but there is a little redness, a kind of tendency to inflammation around them, and she is likewise slightly marked with the small pox; both which trifling blemishes were then imperceptible, and she appeared perfectly beautiful. On entering the box she sat down, and pressed the Dutchess to sit also, which the latter in terms of great respect declining, the Queen in a tone of kindness that it is impossible to forget, said, "Then you will oblige me to stand," rising as she spoke. The Duchess then complied, and they conversed together very agreeably during their stay. Her majesty seemed highly gratified by the entertainments, and expressed her approbation, in what I could not help thinking, rather too familiar a way for a person of her exalted rank: frequently clapping her hands and exclaiming aloud, "Ah! mon Dieu que c'est charmant, ah! que c'est joli."[30] The Royal party soon retired, and we afterwards walked in the Rotunda![31] than which a more brilliant spectacle can scarcely be imagined. The ladies were all splendidly dressed, and their heads adorned with feathers in greater profusion, and far more lofty, than is customary with us. But enough of this, I must now turn to a very different subject, having hitherto neglected to inform you of a singular conversation (and its result) which passed in the Diligence, as we came to this place. We had among the passengers a Mr. H— an English Jew, and two brothers, named Ar—f diamond merchants, who were just returned to their native country after a long residence in London. The former had left Paris some years and resided in a provincial town. Speaking of this circumstance he observed that, his principal reason for quitting the Capital was his dread of assassination,[32] to which he thought it probable that his religion might render him more liable, than other inhabitants; although he admitted he had no proof that persons of his persuasion were among the more frequent Victims. This statement, of course, excited both surprize and curiosity in us, who were foreigners; and the elder Mr. A—f evidently mortified at such discourse, and doubting a representation of facts from so prejudiced a quarter, and about which it had not fallen in his way to inquire, stoutly denied the charge; but the Jew would not give up the point. He said that in a certain part of the City, where there were many houses of ill fame, it was but too common to rob and murder those, who were inveigled into them, and afterwards throw the bodies into the Seine; when taken out they were conveyed to the Petit Chatelet[33] to be owned, and that who ever would take the trouble to visit that place would find that, out of the numbers deposited there were very few (as reported) merely drowned persons; but evidently such as had died by violence. This conversation ended (as that of men frequently does) by a wager between the parties, both of whom agreed to refer the matter to Mr. F—. The Jew was to lose, if, in one week seven bodies under such suspicious circumstances should not be found exposed at the Petit Chatelet. I thought this a monstrous supposition; for though I had often heard of people being drowned in the Seine, and the explicit detail of Mr. H— led me to fear that, the manner in which they met their fate, was but too truly described, yet I could not believe the number of victims to be so great. The result of Mr. F—'s researches has unhappily placed the fact beyond a doubt. Within the last seven days, ten miserable wretches have been exposed, who had marks of violence on their bodies, and of these, there were two dreadfully mangled. But I will say no more on this shocking subject than merely to observe, that there must be either some radical defect in the police, or a degree of ferocity in the people, not to be repressed by the severe penal Laws, which in other countries are found nearly adequate to the purpose. The slight degree of feeling expressed by the lower order in speaking of such things, even when pressed on their senses, evinces a hardness of heart approaching to absolute insensibility, that to me seems quite revolting: I myself asked a young woman, who had been peeping through the gate at the Petit Chatelet, what was to be seen there? "Oh" replied she, with great apparent indifference, "seulement quelques bras et jambes" (only some arms and legs). I have written myself into a train of most uncomfortable thoughts, so lest I infect you with the gloomy ideas that fill my mind, the wisest way will be to say adieu! We shall now soon be out of Paris.

Ever your's,
&c. &c.

LETTER III.

PARIS, 27th April, 1779.

MY DEAR SISTER.

As I do not propose sending this before Monday, I shall have full time to write every particular. I date once more from this sink of impurity, contrary to my expectation. We have been detained thus long that the Lieutenant de Police[34] might have time to make the necessary enquiries about us, but have at last obtained our passports, and thank Heaven shall soon breathe a purer air. From the first place we stop at, I purpose giving you a further account of our accommodations in the superb and elegant city of Paris, famous throughout the world for its superiority over all others, especially in the points of cleanliness and delicacy. I assure you that, so long as I before resided in France, I never till now formed an adequate idea of it: but adieu for the present: I am going to drink tea. How do you think I make it? Why in an earthen pot an inch thick at least, which serves the double purpose of tea kettle and teapot, so it is all boiled up together and makes a most curious mess.

AUXERRE EN BURGOYNE   130 MILLES, DE PARIS.

When I wrote the above I was in a great rage and not without reason, pent up as we were in a street scarce wide enough to admit the light; our chamber paved with tiles, which most likely have never been wetted, nor even rubbed, since the building of the house; add to this two *Commodités*[35] in the same state, on the stairs, and you will not wonder that my constitution was not proof against the shock; the very air I breathed seemed almost pestilential. However thank God I escaped with one of my feveretts[36] of four days continuance. When I began this letter I was but just recovering: no creature to do the least thing for me in the way I had been accustomed to; obliged to prepare for my departure the next morning, though scarcely able to crawl; and to crown the whole a most extravagant bill for being poisoned with Dirt. Well we sat off, and the fresh country air soon restored me to myself—but I have not told you how we travel.

We found the route totally different from what we expected,[37] and that we must be positively under the necessity of going by land to Chalons sur Soane, which is three hundred miles from Paris: now as we could get no remittances till our arrival at Leghorn,[38] it did not suit us to take the Diligence, so after mature deliberation we determined on purchasing two horses, and an old single horse-chaise; but how to avoid being cheated, was the question; for Mr. Fay did not care to depend on his own judgement in horseflesh—He made enquiry and found that there were many englishmen employed in the stables of Noblemen here; so putting a good face on the matter he went boldly to the Duc de Chartres' Castle, and scraped acquaintance[39] with his head groom, who was very proud to see a countryman, and immediately on being told the affair, offered his assistance. Accordingly they went next day to the cattle Fair, where he pitched on an excellent draught horse, only a little touched in the wind,[40] on which account he procured him for six guineas,[41] so there cannot be much lost by him, even if he turn out amiss. But I dare say he will prove a most useful beast, for he has drawn Mr. B—r, and myself in our chaise (which by the bye we bought for seven guineas) at the rate of thirty five miles a day: and does not seem in the least fatigued, though we had our heavy trunk at our back: so much for Azor—now for his help-mate Zemire.[42] In the course of conversation with his new friend, Mr. Fay found that, there was a very pretty mare in the Duc de Lausanne's stables, which had been intended for the course, but would not bear training; so he agreed to give eight guineas for her. Mr. B— was to ride her next day to a horse-race in the Bois de Boulogne,[43] and we were to accompany him in a post chaise. But alas! poor man! it was an unfortunate attempt. It seems he had never been used to riding, and was ashamed to own it, (one of the weaknesses to which I really believe men are almost invariably subject), so wishing to pass for an excellent horseman, he mounted with pretended courage: but through actual fear, reined her in so tight that miss, knowing the weaknes of her rider, reared up on her hind legs, threw him first, and then fell backward over him. We thought by the violence of the fall that he must have been killed, but he came off with a few bruises; we had him bled immediately,[44] put him to bed and left him in good hands till our return. Mr. Fay mounted Zemire, and we proceeded to the course, where we were very agreeably entertained, only it grieved me to see so many beautiful English horses galloping about; I could hardly believe myself in France, for all the gentlemen were dressed after our manner. The Count D'Artois might very well have been taken for a Jockey in his buck-skin breeches, and round hat. The bets were chiefly between him and the Duc de Chartres; the horses were all rode by englishmen: as to our little mare she would fain have been amongst them, but she had now a rider who knew how to manage her, and is punished for her audacity; for Mr. B— has not the courage to mount her again, and she is forced to carry Mr. Fay with a portmanteau of twenty pounds weight—You will wonder at my temerity when I acknowledge having myself ventured to mount Zemire, after Mr. B—'s accident. I first however saw her tried by several persons, and wishing to be able to vary the exercise by riding now and then, during our journey, was induced to make the attempt. She performed twice very well; but on the third day, an umbrella being snapped close to her nose, just as I was going to set off, she began to rear, on which I instinctively abandoned both whip and reins, and throwing my whole weight forward, clasped her round the neck with all my might, this sudden manœuvre fortunately kept her down: I seized the critical moment and alighted in safety with no other injury, than a little fright, and the consciousness of looking rather foolish. Nor has she ever been guilty of the like towards any one; so that my character for horsemanship is completely established. We have been certainly very lucky in our purchases: the horses perform well, and the chaise, without being particularly uneasy, seems very strong. I am told they will bring a good price in the South, but you shall hear.

I have nothing particular to say of the country; perhaps it may be national prejudice from which no person is entirely free, but notwithstanding all their boasting, I do not think it equals my own dear England. It must be allowed that the present season is not the most favourable for making observations, for they cut the Vines close to the stumps in the winter, and as they are not yet much sprouted, one sees nothing but a parcel of sticks in the manner of our hop poles, but not above thirty inches high, which gives an air of barrenness to the prospect. I do not know what my mother would do here, as she is not fond of wine; for there is nothing else to drink. For my own part, and I believe I may answer for my companions, I cannot say that I find any great hardship in being obliged to put up with tolerable Burgundy at about four pence a bottle; it is not at all heady, so no creature thinks of drinking it with water. A pint every meal is the allowance of each. We have all necessaries with us,[45] such as tea, sugar, bread, butter, corn for the horses &c: so we have little to do with the Inns, except at night, when we provide ourselves with meat for the next day. As to breakfast and dinner we fix on a place where there is water at hand, and there sit down under the shade of a tree, and make a fire, while the horses graze comfortably, and eat their corn. Ask my dear father if he does not think this a good plan? at least we find it pleasant, and much more to our taste, than spending more time as well as money, in the wretched public houses we have hitherto met with—I wish we were hardy enough to make the grass our pillow; but that is impossible, so we must submit to be disgusted and pillaged once a day. You may remember my remarking that, I was afraid we should suffer during our journey, for the fineness of the spring which has proved to be the case. The weather has been excessively boisterous for the last fortnight with much rain, than which nothing can be more disagreeable on a journey, especially when conducted on a plan like ours.—We were obliged to stop at Fontainbleau[46] on account of the weather by which means we saw the Palace, and gardens, and were almost wet through, for our pains. It is an immense place; the Chapel has been beautiful, but the paintings are much injured by time. There is an elegant theatre which I was much pleased with. The apartments of the royal family are truly superb. We were shewn the council chamber where the last peace was signed, and I, as an Englishwoman, beheld it with *great pleasure* you may be sure. We saw likewise the gallery of *Stags*, famous for containing above a hundred stags' heads all ranged in order with an account, when they were killed and by whom, and infamous (at least in my opinion) as being the place where Christina, Queen of Sweden, caused Monaldeschi her chief chamberlain to be beheaded,[47] if not absolutely in her presence, at least while she remained in an adjoining room. I cannot bear that woman. She abdicated her crown from sheer vanity but retained that passion for despotism which shewed what kind of feelings she had cherished, while seated on the throne. I think that in her, the faults of either sex were blended, to form a character, which without possessing the firmness of a man or the gentleness of a woman, was destitute of the virtues expected in both. Christina may have been an accomplished female; but she can never be called great, even by her admirers.

The gardens of Fontainbleau are all in the old fashioned-gingerbread-style, ornamented with box in a thousand fantastical shapes.[48] The Swiss who shewed us the Palace, was very thankful for a shilling, which is more than any person in the same situation would be in England for twice as much. The forest of Fontainbleau is thirty miles across, and nobody can hunt there without the Kings permission; he comes here every season.—We found the roads very heavy, but Azor was strong enough to go through them; however we have given him a day's rest, and after dinner shall set off Jehu like.[49]

Now don't you envy us all this pleasure? I assure you I should be very glad to go all the way in the same manner, for we travel without fatigue, and the way of living just suits me; for you know I always preferred wine to beer, but I would not have you imagine that I can shake off all thoughts of home; they return but too frequently, and I really believe now, that my illness at Paris, was brought on principally by uneasiness of mind: but I find myself unequal to this subject. I must make a resolution never to enter upon it; for what service can it do to either of us, to be continually recalling unpleasant ideas; especially when I have need of every possible consolation to support me in the arduous task, which Providence has called upon me to undertake.

I have now literally exhausted my paper, and must therefore leave you to imagine every thing my heart says to all, and how truly

I am,
your affectionate
&c. &c.

LETTER IV.

LEGHORN, 17th June, 1779.

MY DEAR SISTER,

I suppose you have been long uneasy at my silence, but indeed it has not been in my power to write sooner—In my last I gave you reason to imagine we should arrive here in less than three weeks, by way of Marseilles; but after we reached Lyons we were informed, that this would prove a very uncertain and dangerous method; as between the English and French scarcely any vessel can pass free: therefore after mature deliberation, we determined as we had still our carriage and horses, to push our way boldly through Savoye, and cross the Alps to Italy. We stopped several days at Lyons, which as you and all the world know has long been famous for its incomparable silks, and velvets; I think it ought to be so for its asparagus which is the finest I ever tasted; and remarkably cheap. Being a vegetable I am very fond of, and having found it at all times beneficial to my constitution, I wished to eat it freely; but was almost disgusted by the manner in which it was constantly brought to table at the Inn, covered with a thick sauce composed of eggs, butter, oil and vinegar.[50]

Having in vain remonstrated against this cookery, I at length insisted on seeing the Cook himself; and when he made his appearance, arrayed as is customary, in a white waistcoat, cap, and apron, with a meagre face almost as sharp as the large knife he held in his hand, I calmly represented to him that the sauce he had sent up, totally disagreed with my stomach, and requested to have the asparagus simply boiled with melted butter, the poor man looked much distressed "What without oil!" yes! "Without eggs"? certainly! this answer completed his misery, "Ah madame" exclaimed he, with clasped hands and uplifted eyes "de grace un peu de vinaigre".[51] Madame was inexorable, and the shrug of contemptuous pity with which he retreated was ludicrous beyond expression.

On arriving near the Alps, it appeared that I had formed a very erroneous idea of the route, having always supposed that we had only one mountain to pass, and that the rest of the way was level ground; instead of which when we came to Pont de Beauvoisin (50 miles from Lyons, and the barrier between France and Savoye) we heard the agreeable news, that we had a hundred and twelve miles to travel thro' a chain of mountains, to the great Mont Cenis.

You may imagine how uncomfortable this information made us all; with what long faces we gazed upon each other, debating how the journey was to be performed; but being happily you know very courageous, I made light of all difficulties, and whenever there was a hill, mounted Zemire, while the two gentlemen took it by turns to lead me as I had not a proper side saddle, so poor Azor made shift to drag the chaise up pretty well, and in the descents we made him pay for the indulgence. I forgot to mention that they were very particular about our passports at this Barrier, and detained us while the Governor examined them minutely, though justice compels me to acknowledge that in general we were treated with great politeness in our passage through France; no one ever attempted to insult us, which I fear would not be the case were three French people to travel in England; I wish I could say as much for their honesty; but I must confess that here they are miserably deficient, however my being acquainted with the language saved us from flagrant imposition.

Our method was this: we always if possible, contrived to stop at night in a large Town, (as to dinner we easily managed that you know how), but never did we suffer the horses to be put into the stable till I had fixed the price of every thing; for they generally ask four times as much for any article as it is worth. If I found there was no bringing them to reason, we left the house. In particular, at Chalons sur Soane, the first Inn we stopped at, the woman had the conscience to ask half a crown for each bed; you may suppose we did not take up our abode there, but drove on to another very good house, where they shewed us two rooms with six excellent beds in them, at the rate of four sous a bed, for as many as we wanted; so for once I committed an act of extravagance by paying for the whole; or we might perhaps have been disturbed in the night by strangers coming to take possession of those left vacant. For they are not very nice about such matters in France. I have seen rooms with six beds in them more than once during our route. I only mention the difference of price by way of shewing what people may gain by choosing their houses, for we were really better accommodated at less than one fourth of what we must have paid at the other house. Speaking of Chalons reminds me of a very unpleasant circumstance that occurred to us at the following stage. Mr. Fay had most unwisely and contrary to my earnest intreaty, pinned our passports to the book of roads,[52] which he usually carried with him on horse back, and as might be expected, they, in a short time worked themselves loose, and we were on our arrival at the end of the next day's journey alarmed with the idea of their being intirely lost, and that we should be compelled to return all the way to Paris to procure others: happily Mr. Fay went back & found them at a place where we had stopped, I need not tell you what fright and vexation, this folly and obstinacy cost us: but I hope it will have a salutary effect for the rest of our journey.

In further proof of my assertion on the subject of honesty, I must relate a little incident which occurred on our way to Lyons. Mr. Fay had changed as many guineas at Paris, as he thought would be sufficient to bring us to Chalons, and received by weight twenty four livres ten sous,[53] for each, that is seven pence halfpenny profit: well, the last day but one we finished our current money, but as we were in a city, doubted not of being able to obtain nearly the value of our guineas. On inquiry we were recommended—to a very religious goldsmith who by the landlord's account spent almost his whole life in acts of piety: after waiting an hour and a half till he returned from mass, Mr. F. delivered him a guinea, confident of receiving its full value: when behold this conscientious gentleman after the most minute inspection and weighing it in a pair of sugar scales generously offered eighteen livres as a fair price: which so enraged Mr. Fay that he immediately left him and went to another shop, where the utmost they would give was *twelve* livres: only think what wretches! since it was impossible for them to be ignorant of its real value. Mr. Fay declared that he would rather fast all day than submit to become such a dupe. This subjected us to great inconvenience; after discharging the reckoning we had only thirty sous remaining; and sat out with a sum not sufficient to procure a single refreshment for our poor horses; so that at every Inn we were obliged to represent our situation: but found none who had honesty enough to offer us a fair price for our guineas, or the charity to give us even a glass of wine or a morsel of bread. I leave you to guess if our appetites were not pretty keen by the time we arrived at Lyons. I shall never forget how foolishly we looked at each other all day; however a good supper obliterated all grievances, and the next morning we found a way to change our guineas for Louis-d'ors on equitable terms. So much for our starving adventure. To proceed on our journey.

On the 20th we reached Lanneburg, a village at the foot of Mont Cenis situated in what is called a valley, which though really so with respect to the mountains that surround it, is even with the clouds. I had a tolerable proof of its elevation, for the weather was so sharp, that I could not keep a minute from the fire. By the way I must observe, that having travelled through North Wales, I supposed myself to have acquired a tolerable idea of mountains and their appendages, such as cascades, torrents, and apparently air-hung-bridges &c. but the passage of the Alps set at defiance all competition, and even surpasses whatever the utmost sketch of my imagination could have pourtrayed.

The valley of Lanneburg is itself, the most strange wild place you can conceive, in some parts grotesque, in others awfully terrible.[54] The rocks rise around you so fantastically, that you might almost think yourself transported to a place which nature had made a repository of these stupendous productions, rather with a view of fixing them hereafter in appropriate situations, than of exhibiting them here.

But above all, the cascades throughout the road are charming beyond description; immense sheets of water are seen sometimes, falling from rock to rock; foaming fretting and dashing their spray on every side; and sometimes descending in one grand flow of majestic beauty: in short they went so far beyond any idea I had formed of such appearances in nature, that they seemed to communicate new powers of perception to my mind, and if I may so express it, to expand my soul, and raise it nearer to its Creator.[55] The passage has been so ably described by various writers that any formal account I could give you of it, would rather waste your time than add to your information. I shall only tell you how I felt and acted for I know your affection prompts the wish to travel in imagination with the sister you love; come then let us ascend Mont Cenis together.—After various deliberations it was concluded that I should go up across a mule,[56] as the safest way; both the gentlemen determined on walking, which Mr. Fay knew not to be very difficult, having made the experiment the evening before. I was strictly forbidden to touch the reins, being assured that the animal would guide himself, and that any attempt to direct him could hardly fail to prove *fatal*. Under this charge, judge what I must have felt when my mule, in the very steepest part of the ascent and when I had become fully sensible of the "high and giddy height," all at once, thought proper to quit the pathway, and with great sang froid stalk out upon one of those precipitous projections, where only the foot of a wild Goat or Chamois ought to tread. What did I not suffer! I durst not touch the rein, durst not even call to the guide for help. Every instant appeared fraught with destruction, it seemed madness to die without an effort to save one's self, yet to *make* an effort was to invite the fate one dreaded. Happily this dreadful poise between life and death lasted not long; for, the sagacious animal calmly picking its way fell into the track by a path, which no human eye could discern, and the guides gave me great praise for my self-command; a praise I never desire to purchase again by a similar trial. If however anything could render a stranger easy in crossing the heights, it would be the amazing skill and celerity which these people display; the road winds in a zigzag direction; and in the most acute, and of course, in the most dangerous turns they leap from crag to crag as if they held their lives on lease, and might safely run all risks, till the term expired.—The plain, as it is called, at the top of this mountain is six miles across: as we proceeded we found "still hills on hills, and Alps on Alps arise";[57] for we continued to be surrounded by snow top mountains, where reigns eternal frost. The heat of the sun had thawed the passage, so that we met with no inconvenience, but we passed great quantities of ice lodged in the crannies. There is a very large lake on the plain, said to be unfathomable; that I can tell nothing about, but that it contains excellent salmon and trout, am well convinced, for we stopped at the Inn according to the laudable custom of all travellers, for the sole purpose of tasting it. An Inn, say you, at the top of Mont Cenis! Yes, it is really a fact, not that I envy them their situation, but they are not the only inhabitants: for there are more than twenty farm houses, where they make most excellent butter and cheese. Every spot around, where it is possible for the hand of cultivation to scatter seeds for the use of man, is treasured with care and nourished by industry; and you see gardens no bigger than a dining table, and fields like a patch of carpet, from time to time, smiling beneath the rugged battlements of rocks, like the violets peeping in the hedges. Far, among the apparently inaccessible heights of this "cloud capt" region, they pointed out to me a Chapel, vulgarly called notre Dame de Neige;[58] and justly have they named her, for eternal snows designate her dwelling; if however these simple and sequestered beings can there draw near to God, and experience the comfort of religious hope, and providential care, this singular edifice has not been reared in vain, to bless such a region of desolation.

When you read an account of the road, it will readily be perceived that my fellow travellers must have found some difficulty in getting the horses over, as the poor beasts were not accustomed to such a rugged path; for you are to understand that, the people in the neighbouring villages of Lanneburg and Novalese have no other means of subsistence than carrying passengers over the mountain. It is therefore their interest to render it impassable to any but themselves, so that the whole passage of fifteen miles, is covered with great loose pieces of rock, which must be clambered over: the guides skip from one piece to another like goats, and go at the rate of five or six miles an hour; but my unfortunate companions could not proceed at this pace; so every ten minutes we had to wait for them—As I was carried down in an armed chair, fastened to poles and slung upon straps, in the manner of our sedans, between two men and in which I soon felt tolerably at my ease; I had the pleasure of seeing them continually: sometimes in the clouds, and at others nothing visible but their heads, which was rather amusing to me, knowing they were in no danger, especially as Mr. Fay had affected to make very light of it, and even said "I might walk very well if I chose it," but when we reached the bottom, he told a very different tale, and stormed violently at his own sufferings. The drollest part of our procession was, that of the poor mule which bore our chaise in a kind of machine, on its back; and another with the two wheels placed on each side, in the oddest way imaginable. A good night's rest put us all in good humour, and we proceeded cheerfully forty miles along a very delightful road, for the most part planted with double rows of trees, to Turin, where we remained three days and were much amused; but having crossed the mountain, I must allow myself and you a little rest.

JUNE, 26th.—I was more pleased with the Palace at Turin[59] than any other I have met with during our journey, not for its external appearance certainly, for that is unpromising, but the inside simply atones for the deficiency. The rooms are all in long ranges, opening into each other by doors, which by folding within the pannels become invisible. The furniture is beyond description rich and elegant, but the best part of every finely decorated house must ever be the paintings, and this palace seemed to say, "You are already in Italy:" like a true Englishwoman however, I looked more, I believe, at a picture of our Charles the first, and afterwards at one by Vandyke of that unfortunate monarch's three children,[60] than at any other in the collection. The face of the King is exquisitely done, but his dress struck me as too fine, and withal so stiff, that I could not admire it. Poor Charles! we are tempted to forget the errors of the Prince, in considering the amiable qualities and long sufferings of the man: nor is it possible to contemplate the benevolent melancholy of his countenance, and credit every accusation of his enemies. I looked on his mild penetrating eyes, till my own were suffused with tears. As to his children, they are the sweetest creatures I ever beheld; and to see them thus, was perhaps the more pleasant, from a consciousness of its being the only period wherein they could communicate that sensation to a reflecting mind.—There was no tracing the selfish, and eventually, callous libertine in Charles; nor the tyrant and bigot in James;[61] all seems playful grace, and dignified gentleness; and the painter appears to have given a kind of royal polish to the beauty (certainly far beyond nature) which he had so happily depicted in these unfortunate children. Among what I deemed the most curious portraits, were those of Martin Luther, and his wife.[62] I have frequently meditated on this great character, and always felt myself so much obliged to him (especially since my residence in a Catholic country,) that I confess I was disappointed to see him a homely, and rather vulgar looking man. I cannot believe this is a good likeness; at least the one I saw of him in the abbey of St Bertin at St Omers left a very different impression on my mind. The Reformer might not be handsome, in the common acceptation of the word, but surely, penetration courage and firmness must have stampt their expression on his features. Here is a terrible representation of another great man, tho' in my opinion deficient in the first mentioned quality (Sir Thomas Moore)[63] of his head rather, for it appears just severed from the body; his daughter has fainted at the horrible spectacle; and her complexion is so exactly what it should be, that the whole scene appears natural, and you feel too much for her, even to offer her restoratives to life and misery. I would not live in the same room with such a picture for the world; it would be worse than the cave of Trophonious.[64]

I was doomed to experience another disappointment in what is affirmed to be a faithful portrait of Petrarch's Laura,[65] which I had fancied was like the Venus of Apelles,[66] an assemblage of all that was lovely and graceful in woman. You remember my saying, that it was worth all the pains I took in learning Italian, to read his sonnets in praise of this idolized being. So no wonder that I ran eagerly to seize on features that had inspired such verses, and awakened such tender constancy as Petrarch displayed. Judge then how disagreeably I was surprised at seeing a little red-haired, formal looking, old maidish thing, no more like the beauty in "my mind's eye" than "I to Hercules."[67] Petrarch too was as ugly as needs be. Well, well, they are not the only couple seen to most advantage in their Poetic dress. What further I have to say about the Palace, must be very concise. I cannot help informing you though, that we saw the King of Sardinia[68] at mass with his whole family but none of them seem to be remarkable for beauty. Though not esteemed rich, yet he lives in great splendour; the furniture of his state bedchamber, even to the frames of the chairs, is all of massive silver.

The Theatre[69] is a vast building and so magnificent in every respect, that nothing you have seen can give you any idea of it; the stage is so extensive, that when they want to exhibit battles, triumphant entries, or any kind of grand show they have room enough to produce the finest effect, and really seem to transport you to the scene they would represent. It is not uncommon to have fifty or sixty horses, at a time upon this stage, with triumphal cars, thrones &c &c. The King's box, is consistent with his superb Palace; it is as large as a handsome parlour, and lined throughout with mirrors, which have a beautiful effect, as they reflect the stage and thus double the display of its grand processions &c: all the boxes in this Theatre are neat and commodious; furnished with chairs and curtains, so that if the party choose to be retired they are at full liberty; and, as coffee and other refreshments are served, they frequently pay little attention to the Stage, except when some celebrated performer or grand spectacle excites their curiosity. There is a smaller Theatre,[70] which opens when this is closed, but I did not see it. I visited the royal gardens,[71] but thought them very uninteresting, as all appear after those that surround the seats of our English Nobility and gentry; and on running thro' another Palace, an academy and various other places, nothing struck me as sufficiently novel to merit your attention; and, I have written such an intolerably long letter, that I must conclude for the present, tho' I mean to bring you on my journey to-morrow, as I have not yet told you half that is on my mind; but there is such an uncertainty in my present movements, that it is desirable not to lose a single day in forwarding a letter. Believe me however and wherever I may be,

most affectionately yours,
E. F.

IN CONTINUATION.

LEGHORN, 28th June.

I resume my journal of yesterday which I shall now inclose in this; I am still waiting a summons for departure, and anxious to say all I can, to my dear friends, before what may probably be a long adieu. From Turin we sat out on the 26th ultimo, to Genoa, a distance of 130 miles; and now I own my courage begun to fail; for having been some days ill, I grew so much worse, from the motion of the chaise, that we were obliged to stop and get Mr. Fay's horse ready for me to ride, which was a great ease to me; but notwithstanding this relief, on the second evening I was seized with every symptom of fever, and that of the most violent kind; "Well," thought I, "it is all over with me for a week at least;" but thank God I was mistaken, for at two o'clock in the morning, I fell into the most profuse perspiration I ever experienced, which, tho' it exceedingly weakened me, yet considerably abated the disorder, and altho' I felt ill, dispirited, and every way unfit to travel, yet I made a sad shift to pursue my journey.

Unfortunately, in coming out of Alessandria the place where I had been so ill, we had a wide river to ford, and there was no way for poor miserable me to get over, but by Mr. Fay's taking me before him across the mare, which was tolerably well accomplished. When he had landed me safe he went back, and with great difficulty whipped the old horse through; he was up to the girth in water, and I expected every moment, he would break the chaise to pieces for he frequently attempted to lie down. When we had overcome this difficulty we continued in tolerable spirits, until our arrival next day at the Buchetta, an appenine mountain, by the side of which Mont Cenis would appear contemptible; it is near twenty miles over, without any plain at the top, so that no sooner do you reach its summit, than you turn short, and descend immediately. Had the weather proved fine, the prospect from this prodigious eminence must have been glorious; but so thick a fog enveloped us, that we could not distinguish any thing of five yards distance, and the cold was as piercing as with us in January. Never shall I forget the sense of wearisome, overbearing desolateness, which seemed to bow down both my body and mind at this juncture. I felt a kind of dejection unknown before through all my peregrinations, and which doubtless tended to increase the unusual fears that operated on my mind, when we arrived at the end of this day's journey. It was nearly dark; the Inn was little better than a large barn or hovel, and the men we found in it, so completely like all we conceive of Banditti, and assassins, that every horrible story[72] I had heard or read of, instantly came into my head;

and I perceived that the thoughts of my companions were occupied in the same painful way; our looks were the only medium of communication we could use, for we were afraid of speaking, lest we should accelerate the fate we dreaded. Every thing around us combined to keep alive suspicion and strengthen fear; we were at a distance from every human habitation: various whisperings, and looks directed towards us, continually passed amongst the men, and we fancied they were endeavouring to find whether we had any concealed arms. When we retired for the night worn out as we were, not one dared to sleep and surely never night appeared so long. With the earliest dawn we departed, and as the people saw us set out without offering us any injury, we are now persuaded that we wronged them; but yet the impression made upon our minds will not easily be effaced: we feel as if we had escaped some projected mischief.

We arrived pretty early at Genoa, a grand but gloomy disagreeable city, owing to the houses being very high, and the streets so narrow you might almost shake hands across them out of the window. It abounds with magnificent Churches and Palaces, principally built of the most beautiful marble, at least they are faced and ornamented with it. Their roofs flat, and rendered very agreeable gardens, by flowering shrubs, little arbours, covered with wood-bine and jessamine, elegant verandahs, awnings &c. In these the ladies wander from morning to night.—As far as I can hear or see, they are more remarkable for pride than any thing else. Their dress costly, but heavy and unbecoming, except so far as they manage their veils, which are so contrived as to give very good play to a pair of fine eyes. They wear rouge; but apply it better than the French ladies, who may be said rather to plaster than to paint: when the best however is made of this practice it is still a very hateful one in my opinion.—I went to view the Palaces of Doria, Doraggio, and Pallavicini,[73] where are many fine pictures and statues; but the rooms are so large, and so many of them are only half furnished, that they had on the whole an uncomfortable look. I was much pleased with several of the churches; the Cathedral[74] is completely lined with marble, but I was attracted more by the Jesuits' church[75] on account of the paintings, though, I have neither health nor spirits to enter into a particular description of them. The assumption of the Virgin by Guido,[76] is a most delightful performance to my taste. I always admire his pictures, but being simply an admirer, without knowledge on the subject, I seldom hazard a remark as to the manner in which a piece is executed.—The theatre here is large, but not to be compared with that at Turin. The gardens are every where in the same style, all neat and trim, like a desert Island in a pastry cook's shop, with garnish and frippery enough to please a Dutchman. There are many admirable churches in this city; but its chief boast, in my opinion, consists in being the birth place of Columbus, who was undoubtedly a great man, and from his talents, firmness, wisdom and misfortunes, entitled to inspire admiration and pity. I often thought of him, as I passed these streets and was ready to exclaim, you were not worthy of such a Citizen. The velvets, goldwork, and artificial flowers manufactured here, are said to be unrivalled; but I made no purchases for very obvious reasons.

We saw a very grand procession on Corpus Christi day,[77] at which the Doge[78] assisted, and all the principal nobility, clothed in their most magnificent habiliments, and each carrying a lighted taper; several images also, adorned with jewels (as I was informed) to an almost incredible amount, were borne along to grace the spectacle. It is to be lamented that, this noble city should disgrace itself by the encouragement given to assasination, for a man after committing half a score murders, has only to take a boat which nobody prevents him from doing, and claim the protection of any foreign ship, which none dares to refuse, and there he remains in safety.[79] Mr. Fay saw five of these wretches on board one vessel. What you have heard respecting the custom of married women in Italy being attended by their Cicisbeos,[80] is perfectly true. They speak of it with all the indifference imaginable. Surely, after all that has been said, the usage must be an innocent one, if any thing can be called so which tends to separate the affections of husband and wife, and *that*, the constant attendance, the profound respect of another man, must be likely to effect. Altogether it is a vile fashion, make the best of it, and I heartily hope never to see such a mode adopted in old England.

We sold our horses at Genoa, for about three guineas profit—and no more, as Mr. Fay embraced the first offer that was made him. You who know me, will be well aware, that I could not part with these mute but faithful companions of our journey without a sigh. Far different were my sensations on bidding adieu to our fellow traveller Mr. B——r, who left us on our arrival at this place. My first impression of his character was but too just, and every day's experience more fully displayed a mind, estranged from all that was praise worthy, and prone to every species of vice. He professed himself almost an Atheist, and I am persuaded, had led the life of one; it was perhaps fortunate that his manners were as disgusting as his principles were wicked, and that he constantly reminded one, of that expression of the Psalmist "the *Fool* hath said in his heart there is no God";[81] as the comment, he was but a fool, rose to remembrance at the same moment.

We took our passage in a Felucca from Genoa, and arrived here in thirty three hours. My first message was to the Post Office, where was only one letter for me, dated 10th May. I am impatient for more, being kept in daily expectation of sailing, and it would be mortifying to leave any behind. I must now conclude; believe me,

Ever most affectionately your's,
E. F.

P. S. I open this to say, our letters and remittances are arrived. Ten thousand thanks for your kindness, but I have not time to add another word.

LETTER V.

OUTER MOLE, LEGHORN,
ON BOARD THE HELLESPONT,

July 2d, 1779.

MY DEAR FRIENDS,

You may perceive from this date that I have quitted Leghorn, but how I came to take up my quarters *here*, cannot be explained, till after the relation of some particulars which I must first notice, in order to proceed regularly with my journal.

Our letter of introduction from Mr. Baretto of London to his brother,[82] the king of Sardinia's Consul at Leghorn, procured us the kindest attentions from that gentleman and his family, indeed they were so friendly to us in every respect, that I soon felt all the ease of old acquaintance in their society, and shall ever remember them, with sentiments of the most cordial esteem. Through this kind family I saw whatever was worthy of note in Leghorn, and its environs; but my increasing anxiety as to our journey, took from me all power of investigation. When one sees merely with the eye, and the wandering mind is travelling to the friends left far behind, or forward to the unknown clime whither its destiny points, few recollections of places and things will remain on it. But far different will be its recognition of persons. When these have softened an anxious hour by kindness, or relieved its irksomeness, by smiles and gaiety, the heart will register their action and their image, and gratitude engrave their names on the tablet of remembrance. What a romantic flight! methinks I hear you exclaim; but consider, this is the land of Poesy, surely, I may be permitted to evince a little of its spirit. I shall never forget that Leghorn contains the Baretti's, and Franco's. The latter are eminent merchants; the house has been established above a century. The eldest of the present family is above eighty years of age; a most venerable and agreeable old man; with more of active kindness and benevolent politeness, than I ever met with in one, so far advanced in life, and who has seen so much of the world. He not only shewed us every attention during our stay, but has given us a letter recommending us in the strongest terms to a Mr. Abraham, of Grand Cairo; which should Mr. Baldwin, the East India Company's resident, be absent when we arrive there, may prove useful. At all events, we are equally indebted to Mr. Franco's friendly intentions.

We have often boasted of the superiority of the British flag, but alas poor old England! her flag is here humbled in the dust; we have several ships in the mole,[83] but if one dare venture out, so many French Privateers[84] are hovering round, that she must be taken in a few hours. I pity the poor Captains from my heart, but the person for whom I feel most interested, is a Captain Les—r of the Hellespont, (Mr. P—'s relation). I cannot express half what I owe to his civility. From the moment he knew of my probable connection with his family, he has uniformly shown us every possible attention. His situation is very disagreeable, to be forced either to abandon so fine a ship, or incur almost a certainty of being taken prisoner in her, as she must soon venture out; for she has already eaten her head off,[85] by lying here a whole twelvemonth on expence, as such is the deplorable state of our commerce in the Mediterranean, that no one will now underwrite an English ship at any premium. I think the number lying here is seven, and believe they intend soon to make a bold push together; but it will be all in vain; they never can get through the Straits of Gibraltar, unmolested.

4 o'clock p.m. A Hard Gale.

I told you this morning what reason I had to esteem Captain L.—He is now entitled to at least a double portion of my gratitude, if estimated by the service done. As there was no likelihood of meeting with an English vessel, we engaged a passage in a Swedish one, called the *Julius*, Captain Norberg, for Alexandria, at £6 each, (cheap enough you will say); and had all in readiness: so last night I quitted the shores of Europe, God knows for how long: his will be done. Captain L— as his ship lay next but one to our's, and we were not to sail 'till day break, offered us his cabin, because, as he very considerately observed, we could not sleep confortably in our own, amidst the noise of preparing for Sea. I readily complied, well knowing the advantages of his proposal, having already dined several times on board the Hellespont, which is kept clean and in good order, equal to the nicest house I ever saw. This morning the Julius went out to the Road, and we prepared to follow; but just at that time arose a sudden squall of thunder and lightning, succeeded by a very strong gale of wind; the poor Julius was forced to drop anchor, and there she lies, two miles off, pitching (driving piles Captain L— calls it) and has just struck her lower yards; she slipped one cable two hours ago, but the other brought her up. I see her now and would not exchange cabins for a trifle.

Several vessels have been driven in, in distress; one dashed directly against the Hellespont and snapped her Bowsprit[86] short; we had but just time to secure the poop lanthorn from the stroke of another; the *iron* was torn away, so you may guess it blows smartly, but I feel perfectly easy. I am luckily sheltered now, and no one shall persuade me to leave this ship 'till all is over, and the weather settled again. I doubt we shall not be able to sail this day or two, for the wind is rising; but so that we arrive, time enough to save our season at Suez, all will be well. Tea is waiting, and they are tormenting me to death. Adieu. God bless you all, prays,

Your affectionate
E. F.

LETTER VI.

SHIP JULIUS AT SEA,

20th July, 1779.

I HOPE, my dear friends will safely receive my letter of the 2nd Instant, from Leghorn, wherein I mentioned the kindness of Captain L.—and our situation in his Ship. We remained with him 'till Sunday evening, when we embarked on the Julius, and the following morning, sailed with a fair wind; but it changed in less than six hours, and came on so strong, that we were forced to put back again and cast anchor. The gale lasted 'till Wednesday evening; however we made shift to ride it out, though we were continually paying out cable (as it is called;) and expected every moment to be driven on shore.

When the weather moderated, Mr. Franco sent off a letter to Mr. Fay, stating that he had just heard from Mr. Abraham of Grand Cairo, who was about to proceed to Europe, with his family, by the first ship; therefore to guard against any future disappointment, this kind gentleman inclosed a general letter to the Jewish merchants, Mr. Franco's name being well known throughout the East. Having already seven letters of introduction to persons in Grand Cairo, we shall not, I imagine, have occasion to make use of this.

On Thursday the 8th, we ventured to sail once more, and have hitherto gone on pleasantly enough.

Tuesday, 20th July. Since my last date, I have been a good deal vexed at an accident which, perhaps, will appear very trivial. I had a pair of beautiful pigeons given me at Leghorn, which furnished me with much amusement. These pretty little creatures, their wings being cut, ranged at liberty about the ship. At length one of them fell, or rather was blown overboard. I saw it a long while struggling for life, and looking towards the vessel, as if to implore assistance; yet, notwithstanding my fondness for the poor bird, and anxious desire to extricate it from its perilous situation, if such a thing were possible, I could not even wish that, a ship running eight knots an hour, should be hove to, and a boat sent out after a Pigeon. The widowed mate lived only three days afterwards, never touching a morsel of food, from the time the other disappeared, and uttering, at intervals, the most plaintive sounds, which I could not avoid hearing, my cabin being upon deck. For you must know, it is a regulation on board Swedish vessels, that the whole ship's company join twice a day, in devotional exercises; so Capt. Norberg reserved his great Cabin for the purpose, of assembling them together, or we would willingly have engaged it. So much for my little favourites. I shall now advert to a more chearful topic.

My voyage has been rendered very interesting, and instructive, by the conversation of one of our passengers, a Franciscan Friar, from Rome, who is going as a Missionary to Jerusalem; and in my opinion no man can be better calculated for the hazardous office he has undertaken. Figure to yourself, a man in the prime of life (under forty), tall, well made, and athletic in his person; and seemingly of a temperament to brave every danger: add to these advantages a pair of dark eyes, beaming with intelligence, and a most venerable auburn beard, descending nearly to his girdle, and, you cannot fail to pronounce him, irresistible. He appears also to possess, all the enthusiasm and eloquence necessary for pleading the important cause of Christianity; yet one must regret that so noble a mind, should be warped by the belief of such ridiculous superstitions, as disgrace the Romish creed.— He became extremely zealous for my conversion, and anxiously forwarded my endeavours, after improvement in the Italian language, that I might the more readily comprehend the arguments, he adduced to effect that desirable purpose. Like other disputants, we sometimes used to contend very fiercely, and one day on my speaking rather lightly of what he chose to call, a miracle of the Catholic Church, he even went so far as to tell me, that my mouth spouted forth heresies, as water gushes from a fountain.

This morning (the 22d) at breakfast, he intreated me to give up my coffee, as a libation to the bambino (child) Jesus, and on my declining to do so, urged me with the most impressive earnestness, to spare only a single cup, which he would immediately pour out in honour of the Blessed Infant. Professing my disbelief in the efficacy of such a sacrifice, I again excused myself from complying with his request: upon which declaring that he was equally shocked at my willful incredulity and obstinate heresy he withdrew to another part of the vessel, and I have not seen him since.

23d A. M. We are now off Alexandria, which makes a fine appearance from the sea on a near approach; but being built on low ground, is, as the seamen say "very difficult to hit." We were two days almost abreast of the Town. There is a handsome Pharos or light-house in the new harbour, and it is in all respects far preferable; but no vessels belonging to Christians can anchor there, so we were forced to go into the old one, of which however we escaped the dangers, if any exist.

My acquaintance with the Reverend Father has terminated rather unpleasantly. A little while ago being upon deck together, and forgetting our quarrel about the libation, I made a remark on the extreme heat of the weather, "Aye" replied he, with a most malignant expression of countenance, such as I could not have thought it possible, for a face benign like his to assume, "aye you will find it ten thousand times hotter in the Devil's House" (Nella Casa di Diavolo). I pitied his bigotry and prayed for his conversion to the genuine principles of that religion, whose doctrines he professed to teach.

Mr. Brandy[87] to whom Mr. Fay sent ashore an introductory letter, came on board to visit us. I rejoice to hear from him, that there are two ships at Suez, yet no time must be lost, lest we miss the season. This gentleman resides here, as Consul for one of the German Courts, and may be of great use to us. We received an invitation to sup with him to-morrow; he has secured a lodging for us, and engaged a Jew and his wife to go with us to Grand Cairo as dragoman, (or interpreter) and attendant: should we proceed by water, which is not yet decided on, Mr. B— will provide a proper boat. I am summoned to an early dinner, immediately after which we shall go on shore with our Dragoman, that we may have time to view whatever is remarkable.

24th July. Having mounted our asses, the use of horses being forbidden to any but musselmans, we sallied forth preceded by a Janizary, with his drawn sword, about three miles over a sandy desert, to see Pompey's Pillar,[88] esteemed to be the finest column in the World. This pillar which is exceedingly lofty, but I have no means of ascertaining its exact height, is composed of three blocks of Granite; (the pedestal, shaft, and capital, each containing one). When we consider the immense weight of the granite, the raising such masses, appear beyond the powers of man. Although quite unadorned, the proportions are so exquisite, that it must strike every beholder with a kind of awe, which softens into melancholy, when one reflects that the renowned Hero whose name it bears, was treacherously murdered on this very Coast, by the boatmen who were conveying him to Alexandria; while his wretched wife stood on the vessel he had just left, watching his departure, as we may naturally suppose, with inexpressible anxiety. What must have been her agonies at the dreadful event! Though this splendid memorial bears the name of Pompey, it is by many supposed to have been erected in memory of the triumph, gained over him at the battle of Pharsalia. Leaving more learned heads than mine to settle this disputed point, let us proceed to ancient Alexandria, about a league from the modern town; which presents to the eye an instructive lesson on the instability of all sublunary objects. This once magnificent City, built by the most famous of all Conquerors,[89] and adorned with the most exquisite productions of art, is now little more than a heap of Ruins; yet the form of the streets can still be discerned; they were regular, and many of the houses (as I recollect to have read of Athens) had fore-courts bounded by dwarf walls,[90] so much in the manner of our Lincoln's-Inn Fields, that the resemblance immediately struck me.

We saw also the *outside* of St. Athanasius's Church, who was Bishop of this Diocese, but it being now a Mosque were forbidden to enter, unless on condition of turning mahometans, or losing our lives, neither of which alternatives exactly suited my ideas, so that I deemed it prudent to repress my curiosity. I could not however resist a desire to visit the Palace of Cleopatra,[91] of which few vestiges remain. The marble walls of the Banqueting room are yet standing, but the roof is long since decayed. Never do I remember being so affected by a like object. I stood in the midst of the ruins, meditating on the awful scene, 'till I could almost have fancied I beheld its former mistress, revelling in Luxury, with her infatuated lover, Marc Anthony, who for her sake lost all.

The houses in the new Town of Alexandria thro' which we returned, are flat roofed, and, in general, have gardens on their tops. These in some measure, in so warm a country, may be called luxuries. As to the bazars (or markets) they are wretched places, and the streets exceedingly narrow. Christians of all denominations live here on paying a tax, but they are frequently ill treated; and if one of them commits even an unintentional offence against a musselman, he is pursued by a most insatiable spirit of revenge and his whole family suffers for it. One cannot help shuddering at the bare idea of being in the hands of such bigotted wretches. I forgot to mention that Mr. Brandy met us near Cleopatra's needles,[92] which are two immense obelisks of Granite. One of them, time has levelled with the ground; the other is intire; they are both covered with hieroglyphic figures, which, on the sides not exposed to the wind and sand from the Desert, remain uninjured; but the key being lost, no one can decypher their meaning. I thought Mr. B— might perhaps have heard something relative to them; he, however, seems to know no more than ourselves. A droll circumstance occurred on our return. He is a stout man of a very athletic make, and above six feet high; so you may judge what a curious figure he must have made, riding on an ass, and with difficulty holding up his long legs to suit the size of the animal; which watched an opportunity of walking away from between them, and left the poor Consul standing, erect, like a Colossus: in truth, it was a most ludicrous scene to behold.

25th July. The weather being intensely hot, we staid at home 'till the evening, when Mr. Brandy called to escort us to his house. We were most graciously received by Mrs. B— who is a native of this place; but as she could speak a little Italian, we managed to carry on something like conversation. She was most curiously bedizened[93] on the occasion, and being short, dark complexioned, and of a complete dumpling shape, appeared altogether the strangest lump of finery I had ever beheld; she had a handkerchief bound round her head, covered with strings composed of thin plates of gold, in the manner of spangles but very large, intermixed with pearls and emeralds; her neck and bosom were ornamented in the same way. Add to all this an embroidered girdle with a pair of gold clasps, I verily think near four inches square, enormous earrings, and a large diamond sprig on the top of her forehead, and you must allow, that altogether she was a most brilliant figure. They have a sweet little girl about seven years of age, who was decked out much in the same style; but she really looked pretty in spite of her incongruous finery. On the whole, though, I was pleased with both mother and child, their looks and behaviour were kind: and to a stranger in a strange land[94] (and this is literally so to us) a little attention is soothing and consolatory; especially when one feels surrounded by hostilities, which every European must do here. Compared with the uncouth beings who govern this country, I felt at home among the natives of France, and I will even say of Italy.

On taking leave, our Host presented a book containing certificates of his great politeness and attention towards travellers; which were signed by many persons of consideration: and at the same time requesting that Mr. Fay and myself would add *our* names to the list, we complied, though not without surprize, that a gentleman in his situation, should have recourse to such an expedient, which cannot but degrade him in the eyes of his Guests.

It being determined that we shall proceed by water, for reasons too tedious to detail at present, I must now prepare to embark. I shall endeavour to keep up my spirits. Be assured that I will omit no opportunity of writing, and comfort yourselves with the idea, that before *this* reaches you, I shall have surmounted all my difficulties. I certainly deem myself very fortunate in quitting this place so soon. Farewell; all good be with you, my ever *ever* dear Friends prays,

Your *own*,
E. F.

LETTER VII.

GRAND CAIRO, 27th August, 1779.

MY DEAR FRIENDS,

In coming to this place, we were in great peril, and bade adieu to the sea at the hazard of our lives, the Bar of the Nile[95] being exceedingly dangerous. Fourteen persons were lost there, the day before we crossed it, a circumstance that of course tended to increase our anxiety on the subject, and which was told me just before I closed my last letter; but for the world I would not have communicated such intelligence. Our only alternative to this hazardous passage, was crossing a desert, notorious for the robberies and murders committed on it; where we could not hope for escape, and from the smallness of our number, had no chance of superiority in case of attack. The night after we had congratulated ourselves on being out of danger from the bar, we were alarmed by perceiving a boat making after us, as the people said, to plunder, and perhaps, to murder us. Our Jew interpreter, who, with his wife, slept in the outer cabin, begged me not to move our dollars, which I was just attempting to do, lest the thieves should hear the sound, and kill us all, for the supposed booty. You may judge in what a situation we remained, while this dreadful evil seemed impending over us. Mr. Fay fired two pistols, to give notice of our being armed. At length, thank God, we out-sailed them; and nothing of the kind occurred again, during our stay on board; though we passed several villages, said to be inhabited entirely by thieves.

As morning broke, I was delighted with the appearance of the country, a more charming scene my eyes never beheld. The Nile, that perpetual source of plenty, was just beginning to overflow its banks; so that on every side, we saw such quantities of water drawn up for the use of more distant lands, that it is surprising any remains. The machine chiefly used for that purpose is a wheel with earthen pitchers tied round it, which empty themselves into tubs, from whence numerous canals are supplied. Oxen and Buffaloes are the animals generally employed in this labour. It is curious to see how the latter contrive to keep themselves cool during the intense heat that prevails here; they lie in the River by hundreds, with their heads just above water, for hours together.

Rosetta is a most beautiful place, surrounded by groves of lemon and orange trees; and the flat roofs of the houses have gardens on them, whose fragrance perfumes the air. There is an appearance of cleanliness in it, the more gratifying to an English eye, because seldom met with in any degree, so as to remind us of what we are accustomed to at home. The landscape around, was interesting from its novelty, and became peculiarly so on considering it as the country where, the children of Israel sojourned. The beautiful, I may say, the unparalleled story of Joseph and his brethren,[96] rose to my mind as I surveyed those Banks, on which the Patriarch sought shelter for his old age; and where his self convicted sons bowed down before their younger brother, and I almost felt as if in a dream, so wonderful appeared the circumstance of my being here. You will readily conceive that, as I drew near Grand Cairo, and beheld those prodigies of human labour, the Pyramids of Egypt, these sensations were still more strongly awakened; and I could have fancied myself an inhabitant of a world, long passed away: for who can look on buildings, reared, (moderately computing the time) above *three thousand years ago*, without seeming to step back as it were, in existence, and live through days, now gone by, and sunk in oblivion "like a tale that is told."[97]

Situated as I was, the Pyramids were not all in sight, but I was assured that those which came under my eye, were decidedly the most magnificent. We went out of our way to view them nearer, and by the aid of a telescope, were enabled to form a tolerable idea of their construction. It has been supposed by many that the Israelites built these Pyramids,[98] during their bondage in Egypt, and I rather incline to that opinion; for, altho' it has lately been proved that they were intended to serve as repositories for the dead, yet each, being said to contain only one sarcophagus,[99] this circumstance, and their very form, rendered them of so little comparative use, that most probably, they were raised to furnish employment for multitudes of unfortunate slaves; and who more aptly agree with this description, than the wretched posterity of Jacob? I understand there is a little flat, on the tops of the larger Pyramids, from which it is conjectured that the Egyptians made astronomical observations.[100] The largest, is said to be, above five hundred feet high, perpendicularly. The inclined plane must measure much more: the steps are nearly three feet distant of the Pyramids; though I very anxiously wished to have inspected them, and the sphinx,[101] prudence forbade me from making the attempt, as you will allow, when I proceed farther in my narrative.

On the 29th, we reached Bulac the port of Grand Cairo, and within two miles of that city, to my great joy; for on this river, there is either little wind, or else it comes in squalls, so suddenly, that the boats are often in danger of being overset, as they carry only, what I believe is called, a shoulder-of-Mutton-sail, which turns on a sort of swivel, and is very difficult to manage, when the wind takes it the wrong way. It seems indeed almost miraculous how we escaped.

Mr. Fay set out almost immediately to Mr. Baldwin's,[102] who received him with much civility, and sent an ass for me, with directions to make all possible haste, as a Caravan was to set off in three hours.

I must now give you a description of my dress,[103] as my Jewess decked me out, preparatory to our entering the Great City. I had, in the first place, a pair of trowsers, with yellow leather half-boots and slippers over them; a long sattin gown, with wide sleeves, open to the elbows; and a girdle round my waist, with large silver clasps; over that another robe with short sleeves: round my head a fine, coloured, muslin handkerchief, closely bound, but so arranged that one corner hung down three quarters of a yard behind. This is the dress for the House; but as I was going out, she next put on a long robe of silk, like a surplice, and then covered my face with a piece of muslin, half a yard wide, which reached from the forehead to the feet, except an opening for the eyes; over all, she threw a piece of black silk, long and wide enough to envelop the whole form; so, thus equipped, stumbling at every step, I sallied forth, and with great difficulty got across my noble beast: but, as it was in the full heat of the day and the veil prevented me from breathing freely, I thought I must have died by the way. However, at last, I was safely housed, but found a great change had taken place; all thoughts of going were now laid aside. I dare not at present enter into particulars, and can only say that, some thing was wrong, and on that account we were kept in suspense, 'till about a week ago, when just as we had determined to proceed, if possible, another way, matters were adjusted: so to-morrow afternoon we are to enter on the Desert, and shall, please God, arrive at Suez, most likely, on Monday, from whence I propose writing again. The season is so far advanced that a good passage cannot be expected: we have no hopes of reaching Calcutta in less than three months, but at any rate, the voyage is preferable to going through the long Desert, from Aleppo to Bassora.

When I write from India I will give a full detail of the affair to which I allude, though as it is very important, you will, most probably, see the whole in the papers. Adieu for the present it is bed time.

28th. Again I take up the pen to hold a little further converse with my dear friends, while waiting the summons to depart; and as health is the most important of all earthly subjects, shall begin with that. It will, I know, give you pleasure to hear that I have found scarce any inconvenience from the heat, though all of our Party, who have been in India agree that, they never felt the weather so oppressively hot as here; which proceeds from the terrible sandy deserts, that surround the town, causing the air to smell like hot bricks. This however I could have borne, but just on our arrival, there broke out a severe epidemical disease, with violent symptoms.[104] People are attacked at a moments warning with dreadful pains in the limbs, a burning fever, with delirium and a total stoppage of perspiration. During two days it increases; on the third, there comes on uniformly a profuse sweat (pardon the expression) with vomiting, which carries all off.—The only remedies prescribed, are lying in bed and drinking plentifully, even two gallons a day, of Nile water: no nourishment, and not so much as gruel, is allowed until after the crisis; not one has died of the disease, nor, I believe, scarcely one escaped: even the beasts have been affected. Mr. Fay had it three weeks ago, and among all I conversed with here, I remained the only healthy person, and really hoped to have proved the truth of what is asserted by physicians, that nervous persons are not subject to be attacked by contagious distempers, not even by the Plague itself. However, this day sennight, I was seized with most violent symptoms, so that at the three days end, my strength seemed entirely exhausted; but I have, thanks be to Providence, recovered as surprizingly; and am already nearly well. It had every sign of the Plague, except that it was not mortal. Do not be frightened at the name, but I assure you, it is commonly called "la queue de la Peste,"[105] and the general opinion is, that had it arrived in the month of February, the living would scarce have been sufficient to bury the dead.

Grand Cairo by no means answers to its name at present, whatever it may have done formerly.—There are certainly many magnificent houses, belonging to the Beys[106] and other rich individuals, but as a city, I can perceive neither order, beauty, nor grandeur; and the contrast between the great, who seem to wallow in splendour and luxury, and the people at large, who appear to want the common necessaries of life, is not more striking, than disgusting; because, those who are raised above their fellows, do not look, as though they merited the distinction, either by talent, manners or even the most ordinary pretentions. The Christians (who are called Franks)[107] live all together in one street, which is closed at each end every night; a precaution neither unpleasant nor useless. An agreeable variety is given to the appearance of the town by the Mosques, or I should consider the whole wretchedly stupid. A wedding, here, is a gay and amusing spectacle, from the procession which accompanies the Bride in all her movements, drums, hautboys[108] and every other kind of noise and parade they can make, seem indispensible: but the circumstance of completely veiling, not only the face, but the whole figure of the woman, in the enveloping mantle of black silk, before described, gives an air of melancholy to these exhibitions. To show the face is considered here, an act of downright indecency; a terrible fashion for one like me, to whom free air seems the great requisite for existence.

I must not conclude without mentioning a disappointment I met with. As the fertility of Egypt depends on the due increase of the Nile, persons are hired to go round Grand Cairo, twice a day, and report how many inches the water has risen; returning solemn thanks to Almighty God for the blessing. This is continued 'till it gain a certain point, when the Dykes are broken down, and the river flows majestically into the Canal, formed for its reception; while the inhabitants hail its approach with every demonstration of joy. Such was the account I heard, and great was my anxiety, lest I should not be permitted to witness this *August* ceremony. At length the period arrived, but never, sure, were highly raised expectations more miserably deceived: For this famous Canal,[109] being dry nine months out of the twelve, and serving during that interval as a receptacle for the filth of a populous, and not *over* cleanly City, I leave you to judge, how beautifully *pellucid* its waters must appear: nor could St. Giles's[110] itself pour forth such an assembly of half naked, wretched creatures, as preceded this so vaunted stream; crying aloud, and making all sorts of frantic gestures, like so many maniacs. Not a decent person could I distinguish amongst the whole group. So much for this grand exhibition, which we have abundant cause to wish, had not taken place, for the vapours arising from such a mass of impurity, have rendered the heat more intolerable than ever. My bed chamber overlooks the Canal, so that I enjoy the full benefit to be derived from its proximity.

I am now compelled, much against my inclination, to bid you adieu; for I have a thousand things to do, and this immense letter has left me little time.

Ever your's most truly,
&c. &c.

P. S. Not being able to enlarge on the only interesting subject,[111] has induced me to be rather diffuse on others, as I wished to convey *some* information by this, perhaps, *last* opportunity, 'till our arrival in India; for it is doubtful whether I may have any safe channel of conveyance from Suez.

LETTER VIII.

From Mr. to Mr. C.

On Board Ship, in the Red Sea, Near Suez.

1st September 1779.

Honoured Sir,

I seize the chance of three minutes, to tell you that we yesterday arrived at Suez from Grand Cairo, after a journey of three days, over a most dreadful Desert,[112] where every night we slept under the great canopy of Heaven, and where we were every hour in danger of being destroyed, by troops of Arabian robbers. But having a little party of English gentlemen, and servants (among whom I held a principal command) well armed, and under the orders of Major Baillie,[113] and another military officer, we marched the whole way in order of battle, and though we could frequently see superior numbers, they never dared to molest us.

Your daughter behaved most courageously and is extremely well, considering the extraordinary fatigue she has undergone. There is another English lady and her husband on board, which promises to make it an agreeable voyage. The ship is a very fine one, and we have a handsome little chamber, and I hope in all things shall find ourselves well accommodated. We expect to sail in four hours. The ship is called the Nathalia, Captain Chenu, a Frenchman, and apparently a very polite good-natured man, which is a great matter in a long voyage.

I thank God I was never in better health and spirits, tho' I never slept during the whole journey on the Desert, and lived the whole time on bread and water, notwithstanding we had abundance of wine and provisions; but the heat being excessive, I found no other food agree with me so well, and Mrs. Fay by adopting the same diet, preserved her health also; whereas all the rest were knocked up before we got half way over that confounded Desert, and some are now very ill; but I stood it, as well as any Arabian in the Caravan, which consisted at least of five thousand people. My wife insists on taking the pen out of my hands, so I can only say God bless you all.

My Dear Friends

I have not a moments time, for the boat is waiting, therefore can only beg that you will unite with me, in praising our heavenly Protector for our escape from the various dangers of our journey. I never could have thought my constitution was so strong. I bore the fatigues of the desert, like a Lion, though but just recovering from my illness. We have been pillaged of almost every thing, by the Arabs. This is the Paradise of thieves, I think the whole population may be divided into two classes of them; those who adopt force, and those who effect their purpose by fraud. I was obliged to purchase a thick cloak, and veil, proper for the journey, and what was worse, to wear them all the way hither, which rendered the heat almost insupportable.—Never was I more happy, than when I came on board; although the ship having been for six weeks in the hands of the natives, the reason of which I cannot enlarge on here, is totally despoiled of every article of furniture; we have not a chair or a table, but as the carpenter makes them, for there is no buying such things here. Our greatest inconvenience is the want of good water; what can be procured here, is so brackish, as to be scarcely drinkable. I have not another moment. God bless you! pray for me my beloved friends.

LETTER IX.

From Mrs. Fay.

Mocha 13th September 1779.

Thank God my dear friends, I am once more enabled to date from a place of comparative liberty, and an European Gentleman having promised me a safe conveyance for my packet, I shall proceed to give you a hurried and melancholy detail of circumstances of which it has been my chief consolation to know that you were ignorant. You are of course impatient to be informed to what I allude; take then the particulars: but I must go a good way back in order to elucidate matters, which would otherwise appear mysterious or irrelevant.

The East India Company sent out positive orders some time ago, to prohibit the trade to Suez, as interfering with their privileges; but as there never was a law made, but means might be found to evade it, several English merchants freighted a ship (the Nathalia[114]) from Serampore,[115] a Danish settlement on the Hooghly, fourteen miles above Calcutta, whose commander, Vanderfield, a Dane, passed for owner of the ship and cargo. Mr. O'Donnell one of the persons concerned, and who had property on board to the amount of above £20,000, came as passenger, as did Mr. Barrington the real supercargo, also a freighter, and two Frenchmen, brothers, named Chevalier. They left Bengal on New year's day 1779, and came first to Calicut on the coast of Malabar, where they arrived in February; found English, French, Danish and Portuguese Factors, or Consuls there; and trade in a flourishing state, so not apprehending any danger they entered into a contract with one Isaacs, a rich old Jew, who has great influence with the government, to freight them with pepper for Bengal on their return from Suez; that being the greatest town on the Coast for that commodity.—The price was settled and £700 paid as earnest. This business arranged, they proceeded on their voyage; and having luckily disposed of some part of the cargo at this place, reached Suez with the remainder in the beginning of June, landed their Goods to the amount of at least £40,000, and prepared to cross the Desert on their way to Cairo. The company besides those already mentioned, consisted of Chenu the second mate, with some officers and servants, in all twelve Europeans, strengthened by a numerous body of Arabian guards, camel drivers &c., for the conveyance of their property: more than sufficient in every body's opinion; for no one remembered a Caravan being plundered, for altho' sometimes the wandering Arabs were troublesome, yet a few presents never failed to procure a release from them. Thus were they lulled into a fatal security; each calculating the profits likely to accrue, and extremely willing to compound for the loss of a few bales, should they happen to meet with any strolling depredators, not even once supposing their lives were in danger, or intending to use their firearms should they be molested.

On Monday the 14th June they left Suez, and next morning at day break, had travelled about twenty miles (nearly one third of the way) when suddenly an alarm was given of an Attack, as they, poor souls, were sleeping across their baskets (or panniers.[116]) Capt. Barrington on awaking ordered a dozen bales to be given to them immediately: but alas! they were already in possession of the whole; for the Camel drivers did not defend themselves an instant, but left their beasts at the mercy of the robbers; who after detaching a large body to drive them away with their burthens, advanced towards the passengers. Here I must request you to pause, and reflect whether it be possible even for imagination to conceive a more dreadful scene to those concerned, particularly to Mr. O'Donnell, who from a concurrence of fortunate circumstances, had in less than four years realized a fortune of near £30,000; the bulk of which he laid out in merchandise on the inviting prospect of gaining 50 Per Cent, and as his health was in a very weak state proposed retiring to Europe. What must that man have felt, a helpless spectator of his own ruin. But this was nothing to what followed on their being personally attacked. The inhuman wretches not content with stripping them to the skin, drove away their camels, and left them in a burning sandy Desert, which the feet can scarcely touch, without being blistered, exposed to the scorching rays of the sun and utterly destitute of sustenance of every kind; no house, tree, or even shrub to afford them shelter. My heart sickens, my hand trembles as I retrace this scene. Alas! I can too well conceive their situation: I can paint to myself the hopeless anguish of an eye cast abroad in vain for succour! but I must not indulge in reflections, let me simply relate the facts as they occurred. In this extremity they stopped to deliberate, when each gave his reasons, for preferring the road he determined to pursue. Mr. O'Donnell, Chenu, the cook and two others resolved to retrace their steps back to Suez, which was undoubtedly the most eligible plan; and after encountering many hardships, they at length, arrived there in safety. Of the remaining seven who went towards Cairo, only *one* survived.—Mr. Barrington being corpulent and short breathed, sunk under the fatigue the second day; his servant, soon followed him.— One of the French gentlemen was by this time become very ill, and his brother perceiving a house at some miles distance (for in that flat country, one may see a great way,) prevailed on him to lie down under a stunted tree, with his servant, while he endeavoured to procure some water, for want of which the other was expiring. Hope, anxiety, and affection combined to quicken his pace, and rendered poor Vanderfield, the Danish captain, unable to keep up with him, which he most earnestly strove to do. I wept myself almost blind; as the poor Frenchman related his sufferings from conflicting passions; almost worn out with heat and thirst, he was afraid of not being able to reach the house, though his own life and that of his brother, depended on it. On the other hand the heart piercing cries of his fellow sufferer, that he was a dead man unless assisted by him, and conjuring him for God's sake, not to leave him to perish now they were in view of relief, arrested his steps and agonised every nerve. Unable to resist the solemn appeal, for some time he indulged him, 'till finding that the consequence of longer delay must be inevitable destruction to both, he was compelled to shake him off. A servant belonging to some of the party still kept on, and poor Vanderfield was seen to continue his efforts, 'till at length nature being completely exhausted, he dropped and was soon relieved from his miseries by Death. Nor was the condition of the survivors far more enviable, when having, with difficulty, reached the building after which they had toiled so long, it proved to be an uninhabited shed. Giving himself up for lost, the French gentleman lay down under shelter of the wall, to await his last moment, (the servant walked forward and was found dead a little further on). Now it so happened that an Arabian beggar chanced to pass by the wall, who seeing his condition, kindly ran to procure some water, but did not return for an hour. What an age of torture, of horrible suspense! for if "hope deferred maketh the heart sick," the sensation must cause ten-fold anguish at a moment like this.

The unhappy man was mindful of his brother, but utterly unable to undertake the task himself, he directed the beggar, as well as he could, to the spot where he had left him, with a supply of water. But alas! all his endeavours to find the unfortunate men were ineffectual, nor were their bodies ever discovered: It is supposed that they crept for shelter from the sun, into some unfrequented spot, and there expired. The survivor by the assistance of the beggar, reached the hut of a poor old woman, who kindly received him; and through whose care he was soon restored to strength, and arrived safely at Cairo, after as miraculous an escape, as ever human being experienced.

This melancholy story had been mentioned by Mr. Brandy before I landed at Alexandria, (Oh with what horror did I hear his brief recital) and the particulars I soon learnt at Cairo. The subject was in fact closely connected with my fears and sufferings, at that place, and which I hinted at the impossibility of my then revealing, neither could I, for the same reason, give you any account of the Egyptian Government, lest they should intercept my letter, altho' it is necessary you should know a little of it, for the sake of comprehending what I have further to relate, concerning these unfortunate adventurers.

Egypt, then, is governed by twenty four Beys,[117] of whom one presides over the rest, but this superiority is very precarious; for he holds it no longer than 'till some other of the number thinks himself strong enough to contend with him; and as they have here but two maxims in War, the one to fly, the other to pursue, those contests last not long: the vanquished, should he escape assassination retires up the country, 'till Fortune changes her aspect: while the victor takes his place. Thus do their lives pass in perpetual vicissitudes. To-day a Prince, to-morrow a Fugitive, and next day a prince again. These things are so common, that nobody notices them; since they never disturb the inhabitants or compel them to take part in their disputes. In order to be a check on these gentlemen, the Grand Signor sends a Bashaw, to reside among them, whom they receive with great respect and compliment with presents of value, pretending the utmost deference for his authority, but at the same time a strict eye is kept over him, and on the least opposition to their will, he is sent in disgrace away—happy if he escape with life, after refunding all his presents and paying enormous sums besides.

By the above statement you will perceive that, the Beys are in reality independent, and likewise discern the hinge on which their politics turn, for as long as under colour of submission, they consent to receive a Bashaw,[118] it is in their power constantly to throw the odium of every disagreeable occurrence on his shoulders, under pretence of Orders from the Porte. Now briefly to proceed with my little history, some time after the fatal robbery, another ship called the St. Helena, arrived at Suez, under Danish colours with the real owner, a Mr. Moore, on board. He justly apprehensive of a similar fate, refused to land his Cargo 'till the *then* Chief Amurath Bey, had accorded him a solemn permission or rather protection, under which he safely reached Cairo, disposed of his effects, and prepared for his return to his ship with a fresh Cargo. But in the interim, Mr. O'Donnell had been advised to present a memorial to the Beys, by which he reclaimed his property as an Englishman, threatened them with the vengeance of his nation if not immediately redressed, and declared himself totally independent of the Danes. This rash procedure alarmed the people in power, who however still continued apparently friendly, in hopes of a larger booty, 'till the 30th July, when they threw off the mask, seized the Caravan even to the passenger's baggage, and made Mr. Moore a prisoner. You may recollect that in my letter from Cairo, I told you what a hurry Mr. Fay was in, to fetch me from Bulac, not having, as he then thought, a moments time to spare. It so happened that I arrived within an hour after the seizure of the Caravan and when all the gentlemen concerned, were in the first transports of that indignation, which such a daring outrage could not fail to excite; at once exasperated by this treacherous behaviour and alarmed, lest some new crime should be committed against them.

Every one is of opinion that their design was to cut us *all* off, had we gone out ignorant of the seizure of the Caravan. I had scarcely sat down in Mr. Baldwin's parlour, when this terrible news, which seemed to involve the fate of every European alike, burst upon me like a stroke of lightning. Never shall I forget the terrors I felt.—: In a few moments the room was filled with Europeans, chiefly English, all speaking together,—calling out for arms, and declaring they would sell their lives dearly; for not one appeared to entertain a doubt of their being immediately attacked. In the midst of this confusion, Mons. Chevalier (the poor man who escaped from the Desert) cast his eyes upon me, exclaiming "Oh Madam how unhappy you are in having come to this wretched place." This drew the attention of the rest,—and "what shall we do with the lady?"—was every one's question—at last they resolved on sending me to the house of an Italian Physician, as a place of safety; thither I was instantly taken by a native, who even in the distress and confusion of the house, and although the Italian's was only a few steps distant across a narrow lane, felt greatly shocked, because my veil chancing to be a little loose, he could see one corner of my eye, and severely reprehended the indecency of such an exposure.

On reaching my expected Asylum a scene of more serious alarm (if possible) than I had left at Mr. Baldwins awaited me. The lady and her daughter were wringing their hands, and crying out in agony, that they were utterly ruined—; that all the Europeans would be murdered; and they even appeared to think, that receiving another of the proscribed race increased their danger. Imprisonment and massacre in every shape, were the sole subjects of their conversation; and so many terrible images did their fears conjure up, and communicate to my already disordered mind, that there were times, when the reality could have been scarcely more appalling. Oh England! dear England! how often did I apostrophise thee, land of liberty and safety—: but I must not review my thoughts—; a simple narrative is all I dare allow myself to write.

For several days we remained in this harrassing state of suspense, and alarm; at length news arrived that the two ships which had brought these ill-fated adventurers to Egypt's inhospitable shores, were seized by the Government, three days before they took possession of the Caravan. Their prisoners indeed, we already virtually were, not being allowed to quit the City. I should have mentioned that the Bashaw was the tool made use of on this occasion; who pretended he had Orders from Constantinople, to seize all English merchandise and confiscate the Vessels, suffering none but the East India Company's packets to touch at Suez. This Firman[119] was said to be obtained of his sublime highness, by the British resident at the Porte, on behalf of the E. I. Company; whether this pretence was true or false, we could never learn. Many other reports were propagated, as must always be the case in a country under arbitrary government: there being no certain rules to judge by, every one pronounces on the event as his hopes or fears dictate. Some times we were all to be sent prisoners to Constantinople, then we were assured that after a general plunder of our effects, we should certainly be released; and once it was confidently reported that, the *Bowstring*[120] would be secretly applied to prevent our telling tales.

What added much to our mortification and justified our fears was, that all the Christians belonging to the two ships, were on the 10th of August dragged to Cairo in the most ignominious manner, having previously suffered, during their imprisonment at Suez, every species of hardship which barbarity and malice could inflict. The people also at whose house we lodged, behaved to us continually with marked disrespect, if asked a question they seldom deigned to reply, and took care to enlarge perpetually on their condescension in suffering themselves to be incommoded with strangers. To be thus treated, at a time when perpetual solicitude and terror had unbraced my nerves and subdued my spirit, seemed so cruel, that I think it absolutely hurt me more than even our detention; a detention which was certainly harder upon us, than any other Europeans in one sense, since we had no connection whatever with the parties, were coming from a different quarter of the globe; not concerned in trade, and unknown to those who had visited their country on that account: no demon of avarice had led *us* into their power, nor could we afford a prey to *theirs*. These considerations however evident, made no impression on our host, they were rather motives of exultation over us, and what enhanced our misfortune, it was irremediable, for we could not change our abode, without going into another street, where we should have been unprotected.

All the Christians live in one part of the town as I before noticed: during the time when the Plague rages, they visit each other by means of bridges thrown across the streets, from the tops of the houses, and this is a convenience they often resort to at other times, as it saves them from insult, which they often meet below. I find I have written myself into such a strange humour, that I cannot proceed methodically; but I must try to arrange my thoughts and go forward better.

At length the Beys, enchanted by that Deity whose bewitching attractions few mortals can resist, whether on the banks of the Nile or the Thames: in other words, influenced by the promise of three thousand pounds, and an absolute indemnification from Mr. O'Donnell, gave us leave to proceed on our Voyage in defiance of the tremendous order of their master, and thus ended this most disagreeable and distressing business. I will release you from this wearisome letter. I shall have time at Mocha to continue my journal—, Adieu till to-morrow.

Ever most affectionately your's,
E. F.

LETTER X.

INCLOSED IN THE FOREGOING

MOCHA 15th September.

MY DEAR SISTER,

I resume my pen in order to give you some account of our passing the Desert, which being done by a method of travelling totally different from any thing in England, may afford amusement, and even without the charm of novelty could not fail to interest you, as the narrative of one so nearly and dearly connected.

When a Caravan is about to depart, large tents are pitched on the skirts of the City, whither all who propose joining it repair: there they are drawn up in order, by the persons who undertake to convey them. Strong bodies of Arabian soldiers guard the van and rear; others flank the sides—; so that the female passengers, and the merchandise, are completely surrounded, and, as one would hope, defended in case of attack. Each gentleman of our party had a horse, and it is common to hire a camel between two, with panniers to carry their provisions &c.—: across the panniers, which are of wicker, a kind of mattress is thrown, whereon they take it by turns to lie, and court repose, during their journey. Females who can afford the expence, are more comfortably accommodated—; these travel in a kind of litter, called a Tataravan; with two poles fastened between two camels, one behind, the other before. The litter has a top and is surmounted by shabby, ill contrived Venetian blinds, which in the day, increase the suffocating heat, but are of use during the nights which are cold and piercing.—Every camel carries skins of water, but before you have been many hours on the Desert, it becomes of the colour of coffee. I was warned of this, and recommended to provide small guglets of porous earth, which after filling with *purified* water, I slung to the top of my *Tataravan;* and these with water melons, and *hard* eggs, proved the best refreshments I could have taken. The water by this means was tolerably preserved; but the motion of the camels and the uncouth manner in which the vehicle is fastened to them, made such a constant rumbling sound among my provisions, as to be exceedingly annoying. Once I was saluted by a parcel of hard eggs breaking loose from their net, and pelting me completely: it was fortunate that *they were* boiled, or I should have been in a pretty trim; to this may be added the frequent violent jerks, occasioned by one or other of the poles slipping out of its wretched fastening, so as to bring one end of the litter to the ground; and you may judge how pleasing this mode of travelling must be.

At our first outset, the novelty of the scene, and the consolation I felt, on leaving a place which had been productive of so much chagrin, and so many too well founded apprehensions, wrought an agreeable change on my harrassed feelings—; but when we had proceeded some distance on the Desert; when all traces of human habitation had vanished—; when every sign of cultivation disappeared; and even vegetation was confined to a few low straggling shrubs, that seemed to stand between life and death as hardly belonging to either—; when the immeasurable plain lay around me, a burning sun darted his fierce rays from above, and no asylum was visible in front, my very heart sunk within me.—I am sure you will do justice to my feelings, the late Catastrophe being deeply imprinted on my mind, and indeed never absent from it. For the world, you should not have known what was passing there, when I made so light of the journey in my letter from Grand Cairo.

In the midst of these soul-subduing reflections, the guides gave notice of a body, apparently much larger than our own, being within view of us.—All the sufferings related by the poor French gentleman, my active imagination now pourtrayed, as about to be inflicted on me. My dear Parents, my sisters, cried I, will never see me more!—should they learn my fate what agonies will they not endure!—but never can they conceive half the terrible realities, that I may be doomed to undergo! Happily, for once, my fears outwent the truth; the party so dreaded, turned off in pursuit of some other prey, or perhaps intimidated by our formidable appearance, left us unmolested.

It is impossible even amidst fear and suspense not to be struck with the exquisite beauty of the nights here; a perfectly cloudless sky, and the atmosphere so clear, that the stars shine with a brilliancy, infinitely surpassing any thing I witnessed elsewhere. Well might the ancient Egyptians become expert astronomers, possessing a climate so favourable to that study; nor were we less indebted to those Heavenly luminaries; since, by their refulgent light, and unvarying revolutions, the guides cross these trackless Deserts with certainty, and like the mariner, steer to the desired haven.

You will perceive, that my boast of having crossed the Desert, like a lion, was not literally just;—but then remember, it was his strength, not his courage to which I alluded: for it is true that, considering how much I had suffered in Cairo, I really did perform the journey well, and on the second day being convinced by the behaviour of some around me, how greatly dejection increased the actual evils of our situation—I rallied my spirits to the utmost, and lifting up my heart in gratitude to the Almighty, for having thus far supported us, I determined to trust in his goodness, and not desert myself.

On this day I was exceedingly affected by the sufferings of one of our party— Mr. Taylor, going out as assistant surgeon on the Bengal establishment. He complained of illness when we sat out, and seemed overwhelmed with melancholy. He had been plundered of all by the Arabs—had sustained various misfortunes, and of late, appeared to be consumptive. The extreme heat of the weather so overpowered him, that he resigned all hope of life, and at length, in a fit of despondency, actually allowed himself to slide down from his horse, that he might die on the ground. Mr. Fay seeing him fall, ran to assist him in regaining his seat, but he earnestly begged to be left alone, and permitted to die in peace. It was impossible to inspire him with hope and as he appeared to have so little strength, I did not believe that, with so strong a predilection for death, he could have been kept alive—: yet to see a fine young man, a countryman and fellow-traveller expiring amongst us, without striving to the last to preserve him, would have been inhuman. Thank God, our cares so far prevailed that he is still with us, though his disorder is now confirmed, and his melancholy but little abated—He thanks us for life, as if grateful for our attention, but not for the gift. I fear his heart is breaking, as well as his constitution.

When my mind was a little relieved on poor T—'s account, I had leisure to think of the horses;—you recollect how partial I ever was to these noble animals; and we had several with us, of such singular beauty and docility, that they would have attracted the attention, I had almost said the affection, of the most indifferent spectator. The wretched creatures suffered so much from heat and thirst, that their groanings were terrible, and added to this an involuntary rattling in the throat, as if they were on the point of expiring, so that one heard them with a mixture of compassion and horror extremely painful to bear: yet notwithstanding that this continued for many hours, we were so fortunate, as not to lose a single horse in the Caravan.—With the dogs, we were less successful,—three very fine ones sat out with us, but none survived—one of them was the most beautiful Italian greyhound, I ever beheld;—he cost seven guineas at Venice. The first day he got tolerably well forward; but during the second his strength failed, and he appeared to suffer excruciating pain from the heat. When he was in the most frightful state, his tongue hanging out of his mouth, his eyes wildly staring, and altogether presenting the idea of madness, rather than death, his master Mr. T— had the modesty to bring him to me, and request that I would admit him into my Tataravan. I hope no person will accuse me of inhumanity, for refusing to receive an animal in that condition,—self-preservation forbade my compliance. I felt that it would be weakness, instead of compassion, to subject myself to such a risk; and you may be certain, my sympathy was not increased for its owner, when he solemnly assured me, by way of inforcing his intreaty, that it would cost him a less severe pang, to see his own father thus suffering, than he then felt—I was induced to credit this assertion; knowing that when last in England, he had remained there seventeen months without visiting the old gentleman; though he acknowledged having been within 150 miles of his residence. A very short time after this, the poor creature dropt down gasping, but ere he had breathed his last, a brutal Arab cut him to pieces before his masters face; and on his expressing anger at his cruel behaviour, ran after him with a drawn scymiter—you may judge from this incident, what wretches we were cast amongst.

We found Suez a miserable place,[121]—little better than the Desert which it bounds, and were, as probably I have already told you, impatient to get on board, where we found every portable necessary of life had been carried off. We had been pretty well pillaged ourselves, and could therefore sympathize with the losers, as well as lament our own personal inconvenience, however, thank Heaven that we escaped as we did;—if ever they catch me on their Desert again, I think I shall deserve all they can inflict.

Our passage down the Red Sea was pleasant, the wind being constantly favourable, but afforded no object of interest, save the distant view of Mount Horeb,[122] which again brought the flight of the children of Israel to my mind; and you may be sure, I did not wonder that they sought to quit the land of Egypt, after the various specimens of its *advantages* that I have experienced.

The only vessels we saw, were those built for the conveyance of coffee,[123] for which this port is famous;—they are so bulky, clumsy, and strangely constructed, that one might almost take them for floating mountains. I cannot be expected to say a great deal of my shipmates, having been so short a time together, but to own the truth, I do not look forward to much comfort, where the elements are so discordant;—however, as we are to touch at Calicut on the Coast of Malabar, you shall from thence have the particulars: for, by that time we shall be pretty well familiarized with each other. May the detail be more agreeable than my present ideas will warrant me in supposing.

Let me now proceed to say a few words of Mocha, which is a pretty considerable place, walled round, and guarded by soldiers.—It appears to great advantage after Suez, being plentifully supplied with fruit and vegetables;—the provisions not bad, and the water excellent. The worst I know of it, is the excessive heat, which is even beyond that of Cairo. Our sailors have a proverb, that there is only a sheet of paper between that and another place—too shocking to be mentioned—I should yet say there were many sheets; for we have really met with so much kindness and hospitality here, as to make us almost forget the heat.

The principal trade is carried on by Banians[124] and Rajaputs,[125] (as they are called, tho' I cannot yet tell why) who come here from India—make comfortable little fortunes and return. A family of the former, consisting of three brothers, named George, has shewn us every possible attention ever since we landed, and the Chevalier de St. Lubin,[126] a French gentleman, of elegant manners and superior information, has treated us, in the most sumptuous style. It is whispered among the English here, that Mons De St. L— has been on a mission from the French Court to Hyder Ally, for the express purpose of sowing the seeds of discord between him, and the English; and that he has to a great degree succeeded; how far this is true, we cannot yet say, but so intirely was Mr. Fuller, one of our passengers, persuaded of the fact, that he just now proposed we should arrest the Chevalier, who is about to proceed in a day or two to Europe. How far Mr. F— may be politically right, I cannot tell; but my heart revolted at the idea of receiving every mark of attention from a man one hour, and on bare suspicion, making him a prisoner the next; and most truly did I rejoice when this scheme was overruled. There should be very sufficient reasons for conduct, so despotic and apparently ungrateful, and we certainly were not in possession of documents to authorise such a procedure. I am much better pleased that this gentleman should return peaceably to his native country, and forward my letters to you, which he has promised on his *honour* to do, and to secure them amongst his private papers.—I might have written twice as much if I chose.

And now my dear Friends, I must again bid you adieu. I trust my next accounts will be more pleasant, than this sad detail must prove, and that I shall meet letters at Calcutta, with good news of you all. My heart aches with thinking of the distance between us; but after surmounting so many difficulties and happily escaping from so many dangers; I feel inspired with hope for the future.

Ever most affectionately your's
E. F.

LETTER XI.

On Board the Nathalia at Sea.

28th October 1779.

My Dear Friends,

I wrote you from Mocha, in date the 15th September, by the Chevalier de St. Lubin who has most solemnly engaged to forward my letter, and I trust will keep his word.

We have now been six weeks at sea, and in the course of a few days hope to reach Calicut. Our passage across the Indian Ocean, we found very pleasant: the Monsoon being against us,[127] made it tedious, but no boisterous seas had we to contend with, as in the Mediterranean:—all has been calm, easy and free from alarm of every kind hitherto; fortunate indeed may we deem ourselves in having experienced such fine weather; for our ship is not half laden and has not Cargo enough to keep her steady. You will now expect me to say some thing of those with whom we are cooped up, but my account will not be very satisfactory, although sufficiently interesting to us—to begin then.

The woman, of whom I entertained some suspicion from the first, is I am now credibly informed, one of the very lowest creatures taken off the streets in London;[128] she is so *perfectly* depraved in disposition, that her supreme delight consists in rendering everybody around her, miserable.—It would be doing her too much honour to stain my paper with a detail of the various artifices she daily practices to that end.—Her pretended husband having been in India before, and giving himself many airs, is looked upon as a person of mighty consequence, whom nobody chooses to offend; therefore Madam has full scope to exercise her mischievous talents, wherein he never controuls her—not but that he perfectly understands how to make himself feared; coercive measures are *some times* resorted to; it is a common expression of the lady. "Lord bless you, if I did such, or such a thing, Tulloh would make no more to do, but knock me down like an ox." I frequently amuse myself with examining their countenances, where ill nature has fixed her Empire so firmly, that I scarcely believe either of them ever smiled unless maliciously. Miss Howe's description of Solmes, in Clarissa Harlowe,[129] recurs to me as admirably suiting this *amiable* pair—to that I refer you.

Chenu, the Captain, is a mere "Jack in office;"[130] being unexpectedly raised to that post from second mate, by the death of poor Capt. Vanderfield and his chief officer on the *fatal* Desert, is become from this circumstance so insolent and overbearing, that every one detests him. Instead of being ready to accommodate every person with the few necessaries left by the plundering Arabs, he constantly appropriates them to himself. "Where's the Captain's silver spoon? God bless my soul. Sir, you have got my chair, must you be seated before the captain? What have you done with the Captain's glass?" and a great deal more of the same kind; but this may serve as a specimen. And altho' the wretch half starves us, he frequently makes comparisons between *his* table, and that of an Indiaman, which we dare not contradict while in his power; tell me now, should you not doat on three such companions for a long voyage?—but I have a fourth who at least, merits to be added to the triumvirate; his name John Hare, Esqr., Barrister at Law,[131] a man of the very first fashion I assure you, and who would faint at the thought of any thing Plebeian. Taylor was one day shewing him a very handsome silver hilted sword, which he greatly admired, till chancing to cast his eye on the scabbard he read "Royal Exchange." "Take your sword" said he, "its surprizing a man of your sense should commit such an error; for fifty guineas I would not have a City name on any article of *my* dress; now St. James's or Bond street, has a *delicious* sound, don't you think so my dear friend?"—Now would any one suppose this fine gentleman's father was in trade, and he himself brought up in that very City, he effects to despise? very true nevertheless—Quadrille[132] he would not be thought to know; it is only played by the wives and daughters of Tradesmen, in country towns: I want to make you see him; figure to yourself a little mortal, his body constantly bent in a rhetorical attitude, as if addressing the Court, and his face covered with scorbutic blotches.[133] Happily from an affectation of singularity, he always wears spectacles. I say happily, as they serve to conceal the most odious pair of little white eyes mine ever beheld. What Butler says of Hudibras—that

"he could not ope
His mouth, but out there flew a trope,"[134]

may literally be applied to this Heaven-born Orator, who certainly outdoes all I ever heard, in the use of overstrained compliments and far-fetched allusions. But with all those oddities, were he only a good-natured harmless simpleton, one might pity him. At first he took so much pains to ingratiate himself with us, that he became a sort of favorite;—so many confessions of superior abilities in Mr. Fay—such intreaties to spare him, when they should practise in the Courts together,—a studied attention to me in the *minutest* article—effectually shielded him from suspicion, till his end was answered, of raising a party against us, by means of that vile woman, who was anxious to triumph over me; especially as I have been repeatedly compelled (for the Honour of the Sex) to censure her swearing, and indecent behaviour. I have therefore little comfort to look forward to, for the remainder of the voyage.

It is, however, only justice to name Mr. Taylor as an amiable, tho' melancholy companion, and Mr. Manesty[135] an agreeable young man, under twenty, going out as a writer on the Bombay Establishment, from whom I always receive the most respectful attention. Mr. Fuller, is a middle aged man; it is easy to see, that he has been accustomed to genteel society. How different *his* manners from those of H—! Poor man he has, it seems, fallen into the hands of sharpers,[136] and been completely pillaged. He has the finest dark eyes, and one of the most intelligent countenances I ever met with. His trip to Bengal is, I doubt, a last resource. May it prove successful. I have no enmity towards him; for though he has joined the other party, it is evidently with reluctance. Mr. Moreau a musician, going out to India to exercise his profession, is very civil and attentive.

Dissentions have run very high on board. The very day after we sailed from Mocha, a sudden quarrel arose between the Captain, and H— the Barrister;[137] on which the ship was ordered about, and they were going ashore in a great hurry to decide it; but by the interposition of friends, they were prevailed upon to curb their wrath, 'till their arrival at Calicut, as in case of an accident, no officer remained to supply Chenu's place. About a month after, they were reconciled; and so ended this doughty affair.

I had almost forgotten to mention Pierot, the purser[138] of the ship—a lively, well informed little Frenchman,—full of anecdotes and always prepared with a repartée; in short, the *soul* of the party. He sings an excellent song, and has as many tricks as a monkey. I cannot help smiling at his sallies, though they are frequently levelled at me; for he is one of my most virulent persecutors. Indeed, such is our general line of conduct; for, having early discovered the confederacy, prudence determined us to go mildly on, seemingly blind to what it was beyond our power to remedy. Never intermeddling in their disputes, all endeavours to draw us into quarrels are vainly exerted—: indeed I despise them too much to be angry.

During the first fortnight of our voyage my foolish complaisance stood in my way at table; but I soon learnt our genteel maxim was "catch as catch can,"[139]— the longest arm fared best; and you cannot imagine what a good scrambler I am become,—a dish once seized, it is my care, to make use of my good fortune: and now provisions running very short, we are grown quite savages; two or three of us perhaps fighting for a bone; for there is no respect of persons. The wretch of a captain wanting our passage money for nothing, refused to lay in a sufficient quantity of stock; and if we do not soon reach our Port, what must be the consequence, Heaven knows.

After meals I generally retire to my cabin, where I find plenty of employment, having made up a dozen shirts for Mr. F— out of some cloth, I purchased at Mocha, to replace part of those stolen by the Arabs—Sometimes I read French and Italian, and study Portugueze. I likewise prevailed on Mr. Fay to teach me short-hand; in consequence of the airs H— gave himself because he was master of this art, and had taught his sisters to correspond *with* him in it. The matter was very easily accomplished—in short I discovered abundant methods of making my time pass usefully, and not disagreeably. How often since, in this situation have I blessed God, that he has been pleased to endow me with a mind, capable of furnishing its own amusement, in despite of every means used to discompose it.

4th November.—We are now in sight of the Malabar hills, and expect to reach Calicut either this evening, or to-morrow; I shall conclude this letter, and send it under charge of Mr. Manesty, to forward it from Bombay. I am in tolerable health, and looking with a longing eye, towards Bengal, from whence I trust my next will be dated. The climate seems likely to agree very well with me, I do not at all mind the heat, nor does it affect either my spirits, or my appetite.

I remain
Ever affectionately your's,
E. F.

LETTER XII.

CALICUT,[140] 12th February, 1780.

MY DEAR FRIENDS

It was my determination never to write to you, during the state of dreadful Captivity[141] in which we have long been held, but having hopes of a release, think I may now venture to give you some account of our sufferings, which have been extreme, both in body and mind, for a period of fifteen weeks, which we have spent in wretched confinement, totally in the power of Barbarians.

I must premise that, such is the harrassing confusion of my mind, and the weakness of my nerves, that I can merely offer you a simple statement of facts, and even that must necessarily be incorrect; for incessant anxiety and constant anticipation of more intolerable evils, have totally unhinged my faculties. God knows whether I may ever recover them; at present all is confused and clouded.—Reflections on the importance of our speedy arrival in Bengal, which so many circumstances had contributed to prevent, and the apprehension lest our delay should afford time to raise serious obstacles against Mr. Fay's admission into the Court, as an advocate, had long been as so many daggers, piercing my vitals: add to this the heart-breaking thought what immense tracts lie between me and those dear *dear* friends, whose society alone can render me completely happy. Even were the most brilliant success to crown our future views, never could I know comfort, 'till the blessed moment arrive, when I shall clasp you all to my fond heart, without fear of a future separation; except by that stroke, to which we must all submit; and which has been suspended over my head as by a single hair.[142] I trust that I have been spared, to afford me the means of proving more substantially than by words, how inestimably precious, absence has made you in my sight.—Well may it be said that, the deprivation of a blessing enhances its value; for my affection rises now to a pitch of Enthusiasm, of which I knew not that my heart was capable;—but which has been its consolation, amidst all the horrors of imprisonment and sickness: no congenial mind to which I could declare my feelings, sure of meeting with sympathizing affection, as I so delightfully experienced in the company of my beloved sister—But I forget that all this while you are impatient to hear how we fell into so distressing a situation; take then the particulars.

I told you in my last that we expected to reach Calicut very shortly, and accordingly next day, on the (to me ever memorable) 5th November, we anchored in the Roads, and to our great concern saw no English flag up.[143] In a short time we were surrounded by vessels which approached us with an air of so much hostility that we became seriously alarmed,—with one exception; this was the redoubtable

Mrs. Tulloh. She had frequently, in the course of the voyage, expressed a violent desire for some species of adventure,—a passion for some romantic danger, on which she could descant hereafter; and far from congratulating herself on having arrived at Grand Cairo, when the Caravan was setting off in safety, she ever expressed a wish, that *she* had been present during that period of terror and confusion, of which she envied us the participation. On hearing Chenu declare that he feared he must make a *shew* of engaging, notwithstanding the deficiencies under which he laboured, and which evidently rendered the idea of resistance on our part, a *mere* farce; since we had neither arms, ammunition, nor men on board sufficient to abide the contest, she positively insisted on having a chair brought upon deck, in which she was determined to sit, and see the engagement; observing that, it was the next best thing to escaping from shipwreck.—Having no ambition to play the Heroine in this way, I resolved on going below, and exerting, (should it be necessary) my limited abilities in assisting Mr. Taylor, who had agreed to officiate as Surgeon—not feeling myself inclined to brave horrors of this nature, for the mere love of exhibition. Most probably had the matter become serious, she would not have been permitted to indulge her fancy; but by degrees our suspicious visitants sheered off, without venturing to commence an attack, seeing us apparently so well prepared to resist them; and we flattered ourselves that our fears had been altogether groundless.

The next morning H— and two others, going on shore to reconnoitre brought back intelligence, that we might all be safe in the Danish Factory, on condition of our passing for Danes;—as a misunderstanding actually subsisted between Hyder Ally and the English. Mr. Passavant, the Danish Consul,[144] had been on board meanwhile, and given us pretty nearly the same information, and from others we soon learnt a circumstance, which confirmed our apprehension, that some mischief was brewing,—this was the departure of Mr. Freeman, the English Consul, who had left the place some weeks before, taking with him his furniture and effects,—a positive proof that he supposed hostilities were about to commence; as it has been found a common procedure in these cases, for Asiatic Princes to begin a War, by imprisoning the Embassadors or Residents, of course, a wise man will fly when the storm lowers.

Now our most worthy fellow-passengers, had privately agreed to continue their journey by land, and rejoiced in the opportunity of leaving us in the lurch:—they therefore accepted Mr. Passavant's invitation immediately, without consulting us. At first this behaviour affected me a good deal and I resolved to follow them;—Mr. Fay concurring in opinion.—But on calm reflection, we judged it most prudent to learn what reception *they* met with, before *we* ventured on such slippery ground. On Sunday Chenu dined on board; and appeared very earnest for our quitting the Ship: but we did not attend to his persuasions. The Gunner who had charge of the vessel was a very respectable man, and we had lately held many conversations with him; he had a vile opinion of the Captain, believing that money would tempt him to commit *any* act, however atrocious; and had resolved in case an armed force was seen approaching the ship, to cut and run down to Cochin, with all the sail he could set,—but alas! before Chenu left us this day, he ordered all the yards to be struck, saying he should stay six weeks. This was doubtless done to frighten us, and to induce us to go on shore; but having taken our resolution, we were not to be moved; especially as he dropped some dark hints, respecting the situation of those, who *were* there; in so much that we had reason to think our only chance of escaping imprisonment, was by remaining where we were. Meantime intelligence reached us from various quarters, that disputes ran high between the Captain and passengers, about the remaining half of their passage money. As they proposed leaving the ship there, he demanded payment; which they refused till they should arrive in Bengal.

On the 8th came Lewis, Hare's servant, for his own clothes;—he brought news that a challenge had again passed between his master and Chenu, on the occasion of his master's trunks being stopped for the passage money—he left them on the point of deciding it when he came off. You may suppose we became exceedingly anxious to learn the event, but had soon other matters to engross our attention.

During the three days we staid here, after every one else departed, boats full of people, were continually coming on board by permission of our *worthy* Captain, under pretence of viewing the ship,—we thought this rather odd; but John the Gunner being, as I observed before, a prudent steady man, we trusted to his discretion. About four, on Monday afternoon, I was sitting in the round-house at work, when a large boat came along side, with *more* than twenty *armed men* in her;—one of them shewed a written *chit*[145] as he called it from Chenu; notwithstanding which, John insisted on their leaving their arms behind them—this, they at length complied with, and were then permitted to enter. I ran down half frightened to Mr. Fay, who was reading in our cabin, and told him the affair. "Pho," said he, it is impossible they should mean any harm: are we not under the protection of the Danish flag?" this silenced me at once, and he went upon deck to see the issue. All this while our visitors feigned to be mighty ignorant, and inquisitive, peeping into every hole and corner, as if, they never saw such a sight in their lives—purposely dallying on the time 'till just dark, when to my great joy they departed. A heavy squall came on, which they sheltered from under the ship's stern, there another boat met them, and after some parley, they both (as I thought) went away.

But in a few minutes down came Mr. Fay "you must not be alarmed, said he, I have news to tell you:—we are to have a hundred and fifty sepoys on board tonight!" Seapoys:[146] for what! "Why the English are coming to attack Calicut[147]— Chenu has promised Sudder Khan, the Governor, his assistance, who has sent these troops for our defence"—"Oh Mr. F—" replied I, "this is a very improbable story, for God's sake suffer not these people to enter the ship, if you can avoid it; otherwise we are ruined. I see plainly this is a second Suez business;"[148] (for by the same treacherous pretext they gained possession of the ships there) and at *that* instant, all that those unfortunate men suffered, coming fresh into my mind, I really thought I should have fainted—Seeing that I was rendered more uneasy by being kept in suspense, he now acknowledged, that under favour of the night, a large party, headed by a Capt. Ayres,[149] an Englishman in Hyder's service, had already made good their entrance. The Commander had indeed related the above nonsensical tale to our Gunner, as an excuse for his proceeding; but did not seem himself to expect, it would gain belief: however being nearly destitute of Arms and Ammunition (the Arabs had taken care of that) what could we do, but recommend ourselves to the Divine Protection? which I may truly say, was never more earnestly solicited by me.—When the redoubtable Captain Ayres had settled every thing upon Deck, he favoured us with his company below.—As this Gentleman is in great power, and had a large share in the subsequent transactions, I must here devote a few moments to giving you a little sketch of his history.

He was born in London, and at the usual age bound apprentice to a saddler; but being a lad of spirit, and associating with other promising youths of similar talents, and courage, he soon found an employment more suited to his active genius; in a word, he became a Gentleman Collector on the *Highway*.[150] This post he maintained several years, and if we may credit what he relates when in a boasting humour, performed many notable exploits; it is true he sometimes got inclosed within the hard gripe of the Law, but always found means to liberate himself, from it, 'till on one unlucky trial, proofs ran so strong against him, that in spite of money and friends (which in his case were *never* wanting) he was *Capitally convicted*; though, afterwards, pardoned on condition of transportation for life—This induced him to enlist for the East Indies, where he exercised his former profession, and was twice imprisoned at Calcutta on suspicion; but having acted cautiously, nothing positive appeared against him: so by way of changing the scene, he was draughted off for Madras, where finding his favourite business rather slack, and his pay insufficient to support him without it, our hero determined on deserting to Hyder Ally, which resolution he soon found means to put in practice,—carrying with him two horses, arms, accoutrements, wearing apparel, and every thing else of value he could lay hands on, to a pretty considerable amount. This shew of property, (no matter how acquired) gave him consequence with Hyder, who immediately promoted him to the rank of Captain. Being a thorough paced villain, he has during these seven years taken the lead in every species of barbarity.— He even advised his General, who is Governor of this Province,[151] to massacre all the natives by way of quelling a rebellion which had arisen.—The least punishment inflicted by him was cutting off the noses and ears of those miserable wretches, whose hard fate subjected them to his tyranny. In short a volume would not contain half the enormities perpetrated by this disgrace to human nature— but to proceed.

At sight of him I shuddered involuntarily, though at that time ignorant of his real character, such an air of wickedness and ferocity overspread his features. The sergeant who accompanied him was (always excepting his master) the most horrid looking creature, I verily believe, in existence: from such another pair the Lord defend me! Ayres told me, with the utmost indifference that the people at the Factory had all been fighting duels:—that Mr. Passavant the Danish Chief, had sent for a guard to separate them; and that the Governor finding the ship had no owner, as all these disputes arose about dividing the spoil, had thought proper to take possession of her in the *Nabob's* name,[152] until matters were inquired into; after which he *faithfully* promised to restore her, without the least embezzlement—the love of *Justice* alone inducing him thus to act.

Though we perceived the fallacy of these pretences, yet as it was useless to argue with the vile instrument of oppression, we only requested to be set free on shore with our effects. This he engaged for, and even offered to take *charge* of any *valuables* or *money*—You may be sure we pleaded poverty; declaring that except our clothes, (which could be no object in a country where so few are worn) a guinea would purchase all we possessed; in the mean time we requested a guard to protect our persons from insult.—Having pledged his *Honour* for our security, the captain retired. You will believe that sleep did not visit our eyelids *that* night: The fright had disordered me so much, that a violent retching came on, succeeded by a strong fever, which occasioned dreadful pains in my limbs. In the midst of these excruciating tortures, I heard Ayres tell his Serjeant, that orders were come to plunder the Ship, and make all the officers prisoners in the Round-house.

Can any thing be imagined more distressing, than my situation without the means of relief,—no possibility of obtaining advice, and no female to whom I could look for succour or assistance. This was about two in the morning,—these words sounded like the signal of death in my ears. Immediately a party of armed men surrounded our Cabin, and demanded entrance. I clung round my husband and begged for God's sake that he would not admit them; for what could be expected from such wretches but the most shocking treatment. All this while there was such a noise without, of breaking and tearing, to come at their plunder, as convinced me that should we once lose sight of our little property, *every thing was lost:* at first they were pacified on being told that I was asleep, but soon grew out of patience, brandished their scymitears[153] and one man who spoke a little English, threatened with horrible execrations to murder us, if we did not *instantly* comply with their demands, and open the door.—Mr. Fay drew his sword on this declaration, swearing solemnly that he would run the first man through the body, who should presume to enter his wife's apartment. His air of resolution and menacing actions, had their effect so far, as to prevent them from breaking open the door; the top of which being sashed, I beheld through it, their terrific countenances, and heard them incessantly calling "*ao, ao,*" (in English come). This word has made an impression on me, which is indescribable. I can never hear it pronounced on the most common occasion, without trembling: but to return—Mr. Fay now intreated me to rise if possible, being fearful he could not keep them much longer at bay. I endeavoured to comply; but the agonising pains I suffered, and the extreme weakness brought on by fever, rendered it impossible for me to stand upright; there was however no remedy—so by degrees I got my clothes on (I recollect now that I must have been above an hour employed in this business.) Through the glass door, I could see the villains outside, use menacing gestures and urge me to make haste,—vowing vengeance on me if I kept them longer waiting.

Expecting a strict search and being desirous of rescuing something from the general wreck, Mr. Fay contrived to conceal our watches in my hair, having first stopped their going by sticking pins in the wheels; and the little money we possessed, and what small articles I could take without exciting suspicion, were concealed about my person. Thus equipped I crawled out, *bent double*, and in an instant, the Cabin was filled with Seapoys. I must here pause, and intreat my dear sister to imagine herself in my situation at that *dreadful* moment; for no language can I find, that would do justice to my feelings.

But when I came on deck, the scene which presented itself would have appalled the stoutest heart;—mine already weakened by grief and apprehension could not withstand it. A sudden burst of tears alone saved me from fainting. The poor sailors were so distracted, that many of them could scarcely be restrained from jumping over board to escape slavery;—sometimes crying for their wages, and asking the Officers to pay them; who incapable of affording any consolation, walked about like men bereft of reason: no wonder, since this fatal event would, to say the least, occasion them the loss of twelve month's pay, exclusive of their private ventures.

We were immediately ordered on shore, together with the carpenter and ship's steward;—we demanded our baggage, but in vain; at length having represented the necessity of a change of linen, a person was sent down with me, in whose presence I put up a few common things, in a handkerchief, not being allowed to take any thing of value; but having laid out a silk gown the day before, to put on in case I went ashore, I begged hard for that, and obtained it; though my husband was not suffered to take a second coat, or even to change that he had on. Our beds were likewise refused, lest they should contain valuables; and upon deck the bundle was again examined in search of hidden treasure,—but finding nothing, they, contrary to my expectations, searched no further; but permitted us to leave the vessel unmolested; except that they had the cruelty to toss several half extinguished *Blue lights*[154] into the boat, the smoke of which, from the rancid oil and abominable rags used in their composition, almost stifled me.—At this time it rained hard, and continued to do so the whole day, which forced me to creep under the shelter of a kind of half deck, where I sat, bent double, for two long *long* hours, and then a remarkably high surf, prevented large boats from landing,—we had no remedy but to go into a canoe, scarcely bigger than a butcher's tray, half full of water,—so that we reached the shore dripping wet—Compare this account with the many chearful and flattering conversations we have held together on the subject of my arrival in *India*. What a striking difference! It is true we were in the hands of the natives; but little did I imagine that, any power on this Continent, however independent, would have dared to treat *English* subjects with such cruelty, as we experienced from them.

As if to aggravate our miseries by every species of insult, they compelled us to walk above a mile thro' a heavy sand, surrounded by all the mob of Calicut, who seemed to take pleasure in beholding the distress of white people, those constant objects of their envy and detestation.—When we had proceeded about half way, our Guards detained us nearly an hour, in an open Square, till the Governor's pleasure should be known. He sat all the while smoking his Hooka,[155] and looking down upon us; when having sufficiently feasted his eyes, he ordered us to be taken to the English Factory—How I dragged on my weary aching limbs, I know not. The rain still poured and as we went, a lad who had deserted from Madras, and was then a serjeant in Hyder's service, seeing a country-woman in such distress, offered to procure me an umbrella, but could not prevail on the barbarians to stop, while he ran for it, though he was their officer. I thanked the poor lad for his kind intention and Mr. Fay insisted that I should take his hat, while he walked on bare-headed to the place of our confinement.—But here I cannot describe the horror which seized me on finding, we were totally in the power of wretches, who, for, aught I knew, intended to strip and murder us: why else were we sent to an empty house? not a single chair to sit on, or any other bed than the floor. These were my heart-breaking reflections, as I threw myself in despair on a window seat, worn out with fatigue and want of nourishment; without means of procuring even a draught of water to assuage my thirst, which grew excessive; for the offer of a bribe would have been dangerous.

In this miserable condition we remained till two o'clock, when Mr. Passavant having heard of our misfortune, sent us a dinner; but his messenger had very great difficulty in obtaining admittance, with even this temporary relief. From him we learnt that, the other passengers were hitherto unconfined, but expected every moment to be made prisoners. After Mr. Fay had dined, (for my anxiety continued so great, that exhausted as I was, I could not touch a morsel of what was brought) I besought him to look round for some place into which I might crawl, and lie down unseen by the Seapoys, that guarded us. He was averse to this, lest they should imagine that we were seeking to escape, and make that a pretext for ill usage:—but perceiving that the sight of them prevented me from taking that repose, so necessary to recruit my poor worn out frame, he complied with my request, and having discovered a lumber-room leading out of the Veranda which surrounded the house, he assisted me into it—Here with my little bundle for a pillow, I stretched myself on the floor, amidst dirt and rubbish, and enjoyed a fine sleep of more than three hours, when I awoke completely refreshed and entirely free from the dreadful tortures, which had racked me the whole night.—I did not even feel any symptoms of fever.

Surprized and thankful for the change, I joyfully went down to Mr. Fay, declaring that I would continue to make use of the lumber-room to sleep in, and as Mr. Passavant had, during my nap, sent me a rattan couch, tho' by the bye without either mattress, pillow, or musquito curtains, I was just going to have it conveyed there, when the place was found to be swarming with venomous reptiles; perhaps a hundred scorpions and centipedes—happily I slept too soundly to feel them, and I remained unmolested; but had I moved hand or foot, what might have been the consequence!

The next morning we had a visit from Mr. Hare; less, it appeared, to condole with us on such unexampled suffering, than to embrace the occasion of displaying his own eloquence; for which having a very strong passion, it was no wonder, if he thought the misfortunes of others proper subjects to expatiate on. Mounting his rhetorical hobbyhorse,[156] the Orator harangued a long while, though to little purpose, endeavouring to turn our situation into ridicule;—offered to convey letters for us to Bengal;—pretended to be in raptures with the fine view of the Sea from our Veranda, which I hinted to him he might still have time to admire at his leisure, though he affected to be certain of leaving Calicut in a few hours. At length he concluded, by advising me to address a *tender* memorial to Hyder Ally, whose general character for gallantry, would not admit of his refusing any request made by a *fair* Lady. This was wonderfully witty in the speaker's opinion, as you may conceive, how *fair* the Lady in question looked. How a man could break a jest on a creature so bowed down by affliction, I know not: but I envy not his feelings.

I forgot to tell you that, the duel between the *Captain*, and the *Orator*, was prevented by the guard, doubtless to the regret of these heroes. It seems the day they went on shore, Ayres accompanied by another Captain of a pretty similar description, named West, made Mr. Passavant a visit, to look at the strangers.[157] Now as it was of the utmost importance, that they should remain undiscovered by such dangerous people, and as their visitants, though illiterate, were sufficiently acute, all perceived immediately the necessity of being guarded;—accordingly they, every one spoke French, and this, together with their long wide coats, and *preposterous* hats, which had just then become fashionable in England, effectually shielded them from suspicion; when behold, a sudden fit of Patriotism, aided by an irresistible fondness for exhibition, rendered the great Mr. H— incapable of persevering in deception. "What" exclaimed he, "shall *Englishmen* harbour distrust of each other! perish the ignoble idea!—be the consequences what they may, I will no longer restrain myself from embracing my beloved country-men." At the conclusion of this heroic speech, "Suiting the action to the words"[158] advancing theatrically, he grasped the hand of Ayres, and shook it, with such violence as if he meant to demonstrate the excess of his joy and confidence, by dislocating the shoulder of his newly acquired friend.

The most unreserved intimacy, immediately took place between these congenial souls, and it is asserted that unable to keep any secret from his bosom confidant, H— was really so mad, (I may say, so cruel) as absolutely to acknowledge the ship to be English property. I could not have believed that his folly and imprudence would carry him so far; thus much is, however, undoubtedly fact, that the man in the spectacles is constantly pointed out, as the author of every mischief which followed.—It is surprizing how often we find weakness and malignity united, or rather let us say, that providence has thus ordained it, for the benefit of mankind. Probably the former induced H— to injure the party to which he had attached himself:—the latter undoubtedly led him to visit us, for he could not conceal his exultation at the circumstance of our accidental capture in the Vessel, seeming to involve us *exclusively* in her fate. The unfeeling wretch availed himself of this to lay a scheme, that had it been adequately seconded, must have brought on our destruction.

Ayres was first prevailed on by large presents, to dissuade the Governor from confining *them*, and that point gained, he pushed their interest forward thus, "These gentlemen" said he, "have no concern here of any kind; besides, as they are people of the highest consequence, their detention would bring half India on our back, so take my advice and let them go." "Well, but replies Sudder Khan,[159] what must I do with my prisoners?" "Oh keep them by all means" replies *Beelzebub*,[160] "the man is a stout fellow, and after a little breaking in, will make a most excellent soldier: send him and his wife up the country, there feed them on dry rice,[161] he will soon be glad to enlist I warrant you. The chief of the other party Mr. H— is a brother lawyer, so you need not fear, but he will be happy enough to get rid of him; indeed he owned as much to me privately, and pledged his honour that no ill consequence could possibly arise from the transaction;—the person in question not being of sufficient importance for the English to reclaim him solemnly; especially as he came out without leave." You will wonder how I came by all this information;[162] have patience, you shall know in time.

The Governor heard this argument calmly, promised fair, and acted so far agreeably to his professions that, while *we* were closely confined and miserably situated, our worthy fellow passengers enjoyed full liberty to walk about, and amuse themselves as they pleased.—This procedure could not fail to vex us excessively, though we were then ignorant of its real cause, and whenever we ventured to expostulate on our unreasonably harsh treatment with Ayres or any other, who chanced to call, the only answer we could obtain was, with a shrug of affected compassion, "why did you stay on board! nothing can be done for you *now*, you must abide the event." These insinuations created fears, that a distinction would really be made in our eventual disposal, as much to our disadvantage, as the present state of things, but we had no remedy—all avenues to relief were closed.

I think I told you that, our watches were concealed in my hair, being secured with pins to prevent them from going; one of the pins however came out, at the very time I was set on shore. Never shall I forget what a terrible sensation the ticking of the watch caused! I think had it continued long, I must completely have lost my senses; for I dared not remove it, from a fear of worse consequences; but happily it stopped of itself. When we were fixed in our prison Mr. Fay took these watches, (we had three you know) and all the money we had power to secure in chequins,[163] which are of easy conveyance (about twenty-five pounds) and putting them into his glove, hid them in a snug place, as he thought, about the Verandah. The day after we were taken prisoners, a most dreadful hurricane of rain and wind came in, (it was the breaking up of the monsoon) and next morning we found to our extreme grief, that the place where Mr. Fay had concealed our treasure, to which alone we could look for the means of escape, was entirely blown down; and no vestige of our little property remaining. Mr. Fay was in despair from the first; but after he had told me, I searched diligently all round, but in vain. At length it struck me, from the direction in which the wind blew, that if I could make my way into an inclosure, at the back of the house, it might possibly be found there. The seapoys guarded the front, but there being only one door backwards, they seldom took the trouble of going round. I did not tell Mr. Fay of my scheme, as there was nothing he opposed so strongly, as the appearance of seeking to escape; but when he was completely absorbed in contemplating this new misfortune, I stole to the back door. There was a large lock and key inside and to my surprize, when I had turned this, my passage was clear to the stairs, leading to the inclosure; and not a soul in sight. The grass was excessively high and wet, but I struggled to make my way through it and waded about, determined at least not to leave an inch unexplored. Imagine my joy, when in the midst of a deep tuft I found the old glove, with all its contents safe, and uninjured. What a treasure it seemed! how many are there who never felt so much true delight on receiving a magnificent fortune, as we experienced in again beholding this sheet anchor of our hopes, thus unexpectedly restored.

But alas! the little unlooked for liberty I had regained, was too tempting *not* to be enjoyed again; and a day or two afterwards as I was walking about in the grass, I espied a seapoy coming round. I was not certain that he saw me, so I endeavoured to reach the house unobserved. At the moment I turned round to fasten the heavy door, he ran to it, pushing it against me, with such violence that the large key which had unfortunately a very long shank, was by this means struck directly against my right breast, and gave me the most excruciating pain. I fainted through excessive agony, and was with difficulty recovered. Much I fear the consequences of this accident will embitter my future life. Having no other nurse than my poor husband, who was not only ignorant of what ought to be done, but totally without the necessaries for any kind of emollient application,—my case was truly distressing; so that even Ayres who chanced to call, expressed some concern for me, and sent plenty of milk which I used as an embrocation with success. I believe he punished the seapoy for his insolence, but this could not repair the mischief.

At the very time when this painful variety took place in the cheerless monotony of our prison days, the cruel designers who had assisted in dooming us to this wretched abode, fell completely into the pit which they had digged for us.—The evening before Ayres Tulloh and Hare had called on us together, the former was (according to his *general* policy) endeavouring to discover whether we had any concealed property; on which I exclaimed "Captain Ayres how should we have any thing left, except the baggage in the vessel, which is of little value? as the Arabs pillaged us to the utmost of their power; we were altogether a set of poor creatures when we came to Calicut; and you are well aware we have received nothing since." "Answer for yourself Mrs. Fay" cried Hare, "for my *own* part I feel happy in saying, that, I am *not* poor, I have property, *valuable* property and shall not shrink from avowing that I possess it." I marked the eye of Ayres during this bombastic speech, and have since found, that I was not deceived in its expression.

Sudder Khan induced by this and other similar stories, which the passengers had told of their own consequence, determined to frighten them into the payment of a large sum of money. Accordingly next morning (the 13th) he sent a large party of seapoys to the Danish Factory, who peremptorily demanded them as the

Nabob's prisoners.[164] Mr. Passavant at first refused, but on their threatening to fire into his house, was constrained to yield to this outrageous violation of the most sacred rights, and delivered his guests to slavery. God forbid that I should, generally speaking, be capable of rejoicing in the miseries of my fellow creatures, even where they merit punishment, but I must own, (blame me if you will) that for a short time I *did* feel satisfaction in this stroke of retributive justice, in as far as regarded the Tullohs, and Hare, for the vile conduct of these people, and the malevolence of their dispositions, had steeled my heart against them.

It was certainly a curious sight to behold them, after all their airs of superiority reduced to take up their residence with us, whose situation, while singular, was the object of their ridicule and contempt. The scene was however now changed; although *they*, like many others in the world, were able to support their neighbour's misfortunes with stoical firmness, and even render them a source of amusement, each readily discovered when personally attacked by a similar calamity, that close imprisonment is by no means a proper subject on which to exercise wit, and that people when in distress are not precisely in the humour for relishing the pleasantry of others on their troubles. Tulloh fortunately understood Moors,[165] which is the general language among the military throughout India;— by this means he got his trunks on shore the day after the seizure, and saved them from the violent storm, which came on next morning, wherein every one imagined the ship must have been wrecked. How we wished to see her drive on shore! especially when Sudder Khan the Governor who is Hyder's brother-in-law, was seen walking about in great perturbation on the beach anxiously watching the vessel, praying to Mahomet, and from time to time, casting up the sand towards Heaven with earnest invocation and entreaties, that she might be spared, as a present to the great Hyder; very probably fearing that some blame might attach to him in case she were lost.

As it happened, however, all things went wrong for us—The cabin and steerage where our trunks had been placed were soon filled with water, and every thing, such as books, wearing apparel, beds, with laces, buckles, rings &c. was either stolen or totally spoiled. These latter I might have saved, when we were brought on shore, but unfortunately the trunk, which contained my clothes, was just *without* the cabin-door, and two of the wretches who watched us sat on it, so that I could not remove an article. This disaster left us nothing except our lives to be anxious about—why do I say anxious! since life itself on the terms we held it, was hardly worth preserving. The other passenger's baggage was injured but not like our's; for we, not being favorites, had been forced to keep *our* packages at hand, during the voyage, as we had no one to get them up when wanted, whereas the rest had theirs stowed away in the hold and consequently little damage befel them.

Many ships perished in this terrible hurricane. The St. Helena which left Mocha a week after us, met with it, and suffered so much that she was forced to put into Cochin, (a Danish settlement in Latitude 10) with the loss of her masts; and so greatly shattered besides, as to be compelled to undergo a thorough repair.—If this happened to a fine new vessel, one of the best sailors in India, what must have become of us, had we continued five days longer at Sea?—badly found in all respects, and worse manned; not half people enough to work the ship properly, even in good weather, was not this another hairsbreadth escape think you, though by a dreadful alternative? The ways of providence are inscrutable! But to revert to my main subject,—glad shall I be when it is concluded; for I detest matter of fact *writing*, almost as much as matter of fact conversation:—yet this story must be told in my own way, or not at all.

When the gale ceased, the whole cargo was landed and deposited in the Governor's warehouses, where he caused the Gentlemen's baggage to be opened, and like a child pleased with gewgaws,[166] every article which struck the eye, was instantly condemned as his booty. Poor Hare's trunks were stuffed with knickknacks like a Pedlar's box: judge then what agonies he appeared in, when the fatal moment of examination approached, lest they should become, as might be expected, objects of desire to the Governor.—Not a single tooth pick case, knife, or knee-buckle was produced, but what he declared had been received as a pledge of friendship from different relations; parents, brothers, sisters, male and female cousins, to the utmost verge of propinquity, all put in their claims with success. Tulloh serving as interpreter, until he was perfectly weary of the office; ashamed of pleading such trifling causes, and only deterred from throwing up his post, by the earnest entreaties of Hare, who continued stamping, exclaiming and fretting, as if his life depended on the issue. At last a small paper bundle fell into the searcher's hands, he then became outrageous. "For Heaven's sake, cried he my *dear* friend, (almost breathless with apprehension) Oh for Heaven's sake endeavour to preserve *this* parcel for me; should it be taken I am an *undone man*, for I shall never be able to replace the contents; let them take my clothes, my Law books, *every* thing, except my music books—all that I can yield without a sigh." Tulloh imagining that the contents must be of immense value to him from his extreme agitation, earnestly interceded for the parcel; but obtained it with great difficulty, as curiosity and avarice were awakened by perceiving the convulsive eagerness with which the owner petitioned for it.—The former was soon gratified and the latter consoled; for Hare tearing open the parcel discovered to the astonished spectators neither more, nor less, than an exquisite assortment of VENETIAN FIDDLE STRINGS!![167] But, ah! dire mischance! the remorseless waves, (which are neither respectors of persons or things) had pervaded this invaluable treasure and rendered it wholly useless; and to complete his misery the next thing that presented itself to the sad owner's eyes, was a most expensive and finely toned *Tenor violin*, purchased at Venice, and for which the precious strings were intended,—broken all to pieces! I leave you to form any ideas you may think proper on the subject of that extravagant sorrow, such a character was likely to exhibit—and pass on to matters more interesting.

The general introductory letter which, as you may recollect, Mr. Franco gave us at Leghorn, had remained in Mr. F—'s pocket book from that time, 'till we reached Calicut. We had been told that Isaac, the Jewish merchant,[168] who agreed to freight the Nathalia, and received £700 as earnest on that account, was *immensely* rich, and had great credit with Government, of which he held several large contracts for building ships &c. besides being a great favourite with Sudder Khan. Every one also, even Ayres, spoke highly of his general character. But our introduction to Mr. Baldwin had been productive of, or at least connected with so many misfortunes, that my confidence was lost, and I dreaded making further applications, lest similar events should ensue. This was very foolish reasoning you will say, and I am ready to acknowledge it, the only excuse to be made is, that my mind was weakened by calamity. However after Tulloh and the rest of these people joined us, our situation became, if possible, still more distressing and we anxiously sought every practicable mode of relief. Mr. F— therefore petitioned the Governor for leave to go out under a guard, which being granted, he immediately delivered his letter to Isaac, who seemed highly gratified at hearing from Mr. Franco whom he had personally known at Constantinople, when they were both young men, *above sixty* years ago: for Isaac is also considerably turned of eighty, and like him, enjoys full possession of his faculties, both bodily and mental, being equally remarkable for temperance and sobriety. Mr. F— could not speak to our strangely acquired friend except by an interpreter; so that no confidential conversation could take place. He was apparently touched with pity for our sufferings, especially on hearing how much I was afflicted with illness. My spirits were raised by the account my husband gave of his visit, and soon after his favourable report was confirmed, by my receiving a present brought to the Factory, by a servant, belonging to the benevolent Jew, and which in our situation was truly valuable, consisting of a catty[169] of fine tea, a tea-pot, and a tea-kettle. Although these things were expressly sent to me, yet Mrs. Tulloh and her party seized the last mentioned article, and forcibly kept it; so that I was forced to make my tea, by boiling it in my tea-pot. Ah my dear sister, I was at this time ill enough to be laid up on a sick bed, and carefully nursed, yet was I thankful for such food as I should once have loathed, and I still continued to lie on my rattan couch, without a pillow or any covering except my clothes, and surrounded by people whom my very heart sickened to behold.

I will here by way of relaxation transcribe a few passages from my Journal, as nothing happened for some time worthy of a particular recital; reserving to myself, however, the option of resuming the narrative style, whenever I shall deem it necessary.

14th November, 1779.

Mr. Fay was sent for, this morning, to the Governor, who asked him what he wanted? he replied, *Liberty*:—there was no observation made on this answer, nor can we conceive what Sudder Khan can mean by the detention of so many persons, who never bore arms. They gave Mr. Tulloh 30 rupees for our support. All we are able to procure is tough, lean, old beef, goat's flesh, and a not unpleasant rice cake, but too sweet to be palatable with meat; we preserve either with difficulty from our perpetual visitors the crows, having no cup-board or place to put our victuals in.—Of all existing creatures crows are surely the most voracious, and the most persevering—I have seen one with his eye fixed for a full half hour on a person, and the instant that person's eye was averted, pounce on the bread, or whatever had been prepared and bear away the prize. Mem.—Ayres is remarkably like these crows, he has exactly their *thievish* expression of countenance, and the form of his head resembles their's.

15th November, 1779.

The Gentlemen waited all day at the Governor's house, being promised their baggage, but he thought proper to disappoint them—received 10 rupees subsistence money.

18th November.

A most impudent message brought from the Governor, requiring all the gentlemen to enter into the Nabob's service; which they unanimously refused, with every mark of contempt, and were in consequence ordered to be more closely confined—One of Mr. Fay's trunks brought on shore containing wearing apparel, and law books, probably much damaged, yet certainly valuable to him, as he has *none* remaining. Made application for it but without success. Tulloh received 20 rupees.

20th November.

Received notice to prepare immediately to set off for Seringapatam, a large City about three hundred miles distant, where Hyder Ally usually resides—How can I support this journey over the mountains!—Mr. F— is about drawing up a petition, representing the bad state of my health, and entreating permission for me to proceed to Cochin. We hope to prevail on Isaac to present it.

21st November.

Discover that the journey to Seringapatam was merely a vile plot of the Governor's to put us off our guard, and thereby gain possession of what property had hitherto been concealed; thank God this feint miscarried. A letter reached us from Mr. O'Donnell, stating the arrival of the St. Helena at Cochin. He laments our misfortune and promises to take such methods as shall compel the Nabob to do us speedy and effectual justice. Heaven speed his endeavours; this life is horrible.

22d November.

The gentlemen waited five hours at the Governor's for their effects, but returned without them. He takes evident satisfaction in seeing them like slaves attendant on his *nod*—Five ships supposed to be English passed in front of our prison. How peculiarly distressing did I feel this sight!

23d November, 1779.

Mrs. Tulloh being taken ill of a fever, application was made to the Governor for medicines; but this happening to be a high festival, he, like the Pharisees in Scripture,[170] refused to profane it by doing good—Should the woman die in the interim what cares he?

24th November, 1779.

This morning got some medicines from the ship's chest—many flying reports of hostilities having actually commenced between Hyder Ally, and the English—should this really prove true, our fate will be sealed *for life*. Little did I think when pleading the cause of the Chevalier de St. Lubin at Mocha, that he had been raising a storm whose effects would so materially involve us. Mem.—The lady is well again.

28th November, 1779.

It is now certain that the Nayhirs[171] have laid siege to Tellicherry;[172] a settlement of our's about a degree to the northward; seven miles nearer lies Mahey[173] which the French held, 'till we took it from them in March last; but not finding it worth keeping, have since evacuated it, after dismantling the fortifications.

29th November, 1779.

Sudder Khan is about to march a thousand troops into Mahey, under pretence of resuming it in the Nabob's name, but every one guesses this to be merely a feint to cover his real intentions of privately assisting the Nayhirs;—should they succeed in their attack, Hyder will then throw off the mask and declare war; but if the English conquer, he will disavow the whole affair.

30th November.

I have now a lamentable tale to relate. We were this morning hurried away at a moments warning to the fort, crouded together in a horrid dark place scarcely twenty feet square, swarming with rats, and almost suffocating for want of air. Mr. and Mrs. Tulloh secured a small room to themselves; but my husband and I, were obliged to pass the night among our companions in misery—rats continually gnawing the feet of my couch, whose perpetual squeaking would have prevented sleep, had our harrassing reflections permitted us to court its approach.

1st December, 1779.

Luckily discovered a trap-door, which led to some rooms, or rather lofts, where no human foot had trod for many *many* years. These had been the store rooms of Angria the Pirate,[174] and they certainly contain "a remnant of all things"[175]— Broken chairs—tables—looking-glasses—books, even a spinnet[176] was among, the articles, but beyond all repair, and vast quantities of broken bottles, which had been filled with liquors of all kinds: but the rats in their gambols[177] had made havoc among them. I remember when I should have shuddered at the thoughts of sleeping in such a wretched place; but now privacy gave it irresistible charms; so having with difficulty obtained leave to occupy it, we exerted every nerve to get a spot cleared out before dark, for my couch; likewise so to arrange some bolts[178] of canvas which were among the spoils, as to form a sort of mattress for Mr. F—; here we lay down, comparatively happy in the hope of enjoying a tolerable nights rest; my husband being provided with a long pole to keep off the rats; but surely never were poor mortals so completely disappointed and for my own part I may add, terrified.—No sooner was the light extinguished, than we heard a fluttering noise, attended at intervals with squeaking—by degrees it approached the *beds*, and we felt that several creatures were hovering over us, but of what description we were totally ignorant—sometimes their wings swept our faces, seeming to fly heavily—then again they would remove farther off, but still continued squeaking.—Good God! what horrors I felt. Mr. F— protested that whole legions of evil spirits had taken possession of our apartment, and were determined to expel the intruders. The rats also acted their part in the Comedy; every now and then jumping towards the beds, as we could hear; however Mr. F— on these occasions laid about him stoutly with his pole, and thus kept *them* at bay; but our winged adversaries were not so easily foiled;—they persisted in their assaults 'till daybreak, when what should we find had caused all this disturbance, but a parcel of poor harmless bats! whose "ancient solitary reign we had molested."[179] To any one accustomed to see or hear these creatures our terror must appear ridiculous, but to me who had never chanced to meet with any such, the idea never occurred, nor did even Mr. Fay suggest any probable or natural cause of alarm. We cannot help laughing very heartily at it ourselves now, and you are at full liberty to do the same.

2d December.

Ayres called to tell us that two ships of the line, and a frigate had just passed towards Tellicherry.—We shall soon hear news from thence; Oh! that it may change our hard destiny!—The Governor marched at the head of his troops towards Tellicherry.[180]

10th December.

Application was made this morning to the Lieutenant Governor by Mr. Isaac, who I am now convinced is our true friend, representing that this air disagreeing with me I requested permission to remove to Cochin, and that my husband, on account of my extreme ill health, might accompany me. He promised to consult Sudder Khan upon it. The Quelladar or Governor of the Fort, spent some time with us this morning;—he is a fine old man, with a long red beard, and has altogether a most interesting appearance:—and here I may as well give a short description of this place.

Calicut then, is situated on the coast of Malabar in 11° north latitude and 75° east longitude. It was formerly a very considerable town governed by a Zamorin,[181] who also held the adjoining country; but has been some years in the possession of Hyder Ally, of whom you must have heard on occasion of his war with the English in 1770. They would certainly have put an end to the reign of this Usurper, had he not discovered a *method* of influencing the principal persons in power, in consequence of which he obtained a peace, much more honourable and advantageous to himself than to those who granted it. Having acquired by his genius and intrepidity every thing that he enjoys, he makes his name both feared and respected; so that nobody chooses to quarrel with him. I have indeed heard a comparison drawn between him and the King of Prussia, though I think much to the disadvantage of the latter; as supposing their *natural* abilities to be equal,—the great Frederick[182] ought *infinitely* to surpass a man who can neither write nor read, which is the case with Hyder. The lawful Prince of the country of which he has usurped the Government is held by him in actual confinement, though with every outward shew of respect, by which means he prevents the people from rising, lest their legitimate sovereign should fall a sacrifice to his resentment.

The fort must have been formerly a strong place, but is now in a dilapidated state—the walls are very thick, and they mount guard regularly; which was one inducement for sending us here; as Ayres told the Governor it was not worth while to keep a hundred seapoys watching us, when they were wanted elsewhere and that the fort was quite good enough for us to live in;—these arguments prevailed and here we were sent. When I first arrived I was so extremely ill, as to be scarcely sensible of what passed for some hours; but I remember Hare burst into a violent flood of tears, declaring that we were all doomed to death by our removal to this wretched spot, which being completely surrounded by stagnant water, could not fail to produce some of those disorders so fatal to Europeans.[183] We have not however hitherto experienced any complaint. The loft we sleep in is indeed disgusting beyond belief, and the Quelladar, I suppose at the suggestion of Ayres, has ordered the easier of the two ways of entrance, that discovered by Mr. F— to be blocked up; so that there is no way left but by means of a ladder placed almost in a perpendicular direction:—there is a rope by which to hold, or it would be impossible for any person to descend, but even with this assistance, I have great difficulty to reach the bottom.

11th December, 1779.

Peremptorily ordered to make ready for a journey to Seringapatnam.[184] By the Governor's desire delivered an Inventory of our losses: he promises full restitution, but has given no answer to my request. I am full of solicitude on this subject; but would submit to any thing rather than remain in this wretched place.

12th December, 1779.

Mr. F— waited twice on the Lieut. Governor but without effect. What can he mean by thus trifling with us? is it merely a wanton exercise of power, or intended to hide some dark design? these perpetual surmises distract me. Mem. Tulloh received 144 rupees to pay *all* our debts but took especial care not to let us have a single rupee, what wretches we are cast among! my very soul rises at them.

13th December, 1779.

Mr. F— was sent for by the Governor, who told him, that we might both have permission to go to Cochin whenever we thought proper; that he would furnish a boat and pay every incidental expense, besides making entire satisfaction for damages sustained,—Can all this good news be true? How suspicious I grow? what a change from being credulous—yet where is the wonder after being so frequently deceived?

14th December, 1779.

Preparations are going on briskly all day with our fellow passengers, who are eager for their departure, as well they may. Every thing which was taken from them on shore, has been this day restored, but those left in the ship are irrecoverable; of course we benefit nothing by this restitution—Mr. F— could not obtain our promised licence to-day.—These delays, weigh down my spirits, and increase all my complaints. I have still much pain in my breast; Oh that I fear, will prove a fatal blow—I shall have a great loss in Mr. Taylor.[185]

15th December, 1779.

The Governor still withholding our licence under pretence of business, I advised Mr. F— to insist on being *immediately* dispatched, or in case of refusal, by all means to declare himself ready to accompany the others; for I saw clearly that should they once leave us, it must then be entirely at this fellow's option, whether we went all or not, and who would not rather run the risk of even *dying* of fatigue on the journey, than hazard remaining at the mercy of such wretches! I dread, lest this should be part of the old plan of which I have since never heard, and had almost forgotten it. It is much easier to practise against two individuals than a whole company.

16th December.

The Doolies[186] (a kind of shabby Palanquin in which a person sits upright and is carried between two men) arrived this morning about ten. The gentlemen went to take leave, when Tulloh earnestly represented our case, to which the Governor replied, that he could not possibly attend to other matters till they were gone, but pledged his word that nothing should arise on his part to detain us a single hour afterwards; every one agreed with me how dangerous it was to trust such fallacious promises. On my knees I intreated Mr. F— to pursue the method I had before pointed out, but my advice was despised. At nine in the evening the party commenced their journey, having first stripped the place of provisions and every thing else, which having been bought out of the general purse we had an undoubted right to share. They even took my tea kettle, but luckily the man who had it in charge forgot it amidst the hurry of departure, by which means I recovered it. My heart sunk within me at seeing them quit the fort, not from motives of personal esteem or regret you may suppose, for it was impossible to grieve for the loss of some of the company; we parted with as much indifference as absolute strangers; after a fellowship in misfortune sufficient to have united almost any other society more closely than an intercourse of *years* under common circumstances. I went to bed, but in spite of every endeavour to calm the agitation of my mind, passed a *sleepless* night.

ELIZA FAY, *ORIGINAL LETTERS FROM INDIA* (1817)

17th December.

Rose in extreme anxiety which was far from being diminished by a message from the Governor, ordering Mr. F— not to attend him 'till the evening; accordingly at four o'clock he sat out, and as I felt extremely ill, the certain consequence of fretting and want of rest, I lay down and had just sunk into a doze, when my poor husband flew into the room like a madman, uttering a thousand extravagant expressions. Starting up in new and indescribable terror, and wringing my hands, I begged only to know what had happened. "Happened!" cried he "why we are betrayed, ruined, utterly undone; you must leave this place instantly, or you may be made a prisoner here for ever." Where are we to go? I very naturally asked! I *heard* not the answer, my head swam, and I dropped on the floor completely overpowered.—Whatever happened at that *fearful* moment I forget and endeavour to banish from my mind, as the effect of insanity.—How he accomplished it I know not, but Mr. F— actually carried me in his arms down that almost perpendicular ladder which I have described and placed me on a kind of bier: I was in this manner conveyed to my former habitation—I opened my eyes and became for a few moments sensible of the motion, but soon fainted again, and did not recover 'till I found myself once more entering the English Factory as a prisoner.

I now inquired, what was the cause of this change in our abode: and learnt that Mr. F— being refused leave to depart, had became so exasperated as wholly to lose all self-command; and rushing up to the musnud (throne) of the Lieutenant Governor had actually seized him, peremptorily insisting on the immediate fulfilment of his promise. Such conduct might have been expected to bring down *instant* destruction; but fortunately every one present was persuaded that grief and vexation had literally turned his brain; and they are not only much terrified at every species of madness, but from their religious prejudices, regard the sufferers under these complaints with a superstitious awe. Swayed by these mingled emotions the wicked Governor condescended to temporize with my husband, acknowledging that he had no *power* to release us without the Nabob's order which in consideration of my ill health he would endeavour to procure; and to pacify him further, he permitted our return to this place, where we are certainly in every respect more comfortably situated. But these concessions went little towards allaying that fever of passion, which his continual and cruel delays had excited: thence arose the alarm I experienced and which for a time so materially affected my health.

19th December, 1779.

Received five rupees subsistence money which we were informed were the last we should ever have. I cannot conceive what they mean to do with us or what will be our fate at last.

21st December, 1779.

The Governor sent for Mr. F— to offer him a commission in the Nabob's service and on his absolute refusal, swore that he might subsist how he could; that his masters money should no longer be lavished on idlers, then in a rage ordered palanquins. "you shall go to Seringapatam" said he "they will soon teach you better manners there" Mr. F— joyfully acquiesced in this mandate,—we provided necessaries for our journey which was fixed for the 24th; but the other knew better than to keep his word, so this like all our former views, and expectations of liberty ends in smoke, shall I say?

26th December, 1779.

A very melancholy Christmas-day passed yesterday. My dear friends little imagined they were drinking the health of a poor prisoner, (for I know you did not forget us) neither were we forgotten here, if empty compliments can be styled remembrance. All the Europeans and several of the natives attended our Levée.[187] But alas! what relief can mere ceremonious visits afford to misfortune! say rather that *aided by recollection*, such shadowy comforts add *keenness* to afflictions sting. I feel my mind insensibly raised whenever I attempt to expatiate on any subject which tends to revive the ideas of our separation. Even now I tread forbidden ground; for your sakes as well as my own, let me hasten to escape by skipping over this dangerous season of Christmas. I therefore pass on.

10th January, 1780.

The little money saved was nearly expended, and we must soon have been reduced to our last mite had not providence sent us relief from a quarter little dreamed of. Mr. F— wrote about a week ago to Mr. Church, Governor of Tellicherry[188] inclosing a memorial of our case, which he requested might be translated into the language of the country and proper methods used for its safe delivery to Hyder Ally himself. This morning brought in reply, a most generous humane letter from Mr. Church; which, after acknowledging himself honoured by our application, and promising his utmost concurrence in every measure we may think necessary, concludes thus "my heart bleeds for your distresses, and those of Mrs. F—she in particular must have suffered greatly. I have taken the liberty to accompany this letter by an order for two hundred rupees to serve *present* occasions: Any sum you may in future require a line to me shall always command it, as I know the difficulty of procuring remittances where you are. Englishmen ought to feel for each other; we are not without our share of troubles *here*; and I verily believe Hyder is at the bottom of all." Now pray does not this letter deserve more than I have said of it! just thus would my dear father have treated a distressed countryman—Methinks I see his benevolent heart venting itself in tears of sympathy at the recital. Precious tears! why am I not permitted to mingle mine with them! for they will flow in spite of my endeavours to restrain their course.

11th January.

Having now money to bribe with, we began to think of attempting an escape; for besides the silence observed on the fate of our companions, though near a month has elapsed since their departure, we live in continual dread of being forced up the country and perhaps massacred there: Every one who leaves this place must first obtain permission from the Governor, but as these passes only mention generally *so many people* and are granted indiscriminately to whoever applies for them, provided they be not suspected persons, one may easily be procured under feigned pretences (it is a matter frequently done.) A Friar belonging to the Portuguese convent, usually manages these affairs when properly instructed. This information we have from a Native Portuguese named Pereira, an officer in Hyder's service, with whom Mr. F— commenced an intimacy while we were in the Fort, and who is now quartered here at his special request. Tho' I must confess I cannot like this man, yet am I obliged to trust him. The visits we receive from Ayres are terrible trials to one who loathes dissimulation as I do. This wretch has once or twice mentioned a cow that annoyed him by entering the little garden, or paddock, in which it appears his house is placed; this morning he entered the factory with his scymitar in his hand unsheathed, and bloody, and with an expression of diabolical joy informed me that he had just caught the animal entering and being armed had completely chined[189] her. You cannot imagine said he, how *sweetly* the sword did the business; my very heart shuddered with horror and indignation, yet I dared not give vent to those feelings. I doubt not he would murder me with as much pleasure as he killed the cow with; and have no reason to suppose he would be punished for the act.

12th January, 1780.

Some quarrel unknown to me has certainly taken place between Pereira and Mr. F— the looks of the former alarm me; his dark scowling eye is frequently directed towards him, with an expression of dreadful import; yet he appears desirous of forwarding our escape.—He has introduced us to father Ricardo, who engages to provide us all things for our departure to Cochin.

13th January, 1780.

The priest breakfasted with us, and promised to set about the business without loss of time; he is to receive twenty rupees, on our setting off from hence, and twenty more on our arrival at Cochin or Tellichery, through the medium of Isaac, on whom the order from Mr. Church was drawn, by which means we received it without suspicion.

14th January, 1780.

A Licence or Passport is procured for us as two Frenchmen going to Mahey. We have paid twenty rupees boat-hire to a smuggler; these are commonly very courageous men; which is some comfort to me: under Mr. F—'s protection and his, I will endeavour to think myself secure. His house is admirably situated for our purpose, close by the sea side; this is to be our place of rendezvous. The precise time is not yet fixed upon: the intervening hours how anxiously will they pass!

15th January, 1780.

The boatman called to desire we would be at his house at six this evening;—gave him our little baggage (we had been obliged to purchase many necessaries) and four rupees to buy provisions. When it grew dark, Mr. F— put on a sailor's dress and I equipped myself in a nankeen[190] jacket—a pair of long striped trowsers—a man's night cap, and over that a *mighty* smart hat,—with a pair of Mr. F—'s shoes tied on my feet, and a stick in my hand. In this dress Mr. F— declared that I was the very image of my dear father, which highly gratified me. I had tied the clothes we took off, in a handkerchief; with that in one hand and brandishing my stick in the other, I boldly sallied forth,—taking care, however, to secure a retreat in case of accidents, a most fortunate precaution as the event proved.—Father Ricardo met us at the smuggler's according to appointment and we paid him twenty rupees, and gave him security for the other twenty; when this was settled, nothing remained as we supposed, but to step into the boat,—when behold! news was brought that the sailors had made their escape no one knew whither! after waiting two hours in that dangerous situation to see if they would return, and raving in all the folly of angry disappointment against those who had misled me, we made a virtue of necessity and trudged back to our prison, where we luckily effected an entrance without exciting suspicion.

17th January, 1780.

Had all arranged for our escape last night but so many people were about us, that we dared not make the attempt.

19th January, 1780.

Father Ricardo has once more arranged all things for to-night,—we must give more money, but that is no object. Once free and we shall doubtless find means of proceeding on our journey.

5th February, 1780.

Every day has this wicked priest contrived some scheme, to amuse us with false hopes of escaping; every *night* have we lain down in the full persuasion that it was the last we should pass in confinement; and as constantly have we awoke to meet bitter disappointments.—This continued alternation of hope and fear preys on my spirits and prevents me from gaining strength, but yesterday I received a *serious* shock from the behaviour of Pereira, and which excited more alarm than almost any circumstance that has occurred to me—I had long marked his hatred to Mr. F— and dreaded his revenge—I was setting at work when he entered the room—naked from the middle—just as Mr. F— was going into the next room. His strange appearance and the quick step with which he followed my husband caught my attention; and I perceived that he held a short dagger close under his arm, nearly all concealed by his handkerchief and the exigency of the moment gave me courage.—I sprung between him and the door through which Mr. F— had just passed, drawing it close and securing it to prevent his return, and then gently expostulated with P— on the oddness of his conduct and appearance; he slunk away, and I hope, will never trouble us again, especially as he has adopted another mode of revenge which may perhaps be equally effectual, though more slow in its operation. He went to Ayres and informed him that we had endeavoured to escape, mentioning every particular of our scheme, and, as far as I can learn, telling the whole truth; but fortunately naming a different evening from the one on which our unsuccessful attempt really was made on which Ayres exclaimed, "well Pereira you have made up a very fine story, but without a word of truth, for on the very night you mention, F— was setting with me over a bottle of wine; I'll take my oath of that for it was my birth night" this was true likewise, so we were saved for that time; but as Ayres knows that escape is in our heads he will, I fear, guard us with redoubled vigilance, and so far Pereira's design has taken effect.

6th February, 1780.

Mr. F— has completely detected the pious father Ricardo, and his worthy colleague the smuggler, and sorely against their will compelled them to refund his money all to about twenty three rupees, which they pretend has been disbursed. We now discovered, that although our offers might tempt their avarice and lead them to deceive us, yet they dared not persevere in assisting our escape; as the consequence of detection would to them be inevitable death.

10th February, 1780.

At length I begin to cherish hopes of our speedy release, as Sudder Khan returned last night from Seringapatnam; but is encamped without the Town, waiting for a lucky day,[191] till when he dares not enter his own house.—So how long we may still be detained, Heaven knows—Mr. F— and our friend Isaac propose paying him a visit to-morrow.

13th February, 1780.

They went out on Friday and again to-day, but have not yet been able to obtain an audience; and thus we may perhaps be led on a fortnight longer, by his ridiculous superstitions. Mr. Isaac, however, assures my husband, that from all he can learn it is really intended to release us, which makes me comparatively easy; yet it is impossible not to feel severely this delay, at such a critical period; for should Hyder commence hostilities against the English, whilst we remain in his power, not all Isaac's influence will be sufficient to extricate us from it; our doom must be sealed for life.

14th February.

Our indefatigable advocate walked out with Mr. F— (I should have mentioned that the distance is about three miles) but they were again disappointed, Sudder Khan being still closely shut up at his devotions, which are to continue two days longer at least.—How very distressing to be kept in this horrible suspense! But our friend still comforts us with the assurance, that *all* will be well.—He really behaves to me like a father, and as I have now acquired some knowledge of Portuguese, we are enabled to converse tolerably well. I do not recollect having described his person, and will therefore endeavour to give you some, though a very inadequate idea of it.

Isaac then is a fine venerable old man, about eighty-five with a long white beard; his complexion by no means dark, and his countenance benign yet majestic; I could look at him, till I almost fancied that he resembled exactly the Patriarch whose name he bears, were it not for his eye, which is still brilliant. His family I find according to ancient custom in the East, consists of two wives, to whom I am to have an introduction.

15th February.

Saw a letter to-day from Mr. Tulloh, to Mr. Passavant the Danish Factor, dated 19th January, which mentions, that they were fifteen days on their journey to Seringapatam and twelve more confined in a shed, half starved to death, as no one was permitted to assist them except with the coarsest food in small quantities; at length the Nabob[192] granted them an audience, when having listened to their complaint, he sent for Sudder Khan, to answer the charge. "Three successive days" says Tulloh "we were all sent for, and confronted with him, when Hyder commanded him to make instant restitution, however, we have as yet received nothing except that yesterday on taking leave his highness presented us with five hundred rupees for our journey to Madras, besides ordering Palanquins, carriages for our baggage, and every other convenience, likewise a guard of a hundred seapoys to conduct us into the English bounds. I spoke to him for Mr. and Mrs. F— and obtained an order for their release also. Whether the ship will be returned or not, *God Knows*, we are just going to set off." Thus far Tulloh. Now the man who brought this letter, saw them all go and remained at Seringapatam ten days afterward, without hearing further; so I hope we may conclude they are out of *their* troubles. Mrs. Tulloh has now seen enough poor woman to satisfy her taste for adventures. From all I can learn, it would have been utterly impossible for me to have supported the various hardships of their journey, in my precarious state of health; poor Mr. Taylor how sincerely do I pity him.

17th February, 1780.

Mr. Isaac called by appointment about two o'clock and took my husband with him, to wait *once more* on the Governor. He seems to entertain no doubt of bringing back the order for our release. I endeavour to be calm and to rest with confidence on his assurance; but when I contemplate the dreadful alternative, should he meet a peremptory refusal, and recollect the deep machinations that have been practised to keep us here, my heart recoils at the idea. It is now eight in the evening; every thing is packed up and ready for our departure yet they return not. Some obstacle I fear must have been thrown in the way by that vile Sudder Khan to prevent our liberation, and we are destined to remain his wretched prisoners. How shall I support the intelligence? Heaven inspire me with fortitude! I can neither write, nor attend to any thing!

LETTER XIII.

COCHIN,[193] 19th February, 1780.

THANKS be to Providence that I am at length permitted to address my beloved friends from this land of liberty towards which my wishes have so long pointed. After wading through my melancholy journal, you will be enabled in some measure to form an idea of the joy that fills my breast on contemplating the contrast between my present situation, and that from which I have so recently escaped—I will not however indulge in reflections, but hasten to proceed with my narrative, which broke off at a most interesting period in my last letter, when I was every instant expecting the news of our release.

I was not relieved from suspense till near twelve on Thursday night, when the gentlemen returned bringing with them the so anxiously desired passports for ourselves, and such trifling articles as remained in our possession; more than this I find they could not obtain for us, though absolute promises of restitution and remuneration had been frequently held out. This however seemed a slight evil compared with what even *one* days detention might produce; we therefore abandoned all thought of farther application on the subject, and on *Friday* 18th February, at 5 A. M. joyfully quitted our detested prison, and repaired to the house of our steady friend and benefactor Isaac, when we found one of his own sloops prepared to convey us to Cochin, with every necessary refreshment on board.

Thus by the indefatigable exertions of this most excellent man, we are at last released from a situation of which it is impossible for you to appreciate the horrors. To him we are indebted for the inestimable gift of liberty. No words can I find adequate to the expression of my gratitude. In whatever part of the world and under whatever circumstances my lot may be cast; whether we shall have the happiness to reach in safety the place to which all our hopes and wishes tend, or are doomed to experience again the anxieties and sufferings of captivity; whether I shall pass the remainder of my days in the sunshine of prosperity, or exposed to the chilling blasts of adversity; the name of *Isaac the Jew* will ever be associated with the happiest recollections of my life; and while my heart continues to beat, and warm blood animates my mortal frame, no distance of time or space can efface from my mind, the grateful remembrance of what we owe to this most worthy of men. When we were plundered and held in bondage by the Mahometan robbers[194] amongst whom we had fallen; when there was no sympathizing friend to soothe us among our Christian fellow captives; when there was no hand to help us, and the last ray of hope gradually forsook the darkening scene of our distress; kind Providence sent a good Samaritan to our relief in the person of this benevolent Jew,[195] who proved himself an Israelite indeed. Oh my dear sister! how can I in the overflowing of a grateful heart do otherwise than lament, that the name of this once distinguished people should have become a term of reproach! Exiled from the land promised to the seed of Abraham; scattered over the face of the earth, yet adhering with firmness to the religion of their fathers, this race once the boasted favourites of Heaven, are despised and rejected by every nation in the world. The land that affords shelter, denies them a participation in the rights of citizenship. Under such circumstances of mortifying contempt, and invidious segregation, it is no wonder that many of the children of Israel in the present day evince more acuteness than delicacy in their transactions, and are too well disposed to take advantage of those, from whom they have endured so much scorn and persecution. It gives me therefore peculiar pleasure to record their good deeds, and to proclaim in *my* limited circle, that such men as a FRANCO and an ISAAC, are to be found among the posterity of Jacob. These sentiments are not overstrained but the genuine effusions of a thankful heart: as such receive them.

19th February, 1780.

This morning about eleven we arrived at our long wished for Port, and were landed close to the house of our good friend ISAAC which is pleasantly situated by the river side about a mile from Cochin, and rendered in every respect a most delightful residence. Here we were welcomed by the two wives of ISAAC who were most splendidly dressed to receive us, rather overloaded with ornaments yet not inelegant. Indeed I think the Eastern dresses have infinitely the advantage over ours; they are much more easy and graceful; besides affording greater scope for the display of taste, than our strange unnatural modes. They were extremely hospitable and very fond of talking.

I mentioned before, having learned a little Portuguese during my imprisonment, which was of great advantage to me here, for except Malabars, it is the only language they speak, and a miserable jargon indeed is what they call Portuguese here.—However we contrived to make ourselves mutually understood so far as to be convinced that each was kindly disposed towards the other. Had I been differently circumstanced, it would have given me great pleasure to have accepted the pressing invitations of these ladies to pass some time with them—the entire novelty of the scene would have amused me. Novel I may *well* call it, in more respects than one; we were entertained with all the profusion that wealth can command, and generosity display. Though religious prejudices banished us from *their* table, ours was loaded with every delicacy,—all served on massive plate; among many other articles of luxury which I had never seen before, were numbers of solid silver *Peekdanees*,[196] which served the purpose of spitting boxes (excuse the term.) They stood at each end of the couches in the principal room: some of them were nearly three feet high, with broad bottoms; the middle of the tube twisted and open at the top, with a wide mouth, for the convenience of such as had occasion to expectorate. These are not what *we* should call delicate indulgences in England; but in a country where smoking tobacco and chewing betel[197] are universally practised, they must be allowed to be necessary ones.

You will judge what a change these apartments were to me when contrasted, not with our prison in the Fort of Calicut, for our residence there was undoubtedly the *acme* of wretchness, but even with the house in which I had so long lived, without any furniture at all, save my unmattressed couch, an old table and three broken chairs; and where many a time the poor Portuguese lad who served us, had entered at the hour of dinner empty handed, exclaiming that the dogs had carried off all that had been provided. My own face I never saw during the whole period, there not being so much as the fragment of a looking-glass to be obtained.

The younger wife of ISAAC attached herself to me in such a manner as I never before experienced, and really appeared as if she could not bear to part with me, even when I went with my husband to see the town of Cochin, which is truly a very pretty romantic place; but what was far more to my satisfaction, we luckily found Mr. Moore[198] there, who proposed sailing the next day, and kindly offered us a passage on the St. Helena, which you may be sure we gratefully accepted. On our way back we were accosted by a Captain Richardson, whose ship is under repair here, and will be ready in about six weeks. He shook hands with us as country folks, and directly offered us both a passage to Bengal with every accommodation in his house during our stay here,—a most liberal proposal; was it not? and which would have been very fortunate for us, had we missed the St. Helena; in the present case his offer was of course declined, but I shall ever recollect the kindness which dictated it, and trust opportunities will be afforded to evince my gratitude.

On the 21st, at 5 A. M. Mr. F— left me with my new friends, promising to return for me in half an hour, to the great grief of the fair Jewess who was become so fond of me—but alas! I waited hour after hour, and no husband returned. I was in the greatest anxiety and consternation imaginable, dreading lest some new disaster had overtaken us, and that our ill starred journey was again stopped short in its course—It is impossible for you to conceive what I suffered during his absence and how my mind was harrassed by various tormenting conjectures,—those only, who have been subject to such cross accidents as I have so frequently experienced, can judge of my feelings—At length about noon he made his appearance, and very calmly began unpacking the chest as if to replace the things at his leisure—I asked of course what had occurred and if Mr. Moore had changed his intention? "Why, answered he, Moore and all the rest are gone on board, but somehow I dont think he will sail to-day for all that." This reply almost bereft me of my senses, knowing the consequence of being left behind would be a journey by land to Madras, (for he would never have had patience to wait till Captain Richardson's ship was ready) the expense of which alone must amount to eight or nine hundred rupees, not to mention the intolerable fatigue of travelling in this Country. Aware that if I did not exert myself all was lost, I took a hasty leave of our kind friends, and we immediately proceeded to Cochin with our little baggage, and sent out for a boat, but by this time the afternoon breeze had set in and the sea ran so high, that none would venture over the Bar; at last a man agreed to provide a large boat and take us off for sixteen rupees. When we came to the water side, what should this mighty boat prove, but a narrow Canoe with paddles, scarcely big enough to contain us and our four rowers. I hesitated—the people ran round me on all sides, intreating me not to venture, and assuring us both by words and gestures that the danger was imminent. Captain Richardson who was among them declared that, it would be next to a miracle if we escaped: indeed every moment evidently increased the risk; but Mr. F— now seeing the error of his delay, swore to run all hazards, rather than stop any longer at Cochin: a common practice with most people who have brought themselves into difficulties by their imprudence and who seek to regain by obstinacy, what they have lost through folly. Pity such cannot always suffer alone. Finding him positive I commended myself to the protection of the Almighty and stepped in; all the spectators seeming to look upon me as a *self* devoted victim:[199] yet how was it possible to avoid going! had I refused Mr. F— would constantly have upbraided me with whatever ill consequence might have resulted from the delay, and who could wish for life on such terms! "No" thought I at the moment, "rather let me brave death in the line of my duty, than have my future days embittered by reproach, however unmerited." As we proceeded the waves gradually rose higher, and began to break over us: one man was continually employed in baling out the water, though his only utensil was a bamboo, which hardly held a quart. Never shall I forget what I felt on looking round in this situation; every wave rising many feet higher than the boat, and threatening to overwhelm us with instant destruction. I sat at first with my face to the stern, but afterwards moved to the front, and when I saw a wave coming, bowed my head to receive it. We were a mile from the shore, and at least *two* from the ship; was not this sufficient to appal the stoutest heart! yet I can truly say that my mind was perfectly composed, conscious of the rectitude of my intentions,—I could look up boldly to Heaven for protection. Mr. F— will tell you how frequently I begged him not to entertain the least doubt of our safety. "We have never" said I, "been conducted thus far by the hand of Providence to perish; remember my dear parents; is not *their* happiness involved in *our* safety? depend upon it we shall be preserved to become the humble instruments of rendering their declining years happy."

While I was speaking a tremendous wave broke over us, and half filled the boat with water, on which, thinking it would be presumptuous to proceed, we ordered the men to make for the nearest land, but this the wind would not permit, so we were obliged to keep on, and had reached within a mile of the ship, when she began to spread her sails, and in a few minutes got under weigh with a fair wind.—Our people now wanted to quit the pursuit, as she gained ground considerably, but we kept them in good humour by promising more money, and putting a white handkerchief on a stick, waved it in the air. After some time we had the pleasure to see her tack about and lye to so in another half hour we came up with her, having been three hours in the condition I have described,—wet through and nearly frightened to death, being every moment in the most imminent danger. To describe my joy is impossible or my impatience to quit the boat; without waiting for the chair to be lowered I scrambled on board, and had I not been relieved by a violent burst of tears, must have fainted.

Every one in the vessel blamed Mr. F— exceedingly for running such a risk by his delay as the other passengers who went on board in the morning, did not experience the slightest inconvenience. Mr. Moore luckily came in the provision boat, which was six hours in getting on board. This circumstance was the means of saving our passage.

When we reached Ceylon[200] the wind became contrary, which together with a strong current, kept us upwards of three weeks beating off the Island, before we could weather Point de Galle.[201] This will account to you for my letter being scarcely legible.—I am at this moment writing on my knees in bed, and if I had not been contented with this method all the way, I could not have written at all. My father well knows, a vessel has not a very agreeable motion, when beating up in the winds eye.[202]

4th April, 1780.

At length thank Heaven! we are at anchor in Madras Roads, having been six weeks making a passage that with a fair wind we could almost have performed in as many days. Happily for me our society has been very different from the last I was condemned to mix with on shipboard;—of those Mr. Moore, and Mr. O'Donnell are of the most importance to us, our acquaintance with them commenced in Egypt, and as they were indeed (though innocently) the cause of all we suffered there, a very agreeable fellow-feeling has naturally taken place between us. The latter is now obliged to return to India to begin life again, (his losses on the Desert having been followed by many unavoidable expenses, as you will learn from my narrative), and seek a competence under all the disadvantages that an injured constitution added to a deep sense of disappointment and injustice, subject him to.—You may be sure we have had many conversations concerning the sad story of the Desert, and the last moments of those who perished there.—A boat is just come to take us on shore, so adieu for the present. The Roads are very full, there are eight ships of the line and above sixty other vessels, which form a magnificent spectacle.

6th April, 1780.

I was exceedingly alarmed yesterday by the surf. We got safe over it, but another boat upset just afterwards; however, fortunately no lives were lost.—Sir Thomas Rumbold is hourly expected to embark, which is all that detains the fleet; so that perhaps I may not be able to write ten lines more –

6 P.M. As far as I can judge I feel pleased with Madras, and gratified by the reception I have hitherto met with. I shall of course write to you again from thence, being likely to remain here a week or two; at present I must close my letter; but as a matter of curiosity shall just mention the astonishing celerity of the Indian tailors.—Yesterday evening Mr. Fay, not being *overstocked* with clothes to appear in, ordered a complete suit of black silk, with waistcoat sleeves, which they brought home *before nine* this morning, very neatly made though the whole must have been done by candle-light.

I cannot conclude without saying, that although I feel rather weak, my health is improving, and that the pain I suffer from the accident *which* befel me at the Factory, is not so violent as formerly—God grant I may soon be relieved from apprehension on *that* score.

The Governor is gone on board.—Captain Richardson of the *Ganges*[203] under whose especial charge this packet (containing the whole of my narrative from Mocha) will be placed, as I had no safe opportunity of forwarding any letter from Calicut or Cochin, has sent for it. The perusal will cost you many tears but recollect that all is *over*, and my future communications will I trust, be of a very different complexion. May this reach you safely and meet you all well and comfortable. Adieu—God Almighty preserve you prays your own,

E. F.

LETTER XIV.

Madras, 13th April.

My dear Friends,

Agreeably to my promise I take up the pen to give you some account of this settlement, which has proved to me a pleasant resting-place after the many hardships and distresses it has lately been my lot to encounter; and where in the kind attentions and agreeable society of some of my own sex, I have found myself soothed and consoled for the long want of that comfort; while my health has in general reaped great advantages from the same source.

There is something uncommonly striking and grand in this town, and its whole appearance charms you from novelty, as well as beauty. Many of the houses and public buildings are very extensive and elegant—they are covered with a sort of shell-lime which takes a polish like marble, and produces a wonderful effect.[204]— I could have fancied myself transported into Italy, so magnificently are they decorated, yet with the utmost taste. People here say that the *chunam* as it is called, loses its properties when transported to Bengal, where the dampness of the atmosphere, prevents it from receiving that exquisite polish so much admired by all who visit Madras. This may very likely be the case.

The free exercise of all religions being allowed; the different sects seem to vie with each other in ornamenting their places of worship, which are in general well built, and from their great variety, and novel forms afford much gratification, particularly when viewed from the country, as the beautiful groups of trees intermingle their tall forms and majestic foliage, with the white chunam and rising spires, communicating such harmony softness and elegance to the scene, as to be altogether delightful; and rather resembling the images that float on the imagination after reading fairy tales, or the Arabian nights entertainment, than any thing in real life;—in fact Madras *is* what I conceived Grand Cairo to be, before I was so unlucky as to be undeceived. This idea is still further heightened by the intermixture of inhabitants; by seeing Asiatic splendour, combined with European taste exhibited around you on every side, under the forms of flowing drapery, stately palanquins, elegant carriages, innumerable servants, and all the pomp and circumstance of luxurious ease, and unbounded wealth. It is true this glittering surface is here, and there tinged with the sombre hue that more or less colours every condition of life;—you behold Europeans, languishing under various complaints which they call incidental to the climate,[205] an assertion it would ill become a stranger like myself to controvert, but respecting which I am a little sceptical; because I see very plainly that the same mode of living, would produce the same effects, even "in the hardy regions of the North."[206] You may likewise perceive that human nature has its faults and follies every where, and that *black* rogues are to the full as common as white ones, but in my opinion more impudent. On your arrival you are pestered with Dubashees,[207] and servants of all kinds who crouch to you as if they were already your slaves, but who will cheat you in every possible way; though in fact there is no living without one of the former to manage your affairs as a kind of steward, and you may deem yourself very fortunate if you procure one in this land of pillagers, who will let nobody cheat you but himself. I wish these people would not vex one by their tricks; for there is something in the mild countenances and gentle manners of the Hindoos that interests me exceedingly.

We are at present with Mr. & Mrs. Popham[208] from whom we have received every possible civility. He is a brother lawyer, and a countryman of my husbands, and she is a lively woman, her spirits have in some measure restored mine to the standard from which those amiable gentlemen, the Beys of Egypt, and Sudder Khan with his coadjutors Ayres and my worthy ship mates, had so cruelly chased them.

We have made several excursions in the neighbourhood of Madras which is every where delightful, the whole vicinity being ornamented with gentlemen's houses built in a shewy style of architecture, and covered with that beautiful chunam. As they are almost surrounded by trees, when you see one of these superb dwellings incompassed by a grove, a distant view of Madras with the sea and shipping, so disposed as to form a perfect landscape, it is beyond comparison the most charming picture I ever beheld or could have imagined. Wonder not at my enthusiasm; so long shut up from every pleasing object, it is natural that my feelings should be powerfully excited when such are presented to me.

Nothing is more terrible at Madras than the surf which as I hinted before, is not only alarming but dangerous. They have here two kinds of boats to guard against this great evil, but yet, notwithstanding every care, many lives are lost. One of these conveyances called the Massulah[209] boat, is large, but remarkably light, and the planks of which it is constructed are actually sewed together by the fibres of the Cocoa-nut. It is well calculated to stem the violence of the surf but for greater safety it requires to be attended by the other, called a Catamaran, which is merely composed of bamboos fastened together and paddled by one man. Two or three of these attend the Massulah boat, and in case of its being overset usually pick up the drowning passengers. The dexterity with which they manage these things is inconceivable;—but no dexterity can entirely ward off the danger. The beach is remarkably fine.

The ladies here are very fashionable I assure you: I found several novelties in dress since I quitted England, which a good deal surprised me, as I had no idea that fashions travelled so fast. It is customary to take the air in carriages every evening in the environs of Madras: for excursions in the country these are commonly used; but in town they have Palanquins carried by four bearers, which I prefer. They are often beautifully ornamented, and appear in character with the country, and with the languid air of those who use them, which, though very different from any thing I have been accustomed to admire in a woman as you well know, yet is not unpleasing in a country the charms of which are heightened by exhibiting a view of society entirely new to me.

MR. POPHAM is one of the most eccentric beings I ever met with.—Poor man he is a perpetual projector,[210] a race whose exertions have frequently benefitted society, but seldom I believe been productive of much advantage to themselves or their families. He is at present laying plans for building what is called the black town, to a great extent, and confidently expects to realize an immense fortune, but others foresee such difficulties in the way, that they fear he may be ruined by the undertaking. The pleasure he takes in his visionary scheme should not be omitted in the account as of some value, for it really seems to be an uncommon source of enjoyment.

The Black town is that part of Madras, which was formerly inhabited wholly by the natives, but of late many Europeans have taken houses there, rents being considerably lower than in Fort ST. GEORGE, which is a very strong Garrison, built by the English, and where since have been constructed many fine houses, &c.—this is considered of course a more fashionable place to reside in. Between the Black town and the Fort, lies Choultry Plain which being covered entirely with a whitish sand, reflects such a dazzling light, and intolerable heat, as to render it a terrible annoyance especially to strangers. MR. FAY has been exceedingly pressed to take up his abode here, and really many substantial inducements have been held out to him; but as his views have been all directed to Calcutta, where knowledge and talents are most likely to meet encouragement he cannot be persuaded to remain. Besides, a capital objection is, that no Supreme Court being as yet established he could be only admitted to practise as an attorney, no advocates being allowed in the Mayors Court: so that his rank as a Barrister would avail nothing here:[211] I most cordially acquiesce in this determination. But I must suspend my scribbling; MR. P—is waiting to take me to ST. THOMAS'S MOUNT.

17th April, 1780.

I resume my pen, resolved to devote this day to my dear friends, as it is likely to be the last I shall spend in Madras. I found ST. THOMAS' MOUNT a very beautiful place, it is a high hill of a conical form, crowned at the top with white houses, and a Church built by the Portuguese in memory of some ST. THOMAS, who they say, was murdered on this spot by a Brahmin.[212]—The road to this place is delightful, being a complete avenue of the finest trees I ever saw, whose intermingling branches are absolutely impervious to the sun. Not far from hence I was shewn a prodigiously fine Banian[213] tree, the singular nature of which is, that its branches bend down to the ground, take root and thence spring out anew; thus forming innumerable arches. I call it a vegetable Cathedral, and could not help fancying that Banian groves were formerly appropriated to idolatrous worship, since they are admirably calculated for the celebration of any mysterious and solemn rites from which the uninitiated are excluded; and may be properly called "Temples not made with hands."[214] On the whole I felt highly gratified by my little excursion, which was, I believe, not more than seven miles from Madras.

I must now assure you that I have actually seen several of those things with my own eyes which we girls used to think poor Captain S— took traveller's liberty in relating, such as dancing snakes, Jugglers swallowing swords &c. The snakes were to me somewhat alarming, the other a very disgusting spectacle; when they are become familiar I may be amused with the one, since the various forms, the prismatic colours, and graceful motions of the snakes may give pleasure which the other exhibitions never can. When you have seen a man thrust a sword down his throat and are fully convinced that there is no deception, you feel that you have beheld a wonder, and there the gratification ends, for the sight is unnatural and disgusting. With some other tricks of the Juggler, I was however much pleased; his power of balancing was astonishing, and he had a method of throwing four brass balls up and catching them with such amazing rapidity, that they perpetually encircled his head, forming a kind of hat around it; he likewise threaded small beads with his tongue, and performed a number of very curious slights of hand. Dancing girls are a constant source of amusement here, but I was much disappointed in them, they wrap such a quantity of muslin round them by way of petticoat, that they almost appear to have hoops;—and their motions are so slow, formal and little varied, that you see the whole dance as it were at once; they are very inferior to those of the same profession at Grand Cairo though I never saw any there but in the streets, however their dancing is certainly less indecent, at least so far as I could witness it.

There seems to be a strange inconsistency in the character of the natives; they appear the most pusillanimous creatures in existence, except those employed on the water, whose activity and exertions are inconceivable. They will encounter every danger for the sake of reward, with all the eagerness of avarice, and all the heroism of courage; so that if you have occasion to send off a note to a ship, no matter how high the surf may run, you will always find some one ready to convey it for you, and generally without being damaged, as their turbans are curiously folded with waxed cloth for that purpose; so off they skip to their Catamarans,— for the prospect of gain renders them as brisk as the most lively Europeans.

The Hindoos have generally their heads shaved but they preserve a single lock and a pair of small whiskers with the greatest care. Their manner of writing is curious; they write with iron needles, on palm-leaves which are afterwards strung together and form books. Boys are taught to write on the sand; a very good plan as it saves materials and a number can be instructed at the same time. For teaching arithmetic, great numbers of pebbles are used; so that every part of the apparatus is cheap.

The natives of India are immoderately fond of an intoxicating liquor called *Toddy*[215] which is the unfermented juice of the Cocoa-nut or Palmyra tree;—sugar and water is also a favourite beverage. Butter is very scarce and not good; what they call *Ghee* is butter boiled or clarified, in order to preserve it, and is very useful for many purposes, such as frying &c. On the whole one may live very well at

Madras,—to me it appears a land of luxury as you may suppose, when you recollect, how I had been accustomed to fare. We may think ourselves very well off in escaping from the paws of that fell tyger Hyder Ally as we did, for I am assured that the threat of sending us up the country to be fed on dry rice, was not likely to be a vain one; it is thought that several of our countrymen are at this very time suffering in that way: if so, I heartily wish that the War he has provoked, may go forward 'till those unhappy beings are released and the usurping tyrant is effectually humbled.

MR. O'DONNELL has just called and desired me to prepare for an early summons to-morrow. I have ever found him friendly and attentive and must always deem myself highly obliged to him, as he certainly had but too much occasion to feel hurt by the behaviour of MR. FAY, whose temper, you know, is not the most placid in the world. He quarrelled with both him and MR. MOORE during the passage about the *merest* trifles (wherein too he was palpably in the wrong) and challenged them both:[216] Judge what I must have suffered during these altercations, vainly endeavouring to conciliate, and in agonies lest things should proceed to extremities.—On our arrival here, I prevailed on MR. POPHAM to act as a mediator between the parties; who at length, though with great difficulty, convinced MR. F— that he had been to blame, and induced him to make a proper apology to both gentlemen: thus ended the affair but I have reason to think, that had I not been with him, he would not have been invited to proceed farther on the ship; nor am I free from apprehension at present, yet MR. O'D— has proved himself so true a friend and has so materially served my husband, that I trust our short trip from hence to Calcutta, will prove a pleasant one. I understand that several additional passengers are to join us, which may operate as a check on *fiery spirits*.

18th April.

MR. & MRS. P— have completed their hospitable kindness by insisting that we should partake of an *early* dinner (at one o'clock) after which we immediately proceed on board; and heartily rejoiced shall I be, when once over the terrific surf. I leave Madras with some regret having met with much civility and even sympathy here. I must now bid you adieu; in my next I hope to announce that my long pilgrimage is ended. I likewise shall expect to find letters from you, waiting my arrival at Calcutta. My anxiety at times arises to impatience, lest any evil should have befallen you, during the long period in which all communication has been suspended between us: my heart however yet retains its power of conversing with you. Whenever I see any thing new or entertaining I directly imagine how *you* would have looked, and what *you* would have said on the occasion; and thus cheat myself into a pleasing dream of social intercourse with those most dear to me.

Our stay at Madras has been the means of procuring us some respectable recommendations to persons in Calcutta; for we have made several desirable connections here. Hope again smiles on us and I endeavour to cherish her suggestions; for it is as much my *duty* as my *interest* to keep up my spirits, since in my present state of health, without them, I must wholly sink; and now more than ever I feel the necessity of using exertion.

The hot winds prevail here at present, which renders the *weather* peculiarly oppressive, but a few hours will change the scene. Adieu: remember me in your prayers, my beloved parents, my dear sisters, and rest assured of the unalterable affection of your own

Eliza.

LETTER XV.

Calcutta, 22nd May.

My Dear Friends,

I may now indeed call for your congratulations since after an eventful period of twelve months and eighteen days, I have at length reached the place for which I have so long sighed, to which I have looked with innumerable hopes and fears, and where I have long rested my most rational expectations of future prosperity and comfort. I must now in order to keep up the connection of my story return to Madras, and from thence conduct you here regularly.

Mr. F— and Mr. P— both assured me that a massulah boat was engaged, but on arriving at the beach none could be had; so there being no remedy, I went off in a common cargo boat which had no accommodations whatever for passengers, and where my only seat was one of the cross beams. How I saved myself from falling Heaven knows, Mr. F— was under the necessity of exerting his whole strength to keep me up, so he suffered *a little* for his negligence. It was what is called a black surf and deemed very dangerous; there were some moments when I really thought we were nearly gone; for how could I in my weak state have buffetted the waves had the boat overset? When once on board our voyage passed comfortably enough; our society was pleasant; indeed Mr. O'Donnell is ever a host to us in kindness; Mr. M— our supercargo[217] was however more strict in his enforcement of rules than was agreeable to most of us; we were kept more orderly than so many children at school; for if we were in the midst of a rubber at whist, he would make us give over at nine precisely, and we were obliged to keep our score 'till the following evening. But this was of little moment, for as we advanced towards the place of our destination, we were too much interested to think of any thing else. We had a distant view of the pagodas of *Jaggernauth*,[218]— three large pyramidical buildings very famous temples among the Hindoos, who there worship the images of *Jaggernauth* and keep a splendid establishment of the Priesthood attendant on the Idols in the manner of the ancient heathens. I am credibly assured that at stated intervals the principal figure is taken out in an enormous car, with a great number of wheels beneath which his votaries prostrate themselves with the most undaunted resolution; firmly persuaded that by thus sacrificing their lives, they shall pass immediately after death into a state of everlasting felicity. Well may we say that, "life and immortality were brought to light by the Gospel"[219] since in regions where its sacred influence is unknown or unattended to, we see such gross acts of folly and superstition as these, sanctioned by authority: may it please the Almighty disposer of events to hasten the period of their emancipation, that all mankind may hail each other as brothers, and we may be brought together as "one fold, under one shepherd."[220]

Calcutta, you know is on the Hoogly, a branch of the Ganges, and as you enter Garden-reach[221] which extends about nine miles below the town, the most interesting views that can possibly be imagined greet the eye. The banks of the river are as one may say absolutely studded with elegant mansions, called here as at Madras, garden-houses. These houses are surrounded by groves and lawns, which descend to the waters edge, and present a constant succession of whatever can delight the eye, or bespeak wealth and elegance in the owners. The noble appearance of the river also, which is much wider than the Thames at London bridge, together with the amazing variety of vessels continually passing on its surface, add to the beauty of the scene. Some of these are so whimsically constructed as to charm by their novelty. I was much pleased with the snake boat[222] in particular. Budgerows[223] somewhat resembling our city barges, are very common,—many of these are spacious enough to accommodate a large family. Besides these the different kinds of pleasure boats intermixed with mercantile vessels, and ships of war, render the whole a magnificent and beautiful moving picture; at once exhilarating the heart, and charming the senses: for every object of sight is viewed through a medium that heightens its attraction in this brilliant climate.

The town of Calcutta reaches along the eastern bank of the Hoogly; as you come up past Fort William[224] and the Esplanade it has a beautiful appearance. Esplanade-row, as it is called, which fronts the Fort, seems to be composed of palaces; the whole range, except what is taken up by the Government and Council houses, is occupied by the principal gentlemen in the settlement—no person being allowed to reside in Fort William, but such as are attached to the Army, gives it greatly the advantage over FORT ST. GEORGE,[225] which is so incumbered with buildings of one kind or other, that it has more the look of a town than of a military Garrison. *Our* Fort is also so well kept and every thing in such excellent order, that it is quite a curiosity to see it—all the slopes, banks, and ramparts, are covered with the richest verdure, which completes the enchantment of the scene. Indeed the general aspect of the country is astonishing; notwithstanding the extreme heat (the thermometer seldom standing below ninety in the afternoon) I never saw a more vivid green than adorns the surrounding fields—not that parched miserable look our lands have during the summer heats;—large fissures opening in the earth, as if all vegetation were suspended; in fact the copious dews which fall at night, restore moisture to the ground, and cause a short thick grass to spring up, which makes the finest food imaginable for the cattle. Bengal mutton, always good, is at this period excellent—I must not forget to tell you that there is a very good race ground at a short distance from Calcutta, which is a place of fashionable resort, for morning and evening airings.

Through Mr. O'D's kindness we were introduced to a very respectable Portuguese family who received us with the greatest civility, inviting us to take up our abode with them until we could provide ourselves with a house—Mr. Da C— was a widower, but his late wife's sisters, who resided with him, were born at Chandernagore, (a French settlement between twenty and thirty miles higher up the river;) but from long disuse they had lost the habit of *speaking* their native language, though they *understood* it perfectly; so I was forced to make out their Portuguese in the best manner I could, constantly answering in French. In this way we frequently conversed, and I gained much information respecting the customs of the place—the price of provisions, and many other useful matters.

Fortunately, throughout all our difficulties we had preserved our letters of introduction, by keeping them always concealed about us, together with Mr. F—'s admission to the Bar and other credentials, which were essentially necessary to his establishment here: so that my husband became immediately known to Sir Robert Chambers,[226] who behaved to him with the utmost attention; and whose lady[227] after hearing a little of my melancholy story, and finding I was too much indisposed to admit of my paying my respects to her, had the goodness to wave all ceremony, and accompanied by her husband, to visit me at the house of the Portuguese merchant, which was a condescension that I certainly had no right to expect. She is the most beautiful woman I ever beheld,—in the bloom of youth; and there is an agreeable frankness in her manners, that enhances her loveliness, and renders her truly fascinating. Her kindness towards me daily increases; and she seems never weary of listening to my sad story. "She loves me for the dangers I have passed, and I love her that she does pity them."[228]

29th May.

I have delivered my letter of introduction to Mrs. Hastings,[229] on whom I should have waited long ago, had the state of my health admitted of the exertion. She resides at Belvidere-house about, I believe, five miles from Calcutta, which is a great distance at this season and for an invalid. The lady was fortunately at home and had three of her most intimate friends with her on a visit, one of them, Mrs. Motte,[230] a most charming woman. Mrs. H— herself, it is easy to perceive at the first glance, is far superior to the generality of her sex; though her appearance is rather eccentric, owing to the circumstance of her beautiful auburn hair being disposed in ringlets, throwing an air of elegant, nay almost infantine simplicity over the countenance, most admirably adapted to heighten the effect intended to be produced. Her whole dress too, though studiously becoming being at variance with our present modes which are certainly not so, perhaps for that reason, she has chosen to depart from them—as a foreigner you know, she may be excused for not strictly conforming to our fashions; besides her rank in the settlement sets her above the necessity of studying any thing but the whim of the moment. It is easy to perceive how fully sensible she is of her own consequence. She is indeed raised to a "giddy height" and expects to be treated with the most profound respect and deference. She received me civilly and insisted on my staying dinner, which I had no inclination to refuse, but she seemed not to evince much sympathy when I slightly touched on the misfortunes which had befallen me; nay she even hinted that I had brought them on myself,[231] by imprudently venturing on such an expedition out of mere curiosity. Alas! Mrs. H— could not know what you are well acquainted with, that I undertook the journey with a view of preserving my husband from destruction, for had I not accompanied him, and in many instances restrained his extravagance and dissipated habits, he would never, never, I am convinced, have reached Bengal, but have fallen a wretched sacrifice to them on the way, or perhaps through the violence of his temper been involved in some dispute, which he was too ready to provoke—but to return I could not help feeling vexed at Mrs. H—'s observation, to say the best of it, it was unfeeling;—but I excuse her. Those basking in the lap of prosperity can little appreciate the sufferings or make allowance for the errors of the unfortunate; whom they regard as almost beings of another order.

You will expect me to say something of the house, which is a perfect *bijou*;[232] most superbly fitted up with all that unbounded affluence can display; but still deficient in that simple elegance which the wealthy so seldom attain, from the circumstance of not being obliged to search for effect without much cost, which those but moderately rich, find to be indispensable. The gardens are said to be very tastefully laid out, but how far this report is accurate I had no opportunity of judging; the windows being all as it were hermetically closed; sashes, blinds, and every opening, except where tatties were placed to exclude the hot wind.[233] This surprized me very much: but I understand no method is so effectual for that purpose. I was not permitted to take my departure till the evening, when the fair lady of the mansion, dismissed me with many general professions of kindness, of which I knew how to estimate the value.

Next morning we received an invitation to the ball given annually on the King's birthday. This however I was under the necessity of declining on the plea of ill health and Mr. F— could hardly ever be persuaded to attend such formal assemblies.

When my husband waited on Sir Elijah Impey,[234] the Chief Justice, to shew his credentials, he met with a most flattering reception. It so happened that he was called to the Bar from Lincoln's Inn himself, and seemed quite at home while perusing the papers, being acquainted with the hand-writing of the officers who prepared them; and perhaps that circumstance might render him more partial. On Mr. F—'s expressing some apprehensions lest his having come out without leave of the E. I. Company might throw obstacles in the way of his admission to the Bar here, Sir E— indignantly exclaimed "No Sir, had you dropped from the clouds with such documents, we would admit you. The Supreme Court is independent and will never endure to be dictated to, by any body of men whose claims are not enforced by superior authority. It is nothing to us whether you *had* or *had not* permission from the Court of Directors, to proceed to this settlement; you come to us as an authenticated English Barrister, and as such, we shall on the first day of the next Term, admit you to *our Bar*." Sir E— also offered to introduce him to Mr. Hyde which Mr. F— thankfully accepted. Do you not admire the high tone in which Sir E— delivers his sentiments? There exists, it seems, a strong jealousy between the Government and the Supreme Court, lest either should encroach on the prerogatives of the other. The latter not long since committed Mr. Naylor the Company's Attorney for some breach of privilege, who being in a weak state of health at the time, died in confinement—this has increased the difference. I merely mention this *en passant*,[235] for it regards not us, let them quarrel, or agree; so the business of the Court be not impeded we cannot suffer. Mr. F— is already retained in several causes. His whole mind will now, I trust, be occupied with his profession, and as his abilities have never been questioned, I flatter myself that he has every reason to look forward to ultimate success.

20th July.

Hyder Ally has at length thrown off the mask, and commenced hostilities in good earnest. How providential was our liberation at that critical juncture! and my gratitude to Heaven was lately called forth in another instance—I recently conversed with a gentleman who crossed the Great Desert by way of Aleppo.—He assures me that besides the danger from the Arabs, there is so much more from other causes than in going over *that* to Suez, that he is quite confident, *I* never could have survived, the journey; "or," he added, "any European woman"—therefore on the whole we seem to have experienced the lesser evil, though the alternative of falling into the hands of the enemy was horrible! I am concerned to say that dreadful reports are in circulation respecting the excesses committed by Hyder's troops in the Carnatic,[236] but the particulars are too shocking to be repeated.

You have no idea how busy I am. Lady Chambers has been kind enough to lend me some of her dresses, for mine to be made by—I have commenced housekeeping, and am arranging my establishment, which is no little trouble in a country where the servants will not do a single thing, but that for which you expressly engage them nor even that willingly. I just now asked a man to place a small table near me; he began to bawl as loud as he could for the bearers to come and help him. "Why dont you do it yourself" said I? rising as I spoke to assist. *Oh I no English. I Bengal man. I no estrong like English; one, two, three Bengal men cannot do like one Englishman.*—Adieu remember you must write me long letters. You see even the heat has not reduced mine to a single sheet. I trust that I shall never be found incapable of addressing *you*. Mr. F— unites with me in kind remembrances.

I am ever most affectionately your's
&c. &c.

LETTER XVI.

CALCUTTA, 29th August.

MY DEAR FRIENDS,

Ten thousand thanks for the precious packet of letters I yesterday received: you can form no idea of the eagerness with which I flew from my dressing room; and Mr. F— from his study—at the joyful sound of "letters from England." But my very eagerness wrought for a while its own disappointment; for when I laid my hands on the prize, I fell into a kind of hysteric, and it was some time before I could break the seals, and yet would not suffer Mr. F— to deprive me of the gratification for which I had so long panted—over such treasures who would not be a miser—I would not permit a single scrap to escape me till I had devoured the whole. Those only know what that impatient hunger of the heart is after information, and the intercourse of affection, who have been debarred as long as I had been from objects so dear.

I rejoice to find that the Chevalier de St. Lubin performed his promise and that you now are in possession of every event that occurred to us till our arrival at Mocha. To know that we had passed the desert, that object of my dear mother's dread and apprehension, must have set her mind comparatively at ease; Alas! little did she suppose, how far more horrible were the miseries that we had still to undergo! thank Heaven, they are past.—I will quit the subject which agitates me too much.

I am happy to say that our house is a very comfortable one, but we are surrounded by a set of thieves. In England, if servants are dishonest we punish them, or turn them away in disgrace, and their fate proves, it may be hoped, a warning to others; but these wretches have no sense of shame. I will give you an instance or two of their conduct, that you may perceive how enviably I am situated. My Khansaman[237] (or house steward) brought in a charge of a gallon of milk and thirteen eggs, for making scarcely a pint and half of custard; this was so barefaced a cheat, that I refused to allow it, on which he gave me warning. I sent for another, and, after I had hired him, "now said I, take notice friend, I have enquired into the market price of every article that enters my house and will submit to no imposition; you must therefore agree to deliver in a just account to me every morning"—what reply do you think he made? why he demanded double wages; you may be sure I dismissed him, and have since forgiven the first but not till he had *salaamed* to my foot,[238] that is placed his right hand under my foot,—this is the most abject token of submission (alas! how much better should I like a little common honesty.) I know him to be a rogue, and so are they all, but as he understands me now, he will perhaps be induced to use rather more moderation in his attempts to defraud.—At first he used to charge me with twelve ounces of butter a day, for each person; now he grants that the consumption is only four ounces. As if these people were aware that I am writing about them, they have very obligingly furnished me with another anecdote. It seems my comprodore[239] (or market man) is gone away; he says poor servants have no profit by staying with *me*; at other gentlemen's houses he always made a rupee a day at least! besides his wages; but here if he only charges an anna[240] or two more, it is sure to be taken off—So you see what a terrible creature I am! I dare say you never gave me credit for being so close.—I find I was imposed on, in taking a comprodore at all; the Khansaman ought to do that business. Judge whether I have not sufficient employment among these harpies?[241] feeling as I do the necessity of a reasonable economy. It is astonishing, and would be amusing if one did not suffer by it, to see the various arts they will practice to keep a few annas in their hands, for though the lawful interest of money is but 12 per Cent (enough you will say), yet twenty four is given by the shopkeepers, who will lend or borrow the smallest sums for a single day, and ascertain the precise interest to the greatest exactitude, having the advantage of cowrees,[242] 5,120 of which go to make one rupee. The foolish custom which subsists here of keeping Banians,[243] gives rise to a thousand deceptions, as no one pays or receives money but through the medium of these people who have their profit on every thing that comes into the house.

In order to give you an idea of my houshold expenses and the price of living here, I must inform you that, our house costs only 200 rupees per month, because it is not in a part of the town much esteemed; otherwise we must pay 3 or 400 rupees; we are now seeking for a better situation. We were very frequently told in England you know, that the heat in Bengal destroyed the appetite, I must own that I never yet saw any proof of that; on the contrary I cannot help thinking that I never saw an equal quantity of victuals consumed. We dine too at two o'clock, in the very heat of the day. At this moment Mr. F— is looking out with an hawk's eye, for his dinner; and though still much of an invalid, I have no doubt of being able to pick a bit myself. I will give you our bill of fare, and the general prices of things. A soup, a roast fowl, curry and rice, a mutton pie, a fore quarter of lamb, a rice pudding, tarts, very good cheese, fresh churned butter, fine bread, excellent Madeira (that is expensive but eatables are very cheap,)—a whole sheep costs but two rupees: a lamb one rupee, six good fowls or ducks ditto—twelve pigeons ditto—twelve pounds of bread ditto—two pounds butter ditto; and a joint of veal ditto—good cheese two months ago sold at the enormous price of three or four rupees per pound, but now you may buy it for one and a half—English claret sells at this time for sixty rupees a dozen. There's a price for you! I need not say that much of it will not be seen at our table; now and then we are forced to produce it, but very seldom. I assure you much caution is requisite to avoid running deeply in debt—the facility of obtaining credit is beyond what I could have imagined; the Europe shop keepers are always ready to send in goods; and the Banians are so anxious to get into employment, that they out bid each other. One says "master better take me, I will advance five thousand rupees"—another offers seven, and perhaps a third ten thousand: a Company's servant particularly will always find numbers ready to support his extravagance. It is not uncommon to see *writers*[244] within a few months after their arrivals dashing away on the course *four in hand*:[245] allowing for the inconsiderateness of youth, is it surprising if many become deeply embarrassed?—Several have been pointed out to me, who in the course of two or three years, have involved themselves almost beyond hope of redemption. The interest of money here being twelve per Cent, and the Banian taking care to secure bonds for whatever he advances, making up the account yearly and adding the sum due for interest, his thoughtless *master*, (as he calls him, but in fact his slave) soon finds his debt doubled, and dares not complain unless he has the means of release which alas! are denied him.

I should have told you before that Mr. F— was admitted an advocate in the Supreme Court, on the 16th June,—has been engaged in several causes, wherein he acquitted himself to general satisfaction and is at present as busy as can be desired. Every one seems willing to encourage him and if he continue but his own friend, all will, I feel persuaded, go well with us, and we shall collect our share of gold mohurs,[246] as well as our neighbours.—I like to see the briefs come in well enough. The fees are much higher here than in England, so you will say "they ought" and I perfectly agree with you.

Sir R. C— met with an accident some weeks ago (by jumping out of a carriage when the horses were restive) which confined him to his house a long while but he is now recovering; I was a good deal vexed both on his own account poor man, and because Mr. F— was deprived of his friendly aid. I have seen little of my kind patroness since, for she goes scarce any where without her husband—we were to dine with them the very day the circumstance happened. They are gone up the country and will not return for some months.

31 August.

I have received another packet and rejoice to hear you are all going on so well. They talk of a frigate being soon to sail, in which case I shall close and dispatch this.—As I propose sending you a regular supply of Calcutta Gazettes,[247] there can be no necessity to fill my letters with political information. I trust that in a short time Hyder will be effectually humbled.

Mr. H— has visited us several times; and is now quite complaisant to Mr. Fay. This is the way of the world you know, and of course to be expected from such a slave to outward circumstance, such a mere "summer friend"[248] as this man ever evinced himself.—By his account the hardships they underwent would very soon have destroyed so poor a creature as I was at that time: so that the difficulties we fell into, though at the moment of suffering so deplored, proved eventually our safe guard in more respects than one. Had we not touched at Calicut, I am fully persuaded we should have been shipwrecked, and had not my illness furnished a pretext for detaining us there after the rest, I should have died among those cruel people in the most shocking way imaginable, since they were for a long while absolutely destitute of every necessary. What short-sighted beings we are!

how futile, how defective our best formed calculations! I have sometimes pleased myself (I hope not improperly) with the idea, that the power of discerning clearly the beneficent designs of providence during our earthly pilgrimage, and of perceiving that in a thousand instances like these, a rough and stony path has led to safety and ultimate happiness, may be intended to form part of our enjoyment in a future state, wherein we are taught that to contemplate the Supreme Being in his perfections will constitute the height of bliss.—Let me have your sentiments on the subject; its discussion can do neither of us harm and may lead to improvement.

8th September.

I have nothing particular to add—my health continues very good considering all things. This is a dull time: vacations are always so to professional people. God bless you and grant us a happy meeting—our prospects are good; nothing but the grossest misconduct can prevent our success. Adieu

Yours most affectionately
E. F.

LETTER XVII.

CALCUTTA, 27th September.

MY DEAR FRIENDS,

The bad news I hinted at some time ago is already avenged; and a much more serious affair has happened since, but for the present I must relate what has occupied a great deal of attention for some days past: no less than a duel between the Governor General and the first in Council, Mr. Francis;[249] there were two shots fired, and the Governor's second fire took place; he immediately ran up to his antagonist and expressed his sorrow for what had happened, which I dare say was sincere, for he is said to be a very amiable man. Happily the ball was soon extracted; and if he escape fever, there is no doubt of his speedy recovery. What gave occasion to the quarrel is said to have been an offensive Minute entered on the Council books by Mr. Francis, which he refused to rescind; but being unacquainted with the particulars, I have as little right as inclination to make any comments on the subject—It always vexes me to hear of such things. What a shocking custom is that of duelling! yet there are times when men may be so situated that, as the world goes, one knows not how they could act otherwise; much may be effected by the judicious interference of friends, but those qualified for the task are rarely to be met with. Mr. Francis is highly respected here, and being now at the head of what is called the opposition party, his death would be severely felt by many who affect great indifference about the event.

Since I wrote last we have had a good deal of trouble with our Mohametan servants, on account of an old custom; not one of them would touch a plate on which pork had been laid—so that whenever we had any at table our plates remained, till the cook or his mate came up to change them. This being represented as a religious prejudice, I felt it right to give way, however ridiculous it might appear, in fact it was an inconvenience we felt in common with the whole settlement, except the gentlemen of the Army who had long before emancipated themselves from any such restraint; finding this to be really the case the whole of the European inhabitants agreed to insist upon their servants doing the same as those of the officers at the Fort, or quitting their places. They chose the latter alternative, and as their prejudices run very high in all religious matters, we were in doubt whether they would not prefer suffering the greatest extremity rather, than touch the very vessels which contained this abhorred food,—but behold in about four days they came back again requesting to be reinstated; and acknowledging that the only penalty incurred by touching the plates was the necessity of bathing afterwards: from this you may judge of their excessive idleness; however all now goes on well and we hear no more of their objection –

The serious affair at which I hinted in the beginning of this letter, was the cutting off Col. Baillie's detachment[250] with dreadful slaughter. I trust we shall soon have ample revenge, for that fine old veteran Sir Eyre Coote[251] is about to take the field and his very name will strike those undisciplined hordes with terror—Oh how I feel interested in the event!

Nothing surely can be more disagreeable than the weather here at present, it is very hot with scarcely a breath of air stirring; and such swarms of insects buzzing about, but beyond all the bug fly is disgusting—one of them will scent a room; they are in form like a ladybird but their smell is a thousand times more offensive than that of our bugs. A good breeze would disperse them all, but that we must not expect till the monsoon changes, that is, about the middle of next month.

I never told you that one of the Captains who had charge of us at Calicut made his escape some months ago, and came to ask our assistance till he could get employment up the country. Mr. F— gave him a lower room, and he remained with us several weeks: his name is West.[252] This was the man from whom we collected intelligence of the plots laid against us there, and which had nearly proved successful. West is a stout fellow accustomed in his early days to labour, and seasoned to the climate;—he is gone up to Patna, in charge of some boats and is to remain there. Ayres used to treat him very ill at times, and *he* says attemped more than once to assassinate him, because he refused to concur with a party that Ayres headed, consisting of six or eight abandoned wretches whose intention it was to cut off several of the more opulent natives *secretly*, and possess themselves of their effects; while they should contrive to fix the guilt of the transaction on some persons who were obnoxious to them. West threatened to reveal the whole plot, on which they pretended to abandon it, but he soon found their object was to rid themselves of him; and he effected his escape in a canoe (at the utmost risk of perishing in the attempt) to Cochin, from whence he easily got a passage to Bengal. What a horrible fellow is that Ayres! surely he will meet his deserts: should the English take him he will be shot instantly as a deserter.

We have found out a nephew of Isaac's named Daniel, he is a man of no great consequence here, either in point of situation or circumstances though not absolutely poor:—we asked him to dinner, and endeavoured by every means in our power to evince the grateful sense we entertain of his worthy uncle's kindness and beneficence.

3rd November.

Since my last date I have the pleasure to acknowledge the receipt of another packet from England, with the gratifying intelligence that you were all well on the 7th of April. My time has passed very stupidly for some months, but the town is now beginning to fill,—people are returning for the cold season. Term has commenced, and Mr. F— has no reason to complain of business falling off; if *he* fall not from it, all will be well. My first Patroness Lady C— is returned from her tour but Sir Robert having purchased an elegant mansion in Calcutta, (for which he is to pay £6,000, in England) her Ladyship has full employment in arranging and fitting up her new abode; so that I see but little of her; she is however always kind and full of condescension towards me when we do meet.

19th December.

Mr. Fay has met with a gentleman here, a Dr. Jackson[253] who comes from the same part of Ireland, and knows many of his connections; they soon became intimate. Dr. J—— is physician to the Company, and in very high practice besides; I have been visited by the whole family. The eldest son a fine noble looking young man, is a Lieutenant in the Army, and has lately married a very pretty little woman, who came out in the same ship under the protection of his mother; as did Miss C——y a most amiable and interesting young Lady, who now resides with them. They have not been long arrived. The Doctor's Lady is a native of Jamaica and like those "children of the sun,"[254] frank and hospitable to a degree—fond of social parties in the old style "where the song and merry jest circulate round the festive board"[255] particularly after supper. Dinner parties they seldom give; but I have been present at several elsewhere since the commencement of the cold season. The dinner hour as I mentioned before is two, and it is customary to sit a long while at table; particularly during the cold season; for people here are mighty fond of grills and stews, which they season themselves, and generally make very hot. The Burdwan stew[256] takes a deal of time; it is composed of every thing at table, fish, flesh and fowl;—somewhat like the Spanish Olla Podrida,[257]—Many suppose that unless prepared in a silver saucepan it cannot be good; on this point I must not presume to give an opinion, being satisfied with plain food; and never tasting any of these incentives to luxurious indulgence. During dinner a good deal of wine is drank, but a very little after the cloth is removed; except in Bachelors parties, as they are called; for the custom of reposing, if not of sleeping after dinner is so general that the streets of Calcutta are from four to five in the afternoon almost as empty of Europeans as if it were midnight—Next come the evening airings to the Course, every one goes, though sure of being half suffocated with dust. On returning from thence, tea is served, and universally drank here, even during the extreme heats. After tea, either cards or music fill up the space, 'till ten, when supper is generally announced. Five card loo is the usual game and they play a rupee a fish limited to ten. This will strike you as being enormously high but it is thought nothing of here. Tré dille and Whist[258] are much in fashion but ladies seldom join in the latter; for though the stakes are moderate, bets frequently run high among the gentlemen which renders those anxious who sit down for amusement, lest others should lose by their blunders.

Formal visits are paid in the evening; they are generally very short, as perhaps each lady has a dozen to make and a party waiting for her at home besides. Gentlemen also call to offer their respects and if asked to put down their hat, it is considered as an invitation to supper. Many a hat have I seen vainly dangling in its owner's hand for half an hour, who at last has been compelled to withdraw without any one's offering to relieve him from the burthen.

Great preparations are making for the Christmas, and New year's public balls;—of course you will not expect me to write much till they are over; nor to own the truth am I in spirits, having great reason to be dissatisfied with Mr. F—'s conduct. Instead of cultivating the intimacy of those who might be serviceable or paying the necessary attention to persons in power; I can scarcely ever prevail on him to accompany me even to Dr. J—'s who is generally visited by the first people; but he cannot endure being subjected to the forms of society—some times he has called on Sir R. C— but the other Judges he has never *seen*, except on the bench since his admission: he did not even accept Sir E. I—'s obliging offer to introduce him to Mr. Hyde,[259] but suffered Mr. Sealy to perform that ceremony, and when the Chief Justice advanced to accompany him, he was forced to acknowledge that he had been already introduced,—upon which the great man turned on his heel and hardly ever noticed him afterwards. This happened on the day Mr. F— was admitted to the bar at Mr. H—'s public breakfast at whose house the professional gentlemen all meet on the first day of every Term and go from thence in procession to the Court House. I will now close this letter in the hope of having better accounts to give you in my next.

Your's affectionately
E. F.

LETTER XVIII.

CALCUTTA, 27th Jan., 1781.

MY DEAR SISTER,

Since my last we have been engaged in a perpetual round of gaiety—keeping Christmas, as it is called, though sinking into disuse at home, prevails here with all its ancient festivity. The external appearance of the English gentlemen's houses on Christmas-day, is really pleasing from its novelty. Large plantain trees are placed on each side of the principal entrances, and the gates and pillars being ornamented with wreaths of flowers fancifully disposed, enliven the scene.

All the servants bring presents of fish and fruit from the Banian down to the lowest menial; for these it is true we are obliged in many instances to make a return, perhaps beyond the real value, but still it is considered as a compliment to our *burrah din* (great day). A public dinner is given at the Government house to the gentlemen of the Presidency, and the evening concludes with an elegant Ball & Supper for the Ladies. These are repeated on New year's day and again on the King's birth day.[260] I should say have been, for that grand festival happening at the hottest season, and every one being obliged to appear full dressed, so much inconvenience resulted from the immense croud, even in some cases severe fits of illness being the consequence, that it has been determined to change the day of celebration to the 8th of December which arrangement gives general satisfaction.—I shall not attempt to describe these splendid entertainments farther than by saying that they were in the highest style of magnificence: in fact such grand parties so much resemble each other, that a particular detail would be unnecessary and even tiresome.

I felt far more gratified some time ago, when Mrs. Jackson procured me a ticket for the Harmonic[261] which was supported by a select number of gentlemen who each in alphabetical rotation gave a concert, ball, and supper, during the cold season; I believe once a fortnight—that I attended was given by a Mr. Taylor, which closed the subscription and I understand it will not be renewed, a circumstance generally regretted as it was an elegant amusement and conducted on a very eligible plan. We had a great deal of delightful music, and Lady Chambers, who is a capital performer on the harpsichord played amongst other pieces a Sonata of Nicolai's[262] in a most brilliant style. A gentleman who was present and who seemed to be quite charmed with her execution, asked me the next evening, if I did not think that *jig* Lady C— played the night before, was the prettiest thing I ever heard? He meant the rondo which is remarkably lively; but I dare say "Over the water to Charley" would have pleased him equally well.

Mrs. H— was of the party; she came in late, and happened to place herself on the opposite side of the room, beyond a speaking distance, so strange to tell, I quite forgot she was there! After some time had elapsed, my observant friend Mrs. Jackson, who had been impatiently watching my looks, asked if I had paid my respects to the Lady Governess? I answered in the negative, having had no opportunity, as she had not chanced to look towards me when I was prepared to do so. "Oh, replied the kind old lady, you must fix your eyes on her, and never take them off 'till she notices you; Miss C— has done this, and so have I; it is absolutely necessary to avoid giving offence." I followed her prudent advice and was soon honoured with a complacent glance, which I returned as became me by a most respectful bend. Not long after she walked over to our side and conversed very affably with me, for we are now through Mrs. Jackson's interference on good terms together.

She also introduced me to Lady C— and her inseparable friend Miss Molly Bazett.[263] It was agreed between them when they were both girls that, whichever married first the other was to live with her, and accordingly when Sir E— took his lady from St. Helena, of which place her father was governor, Miss Molly who is a native of the island accompanied them to England and from thence to India, where she has remained ever since;—thus giving a proof of steady attachment not often equalled and never perhaps excelled.

19th February.

Yesterday being the Anniversary of our release from imprisonment, we invited Dr. Jackson's family, Mr. O'Donnell and some friends to assist in its celebration; I call it my 'Jubilee Day' and trust my dear friends at home did not forget the occasion.

This reminds me to tell you that Sudder Khan and Ayres our chief enemies have both closed their career of wickedness. The former died of wounds received before Tellicherry; and the latter having repeatedly advanced close to the lines of that place, holding the most contemptuous language and indecent gestures towards the Officers; setting every one at defiance and daring them to fire at him, (I suppose in a state of intoxication, miserable wretch!) was at length picked off, to use a military phrase.—Too honourable a death for such a monster of iniquity. My hope was, that he would have been taken prisoner, and afterwards recognised and shot as a deserter.

Poor West is also dead; he never reached his destination—the boat he went up in, by some accident struck on a sand bank and nearly all on board perished.

26th March.

A Frigate being ordered to sail for Europe with dispatches from Government, I shall avail myself of the occasion, and close this letter with a few remarks on our theatrical amusements.

The house was built by subscription;[264] it is very neatly fitted up, and the scenery and decorations quite equal to what could be expected here. The parts are entirely represented by amateurs in the drama—no hired performers being allowed to act. I assure you I have seen characters supported in a manner that would not disgrace *any* European stage. *Venice Preserved*[265] was exhibited some time ago, when Captain Call (of the Army) Mr. Droz (a member of the Board of Trade) and Lieutenant Norfar,[266] in Jaffier, Pierre, and Belvidera shewed very superior theatrical talents. The latter has rather an effeminate appearance off the stage, yet I am told he is a very brave Officer when on service; and though always dressed as if for a ball, when he makes his appearance, is among the most alert in a moment of danger. I cannot imagine how he contrives it, for the present mode of arranging the hair requires a great deal of time to make it look tolerable; however this is said to be the case.—One of the chief inconveniences in establishments of this kind, is that the performers being independent of any controul, will some times persist in taking parts to which their abilities are by no means adequate;—this throws an air of ridicule over the whole, as the spectators are too apt to indulge their mirth on the least opening of that kind: in fact many go to see a tragedy for the express purpose of enjoying a laugh, which is certainly very illiberal and must prove detrimental to the hopes of an enfant institution like the one in question:—for my own part I think such a mode of passing an evening highly rational; and were I not debarred by the expence should seldom miss a representation—but a gold mohur is really too much to bestow on such a temporary gratification. Adieu—I shall write again soon.

Your's most affectionately
E. F.

LETTER XIX.

CALCUTTA, 26th May.

MY DEAR SISTER,

You must have perceived that the style of my letters for some months past has been constrained, nor could it possibly be otherwise; for not wishing to grieve your affectionate heart by a recital of the melancholy change in my prospects, occasioned by Mr. F—'s imprudent behaviour, I was reduced to enlarge on less important subjects. Some hints however escaped me which must have led you to suspect that all was not going on properly; but his conduct of late has been such that no hope remains of his *ever* being able to prosecute his profession here.

Ever since our arrival he has acted in every respect directly contrary to my advice—By constantly associating with persons who had distinguished themselves by thwarting the measures of Government,—he soon became equally obnoxious. On one occasion when a tax was proposed to be levied on houses, several meetings were held at our house, wherein he openly insisted on the illegality of such a procedure, and encouraged his *new* friends to assert their independence. I remonstrated in the strongest terms against measures so pregnant with evil, and which must terminate in utter ruin, if not speedily abandoned; the character of our *chief ruler*[267] being well known;—he will never *desert* a friend or *forgive* an enemy; what chance then has an individual who rashly incurs his resentment of escaping its baneful effects? all this and more I repeatedly but alas *vainly* urged—my representations were as heretofore treated with contempt: he still persevered, giving himself entirely up to low and unworthy pursuits, while his professional duties were wholly neglected and his best friends slighted.

We were frequently invited to parties which he as constantly evaded, leaving me to make what excuses I could for his absence.—My dear kind Patroness Lady C—, still continues on my account to shew him attention as do the Jacksons and some few others: she has lately added a son to her family;[268]—I was with her at the time, and the sweet infant seems to have formed closer ties between us. On a late occasion however she was compelled to speak plainly. The christening is to take place in a few days; Sir Elijah and Lady Impey have offered to stand for the child, and Lady C— wishes me to be present, but Sir E— positively refuses to meet Mr. F— who of course cannot be included; so unless I can reconcile him to the omission I must remain at home also.

3d June.

The grand ceremony is over. I had no difficulty with Mr. F— he declared himself pre-engaged the instant I mentioned the subject, and insisted that I should make some apology for him which was readily promised—You may suppose that I could not under such circumstances enjoy much pleasure though Sir E— and his Lady behaved very graciously. But the idea that my husband was so totally proscribed where he might have figured among the foremost pierced my very soul; yet was I forced to put on the appearance of cheerfulness, that I might seem to receive as a compliment what was certainly so intended. The public countenance of Lady C— and being admitted to such a select party cannot but operate favourably for me at this crisis, when I shall stand so much in need of support.

24th June.

Though term is now far advanced, Mr. F— has scarcely a brief. The attorneys are positively afraid to employ him; and causes have actually come on with two advocates on one side and one on the other, rather than permit him to appear in them. What a noble opportunity of making an ample fortune is thus wantonly thrown away! Heaven grant me patience. I have only this reflection to console me, that every effort in my power has been made to ward off the blow which is now inevitable.

I yesterday confided to Lady C— my real situation: who (on my stating that Mr. F— must certainly be obliged to quit the Settlement very shortly,) with the utmost kindness insisted on my making her house, my home whenever that event should take place; and Sir R— has in the most cordial way inforced the invitation.— Thus through the goodness of Providence am I provided with a secure and highly respectable asylum, till a passage to Europe can be obtained on moderate terms, a difficult matter to accomplish.

17th July.

On the last day of the present month we must quit our house; and when my husband and I may reside under the same roof together again, Heaven alone can tell. It is astonishing to see with what apparent unconcern he supports the shock: but the acquisition of a new Patron has raised his spirits. Colonel Watson,[269] a man of superior abilities and immense fortune has been long a determined opposer of Government, and the *bitter* enemy of Sir E. I— against whom he has set an impeachment on foot, to prosecute which it is requisite that a confidential agent should serve the process on the defendant here, and proceed to England with the necessary documents. Mr. F— has contrived to get himself appointed to this office: he has drawn up a set of articles many copies of which are preparing by Bengalee writers, who though they profess to understand English and are tolerably correct in copying what is put before them, know not the meaning of any thing they write; a great convenience this to such as conduct affairs that require secrecy, since the persons employed, cannot, if they were so disposed, betray their trust. Colonel W— never comes here; all is carried on with an air of profound mystery—I like not such proceedings and doubt if any good can come of them, but I dare not interfere nor drop even a hint which might lead to suspicion that any thing extraordinary is going forward. The duty of a wife which is paramount to all other civil obligations, compels me silently to witness what is beyond my power to counteract; although the character of a highly revered friend is obliquely glanced at, and may be in future more seriously implicated in the business—you will guess to whom I allude. Adieu you shall hear from me again when I change my abode.

Your's affectionately
E. F.

LETTER XX.

CALCUTTA, 28th August.

MY DEAR SISTER,

Since I wrote last, my feelings have been harrassed in various ways almost beyond endurance—Mr. Fay quitted me on the 31st ultimo, and the rest of that day was devoted to the distressing (however just and necessary) task of delivering back such articles of furniture as had not been paid for, to the persons who supplied us with them; and also returning what had been borrowed of different friends for our convenience; what remained was taken possession of next morning, by a man to whom my unfortunate husband had given a bond for money advanced on the most exorbitant terms, to support his extravagance. Thus am I left destitute of every thing but my clothes, to endure the wretched effects of his imprudence, with a constitution weakened by the sufferings and privations, I underwent during my eventful journey, added to the dread which I cannot avoid feeling lest that unlucky blow I received in Calicut should be productive of serious consequences.

Lady C— welcomed me as a sister, she wishes me to accompany her every where but time alone can reconcile me to general society:—The very day of my removal here, a circumstance was disclosed that determined me no longer to bind my destiny with that of a man who could thus set at defiance all ties divine and human. After consulting my legal friends I demanded a separation, to which he having consented, a deed was drawn up by Mr. S— under the inspection of Sir R. C—, in the fullest manner possible rendering me wholly independent of Mr. F—'s authority, with power, to make a will &c. in short conceived in the strongest terms our language could supply. I have appointed Mr. G. Jones Solicitor of Lincoln's Inn and Mr. Mc Veagh one of the masters in Chancery here to act as my Trustees. Two more respectable men I could not have chosen. You my dear sister, who know better than any one, what exertions I have used, and what sacrifices I have *vainly* made for this most ungrateful of beings, will not be surprised to find that even *my* patience was not proof against this last outrage.

But let me dismiss the hateful subject merely stating that the deeds were signed on the 11th instant. His secret[270] is safe with me, though when we met on that occasion he had the insolence to hint his belief that out of *revenge* I should divulge it. So let him *still* think, for I deigned no reply except by a look; when I with secret triumph beheld his hitherto undaunted eye sink beneath the indignant glance of mine.

"Tis Conscience that makes cowards of us all."[271]

5th September.

Sir Robert being appointed President of the Court at Chinsurah,[272] is gone up to take possession of his charge, accompanied by Lady C— and the family. So here am I left alone to ramble over this great house and meditate on irreparable evils. Sir R—has however kindly entrusted me with the keys of his immense library, which will furnish a rich treat when my mind acquires sufficient calmness to look beyond itself in search of amusement.

The acquaintance of Mrs. Wheler[273] I have found a most valuable acquisition. I went with Lady C— to pass a day with her at the gardens, and have been treated with the utmost attention ever since. She has authorised me to look up to her as a steady patroness on all occasions. Mr. H— being gone up the country on political business Mr. Wheler of course takes the chair during his absence so you may judge what influence Mrs. W— possesses; but "she bears her honors so meekly" and contrives to soften the refusals which she is frequently compelled to give by so much affability and sympathy, as to conciliate all parties and render herself generally beloved.

I have never mentioned yet how indifferently we are provided with respect to a place of worship; divine service being performed, in a room, (not a very large one) at the Old Fort; which is a great disgrace to the settlement. They talk of building a Church and have fixed on a very eligible spot whereon to erect it but no further progress has been made in the business.

I now propose, having full leisure to give you some account of the East Indian customs and ceremonies, such as I have been able to collect, but it must be considered as a mere sketch, to point your further researches. And first for that horrible custom of widows burning themselves[274] with the dead bodies of their husbands; the fact is indubitable, but I have never had an opportunity of witnessing the various incidental ceremonies, nor have I ever seen any European who had been present at them. I cannot suppose that the usage originated in the superior tenderness, and ardent attachment of Indian wives towards their spouses, since the same tenderness and ardour would doubtless extend to his offspring and prevent them from exposing the innocent survivors to the miseries attendant on an orphan state, and they would see clearly that to live and cherish these pledges of affection would be the most rational and natural way of shewing their regard for both husband and children. I apprehend that as personal fondness can have no part here at all, since all matches are made between the parents of the parties who are betrothed to each other at too early a period for choice to be consulted, this practice is entirely a political scheme intended to insure the care and good offices of wives to their husbands, who have not failed in most countries to invent a sufficient number of rules to render the weaker sex totally subservient to their authority. I cannot avoid smiling when I hear gentlemen bring forward the conduct of the Hindoo women, as a test of superior character, since I am well aware that so much are we the slaves of habit *every where* that were it necessary for a woman's reputation to burn herself in England, many a one who has *accepted* a husband merely for the sake of an establishment, who has lived with him without affection; perhaps thwarted his views, dissipated his fortune and rendered his life uncomfortable to its close, would yet mount the funeral pile with all imaginable decency and die with heroic fortitude. The most specious sacrifices are not always the greatest, she who wages war with a naturally petulant temper, who practises a rigid self-denial, endures without complaining the unkindness, infidelity, extravagance, meanness or scorn, of the man to whom she has given a tender and confiding heart, and for whose happiness and well being in life all the powers of her mind are engaged;—is ten times more of a heroine than the slave of bigotry and superstition, who affects to scorn the life demanded of her by the laws of her country or at least that country's custom; and many such we have in England, and I doubt not in India likewise: so indeed we ought, have we not a religion infinitely more pure than that of India? The Hindoos, or gentoos are divided into four castes or tribes called the Brahmin, the Khutree, the Buesho, and the Shodor: their rank in the land, declines gradually to the last named, and if any of them commit an offence which deprives them of the privileges that belong to their respective castes, they become Parias,[275] which may therefore be called a filthy tribe formed as it were of the refuse of the rest. Those are indeed considered the very dregs of the people, and supply all the lowest offices of human life. They all profess what is called the religion of Brahma,[276] from the caste which bears his name all the priests are chosen, who are treated in every respect with distinguished honour and reverence. Their religious Code is contained in a book called the Veda, which only the Brahmins are allowed to read; it is written in a dead language called the Sanscrit. They worship three Deities, Brahma, the creator, Vistnoo the preserver, and Sheevah the destroyer. But they profess to believe them only the representations or types of the great spirit Brahma (the Supreme God) whom they also call the spirit of wisdom, and the principle of Truth: none but Hindoos are allowed to enter temples, but I am told the Idols worshipped there are of the very ugliest forms that imagination can conceive; and to whom Pope's description of the heathen deities may, in other respects, be strictly applied.

"Gods changeful, partial, passionate unjust.
Whose attributes *are* rage, revenge, or lust."[277]

I lament to add to such wretched objects as these, numbers of the deluded natives are devoted in the strongest and most absolute manner possible. A certain sect named Pundarams[278] live in continual beggary; extreme hunger alone induces them to ask for food, which when granted, they only take just what will preserve life, and spend all their days in singing songs in praise of Sheevah; another sect add a tabor, and hollow brass rings about their ancles to increase the noise with which they extol *their* deity. I consider both these as a species of monks but believe the holy fathers fall far short of the Jogees[279] and Seniases[280] of India, in their religious austerities. These not only endure all possible privations with apparent indifference, but invent for themselves various kinds of tortures which they carry to an astonishing length; such as keeping their hands clenched 'till the nails grow into them,—standing on one foot for days and even weeks together—and hiring people to support their hands in a perpendicular position.

Their expiatory punishments are some of them dreadful. I myself saw a man running in the streets with a piece of iron thrust through his tongue which was bleeding profusely. On the Churruk Poojah[281] (swinging feast) hundreds I have heard, are suspended at an amazing height by means of hooks, firmly fixed in the flesh of the back, to which sometimes a cloth is added round the body to afford the miserable victim a chance of escape, should the hook give way. I, by accident, (for voluntarily nothing should have tempted me to witness such a spectacle) saw one of these wretches, who was whirling round with surprizing rapidity, and at that distance scarcely appeared to retain the semblance of a human form. They firmly expect by this infliction to obtain pardon of all their offences, and should death be the consequence, they go straight to heaven—thus changing the horrid state of privation and misery in which they exist here, for one of bliss: if such be their real persuasion, who can condemn the result.

Indeed under other circumstances it is found that, notwithstanding their apparent gentleness and timidity, the Hindoos will meet death with intrepid firmness—they are also invincibly obstinate, and will *die* rather than concede a point: of this a very painful instance has lately occurred.—A Hindoo beggar of the Brahmin caste went to the house of a very rich man, but of an inferior tribe, requesting alms; he was either rejected, or considered himself inadequately relieved, and refused to quit the place. As his lying before the door and thus obstructing the passage was unpleasant, one of the servants first intreated, then insisted on his retiring, and in speaking pushed him gently away; he chose to call this push a blow, and cried aloud for redress, declaring that he would never stir from the spot 'till he had obtained justice against the man: who now endeavoured to sooth him but in vain; like a true Hindoo he sat down, and never moved again, but thirty-eight hours afterwards expired, demanding justice with his latest breath; being well aware that in the event of this, the master would have an enormous fine to pay, which accordingly happened. I am assured that such evidences of the surprizing indifference to life, the inflexible stubbornness, and vindictive dispositions of these people are by no means rare; it seems extraordinary though, that sentiments and feelings apparently so contrary to each other should operate on the same minds; seeing them so quiet and supine, so (if it may be so expressed) only half alive, as they generally shew themselves, one is prepared for their sinking, without an effort to avert any impending danger; but that they should at the same time nourish so violent and active a passion as revenge, and brave even death so intrepidly as they often do in pursuit of it, is very singular:—but enough of these silly enthusiasts.

I had lately the opportunity of witnessing the marriage procession of a rich Hindoo. The bride (as I was told) sat in the same palanquin with the bridegroom, which was splendidly ornamented;—they were accompanied by all the relations on both sides, dressed in the most superb manner;—some on horse back, some in palanquins, and several on elephants;—bands of dancing girls and musicians I understood preceded them;—and in the evening there were fireworks at the bride's father's house and the appearance of much feasting &c. but no Europeans were present. This wedding was of a nature by no means uncommon here; a rich man had an only daughter, and he bargained to dispose of her, or rather to take for her a husband out of a poor man's family, but of his own *Caste:* for this is indispensable. In this case the bridegroom is brought home to his father-in-law's house and becomes a member of the family; so that although the law prohibits a man from giving a dowry with his daughter, yet you see he does it in effect, since he gives a house to a man who wants one; gives in fact, a fortune but saddled with an encumbrance;—perhaps in a few years the old man may die, and the young one having fulfilled the wishes of his parents, and provided for his own wants, may employ some of his female relations to look round among the poorer families of his caste for a pretty girl, whom he will take as a second wife, tho' the first always retains the pre-eminence, and governs the house; nor can the husband devote more of his time to one than the other,—the law compelling him to live with them alternately, you may be sure the account is strictly kept. My Banian Dattaram Chuckerbutty has been married between twenty and thirty years, without taking a second lady, and he boasts of being much happier with his old wife (as he calls her) than the generality of his friends are amidst the charms of variety. For my own part, I have not a doubt but he is in the right.

The Hindoo ladies are never seen abroad; when they go out their carriages are closely covered with curtains, so that one has little chance of satisfying curiosity. I once saw two apparently very beautiful women: they use so much art however, as renders it difficult to judge what claim they *really* have to that appellation— Their whole time is taken up in decorating their persons:—the hair—eye-lids— eye-brows—teeth—hands and nails, all undergo certain processes to render them more completely fascinating; nor can one seriously blame their having recourse to these, or the like artifices—the motive being to secure the affections of a husband, or to counteract the plans of a rival.

27th September.

The Hindoos who can afford to purchase wood for a funeral pile, burn their dead; one cannot go on the river without seeing numbers of these exhibitions, especially at night, and most disgusting spectacles they are. I will not enlarge on the subject. This mode however is far superior to that of throwing them into the river as practised by the poor; where they offend more senses than one. I have been frequently obliged to return precipitately from a walk along the river side, by the noisome exhalations which arose from these wretched objects.

Some of the Hindoo customs respecting the sick are really shocking—When a person is given over by the Brahmins, (who are physicians as well as priests) the relations immediately carry him, if within a reasonable distance, to the banks of the Ganges, where he is smeared with the mud, quantities of which I am told are thrust into his mouth, nose, and ears. This treatment soon reduces him to a dying state; nor is it desirable that he should recover, since he must in that case lose caste; for it is an established rule, that whoever removes from the spot where the sacred rites have been performed, becomes an outcast. Dr. Jackson was once fortunate enough to be called in to attend the wife of a Hindoo Rajah[282] whom they were on the point of taking to the river when he arrived—he assured the Rajah that he perceived no dangerous symptoms and would answer for her doing well.— Luckily the tremendous ceremonies had not commenced: The event justified our good Doctor's predictions—the lady is still living and his success in this instance, has led to several others, highly gratifying to the best feelings of humanity and certainly beneficial to his fortune.

This letter has run to such an enormous length that I must now conclude, with wishing that I may soon hear good news of you. I remain,

Your's most affectionately
E. F.

LETTER XXI.

CALCUTTA, 17th December.

MY DEAR SISTER.

Sir R— and Lady C— have been down since I wrote last, and remained here during term, but are now gone up again, though much distressed. Mrs. C— prefers staying here.—A melancholy event has occurred in the family; the sweet little boy just turned of six months old, to whom I was so fondly attached, died a few weeks ago. Dear interesting child! I shall *long* lament his loss. He was not ill more than three days; so rapid is the progress of disease in this country.

Mr. and Mrs. Hosea[283] are arrived in Town and have taken accommodations on the *Grosvenor*, Captain Coxon. I was in hopes of being able to take my passage with them but am disappointed.

Mr. H— was Resident at one of the upper stations; he is a man of high character and generally esteemed; and his wife one of the most amiable women I ever knew; it is impossible to do otherwise than love her. As she daily looks to be confined, her leaving Calcutta till after that period, is out of the question, so they must suffer the *Grosvenor* to proceed to Madras without them, where she is expected to remain a month at least, and the family and baggage of Mr. H— are to follow in a Country ship at the risk of arriving too late.

The agreement is that, if she sail from thence before a certain day a small sum is to be forfeited; but *after* that day, should Captain Coxon be compelled to proceed on his voyage without them, he is still to receive ten thousand rupees, that is half the passage money by way of compensation. I state these particulars to shew what large sums are exacted of passengers.

The society of Mrs. Chambers,[284] who is a fine looking respectable old lady, well informed and chearful, with that of Mrs. H—, who has charming spirits, enables me to pass the time far more pleasantly than when I was left here during the rains. Besides I often visit at Dr. Jackson's, and have made acquaintance with several agreeable families, who allow me to call on them without formality; the very idea of which is hateful to me at present: so cruelly fallen are my once highly and justly raised expectations. For what place do I now hold in the Society with which I am permitted to mix? Alas, none except by sufferance: but most ardently do I wish to escape from this fatal spot the scene of so many severe afflictions, and seek comfort with those who have never failed to afford it. There I shall not be constantly reminded of past hopes, now alas! sunk in disappointment. Think not these observations proceed from a repining spirit, or unmindfulness of favors received; I have been most beneficently treated and my views have been furthered in a way which I had no right whatever to expect. Can attentions like those be forgotten? No! it forms my proudest boast that *I have* such friends, and while life remains I must ever cherish the remembrance of their generous exertions. The approaching season always inspires melancholy reflections—I will therefore pass it over, and look forward to the next, when by the blessing of Providence I hope to be with my beloved family.

27th January, 1782.

My dear Mrs. H— has thank heaven, got happily over her confinement, which took place three weeks ago; and all is now bustle and preparation for their departure.—Sir R—'s eldest son, Thomas, goes under their care; he is a charming boy, nearly seven years of age, which is rather late; but no good opportunity has occurred 'till now;—a Miss Shore (the daughter of an intimate friend) about the age of Thomas, also proceeds with them. Mrs. H— takes one little girl of her own, sixteen months old; the baby is to be left with Lady C—: she promises to be a lovely child.

We are to have the christening to-morrow when I shall take my leave of large parties; except one, which I must attend. Mrs. H—'s infant daughter is to be christened early next month and Sir R—'s whole family is invited. At present I devote myself entirely to Mrs. H— who I really think has a friendship for me. Would it were in my power to accompany her, but that for many reasons is impossible.

Another Indiaman (The Dartmouth Captain Thompson) has just sailed, but *she* too is absolutely *crowded* with passengers; so I must have patience—It is almost incredible what quantities of baggage, people of consequence invariably take with them; I myself counted twenty-nine trunks that were sent on board, for Mr. and Mrs. H— exclusive of chests of drawers and other packages, with cabin stores &c. and more still remain to be shipped. This separate passage to Madras will add greatly to the expense; for Captain Coxon would not have charged a rupee more, had they embarked with him at Bengal; even removing so much baggage from one ship to another will occasion no small inconvenience.

CHINSURAH, 10th February.

My time has been too much taken up for this fortnight past to afford leisure for writing. I have another melancholy event to record; but let me proceed regularly.

Our friends left us on the second Instant. Poor Mrs. H— was dreadfully affected at parting with her infant; it seemed cruel for a mother to abandon her child only twenty-five days old; but it must in all probability have fallen a sacrifice. Her anxiety in other respects was great. Admiral Suffren is said to keep a sharp look out after English ships going down the Bay; but, I trust, Sir E. Hughes will find the French fleet better employment than cruizing about after our vessels.[285]

Sir R— and Lady C— felt severely the shock of their son's departure but poor Mrs. C—, whose very soul seemed treasured up, if I may so express myself, in her grandson, sunk under the blow. On the fifth she was seized with a violent illness, of which on the seventh she expired. Sir R— is deeply afflicted, and I should be surprised if he were not, for, to him she was ever an exemplary parent; and gave an irrefragable proof of strong maternal affection, by accompanying him to this country at her advanced period of life. Her death is generally lamented, as a most charitable humane good woman. "Let her works praise her."[286] She was in her seventieth year. We came up here immediately after the funeral which took place the next day, and was most numerously attended; I may say by almost the whole settlement—gentlemen as well as ladies. Her character demanded this testimony of respect and that it was paid, affords me pleasure.

You will expect me to give you some account of this place; but after having told you that it contains many very fine houses,—is regularly built,—and kept remarkably clean; nothing more remains to be said. One cannot expect much chearfulness among the inhabitants, though they are treated with the utmost kindness, and all private property is held sacred.

A strange circumstance occurred at the time of its capture, which will probably become a subject of litigation. A King's ship, either a frigate or a sloop of war, was lying off Calcutta, when news arrived that the Dutch had commenced hostilities.[287]—The Captain accompanied by a party of his officers and seamen, proceeded with all expedition to Chinsurah, which he reached about 2 A. M. next day, and summoned the place to surrender to *His Majesty's* Arms. The Governor being totally unprovided with the means of resistance complied; so that when a detachment of the Company's troops marched in at seven o'clock to take possession they found the business already settled, and had the laugh most completely against them. The Captain was soon induced to relinquish his capture, but insisted that his people were entitled to prize money,[288] and has put in his claim accordingly—Is it not an odd affair?

21st February.

Sir R—is going to dispatch some letters for England and I will profit by the occasion, having at present nothing further to communicate. All remains in uncertainty.

I am,
Your affectionate
E. F.

LETTER XXII.

CALCUTTA, 17th March.

MY DEAR SISTER,

This is in all probability the last letter I shall write from Bengal. Mrs. W— has been indefatigable in her exertions; and has at length secured a passage for me on the Valentine, Captain Lewis; a fine new ship—this is her first voyage. I shall have a female companion too, which is certainly desirable. Colonel and Mrs. Tottingham with their family accompany us, besides these we shall have seven military gentlemen, two of the company's civil servants, and thirteen children, under Captain Lewis's immediate protection. The ship is expected to sail in the beginning of next month. I dined in company with Captain Lewis yesterday at Mrs. W—'s, and we were both much pleased with his behaviour.—When we retired after dinner my good friend congratulated me on the prospect of sailing with such a commander, for many of them assume airs of consequence, but Captain Lewis does not seem at all that way disposed; and should the passengers prove agreeable, I really think we may promise ourselves a comfortable voyage.

I am using every effort in preparing my baggage, and Lady C— with her usual kindness renders me every assistance; nor have my other friends been neglectful of any thing that can contribute to my comfort both on the passage and after my arrival in England; till my health shall, with the blessing of Providence, be restored, when I may be enabled to seek out some decent means of support.

I had a very eligible proposal made me of entering into partnership with a most amiable lady who has lately engaged in the school line, but was compelled to decline it, my complaints requiring a change of climate, and that I should consult those medical friends who have been accustomed to prescribe for me. I much regret this circumstance, having no doubt but we might have suited each other extremely well, for she has proved herself a sincere friend in many instances and must ever possess my grateful esteem.

28th March.

I had the pleasure last evening, of being present at the marriage of Captain P. M— and my young friend Miss T—; the wedding was kept at Dr. J—'s and of course they intended to have a little ball; but hardly any one could be prevailed on to dance so late in the season. I had given a solemn promise that nothing should induce me to run the risk, so to comply was out of the question.—At length Mrs. J—, senior, who is turned of sixty-five, opened the ball with a very good minuet, and afterwards footed it away for about two hours, as gaily as the youngest: her example took effect, and they made up a tolerable set. The dance was succeeded by a magnificent supper, to which nearly thirty persons sat down. After the customary toasts we retired, and I reached home before one. May they be happy is my sincere wish.

This is a terrible season for reaching the ships, none but stout vessels can venture down. Colonel T— pays seventy pounds for a sloop to convey his family. I am in this respect fortunate. Sir R— and Lady C— are going to a place called Bearcole for the benefit of sea-bathing, and I shall accompany them to Ingellee; which is within a tide of the Valentine: my friends will then proceed by land to the bathing-place; and one of the sloops by Sir R—'s orders will convey me and my baggage to the Barrabola head where the ship is lying at anchor to complete her cargo.

5th April.

I have every thing now ready and only wait for the completion of Sir R—'s preparations. I feel very impatient to get to sea, being persuaded that it will have a salutary effect on my health,—change of scene and company will also be of service. I have taken leave of every one, and for many shall preserve sentiments of the most grateful esteem.

ON BOARD
THE
VALENTINE

BARRABOLA HEAD, 14th April.

I left Calcutta, on Tuesday the ninth Instant with Sir R— and Lady C— the latter I am concerned to say is in a very weak state, but trust sea bathing will be beneficial. We had a boisterous trip of it down to Ingellee, and every one but myself was dreadfully sea-sick.

My kind friends quitted me on Saturday evening.—I felt quite forlorn at our separation. To be thrown among strangers after experiencing for near nine months, the attentive hospitality of such a family as I was torn from, almost overcame my fortitude,—but I soon lost every other sensation in that overwhelming one of sea-sickness, which lasted the whole way, nor could I go on board till the afternoon.—I shall keep this open till the Pilot goes, that you may have the satisfaction of hearing that we have passed the *first* dangers.

20th April.

Our commander is by no means the placid being we supposed.—I doubt he will prove a very tyrant—instead of paying attention, or shewing respect, he *exacts* both, and woe be to those who fail in either. We are still waiting for the remainder of our Cargo and Captain Lewis vents his rage in drinking "*confusion to the Board of Trade*" every day.

28th April.

We had a narrow escape last evening though I knew not of the danger till it was over. I was seized after tea with severe spasms in the stomach, and had the doctor with me; when suddenly the ship began to pitch and toss violently; and I heard Captain Lewis, call out in a *voice* of thunder "Stand by the sheet anchor, heave the lead." Presently all was quiet again, nor had I the least suspicion till next morning of our having been *adrift* on the Barrabola sand; and what might have been our fate Heaven knows, had not the sheet anchor brought us up; for it is a most dangerous place, surrounded by shoals and out of sight of land.

It is pleasant to see Captain Lewis so alert on perilous occasions; he appears to be an excellent seaman, but the roughest being surely that nature ever formed, in language and manners. The oaths he swears by, are most horrible and he prides himself in inventing new ones. How were Mrs. Wheler and I mistaken? I see he must be humoured like a child, for the least contradiction makes him almost frantic.

2nd May.

Now I must indeed say farewell—the Pilot is just quitting us, and has promised to put this on board the first vessel that sails for England; there is one under dispatch. God bless you. Within six months, I trust we shall all meet in health and safety.

I am,
Your's affectionately
E. F.

LETTER XXIII.

St. James's Valley, St. Helena. 24th September, 1782.

My Dear Sister,

A more uncomfortable passage than I have made to this place, can hardly be imagined. The port of my cabin being kept almost constantly shut, and the door opening into the steerage; I had neither light nor air but from a scuttle:[289] thereby half the space was occupied by a great gun, which prevented me from going near the port when it *was* open.

Mrs. F— at first took her meals in the Cuddy, but the gentlemen were in general too fond of the bottle to pay us the least attention; after tea, we were never asked to cut in at cards, though they played every evening. Captain Lewis swore so dreadfully, making use of such vulgar oaths and expressions; and became so very rude and boisterous, that Mrs. F— withdrew intirely from table, and never left her cabin for the last thirteen weeks: but the Colonel took care to send her whatever was necessary; I had no one to perform the like kind office for me, and was therefore forced to venture up among them, or risk starvation below.

The table was at first most profusely covered; being our Captains favourite maxim "never to make two wants of one"; Every one foresaw what must be the consequence, but he would not listen to reason. Thus we went on till the beginning of August, when he declared that we had rounded the Cape of Good hope; offering to back his opinion by receiving twenty guineas, and return a guinea a day till we reached St. Helena: but no one accepted the bet; yet doubts seemed to hang on the minds of many. However on the 5th at noon, hearing that we were in Latitude 33. 32 S. I began to think with the Captain that, it was needless to *spare* our stock, since a few days would bring us a fresh supply—but alas! at 4 p. m. land was perceived on the *East* coast of Africa; so near, that before we tacked *flies* were seen on the shore—had this happened during the night, nothing could have saved us from shipwreck.—Can I sufficiently bless Providence for this second escape?

On examining the state of our water and provision, after the error was discovered, we were put on an allowance of a quart of water a day, for all purposes; and for nearly a month before we arrived here, we were forced to live on *salt* provisions; even the poor children and the sick, had no better fare.

While off the Cape, we encountered very stormy weather but happily sustained no injury, except the loss of a fore-top-mast which was easily replaced—Captain Lewis, one day, thought fit to refuse me a passage through his cabin, for which I had expressly stipulated. I retired, and in a few minutes he came down to apologize for his behaviour, and a most curious apology he made. He began by saying that he had been beaten at *piquet*,[290] and that losing always made him cross, "besides, said he, to tell you the truth I do not like ladies, not, (with a great oath) that I have any particular objection to you, on the contrary I really think you are a quiet good sort of woman enough; but I cannot *abide* ladies, and I declare that, sometimes when you come up to me upon deck, and say, 'how do you do Captain Lewis' it makes my back open and shirt (*sic*) like a knife"—so much for this gentleman's *respect* and politeness! I was forced to appear satisfied and he seemed very penitent for some days; till another cross fit came on.

Judge if I did not rejoice at the sight of this romantic Island;[291] though its appearance from the sea is very unpromising,—inaccessible rocks, and stupendous crags frowning every side but one, nor is there any anchorage except at that point— The town is literally an ascending valley between two hills, just wide enough to admit of one street. The houses are in the English style, with sashed windows, and small doors. Here are back-gardens, but no gardens; which makes the place intensely hot for want of a free circulation of air; but when you once ascend *Ladder Hill*[292] the scene changes, and all seems enchantment. The most exquisite prospects you can conceive burst suddenly on the eye—fruitful vallies,—cultivated hills and diversified scenery of every description. The inhabitants are obliging and attentive, indeed, remarkably; so altogether I find it a most welcome resting place. After being kept on salt provisions for a month, one is not likely to be very fastidious; former abstinence giving more poignant relish to the excellent food, which is set before us.

Lord North, and the Hastings,[293] China ships, arrived soon after us, but we are all still detained for Convey—how vexatious.

18th October.

Yesterday Captain Lewis gave a grand entertainment on board the Valentine. I was obliged to preside for Mrs. F— would not venture on the water till there was a necessity for it. We had a most brilliant party. I danced a good deal, but find no inconvenience from it. It is odd enough, that he should have fixed on your birth day. You may be sure I silently drank my own toast. Mrs. Comettee and the other ladies seemed highly gratified, and well they might, for no expence was spared to render it completely elegant.

20th October.

The *Chapman*[294] is just arrived, in a most dreadful state, having lost near fifty of her Crew in her passage from Madras, from whence she sailed in Company with the Dartmouth,[295] which was wrecked off the Carnicobar island[296] the *very ship* I was, as I *then* thought, so *unfortunate* in *missing*: so that in this instance, as in many others, I may justly impute my safety to that Providence which

"From hidden dangers, snares and death,
Has gently steered my way."[297]

11th November.

Among the passengers in the *Dartmouth* were Mrs. I— and her infant son, a most interesting child, three years of age, who were wonderfully preserved through sufferings, enough to overwhelm the strongest constitution; and proceeded to St. Helena on the *Chapman* on board which were Mr. Casamajor and his mother,[298] who secured accommodations on the *Lord North*, not choosing to venture farther on the *Chapman*. Upon which I was applied to, to accompany Mrs. I— who could not well proceed without a female companion, and was not able to procure accommodations on the other ships—I instantly determined on accompanying her for the express purpose of endeavouring to soften the inconveniences under which she laboured, and to soothe her mind harrassed by the many hardships of her distressing voyage.

25th November.

This day we left St. Helena in company with the *Lord North, Valentine, and Hastings*. The Chapman unfortunately sails very ill and cannot keep up with the other ships. Captain Lewis told me at St. Helena in order to prevent my quitting the *Valentine*, that we should be left in the lurch the first fair opportunity; and so it happened long ere we reached England.

Our passage was tremendous, the Sea breaking over the ship and continually carrying some thing or other away; nor had we any naval stores to replace what was thus lost. Captain Walker and Mr. Gooch, the second officer, were daily employed with the people, repairing the sails and rigging, nor did they shrink from any labour. I never beheld such exertion: very frequently they were obliged to take the wheel, for scarcely a sufficient number could be found to keep watch.

On entering the channel the weather was so thick that no observation could be taken for five days. One night after remaining several hours in dreadful suspense respecting our situation, Captain Walker came down about half past ten o'clock, to tell us that we were off Scilly.[299] What a declaration! off Scilly! on a stormy night in the beginning of February! This intelligence was not likely to tranquillize our feelings. Mrs. I— and myself passed a sleepless night, and in the morning, one of the sailors ascertained the place we were driven into to be St. Ive's Bay, a most dangerous place; but thanks to providence, we sustained no injury, except being forced round the Land's End, which was to us a serious misfortune, being utterly unable to beat back into the English channel, our men being worn out with illness and exertion, and our stores of every kind nearly exhausted.

No Pilot would venture to stay on board: The *Chapman* having no poop, looked so unlike an Indiaman,[300] that she was taken for an American, and we poor forlorn creatures set down at once as prisoners. "Why don't you release those women," said they, "We will have nothing to do with you, we know better." We found afterwards that although the preliminaries of peace had been some time signed,[301] no account of the important event had reached this remote spot. Captain Walker now proposed proceeding to Milford Haven to refit, but the indraught, as it is called, having brought us off Lundy, he changed his resolution and took a pilot on board for King road, where we anchored at 7 A. M. on the 7th February 1783.

THE END OF THE FIRST PART.

PART SECOND

CONTAINING AN ABSTRACT OF THE AUTHOR'S THREE SUBSEQUENT VOYAGES TO INDIA.

LETTER I.

To Mrs. L.——

BLACKHEATH, 12th February, 1815.

MY DEAR MADAM,

The interest which you are pleased to take in my welfare, and the kind inquiries you make respecting the voyages I have performed since my first memorable one, induce me to offer you a simple statement of facts relative to them; though to accomplish this even in the briefest manner, some circumstances must be revealed which I would rather consign to oblivion, and some wounds must be re-opened, which time has mollified, if not healed.—The manuscript submitted to your perusal,[302] closes with an account of my arrival in England, and thus ended my first eventful visit to India; a period which according to my own estimation, had comprized a whole life of suffering and anxiety, and dissolved for ever the strongest tie the human heart can form for itself; a period in which physical and moral evils had alike combined to inflict whatever can wound the heart to its inmost core, and destroy that confidence in our fellow creatures, without which the world seems indeed "a howling wilderness,"[303] peopled with terrific monsters, each prowling either by violence or fraud for his defenceless prey.

Happily for me gentler beings had blended in my path their benign influences; my sorrows had been cheered and consoled by many. I was still young, and with buoyant spirits relieved in some degree from their late severe pressure, hailed my native land; yet a sigh of regret would mingle with my joyful anticipations, at quitting the society wherein, though assailed by tempestuous winds and mountainous seas, I had so frequently enjoyed, "The feast of reason and the flow of soul"[304] amidst congenial minds.

For ever blest be the moment when I quitted the *Valentine*; from that circumstance arose a friendship which has constituted one of the sweetest enjoyments of my life, and which still remains unbroken, though my friend[305] and I seldom meet; but her letters are invaluable. Few possess such epistolary talents: they have been my chief solace and consolation in distress; but to proceed: Mrs. I——n, her little boy and myself went on to town, where a dreadful shock awaited me; my dear mother was no more; the tie to which a daughter most fondly clings was rent asunder; tho' I had still a father and two most affectionate sisters remaining, it was long ere I could justly appreciate their worth, or draw consolation from their society. For nearly a whole year I laboured under very severe indisposition,[306] and incurred great expence for medical attendance, not less than £150. I was several times considered in imminent danger; Mrs. I——n too was long, after her arrival, affected with the most distressing nervous debility. All this is not to be wondered at, for during the passage from St. Helena, both of us were in an infirm state, and our health had suffered much from the circumstances in which we were placed. It is true we experienced all possible relief from the kindness of those around us, whom we daily beheld subjected to privations and exertions the most trying, yet ever affording us comfort and attention. In each benevolent act Captain Walker was amply assisted by Mr. Gooch, and the Surgeon Mr. Crowfoot, a most worthy and scientific young man, to whose skill I was probably more indebted for the prolongation of a precarious existence, than I was aware of at the time. My health being in some measure restored, I tried various plans in pursuit of independence; but none seemed to promise success; my friends wished me to remain at home; but Calcutta appeared the most likely theatre of exertion; and you cannot wonder that my heart warmed towards a place, where I had met such friendship and generosity, and where so much general encouragement was given to the efforts of respectable individuals. I still bore in mind the offer[307] which had been made to me in Bengal, and determined to pursue this plan; and having become acquainted with a Miss Hicks, a young woman of the strictest integrity, and who possessed many valuable qualifications, I engaged her to accompany me as an assistant. Captain Walker[308] was about to proceed to Bombay, in command of the *Lord Camden*, and offered me a passage on very moderate terms, provided I took charge of four ladies, who wished to have a protectress during the voyage. Being desirous of seeing Bombay, I felt little reluctance to comply, especially as my friend Mr. Gooch held the same station in the *Camden* which he had, so meritoriously filled, in the *Chapman*. The passage to be sure, would be rather circuitous, but in a fine new ship, navigated by persons of whose nautical abilities I had such indubitable proofs, *that* appeared of little moment. The prospect of strengthening my connections in India, influenced me still further. Having therefore arranged my plans on a general ground, allowing for the deviations which in such a case as mine, might be allowed to arise from circumstances, I embarked on the *Lord Camden*, and sailed from the Downs for India, on the 17th March 1784.—Here let me pause for the present; I will soon resume my pen.

I am &c.
E. F.

LETTER II.

To Mrs. L.———

15th February, 1815.

My Dear Madam,

For some days we had rather boisterous weather, but this subsided as we approached the Canary Islands, where (to my great mortification) we did not stop.— On the third of April had a view of the peak of Teneriffe which is said to be 2,000 feet high, perpendicularly. It must have been formerly a considerable Volcano; so lately as the year 1704[309] there was an irruption from it which did immense damage. On the 10th we passed the Cape-de-Verd Islands, but to my regret without touching at any; for curiosity was ever with me a predominant feeling. The Island of Fogo has a Volcano, which sometimes flames out in a terrible manner, and discharges pumice stones to a great distance. The weather at this time was intensely hot, but we had plenty of apples on board, which afforded great refreshment; and soon after they were finished, we spoke a Danish ship,[310] whose captain made the ladies a handsome present of oranges and pine apples. It is not easy for you, my dear madam, to conceive the importance of such accommodations; but those who have been many weeks, perhaps months, shut up in a floating prison, without the power of procuring refreshments which even health demands, will be well aware of their value.—At length the trade winds[311] visited us, "and bore healing on their wings;"[312] we passed the Tropic of Capricorn very pleasantly, but soon afterwards a change took place: such are the vicissitudes of a sea life. I have not yet mentioned the names of the ladies who accompanied me, there were Mrs. Pemberton, and Misses Turner, Bellas, and Fisher, who with Miss Hicks and myself occupied two thirds of the roundhouse;[313] and I note it as rather a singular circumstance, that we were only five times on deck during the passage, which was owing to a previous arrangement between the Captain and me, to guard against imprudent attachments, which are more easily formed than broken; and I am happy to say the plan succeeded to our wish—About this time, Captain Walker fell dangerously ill, but fortunately recovered before the 8th of June, when the birth day of Miss Ludlow, a Bristol lady, who subsequently became Mrs. Walker, was celebrated in high style: all the ship's company had a dinner of fresh provisions, and we sat down to a most sumptuous repast, vegetables and fruit having been provided in England, and salad raised purposely for the occasion.

We were now going at the rate of eight knots an hour, *off* the Cape, with a heavy swell; but the young folks, nevertheless, so earnestly solicited for a dance, that the Captain could not refuse; so all the furniture being removed out of the cuddy, I led off, by particular request; but had only gone down one couple, when a tremendous *lee lurch*[314] put us all in confusion. I declined standing up again, but the rest during three or four hours, tumbled about in the prettiest manner possible, and when no longer able to dance, made themselves amends by singing and laughing; no serious accident happened to any one, and the evening concluded very agreeably.

On the 11th June we struck soundings at 7 A.M. off Cape L'Aguillas,[315] this exactly confirmed Capt. Walker's observations, and was matter of greater rejoicing to me, than can be imagined by persons who were never brought into danger, by the ignorance or inattention of those intrusted with the command. The next day we shipped so many seas[316] from the heavy land-swell, as to extinguish the fire; we were therefore constrained to put up with a cold dinner: however our good Captain, ever provident, produced a fine round of beef, preserved by Hoffmann, which well supplied the deficiency.

On the 24th June, we anchored in the Bay of Johanna,[317] one of the African Isles to the northward of Madagascar. It is a fertile little spot. We here met with plenty of refreshments and very cheap. The oranges are remarkably fine: I took a good quantity of them: their beef is pretty good: Captain Walker purchased several bullocks for the ship's use and to supply our table. The inhabitants are very civil, but are said to be the greatest thieves in existence. We were much amused with the high titles assumed by them. The Prince of Wales honoured us with his company at breakfast, after which Mr. Lewin[318] one of our passengers, took him down to his cabin, where having a number of knick-knacks, he requested his royal highness to make choice of some article to keep in remembrance of him; when to Mr. L's astonishment he fixed on a large mahogany book-case, which occupied one side of the cabin; and on being told that could not be spared, went away in high displeasure, refusing to accept any thing else. The Duke of Buccleugh washed our linen. H.R.H. the Duke of York officiated as boatman, and a boy of fourteen, who sold us some fruit, introduced himself as Earl of Mansfield. They seem very proud of these titles—We all went on shore, and while those who were able to walk, rambled about to view the country, which they described as very delightful, I awaited their return in a thatched building erected for the accommodation of strangers. We were careful to return before sun-set, the night air being reckoned very pernicious to Europeans.—These people are almost constantly at war with those of the adjacent Isles. Being in great want of gunpowder, they prevailed on Captain Walker to give them the quantity that would have been expended in the customary salutes.

On the 2nd July we left Johanna, with a pleasant breeze, but were soon driven back and experienced great fatigue for many days, from a heavy rolling sea, but on the 20th, at day break, we saw Old-woman's Island,[319] and at 11 A.M. cast anchor at Bombay. An alarming accident happened while saluting the Fort; the gunner's mate reloaded one of the guns without having properly cleansed it, in consequence of which he was blown off into the water. Never did I behold a more shocking sight. The poor creature's face was covered with blood, yet he swam like a fish till a boat reached him. Thank God he escaped with some slight hurts, and to my surprize was upon deck next day.

On the 21st we went on shore with Mr. Coggan[320] the Naval store-keeper, who was Miss Turner's brother-in-law. We landed in the dock-yard, where the many fine ships building and repairing with the number of Europeans walking about, almost persuaded me, I was at home, till the dress and dark complexion of the workmen destroyed the pleasing illusion—Mrs. Coggan received me very kindly, and by her hospitable treatment, rendered my stay at Bombay as agreeable as possible. On Saturday the 24th we received a visit from the Governor (Mr. Boddam)[321] which I find is to be considered as a great compliment. We went to church, on the 25th, and in the evening sat up to receive company as also the two following evenings, a tiresome ceremony to me who detest parade and was merely a traveller; but Mrs. Coggan assured me it would be an affront to the settlement if I submitted not to the established custom. The like usage formerly prevailed in Bengal, but is now abolished. On the 29th we went to pay our respects to the Governor at *Perell*[322] his country seat, a delightful place and a charming ride to it. Indeed all the environs are beautiful; in this respect it has greatly the advantage of Calcutta; but the town itself is far inferior. They have a handsome church and a good assembly-room, where they dance all the year round.

We dined one day at Mr. Nesbit's,[323] chief of the Marine, who gave us a repast in the true *old* Indian style. "The tables they groaned with the weight of the feast." We had every joint of a calf on the table at once; nearly half a Bengal sheep; several large dishes of fish; boiled and roasted turkies, a ham, a kid, tongue, fowls, and a long train of et ceteras. The heat was excessive, the hour two, and we were thirty in company, in a lower roomed house, so you may conceive what sensations such a prodigious dinner would produce. It is however a fact that they ate with great appetite and perseverance, to my astonishment, who could scarcely touch a morsel.

On the 1st August, the *Camden* being ordered to Madras without any prospect of proceeding from thence to Bengal, Captain Walker secured a passage for Miss Hicks and myself on the *Nottingham*, Captain Curtis, who offered us the best accommodations and refused to accept of any remuneration. He afterwards disposed of his ship, but under the express stipulation that we should retain our cabin. I dined on the 8th at Mr. D. Scott's with our fellow passengers Mr. and Mrs. Lewin; and a very agreeable day we passed, the whole of the cuddy passengers being invited, so that we sat down once more together, assuredly for the last time. On the 23d I dined with Miss Bellas at her uncle's gardens where I met with a most cordial reception, and was introduced to Captain Christie whom she married before I quitted the settlement; and alas! I must add survived her marriage only thirteen weeks. She died, as I afterwards heard, of a confirmed liver complaint. Her health was very bad during the whole passage; for on the least motion she constantly became sea-sick, and never overcame it: she was a most amiable young woman and generally beloved. I shall ever cherish her memory with affection. On the 25th Captain Curtis introduced the new Commander Captain Ross to me, and made as many apologies for quitting the ship, as if he had been accountable to me for his conduct. "But however" said he "go when you will, I will see you safe on board and clear of the Reef," which is a ridge of rocks at the entrance of Bombay harbour. This promise he performed on the 4th September, when having taken leave of our friends, he accompanied us on board the *Louisa*, for so was the *Nottingham* named in honour of the new owner's wife. He staid until seven in the evening, and then went on shore with the Pilot; first calling up all his late servants, whom he charged to pay me the same attention as if he were present. I shall ever esteem him. Our friendship continued unabated while I remained in India; he afterwards commanded the *Swallow Packet*, and mine was the first and the last house he entered on each voyage: since my return home I have seldom seen him, but that alters not my sentiments.—It was natural that I should quit Bombay with favourable impressions. I had been treated with much kindness and mixed with the first society on the Island: I refer you to other travellers for descriptions, observing only that provisions of all kinds are good, but rather dear, except fish, which is here in high perfection and very plentiful.

On the 15th September we anchored in Anjengo roads,[324] to take in coir rope and cables for which this is the great mart. They are fabricated of the outer rind of the cocoa-nut, whose quality is such that the salt water nourishes it, and it possesses also an elasticity which enables it to contract or dilate itself, in proportion to the strain on it. This property is peculiarly useful in these seas, where squalls frequently come on with frightful violence and rapidity, and the preservation of an anchor is an object of importance. The surf runs very high here, and is at times extremely dangerous. Captain Ross brought off an invitation from Mr. Hutchinson[325] the chief, to dine with him; but no one chose to venture on shore. I have not forgotten the fate of Mrs. Blomer, who was drowned some years ago with seven others in attempting to land on the beach.

Here is a pretty strong Fort on the sea side. Every one who went on shore spoke with rapture of the country. The vicinity of the great chain of mountains which separates the coast of Malabar from that of Coromandel, and which are said to be the highest in the world, (the Alps and Andes excepted) gives an awful termination to the prospect. The water is here so indifferent that few Europeans attempt to drink it. Formerly Anjengo was famous throughout India for its manufactures of long-cloth and stockings, but these have fallen to decay. We left this dangerous place on the 22nd; the wind several times blew so strong, we had great apprehensions of being driven on shore; and a very narrow escape we certainly had; for on examining the anchor, only one fluke was found remaining; the other must have been so nearly broke by the strain on it, that it would not bear heaving up. Our passage was remarkably tedious, though we had a pleasant man in command, who kept an exceeding good table, but not expecting to be more than five or six weeks at sea, instead of *twelve*, our stock of fresh provisions was quite exhausted long ere we reached Calcutta, and only distilled water[326] to drink. On the 27th November we arrived, and to my great surprise after all that had been said against the probability of such an event taking place, found the *Camden* had been some time in the river. Mr. Baldwin the chief officer died soon after, and my friend Mr. Gooch succeeded him. In this situation he remained for several voyages, with Captain Dance till he obtained the command of the *Lushington*, and I had frequently the pleasure of seeing him during my residence in Bengal. Being now about to enter on a new scene, I will take leave for the present and remain,

Your's &c.
E. F.

LETTER III.

To Mrs. L.——

BLACKHEATH, 19th February, 1815.

My dear Madam,

At Calcutta I met with great kindness from many whom I had formerly known, and who now appeared desirous of forwarding any plan, I might adopt. At length with the approbation of Captain Walker, and several other friends, I determined on placing Miss Hicks in business as a milliner. It was agreed that my name should not appear, although I retained in my own hands the entire management of the concern, allowing Miss H. one third of the profits. Mr. Berry purser of the *Camden* had the goodness to open a set of books, and to give me every necessary instruction how to keep them in proper order, which afterwards proved very advantageous in the prosecution of my concerns. You are aware how many difficulties both from within and without must have opposed themselves to this design, and how much even the same feeling operated in contrary directions; at least, if the wish for independence may be termed pride, to which it is certainly allied. Soon after, a proposal was made me to engage in a seminary for young ladies, on so liberal a plan, that I have since frequently, regretted not having complied with the solicitations of my friends; but I had in fact gone rather too far to recede, having made several large purchases, which could not be disposed of suddenly but at considerable loss. Within four months after our arrival, Miss Hicks married Mr. Lacey;[327] and the following Christmas lay in of a fine boy, but unfortunately lost him at the end of six weeks; after which her health declined so fast, as to render it absolutely necessary that she should proceed to Europe. I took that opportunity of sending home for education, a natural child of my husband's, whose birth had caused me bitter affliction; yet I could not abandon him, though he was deserted by his natural protector. They accordingly embarked on the 5th of September 1786, on the *Severn Packet*[328] Captain Kidd, with every prospect of a favourable passage; but on the 9th, owing to the rapidity of the current, the vessel struck on a sand, called the Broken Ground, just below Ingellee, and every European on board unhappily perished, except the second officer in whose arms the poor little boy expired; but Mrs. Lacey supported herself in the fore chains with exemplary fortitude, till a tremendous sea broke over them, and he saw her no more, but by great exertion reached the shore on a broken spar. I felt her loss severely, for she possessed a mind and spirit that would have graced any station.

After this melancholy event I was compelled to conduct business in my own name, but on a more extensive scale, and succeeded tolerably well, till the unlucky year 1788,[329] when such immense investments were brought out, that nearly all concerned in that branch of commerce, were involved in one common ruin. Yielding to the storm, for I had large consignments which I was compelled to receive, my brother having become security for them at home, I solicited and obtained the indulgence of my creditors for eighteen months under four trustees, Messrs. Fairlie, Colvin, Child, and Moscrop, whose names were sufficient to sanction any Concern; and such was the confidence reposed in my integrity, that every thing remained in my own hands as formerly. Never, I am proud to say, was that confidence abused; pardon the seeming vanity of this assertion; in justice to my own character, I must say thus much, and can boldly appeal to those who are best acquainted with the whole transaction for the truth of my statement. Having received several consignments from my kind friends at home, which sold to great advantage, and various other means suggesting themselves, wherein I was benevolently assisted by many who saw and compassionated my arduous struggles after independence, I succeeded in settling either in money or goods, every claim on me, and again became possessed of a little property; when in the beginning of 1794, anxiety to see my dear friends, led me to resolve on returning once more to Europe. I must here mention what operated as a strong encouragement to prosecute the plan immediately. In May 1791 Mr. Benjamin Lacey[330] brother of my lamented friend's husband came to Bengal, bringing out a small investment for me. I received him into my family, and altho' only nineteen years of age, he evinced such abilities, that I soon obtained a situation for him, where he conducted himself so much to the satisfaction of his employers, as to be intrusted with confidential commissions to Madras and elsewhere, which he executed with judgment and integrity. This young man happening to be in Calcutta, I embraced the opportunity of leaving to him the management of my concerns. As a proof that my confidence was not misplaced, allow me here to notice, that altho' my stock and bills were delivered over to him without inventory, or engagement on his part when I left India, he in the course of *eleven* days after, transmitted regular accounts of the whole, and where placed, making himself answerable for the proceeds in the strongest manner; so that had we both died, my friends would have found no difficulty in claiming my effects. Having by his assistance laid in a small investment, I embarked on the 25th March on board the American ship *Henry*, Captain Jacob Crowninshield,[331] bound for Ostend; and on the 29th the pilot quitted us. I found the *Henry* a snug little vessel, Capt. C. a well behaved man, and his officers, though not of polished manners, yet in their way disposed to offer me every attention that could render the passage agreeable. I suffered at times from the heat, but on the whole enjoyed better health than during my former voyage. Having only one passenger on board besides myself, but little occurred to relieve the monotony of a sea life: I frequently played chess, and was almost constantly beaten. Cards and backgammon had their turn, but I grew tired of all; till at length, on the 2nd July we anchored off St. Helena.

I went on shore in the afternoon and learnt with some vexation that a large fleet sailed only the day before. I wished to have written, specially as we were not bound direct to England. Many changes had happened in this curious little

Island, during my twelve years absence. Few recollected me; but Captain Wall of the *Buccleugh* formerly chief officer of the *Valentine*, behaved with the greatest attention,—I shall ever acknowledge his kindness. Fresh provisions were very scarce, a drought had prevailed until this season for four years, and it would require three good seasons to repair the damage sustained, by their stock perishing for want of water—A circumstance happened during our stay, the like of which was not remembered by the oldest inhabitant, though from the appearance of the place, one would conclude such events were common: a large fragment of rock, detached by the moisture, fell from the side of Ladder Hill, on a small out-house at the upper end of the valley; in which two men were sleeping in separate beds. The stone broke thro' the top and lodged between them, the master of the house was suffocated, it is supposed, by the rubbish, as no bruises were found on his body; the other man forced his way through, and gave the alarm, but not time enough to save his companion. This accident has caused many to tremble for their safety, since all the way up the valley, houses are built under similar projections, and will some time or other probably experience the same fate. Among the Alps such things are common. An unpleasant affair also occurred to me. I had, when last here, given a girl who had attended me from Calcutta, and behaved very ill, to Mrs. Mason, with whom I boarded, under a promise that she should not be sold, consequently no slave paper passed. Mr. Mason, however, in defiance of this prohibition, disposed of her for £10. This act militating against the established regulations, advantage was taken of my return to the Island, to call upon me as the original offender, not only for that sum, but a demand was made of £60 more, to pay the woman's passage back to Bengal with her two children!!![332] After every effort, I could only obtain a mitigation of £10, being forced to draw on my brother Preston[333] at sixty days sight in favour of the Court of Directors, for £60, a sum that I could ill afford to lose, but the strong hand of power left me no alternative. On the 6th July we quitted St. Helena, and on the 11th anchored off Ascension. Our Captain and the gentlemen went on shore to look at the Island. The following remarks I extract from his journal. "The soil near the sea, appears dry and barren in the extreme, like cinders from a fire; indeed the whole Island bears evident marks of the former existence of volcanoes, several craters still appearing on the hills; perhaps it owes its origin to some great convulsion of nature, as I am persuaded does St. Helena: altho' the sea coast presents a dreary view, yet on walking farther the prospect becomes enchanting; a most delightful verdure covers the *smaller* hills, and the vallies; and no doubt they afford plenty of water, tho' not being very well, I was too much fatigued to examine. The 2nd officer saw five or six goats, but could not get near enough to fire at them."

Numbers of man-of-war birds[334] and eggs were taken, which proved to be good eating; they likewise caught the finest turtle I ever saw, weighing near 400lbs., but by an act of unpardonable negligence in people so situated, it was suffered to walk overboard in the night. We had however the good luck to catch a fine albercuore[335] which weighed near 100lbs., its flesh when roasted resembled veal; we were fortunate in having an excellent cook on board, who really made the most of our scanty provisions. On the 3rd of August, three large ships hove in sight, one of which bore down towards us and fired several guns to bring us to. They sent a boat on board with orders for our Captain to attend the commander; he came back, to our great joy, in about half an hour, having been treated with much civility by the French Captain. It was now we heard the distressing news of Ostend being in the hands of the French;[336] indeed they boasted of having gained the advantage every where, except in the West Indies.—These were three frigates mounting from 28 to 32 guns, they had been 20 days, from Brest and had taken 22 prizes. We had been assured by Captain Wall, that the French dared not shew their *noses* in the channel, but I with sorrow now witnessed the contrary, not on my own account, being safe enough on board an American; but Captain C. informed me, there were more than 200 English prisoners on board those ships.—He now acquainted me with his determination to proceed to America, and very politely offered me a passage, that I might witness the disposal of my property, which I of course declined, not feeling the least desire to prolong my voyage. So having arranged my affairs in the best manner possible under existing circumstances, I took a final leave of the *Henry* on the 4th September, and landed with my baggage at Cowes in the Isle of Wight.—From this place I soon reached London; pleased as I went, to behold scenes from which I had been so many years banished, and anticipating the delight with which my dear father[337] would receive his long absent child. Alas! I was doomed to behold him no more. He expired only four months before my arrival—The remainder of my family I had the happiness of finding in perfect health—The property sent to America came to a tolerable market, but Captain Crowninshield instead of making the returns in cash, sent a ship called the *Minerva*, with his younger brother Richard Crowninshield[338] in command of her, which ship it was proposed that I should take out to India under certain conditions. She was a fine new vessel of about 300 tons burthen; I had her coppered, and proposed her first making a voyage to America, and on her return sailing for Bengal about Christmas: But when completely fitted for sea, with a *picked* cargo on board for Boston, she took fire by the bursting of a bottle of aquafortis, which had been negligently stowed among other goods, and though immediately scuttled and every precaution taken, sustained material damage. This involved me in a series of misfortunes. Mr. P. Wynne who had shipped to the amount of £428 on the *Minerva*, by mere accident discovered that, contrary to the general opinion, the Captain was responsible for all goods committed to his charge under regular bills of lading; and accordingly commenced an action against him, in which he was successful, the whole debt and costs near £600 falling on the Captain, and from his inability, on me: this decision caused a change in the tenor of bills of lading, which now contain clauses against fire and several other casualties, whereas before "the dangers of the seas" were alone excepted. Thus did my loss operate to the advantage of others. To prevent the total wreck of my little property, I was compelled to proceed immediately on the original plan, as affording the only chance of attaining independence, and ultimately securing a home in my native country.

Having resolved never again to travel alone, I engaged a Miss Tripler as a companion, for two years, at £30 per annum; but had soon cause to regret the agreement. A proposal being made by my dearest friend Mrs. Irwin to take out a young lady, who had been educated in England, and was going to rejoin her friends in Bengal, I felt no disposition to refuse, having frequently seen Miss Rogers and knowing her to be a most amiable little girl; besides as I had a piano-forte, and a pair of globes with me, and a good collection of books, I was pleased with the idea of contributing to *her* improvement, and amusing myself at the same time—The ship being obliged to touch at Guernsey, I determined to join her there; so, on the 17th July she sailed for that place. Miss Tripler and my Bengal servant proceeding on her, as the most saving plan. Here let me pause, reserving the account of my third voyage for another letter.

I remain truly your's
E. F.

LETTER IV.

To Mrs. L.——

BLACKHEATH, 24th February, 1815.

My Dear Madam,

On Sunday the 2nd August 1795 at 5 A.M. Miss R——s and myself, accompanied by Captain Richard Crowninshield quitted London for Southampton, from whence the packets sail for Guernsey. I did not leave my sister and nieces without deep regret; they were *always* very dear to me, but now, having lost my parents, the tie was drawn still closer; abstracted from this consideration, I rather rejoiced at quitting England, as the whole time of my stay had been imbittered by a succession of losses and disappointments, arising partly from my individual misfortune respecting the ship, and partly from the general state of commerce at this inauspicious period. Alas! in the number of wretched Emigrants[339] whom I saw crowding the port of Southampton, I felt that I had but too many fellow-sufferers, and it was easy to read in many a sorrowful countenance that, "the times were out of joint."[340]

On arriving there, we were advised to go on by land to Lymington, and embark from thence; this gave me an opportunity of passing a few hours at Newtown Park,[341] a short mile from *Lymington*, the residence of Mrs. I——'s sister Mrs. P——n. The house and grounds are strikingly beautiful, and an Observatory at the top of the former, commands an extensive view over the Isle of Wight, and great part of the channel; and Mrs. P——n assured me, that not long before, she saw from thence near four hundred vessels sail together. The wind becoming fair, we embarked on the 5th August, and next evening safely reached the *Minerva* at Guernsey. We found all on board greatly fatigued, the ship having arrived only the night before, after a most harrassing passage of eighteen days. What an escape we had! On the 8th we went on shore; passed through the market, which appears to be well supplied, particularly with fruit, vegetables, poultry, and butter; we took a quantity of the latter, which lasted perfectly good all the way out. I was pleased with the market people, they were so remarkably clean and civil. The women wore bonnets with enormous stiffened crowns, underneath which, they had becoming laced mobs. Provisions are in general good and cheap; the fish excellent; such delicious soles I never tasted any where. We went to church and heard prayers both in French and English; a dialect of the former prevails here, but it is a vile jargon, I could scarcely understand one word in ten. This must be a very healthy place; I saw here a lady who, at the age of ninety-four, had full possession of her faculties, and I heard there were several others on the island nearly of the same age. Mr. Tupper, a gentleman to whom I had a letter, was in his 76th year; he and his whole family paid Miss R—s and myself the greatest attention. I was surprised to see the magnificent style in which their house was fitted up, the drawing room stove was of silver, the curtains rich silk, with gilt cornices; the chimney piece cost eighty pounds, and every other article corresponding; but even these were trifling, when compared with the many capital paintings and valuable prints which adorned every room in the house. I afterwards found that the prevailing taste with the wealthy here, is for expensive houses; for the roads are so bad and steep, that single horse chaises are the only carriages in use. On the 17th August, Mr. J. Tupper came by appointment to shew us the Island, of which we made almost the tour. The lands are highly cultivated, but such roads I never saw; they are barely wide enough to admit a chaise; fortunately we met only one, which backed for us to pass. I admire the exact manner in which the hedges are kept, they add great beauty to the prospect. I have seldom seen more picturesque views; the land and sea vallies are particularly striking. Their parties, though elegant, are by no means expensive; for liquors are duty free, and the best wines do not cost more than 16*s*. per dozen, except claret, which is at from 25 to 28*s*. The hospitality with which we were all treated by this worthy family, excited the most grateful emotions; and I bade them adieu with sincere regret.

I am yours truly,
E. F.

LETTER V.

BLACKHEATH, 25th February, 1815.

MY DEAR MADAM,

We were a pretty large party on board; Mr. Campbell, fresh from the Highlands of Scotland, on whom the officers were continually playing their jokes; Mr. Smith, a youth going to the Madeiras, and Mr. Regail, who was one of the most interesting young men I ever met with: his manners were elegant, his mind highly polished, and his disposition placid and benevolent; but he appeared bending beneath a deep dejection; he never joined in conversation, if it were gay; he ate no more than barely sufficed nature, and tho' from politeness and native suavity, he never refused to join our evening parties at cards, yet his depression was visible even in the moments of amusement. He had been brought up in Russia, and had, for his age (which could not be more than 24) seen much of the world, and evidently mixed in the first society, and I apprehend some singular blight had happened in his fortunes.

On the 7th September we landed at Funchall, the Capital of Madeira. I was exceedingly delighted with our approach to the Island: the town is built on rising ground, and as you draw near to it, appears imposing and magnificent, having several churches and convents. Behind the town the ground rises abruptly into steep hills, covered with vineyards, and ornamented with pleasure houses, at once exhibiting the appearance of prosperity and cultivation, and the charms of picturesque and romantic scenery.—A Mr. L— to whom I had letters, went with us to a Hotel; for unfortunately his lady being in England, he could not entertain us at his own house. Living in this manner was very expensive and disagreeable also, we paid 5*s*. each for dinner, exclusive of wine; and neither the waiter, nor any other servant, understood a word of English, or any other language we could speak. It was only with the landlady we could have any communication. We found Funchall much less beautiful than its first appearance promised; the streets were ill paved, narrow, dirty and solitary; but the great church[342] is a handsome building, and the hospital a very excellent one, before which is a fine fountain, which is always a refreshing sight in a country like this. The American Consul[343] visited us the next morning, and invited us to his country house, for which we sat out at 5 o'clock. Miss R—s and I were in silk net hammocks, slung upon poles, and each carried by two men, who went at a great rate, considering the road lay up a steep hill; this is the only mode of conveyance, except riding on horse back, as no wheel carriages can be used in a country so hilly—They employ a kind of dray or sledge drawn by oxen to transport goods.

We found a large party assembled; the lady of the house, a pleasant Irish gentlewoman, had all the frankness and hospitality of her country, and with her husband, a most amiable and companionable man, made us quickly forget we were strangers. Even the Portuguese ladies, seemed familiar with us, tho' unluckily we could not converse with them. We had a ball at night, but the weather being too warm for dancing, we exchanged it for whist. I cannot help observing here, how frequently people who travel, will find an advantage in knowing some thing of this game, as they may sit down with persons of different nations and languages and enjoy with them an amusement, that for the time, admits of an interchange of ideas and facilitates good-will, even where conversation is denied. We sat down above thirty to an elegant supper; the grapes I found delicious here, but the season for other fruits was over. The vineyards are tended with unusual care; the grapes of which wine is made, are not suffered to ripen in the sun, which they told me is the reason of the superior flavour in Madeira wine. The Consul's house was most delightfully situated; it overlooked the whole town of Funchall, the surrounding country, and the wide spreading ocean; it had a beautiful garden, which produced abundance of peaches, apricots, quinces, apples, pears, walnuts, bananas, guavas, and pine-apples, and behind rose a fine grove of pine trees. I quitted this paradise with regret, and found my ride down-hill very fatiguing and disagreeable.

We staid here till the 21st, and by means of our first friend, spent several pleasant days, and gay evenings, but the weather was so intolerably hot, and the travelling so disagreeable, that if I had not been detained by business, I would much rather have passed my time on board. One day we went with the American Consul to visit a Convent of Ursulines; we found the Chapel door open, but were not suffered to pass the threshold: the nuns were very chatty, and like most ignorant persons, exceedingly curious, asking a hundred ridiculous questions. How very differently do human beings pass the time allotted them in this probationary existence! Surely, to consume it in supine indolence or "vain repetitions" can never render us more acceptable to Him, who is the fountain of light and knowledge. We ate some preserved peaches with them, which the Consul paid for, and then took our leave; but were forced to submit to a salute from the sisters, which we would gladly have dispensed with, for they all took an enormous quantity of snuff. These are the only nuns I ever saw who do not conceal their hair. On leaving these pious ladies, we went to Golgotha, or the chapel of skulls,[344] (as it is called) being entirely lined with skulls and other human bones. What an idea!

We drank tea the same day, with Signor Esmerado, whose large house and extensive grounds once belonged to the Jesuits. This is one of the richest families in the Island; the display of plate surprised me; the tea tray was the largest I ever saw, and of massive silver; wine and sweetmeats, were served in the same costly style. After tea there were several minuets danced; they with difficulty suffered us to depart, and were the means of introducing us to another pleasant evening party, where the lady of the house played remarkably well on the piano-forte, and sung in a style of superior excellence.

One day we went on horse-back, to visit the church of Nossa Senhora de la Monte, (our Lady of the Mount) about three miles from Funchall, upon a very high ground which must have cost a large sum in building. The ascent to it, is at least by a hundred steps. The church is not large, but richly ornamented: there is a wonder-working image of the virgin, in a chrystal shrine, very small, not more than two feet high, it looks exactly like a doll; but her little ladyship, however insignificant her appearance, had more votaries than any other saint on the Island. Here we saw some paintings, which considered as the work of a self-taught Genius, (and I was assured this was a fact) had extraordinary merit. In this little excursion, I was surprised to see the diversity of climate exhibited in a short distance; the vintage was over, below; while the grapes around us were like bullets, and I am told they never completely ripen; we observed the same effect in Mr. Murray's plantation,[345] half a mile lower. This gentleman, who was the English Consul, had laid out above £20,000 in improving a spot, which after all, will never bring any thing to maturity; yet it is a most charming place; there are three ranges of gardens, one above another, the lower are very large and well laid out, on a level, artificially formed, in the midst of which stands a good house, but not sufficiently elegant to correspond with such extensive grounds. In these are several reservoirs, containing gold and silver fish, which are supplied with water by small cascades, as as to be kept constantly full: Nor are Mr. Murray's improvements confined to his own estate; the road up to the mount and the wall which secures it, with many fountains, conduits, and reservoirs, were made by him. He has also opened many cross-paths, winding round the hill in the prettiest manner imaginable, with stone seats, and alcoves, to rest on from time to time; and has planted the hollows with chestnut trees, entirely at his own expence. Poor man! he had been obliged by ill health to abandon his little paradise, and was at this time in Lisbon. We afterwards called upon the British Vice-Consul Mr. C———k,[346] at his country seat, which was remarkable for its extensive prospect; we thought him and Mrs. C. very good kind of people, but were surprized to find that altho' the latter was English, she had resided abroad from infancy, and knew scarcely a hundred words of her native language.

Altho' we were certainly treated with much kindness and hospitality at this place, yet were we assured, that the inhabitants had little enjoyment of society with each other; that being all engaged in one line of merchandize, the pursuits of interest, were found to jar with those of good-fellowship; and that on the whole, Madeira was an unpleasant residence, except to the sick, and the way-faring.

I am yours truly
E. F.

LETTER VI.

To Mrs. L.——

BLACKHEATH, 28th February, 1815.

My dear Madam,

We were much tossed by the equinoctial gales on quitting Madeira, as might be expected; but on the 23rd September we obtained a sight of the peak of Teneriffe: all that day we kept standing in for the land, but to little purpose, as the mountains are too high to admit of approach, except in a calm. On the 26th we cast anchor in the road of Oratavia:[347] the visit-boat came out, and as soon as our bill of health had been examined, the Captain was permitted to go on shore. I sent by him a letter which, Mr. P—— the American Consul at Madeira, had given me, and received in reply a most cordial invitation from Mr. and Mrs. Barry[348] for Miss R—s and myself, to take up our abode with them during our stay with which we thankfully complied in the evening. The appearance of this country, pleased me much better than Madeira, as it is more cultivated and better inhabited: the city of Oratavia constitutes a fine feature in the beautiful scene. We were received most kindly by the worthy couple who invited us, and at whose house we met with the best society in the Island. I greatly prefer the Spanish ladies to the Portuguese, finding them more easy in their manners, and much better educated. Many spoke French and Italian with facility, and several had been so connected with the English, as to have attained enough of the language, to be tolerably intelligible in it: their persons were pleasing, and some would have been really handsome, but for the presence of Mrs. Barry, who altho' in her thirty-fourth year, I thought the most beautiful woman I ever beheld. She was in England just before Sir Joshua Reynold's death, and he declared repeatedly, that would his health permit him ever to take another picture, it should be Mrs. Barry's. Her height was commanding, with just enough of the *enbonpoint*[349] to be agreeable. Dimples have been called "the first of the graces." I never saw a countenance display more of them; her smile was perfectly fascinating.

I was disappointed in my intention of ascending the Peak of Teneriffe, the season being too far advanced; and I was assured by many, that I was quite unequal at any time to have endured the fatigue. After travelling 15 miles over loose stones and rugged ascents, you find yourself still at the foot of the Peak; here it is necessary to remain till two in the morning, when the task of clambering begins, over pumice stone and ashes, and should you reach the top by sunrise, you may esteem yourself very fortunate: four hours are generally allowed for the ascent, and after all, should the Peak be enveloped in clouds, which is frequently the case, you have your labour for your pains; but on a clear day the view is truly sublime; you can distinctly see the seven Canary Islands; some assert that both the Continent of Africa and the Island of Madeira have been seen from hence; but I cannot suppose the human vision capable of extending so far, tho' I do not doubt that both places are comprehended within the immense horizon such a prodigious height may command. Having heard a very good account of Santa Cruz,[350] which is between 20 and 30 miles across the Island, we determined to visit it, little aware of the roads we must encounter. Ladies here travel on Asses, on which are placed a sort of armed chair, with cushions and a foot-stool; this plan appeared to be easy, but we soon found that the roads at Madeira, were bowling greens compared to these; how the poor animals that bore us, contrived to keep their legs, clambering over the rocks that from time to time had fallen in the path, I know not; the shocks they gave me I shall never forget. Mr. Barry had provided a cold turkey, wine &c. for a repast, and when ready for it, we went into a peasant's cottage, and dined comfortably, endeavouring to laugh away our fears and fatigues; the remains of our meal afforded a feast to the peasants, who live in a most wretched style, seldom tasting either meat, eggs, or milk: the mother of the mistress of the cottage was near eighty, and to see, with what eagerness the poor old creature watched every morsel we put into our mouths, was really affecting. Notwithstanding their coarse fare, the common people here, are a stout, hardy race; fair complexioned, well featured, and remarkably lively, as we found by our attendants, for as each animal has a man to guide it, we were almost stunned by their incessant chatter. Soon after dinner, we renewed our journey; my animal fell down, but I was not hurt, and for the next five miles, our road was easy, and lay over a delightful plain which brought us to the ancient city of Laguna,[351] the Capital of the Island, which is tolerably large, well inhabited, and has two good churches, with several convents; from thence the road to Santa Cruz lay entirely on the descent, over large stones and fragments of rock. The jumbling was horrible, and *pour surcroit de malheur*,[352] so strong a wind blew from the sea, that my whole strength was scarce sufficient to hold my umbrella; yet I did not dare give it up, the rays of the sun were so powerful, and the reflection from the stones intolerable. I was at one time so exhausted, that I declared I must give up the journey, but the creature I rode, carried me on in spite of me, and stopped not until we arrived at the house of Mr. R——y in Santa Cruz,[353] who gave us all a hearty welcome. This gentleman lived in a most delightful situation fronting the Mole, where notwithstanding our fatigue, we walked in the evening, when our good host got tipsy for joy, and with great difficulty allowed *us* to retire. Alas! weary as we were, the musquitoes would scarcely permit us to sleep; my companion suffered terribly from them.

Santa Cruz is indeed a fine place, and the country around, well deserves the pen of Mrs. Ratcliffe[354] to celebrate its cloud-capt mountains, vallies teeming with abundance, that in the language of Holy Writ, seemed to "Laugh and sing"[355] beneath the eye of their majestic mountains; and here to render every *coup d'oeil* complete, the vast Atlantic occupies the front, and offers its immense world of waters to our contemplation.

The most curious, perhaps I ought to say the most *interesting* circumstance that happened to me in this expedition, was the violent passion our kind entertainer conceived for me, and which was certainly opened in a manner perfectly new. "My *dare* soul, what shall I do to *plase* you? Is it fifty pipes of wine you would like? but why will I talk of wine? you shall have my house, my garden, all I have in the world! at nine o'clock to-morrow I will resign every thing up to you, and by J—s if you'll consent to marry me, I'll be drunk every day of my life just for joy." Irresistible as the last argument was, my heart of adamant withstood it. Poor R——y! never did a kinder heart, a more generous spirit exist, and but for a fault which indeed proceeded really from the warmth of his heart, he would have been a most agreeable companion; he was beloved by every one. Poor man! let me here close his history, by recording that he was since killed by a shot in the streets of Santa Cruz, at the time of Lord Nelson's attack[356] against it. We returned soon after this declaration, and found the road present objects of new beauty, because we were a little more at ease in our conveyance, from habit.—We found a new guest with Mrs. Barry, a Mr. Edwards, who was just arrived from Turkey and attended by a native of that country; he was completely a citizen of the world, held a commission in the service of the Grand Signior, had been every where, and seen every thing; he was elegant, accomplished, and every way agreeable. Our fellow voyager Mr. Campbell, during all the time we were at Teneriffe, continued the butt of the Captain's jokes, in which others were too ready to join him; on our return, they persuaded him that his legs were swelled, which was ever the precursor of mortal disease in the Island, and the poor fellow submitted to be swathed in flannel, and dosed with every nauseous mess they gave him, with the utmost patience, until Mr. Barry's good nature released the victim, who was to be sure the most ignorant creature in the ways of the world, I ever met with.

I cannot omit to mention, that when we left Santa Cruz, one of Mr. B.'s servants walked over from Oratavia that morning, and returned with us apparently without fatigue, as he laughed and talked all the way home, tho' the real distance was fifty miles, and the badness of the roads of course rendered the exertion much greater, but I was assured this was not remarkable.

On the 6th October after breakfast, we took leave of our kind hosts: and here instead of putting on a semblance of concern, I was obliged to stifle my actual emotions, lest they should appear affected. I never recollect being equally moved at a separation, after so short an acquaintance. But Mrs. Barry is so truly amiable, and we were treated with such generous hospitality by both parties, that it seemed more like a parting between near relations, than casual acquaintances. Since then Oceans have rolled between us, and time and sorrow have combined to efface the traces of recollection in my mind of a variety of circumstances; yet every thing I then saw and enjoyed, is still fresh in my memory. Adieu, my dear madam, for a while: believe me

Yours truly
E. F.

LETTER VII.

To Mrs. L.——

BLACKHEATH, 1st March 1815.

MY DEAR MADAM,

On the 7th October 1795, we set sail from Oratavia with a fair wind, and as it continued, I was sorry we were obliged to stop at St. Iago, where we anchored, on the 13th, in Port Praya Bay.[357] This Bay makes a noble appearance; the surrounding hills rising like an amphitheatre from the sea. The next morning we went on shore about eight o'clock, but were excessively incommoded by the sun, which in these climates rises very rapidly when once above the horizon. Signor Basto the Commandant of the Island,[358] received us very politely, and most of the principal inhabitants came out to pay their respects to, and gaze at, the strangers; among the rest a tall Negro priest, whose shaven crown had a strange appearance. Signor B. led us to a summer house which he had built for the sake of *coolness*, and where there was indeed wind; but the air from a brick-kiln would have been equally pleasant and refreshing; while the glare was insupportable, as the place was open on all sides; fortunately I had brought a pack of cards, so to whist we sat, and his Excellency the Governor joined us, and did us the honour to play several rubbers; and as he spoke neither English nor French, I know not how we could have amused each other better, as I have observed before. An elegant dinner was provided for us, at which I was obliged to preside. In the evening we walked out to see the country, which is well cultivated and highly picturesque; but the inhabitants make a wretched appearance, generally living in huts, even when they are rich. The sugar-cane raised here is remarkably strong; they have also very good cotton, which they manufacture into a pretty kind of cloth; but it is very dear, and exceedingly narrow, being only about a quarter wide. After tea we returned on board, tho' Signor Basto offered to accommodate us with a house to ourselves; but as it is considered dangerous to sleep on shore, we declined his offer, and bade him adieu with many thanks for his civilities. In the course of the day we learned, that this place is so unhealthy, that out of twenty who land here, fifteen generally die within six months. What a pity! every production of warm countries thrives here in abundance, but Man, who cultivates them, sickens and dies.

Our Captain here laid in a stock for a long voyage, and we set sail with a pleasant gale; the day following we caught a fine dolphin; I never saw any thing so beautiful as the colours it displayed when dying. On the 29th October we crossed the Line, and again poor Mr. C—ll was the butt of the party; he had been taught to expect a great shock on passing it, and really stepped forward to look at it, but the boatswain, who was his countryman, advised him to keep aloof; he however declared very seriously that, "he felt a very great shock, he must say, at the time." Nothing further occurred worthy of notice till our arrival at Madras, which took place on the 25th January 1796. I found this town much improved since my former visit, and was particularly pleased with the Exchange, which is a noble building, ornamented with whole length pictures of Lord Cornwallis, Sir Eyre Coote, and General Meadows. The Theatre and Pantheon,[359] where the assemblies are held, are three miles from Madras. At this place we parted with poor Mr. Campbell. I shall never forget the agony of tears I one day found him in. "What is the matter" said I. "Miss Rogers is going away and I am *here*," answered he; the words were very comprehensive; many young people will be aware that they express love and misery in the extreme. Poor Mr. C— must mourn in vain, for alas! "his love met no return."[360]

On the 6th February we again set sail, and were fortunately but little annoyed by the surf. On the 22nd we reached Fulta,[361] where the pilot being over-anxious to get forward, made sail at night, when the soundings suddenly shallowing he found it necessary to cast anchor, tho' not quite early enough, for in swinging round the ship struck. At first she lay easy, having made a bed in the sand, but when the tide came in, she heeled terribly, and it was the opinion of most on board, that she would never be got off. The chief officer advised us to secure whatever valuables we had, about our own persons, for fear of the worst; (which precaution I had already taken) and used all possible means for the preservation of the vessel himself. Happily the rising tide floated her off.—You cannot judge of the acuteness of my feelings on this occasion; to see all my hopes and cares frustrated; and the quick transition from sorrow and disappointment on seeing the ship afloat again, without having sustained the least injury, can only be imagined, by those who have experienced such changes.

On Wednesday the 24th February we reached Calcutta in safety, where we remained several months. Here we found a resting place after a long voyage, diversified by many pleasant and perilous occurrences, and here therefore I shall make a pause in the narrative.

I remain,
My dear Madam,
Yours truly,
E. F.

LETTER VIII.

To Mrs. L.——

BLACKHEATH, 3d March, 1815.

MY DEAR MADAM,

On Wednesday the 24th February 1796 (as I mentioned in the conclusion of my last letter) my feet once more pressed the ground of Calcutta. Miss R——s, Miss Tripler, and myself, went directly to a large house which Mr. Benjamin Lacey had taken for us by my desire. We procured a freight for the *Minerva* and sent her off, within a month after her arrival. The ship had been detained so long on her passage from various causes, that our goods came to a very bad market; we were compelled therefore to sell part by retail, and dispose of the remainder by auction. A small copper bottomed ship called the *Rosalia*, a very fast sailer, was purchased, and the command given to Capt. Robinson, an American, who came out with us, and on the 26th of August following, I embarked on her, with Mr. Benjamin Lacey and Miss Tripler, for the United States, after bidding a painful adieu to my dear young friend and companion Miss R——s, whose place Miss Tripler had neither inclination nor ability to supply; but having fettered myself by an engagement, I was forced to submit; besides I could not well have proceeded alone.—We set sail with a fair wind, but a very strong current running astern. On the night of the 29th the water broke with such violence against the ship, that I called for dead-lights,[362] but was assured by the Captain that there was not the *least* occasion for them; loth to be thought cowardly or an ignorant sailor, I instantly gave up the point, but had great reason to lament my acquiescence: in less than a quarter of an hour, a most tremendous sea broke in at the starboard side of the cabin, and half filled it with water, which soaked a bale of valuable muslins, with me their unfortunate owner. On this the pilot bawled out, that if the dead-lights were not put up instantly, he would cut cable and get under weigh; so at length they were fixed.—In the morning we had the additional mortification to find, that the ship had sprung a leak, and what was worse than all, that she appeared generally too weak to support the voyage; but as it would have been wrong to give her up without a trial, we proceeded with the tide to Ingillee, in the faint hope of the leak closing.—On the 30th we reached the lower buoy of the Barabulla. Our leak still continuing to increase, on the 1st September we were obliged to put back for Calcutta. In the evening of the 4th, we anchored off Cooly Bazar,[363] and the next day went on shore at Calcutta, where the *Rosalia* was examined, and pronounced totally unfit for the voyage.

On the 11th September I went on board the *Swallow Packet* with Captain Simson, who was a Guinea pig[364] (as it is called) on board the *Camden* when I came out in 1784. He has been a very fortunate young man, so early in life to obtain a command. We had a very elegant repast or Tiffin, and I must say, Captain S. seemed heartily glad to receive his old shipmate. Mr. L— and Miss T— having accompanied me, the former was suddenly taken ill with an ague and fever: this added to the fatigue, loss, and disappointment, I had so lately endured, was very near too much for me. I brought him back, procured the best advice for him, and in a few days he was relieved; but before he was able to crawl out, I was in the same situation with a similar intermittent, but escaped the cold fit: I was exceedingly reduced but restored by the free use of bark,[365] and other prescriptions from Dr. Hare,[366] who never failed to relieve me.

On the 22nd October Mr. Lacey engaged for our freight and passage, on board the *Hero*, Captain Jackson, bound to New York, to sail between the first and the tenth of December. As soon as my strength returned, I bustled about my business, endeavoured to repair my losses, visited my friends, and bade them farewell, and every necessary preparation being completed, on the 18th of December we went on board at Garden Reach, and reached Culpee the 22nd, after a tedious passage, kedging[367] all the way. Here we went on shore, and laid in provisions. On Christmas day we anchored off Kedgeree. On New Year's day we got under weigh; but unfortunately the wind failed us; and at six in the evening, the Pilot received instructions not to take us out till further orders. This was a sad beginning of the New Year; the embargo lasted 18 days, after which we proceeded, though very slowly, and on the 30th arrived at Vizagapatam,[368] where we ran some risk from the *Hero* being mistaken for a French Frigate. On the Captain's going on shore, I sent a letter from my good friend Mrs. Child, to Captain Hodson,[369] who returned me a pressing invitation, and the next day I found him on the beach with four palanquins for me and my friends. We proceeded to Waltair, where Mrs. Hodson, Mrs. Child's sister, gave us a most cordial reception, and insisted on our staying till the ship was ready to sail. The next morning I breakfasted with Captain Pitman,[370] one of the most elegant young men I ever saw. He obligingly drove me in his Curricle[371] round Waltair, and shewed me Sardinia Bay, and several other spots remarkable for their beauty.

His own house was charmingly situated on a hill, half way between Vizagapatam and Waltair. Land here is considered of so little value, that every person who built, took in as much as he could employ.

To one whose eye has been fatigued with viewing the flat country of Bengal, this place appears delightful, but yet diversified prospects do not repay the want of fertile plains. Here I bought some beautiful sandal-wood and ivory boxes, for which this place is famous. Captain and Mrs. Hodson behaved to us with unbounded kindness. In the evening we quitted Vizagapatam. The town makes an agreeable appearance from the sea, not unlike St. James Valley in St. Helena. All who can afford it, live at Waltair, which however does not contain above ten houses.

On Friday the 24th February I once more landed on Madras Beach, and the day following saw many of my friends; among others Captain Gooch, who looked remarkably well: there is nothing more pleasant than to meet unexpectedly an old friend, after a long absence and in a foreign country. He dined with us, and every one was charmed with his behaviour, so different from many who on getting into commands, fancy that insolence establishes superiority.

On the 27th we dined at St. Thomé, with Mr. Stevens, Mr. B. L—'s agent; in the evening we sat down to vingt-un, at a rupee a fish,[372] which Mr. S. assured us was very low. I lost only two dozen. We rose from the card table at half past eleven, and for the honour of Madras hospitality, were suffered to get into our palanquins at that time of night, without the offer of a glass of wine to support us during a four miles' jumble, or a shawl to keep us from the damp air.

On the 2nd of March Captain Gooch paid us a farewell visit: I was a good deal affected at parting; how many thousand miles had each to traverse before we met again! At 5 P. M. we left Madras; there was scarce any surf, but the sea ran high. I found every thing very dear here, consequently made few purchases.

On the 4th of March we got under weigh at day break, and set sail for a new country, towards which I now looked with eager expectation. On the 15th I had the misfortune to fall into the after-hold, which opens into the great cabin; the steward having carelessly left the scuttle open, while he went for a candle. I was taken up senseless, having received a severe blow on the head and many bruises, but thank heaven, no material injury. There was a large open case of empty bottles under the opening, and had I fallen the other way, I must have gone directly on it; judge what the consequences must have been.

About the 20th we began to be troubled with calms and southerly winds, when our Captain politely accused Miss Tripler and me of being two Jonahs,[373] saying he never knew a good voyage made, where a Woman or a Parson was on board. I had a very agreeable revenge, for that very afternoon a breeze sprung up, which proved to be the trade wind, and for some time we enjoyed a fine run; but the ship was the most uneasy I ever sailed in, rolling and pitching on every occasion. On the 23rd of April a violent gale came on, and for several days we had very unpleasant weather. I was in great fear of the passage round the Cape,[374] and we were all in trouble, as provisions ran very short: all our wine and spirits were expended, and we had neither butter, cheese, nor coffee remaining. On the 18th of May we arrived off False Bay,[375] and on the 20th at noon, Mr. D. Trail the Harbour-Master came on board, and we cast anchor soon after. Mr. Lacey wrote to Lord Macartney for leave to proceed to Cape Town, as without his permission no passengers are suffered to land. We received a visit from Mr. Gooch First Lieutenant of the *Jupiter*, an elder brother of Captain Gooch, of whose arrival at Madras we brought the first news. I called by invitation on Captain Linzee to look at the *Dort* late Admiral De Lucas' ship. Captain L. has been three years a Post Captain, tho' not yet four and twenty. When in command of the *Nemesis*, he cut out two French vessels from some Mahomedan Port in the Mediterranean, and was afterwards taken himself. He but just saved his distance now, for hearing at Cape Town on his arrival ten days ago, that the *Dort* was under sailing orders, he sat off on horse-back, and arrived but twelve hours before she was to have sailed. Mr. Gooch brought Mrs. Losack the wife of the Captain of the *Jupiter*, to visit me, and they took us with them on board that ship, where we drank tea and supped.

On Monday the 22d we went on shore at noon, and were received by Major Grimstone the Commanding Officer, who politely apologized for detaining us so long. At one, six of us mounted a waggon with eight horses, which to my great surprize were driven by one man in hand, at the rate of six miles an hour, over loose stones, or whatever else came in the way; so that we were almost jumbled to death. We passed three beaches, and to avoid quick-sands, they drove through the surf; the roaring of which, the horses splashing as they gallopped along, added to the crack of the driver's long whip, formed altogether a charming concert. As the driver cannot wield these enormous instruments with one hand, another man sits by to hold the reins, while by lengthening or shortening his arm he dexterously contrives to make every horse in turn feel the weight of the lash. At length we reached Cape Town in safety, but were terribly tired and bruised. Between the beaches, the road (such as it is) passes along stupendous mountains, from whose craggy tops, masses of stone are continually falling, some of them large enough to crush a church; many have rolled into the sea, where they form a barrier against the surf, and may defy its force for ages.

We heard that the former Governor, General Craig,[376] sailed from hence on Tuesday preceding; he was once forced to put back, but the second attempt succeeded.

There were no less than six vessels here. The flag was struck on the 15th, and would not be hoisted again until the 15th August, during which interval the Dutch suffered no ships to remain in Table Bay. Our people are not so cautious; perhaps, experience may render them so. I like the appearance of the place; for altho' the houses are generally low, they occupy much ground; being built of stone, or covered with plaster, and containing five or six rooms on a floor, they look well; and though with only one upper story, yet the ceilings being lofty, they do not seem deficient in height. The church is handsome; the service is performed in Dutch and English; there are no pews but benches and chairs, which I greatly prefer, as it gives the idea of social worship more, and is consistent with that equality, which in the more immediate presence of God, becomes his creatures, as being equally dependant on Him. It is true this was partly lost here, because the Governor and his family use benches, covered with crimson velvet. We sat off after service for Simon's Town and reached the ship at 4 P. M. On Monday Mr. Gooch took us in the morning to see the *Tremendous*, Admiral Pringle's ship. Here we saw furnaces for heating balls.

On Wednesday the 31st we dined on board the *Dort*, where we met Captain and Mrs. Losack, Lord Augustus Fitzroy, Captain Holles of the *Chichester*, and Captain Osborne of the *Trusty*; we went and returned in Captain L—'s barge. Next day we dined on board *L'Imperieuse* with Lord Augustus Fitzroy. In addition to our yesterday's party were Captain Stevens of the *Rattle-Snake*, Captain Granger of the *Good Hope*, Captain Alexander of the *Sphinx*, Mr. Pownall Naval Officer and his wife, and Mr. Trail. His Lordship gave us a most magnificent dinner, and to my great joy, was too much the man of fashion, to urge the gentlemen to hard drinking, as had been the case on board the *Dort*. He has an excellent band. When we retired Mrs. Losack and Mrs. Pownall entered into conversation, about the Cape, which they both agreed was the vilest place imaginable; Mrs. L—is a fine dashing lady. Since her marriage, the *Jupiter* has been on a cruize. I asked her if they were ever fired upon. "Oh yes, from a battery and returned the fire." "Did you go below?" "Not I indeed." "Then I suppose you must have been greatly alarmed for fear of being shot?" "Why to tell you the truth I was so much engaged in observing how they loaded the guns and manœuvred the ship, that I *never* once thought of danger." There is a courageous lady for you!

We played at whist in the evening and retired at eleven. Captain Alexander took us on board in his Barge. On the 4th of June the Admiral, at one, fired two guns, then all the Men of War in the Harbour followed with twenty one each: the effect produced by the reverberation from so many stupendous rocks was most noble! Mr. Gooch and the Doctor came on board to take leave, and on going away, the boats crew gave us three cheers, which our people returned. On the whole, our time passed here pleasantly; the politeness of my Countrymen, contrasted with the manners of our American officers served to soothe the irritation of our minds, and teach us to endure that for a season, with patience, which we had often found to be a trial of our spirits and temper, in the hopes of meeting by and by with Gentlemen.

On the 5th of June the wind was as foul as it could blow, and split our only main sail. It is a great misfortune to sail in a vessel ill provided with stores and necessaries: we had an opportunity of observing this day, what a good ship can perform; *L'Imperieuse* Frigate being ordered on a cruize, got under weigh at noon, passed us at 3 P. M. and was safely out before night. Lord Augustus was polite enough to hoist his colours while going by, and struck them immediately afterwards. Our Captain was too much of a Yankee[377] however to return the compliment. I forgot to mention, that yesterday four large ships came in; they proved to be the *Rose*, the *Hillsborough*, and the *Thurlow* East India-men, under convoy of H. M. 74 Gun ship the *Raisonable*.

On the 8th of June we were still in sight of Simon's Town, though we were out two days. On the 11th of July we crossed the equinoctial Line, and I felt satisfied in thinking, that I was once more in my own hemisphere. There are cases in which it is wisdom to please ourselves with trifles; at this time my spirits were very low, and sunk with what I might now term a presentiment, as I approached another people and another world, which was eventually the grave of that property, for which I had toiled so long. On the 28th of August a pilot came on board from Philadelphia, and from him we had the mournful account, that a sickness raged in the city, almost as fatal as that which ravaged it a few years before, and that a general distress prevailed in America: frequent Bankruptcies, Trade at a stand, and an open war with France daily expected, as they took every thing from America which fell in their way—As we did not like to proceed to Philadelphia after hearing this account, we tacked and stood to the northward, but we had a succession of vexatious hindrances, having narrowly escaped shipwreck in Egg Harbour,[378] and did not reach New York till the 3rd of September, when we landed at 6 in the evening, and went immediately to a house recommended by my friend Captain Crowninshield, most happy to part with the strange beings with whom we had been so long and painfully immured.

Now having arrived in the land of Columbia, I will bid you adieu for a while.

I am, My dear Madam,
Yours truly,
E. F.

Advertisement

The work had been printed thus far when the death of the author took place. The subsequent parts of her journal, not appearing to contain any events of a nature sufficiently interesting to claim publication, no additional extracts have been deemed necessary by the administrator, who from a view of benefiting the estate has been induced to undertake the present publication.

Editorial notes

Abbreviations

EIC	East India Company
Hobson-Jobson	H. Yule and A. C. Burnell, *Hobson-Jobson: The Anglo-Indian Dictionary* (Cambridge: Cambridge University Press, 2011)
OED	Oxford English Dictionary

Notes

1 *exhibits a faithful account of certain remarkable occurrences*: Fay voices a common dilemma for travel writers often addressed in prefatory materials: in a market crowded with published travel narratives competing for readers' attention, Fay needs simultaneously to claim the extraordinary for her experiences and to insist on their authenticity. Both of these claims – to novelty and to eyewitness experience – work to provide authority for her text. Isabella Baudino, after Philippe Lejeune, describes this as the 'autobiographical pact' required of women publishing in the travel genre during their lifetimes. See I. Baudino, 'British Women Travellers as Art Critics and Connoisseurs (1775–1825)', *19: Interdisciplinary Studies in the Long Nineteenth Century* 28 (2019), p. 2.

2 *her husband the late Anthony Fay Esq*: Born in Ireland, Anthony Fay was admitted to Gray's Inn on 10 November 1772 (the same year the couple married in London) and to Lincoln's Inn on 4 July 1778. In April 1779, husband and wife embarked for India with the intention of practising at Calcutta. Anthony Fay was admitted as an advocate to the Supreme Court of Calcutta on 16 June 1780 after his arrival. But the behaviour which may well have motivated the journey to India (Eliza Fay explains that she undertook the voyage 'with a view to preserving my husband from destruction' as a result of his extravagance, 'dissipated habits' and 'violence of temper') re-emerged on arrival. He fathered an illegitimate child, and Eliza Fay demanded a private deed of separation (signed 11 August 1781). Anthony Fay subsequently returned to Britain

to present a petition to parliament against Sir Elijah Impey (Chief Justice of the Calcutta Supreme court). Very little is known of him after this period except a couple of references in the *Times* in the year 1794. Fay was a widow by 1800.

3 *Lincolns Inn*: Lincoln's Inn is one of London's Inns of Court, historically responsible for providing and overseeing legal education in Britain. At the time Anthony Fay was studying the law, there were no formal requirements for being called to the Bar other than having eaten five dinners a term at Lincoln's Inn.

4 *seized by the officers of Hyder Ally*: Also known as Hyder Ali or Haider Ali (1720–1782), the Sultan and ruler of the kingdom of Mysore in southern India. A leader of strong military and administrative skills, he offered resistance against the military advances of the British EIC during the First and Second Anglo-Mysore Wars (1766–1769; 1780–1784), allying with France and significantly developing Mysore's economy. He left his eldest son, Tipu Sultan (1750–1799), an extensive kingdom bordered by the Krishna River in the north, the Eastern Ghats in the east, and the Arabian Sea in the west. Fay locates her first voyage historically in the period following the British seizure of the French port of Mahe in 1779 and in the lead-up to the Second Anglo-Mysore conflict. The mention of their incarceration so conspicuously in the Preface provides evidence of the 'extraordinary' events Fay promises her readers, and perhaps also makes strategic reference to the notorious incident of 'The Black Hole of Calcutta' (20 June 1756) nearly 25 years earlier.

5 *important circumstances . . . respectable individuals*: Fay's *Original Letters* would have garnered greatest notoriety for its accounts of Warren Hastings (1732–1818), the first de facto Governor General of India from 1773 to 1784, and of the circle of men appointed to the council and court at Calcutta after the Regulating Act for India of 1773, including Sir Elijah Impey, Philip Francis, and Sir Robert Chambers. In 1787, after his return to England, Hastings was arrested and tried in the House of Lords for crimes and misdemeanours in India; he was eventually acquitted in 1795. His impeachment and trial dominated news coverage in the late 1780s and galvanized Parliament to reconsider the legal and sovereign status of India and how it could best be governed.

6 *"the harmless tenor of her way"*: Deliberately misquoting line 76 of Thomas Gray's *Elegy Written in a Country Churchyard* (1751): 'They kept the noiseless tenor of their way'.

7 *"pains and penalties"*: Usually referring to Parliament's power to impose punishments on individuals via legislative act – called bills of attainder – so long as the punishment was less than death. Fay uses the term here to refer to the power of reviewers and the public to penalize female authors without trial.

8 *in terrorem*: In or by way of alarm; here, to alarm women writers.

9 *addressed to a lady*: Nira Gupta-Casale suggests that this is a fictional addressee for the final letters, designed to prolong the appearance of a correspondence in the final section of the *Original Letters*. See N. Gupta-Casale, 'Intrepid Traveller, "She-Merchant", or Colonialist Historiographer: Reading Eliza Fay's *Original Letters*', in S. Towheed (ed.), *New Readings in the Literature of British India, c. 1780–1947* (New York: Columbia University Press, 2007), pp. 65–91.

10 *it was agreed that, my Letters should not in general be addressed to anyone . . . style of journals*: Fay adopts a form common to much correspondence – particularly travel letters – and preserved in many printed travel accounts of the eighteenth and nineteenth centuries. This style of journal 'newsletter', written over many days, even weeks, and posted when carriage became available, was not specifically addressed to a single correspondent, but intended to be shared among family and friends. This more 'open' or public style of letter-writing inevitably shaped a letter's contents, since its topics and materials needed to be appropriate for multiple, even unanticipated, readers in a culture where letters were eagerly anticipated, passed among the family circle, and read aloud. The reasonably public and performative nature of 'private' letters often leads to the mistaken assumption that they were written specifically for publication; instead, it is more accurate

to recognize letter writing as an important skill for men and women, and to understand that the audience for a letter often extended far beyond its nominal addressee.

11 *allons donc*: 'Let's go' (French).

12 *Mr. B—... Captain Mills recommended*: Mr. B— remains unidentified, but Mr. B— returns in the narrative to confirm Fay's early prejudices at Genoa in Letter IV.

13 *the Diligence*: A public stagecoach; the term is shortened from *carrosse de diligence*, meaning 'coach of speed'.

14 *Monsr. Pigault de l'Epinoye*: Charles-Antoine-Guillaume Pigault de l'Espinoy, better known as Pigault-Lebrun, (1753–1835), a French novelist and playwright who had attracted some notoriety for two elopements in his youth (including with a Miss Crawford, daughter of an English merchant at Calais), and twice being imprisoned by *letter de cachet*. Having already been formally presented to Pigault-Lebrun, Fay was able to call on him without the letters of introduction that would normally have been required to make an acquaintance. Pigault-Lebrun claimed a connection (on his mother's side) with Eustache de Saint Pierre, perhaps the best known of the six 'Burghers of Calais' who surrendered to Edward III in August 1347.

15 *the six brave Citizens of Calais... our third Edward*: Referring to the Burghers of Calais, recounted by the chronicler Jean Le Bel (c. 1290–c. 1370), and reworked by Jean Froissart (c. 1333–c. 1400). Besieged by English forces and without any hope of being rescued by King Philip VI of France, the inhabitants of Calais decided to negotiate with the English King Edward III, who agreed to take them prisoner with the exception of six of them, who would be required to appear in public with halters round their necks. Six burghers prepared themselves to be sacrificed and were ordered to be beheaded, but Queen Philippa of Hainault, Edward's wife, managed to change his mind and save them.

16 *humstrums*: The *OED* gives the meaning as a 'musical instrument of rude construction or out of tune; a hurdy-gurdy' but Francis Grose's *Classical Dictionary of the Vulgar Tongue* (London: S. Hooper, 1785) gives a much more detailed description of 'a musical instrument made of a mopstick, a bladder, and some packthread, thence also called bladder and string, and hurdy gurdy; it is played on like a violin, which is sometimes ludicrously called a humstrum; sometimes instead of a bladder, a tin canister is used' (n.p.). The wider appearance of the term across the eighteenth and nineteenth centuries suggests that 'humstrums' could be used to describe poorly constructed instruments, music badly played, or even the itinerant musicians who played it.

17 *the discipline of a horse-pond*: The ducking of an individual – frequently a thief or 'scold' – into a local pond or stream was a punishment often administered spontaneously by members of the public or even a mob (and in popular mimicry of lawful punishments such as the gibbet or pillory). Fay's language echoes the commonplace phrasing of British newspapers; see D. Lemmings, *Law and Government in England during the Long Eighteenth Century* (Basingstoke: Palgrave Macmillan, 2011), p. 6.

18 *were set down at the same inn... before*: Although nothing has been discovered of Fay's earlier travels, the scant evidence from her letters suggests she had previously visited Calais, Paris, and Versailles, likely with her family and taking the same route as she describes now.

19 *tell it not in Gath*: Quoting II Samuel 1:20.

20 *a famous palace belonging to the Prince of Condé*: The Château de Chantilly, located approximately 60 miles north of Paris and one of the principal estates of the House of Condé. Long known for its library and collection of fifteenth- and sixteenth-century paintings, the Chateau is also famous for staging the premiere of Moliere's *Les Précieuses Ridicules* in 1659 and hosting King Louis XIV in 1671.

21 *St Denis... Kings of France*: The *Basilique Royale de Saint-Denis*, a large medieval church in the city of Saint Denis, now a northern suburb of Paris. A holy site as early as 250 AD, it became a place of pilgrimage after 636 AD when the relics of Saint Denis

were transferred there, after which it became the customary burial place of French kings. Construction was almost continuous on the building through to the thirteenth century, producing a cathedral of enormous architectural influence in the Gothic style. In 1793, fewer than 20 years after Fay's visit, the cathedral was a target of anti-monarchical sentiment during the French Revolution. It survived, and restorations began under Napoleon.

22 *Library . . . sword of our illustrious Talbot*: The Saint-Denis Abbey Library was famous for its collection of medieval manuscripts compiled in the thirteenth, fourteenth, and fifteenth centuries. Many of these were translated and copied with the aim of compiling a history of the French monarchy; these eventually were called *Grandes Chroniques de France*. By 'our illustrious Talbot' Fay means Sir John Talbot (c. 1387–1453), first earl of Shrewsbury and first earl of Waterford, a noted military commander during the Hundred Years War with France and celebrated in William Shakespeare's *Henry VI, Part 1*. Known as 'the English Achilles' and 'the Terror of the French', he retook Saint Denis while defending Paris as lieutenant-general in 1435. The siege was the last military effort in which the forces of England and Burgundy worked together, and by its end Burgundy had made peace with France. Talbot ultimately was unable to prevent the French conquest of Normandy. Pressed on three sides by forces superior to his own, he withdrew to Rouen in 1449 and surrendered himself (and his sword) as hostage, and was released in 1450 only after the conquest of the region was completed. His death, which occurred three years later while leading charge against artillery, came to symbolize the passing of the chivalric era.

23 *an eye of St Thomas the apostle*: One of the 12 apostles of Jesus, Thomas speaks in John 11:6, John 14:5, and (most significantly) John 20:24, where he states that he will not believe that Jesus has risen from the dead unless 'I shall see in his hands the print of the nails, and put my finger into the print of the nails, and thrust my hand into his side, I will not believe'. When Jesus next appears, he invites Thomas to 'reach hither thy hand, and thrust it into my side: and be not faithless, but believing' (John 20:27). The episode is the foundation of the term 'doubting Thomas', denoting a sceptic who refuses to believe except from first-hand, usually ocular, experience. The Abbey of Saint-Denis would thus have been especially proud to hold an *eye* of St. Thomas, and it is not surprising that it becomes a vehicle for Fay's anti-Catholic satire.

24 *at the sight of these absurdities . . . cunningly devised Fables*: Here, Fay shows an almost textbook Protestantism, foregrounding her religion's rejection of icons, idols, and relics and derogating Catholicism's celebration of such devices as 'cunningly devised Fables'.

25 *as if there were no War, or even dispute between us*: By 1779 France had joined the side of the American colonies in their War of Independence (1775–1781) against Great Britain.

26 *This you know is not the region of Politics*: Fay here refers wittily to two kinds of censorship: that of Parisian politeness (where politics is rarely, if ever, mentioned in conversation) and policy (where foreign letters are routinely read and objectionable parts suppressed).

27 *passports*: Passports in the late eighteenth century were not like the small booklets we have today. Usually they were a single sheet of paper authorizing a person to pass out of, or into, a country or canton. Given that France and Britain were at war in 1779, the Fays would have required passports for almost every stage of their journey, particularly as they were travelling overland. Here, Fay and her husband appear to be waiting for the return of their passports, already granted, from the local official (usually a Prefect or, in the smaller towns, the mayor or local executive).

28 *Colissée . . . Ranelagh*: Built in 1769 and patterned on the Vauxhall (opened c. 1659) and Ranelagh (opened 1742) pleasure gardens, the *Colisée* was located on the Champs-Élysées and consisted of extensive gardens, a grand rotunda, and side

buildings. Like its English predecessors, it was designed as a kind of amusement park, in which visitors could walk during summer evenings among trees and classical ruins, hear music, shop, eat dinner, attend theatrical performances and spectacles, and watch fireworks.

29 *the Queen ... Duchess D'Alençon*: Marie Antoinette (1755–1793), wife of King Louis XVI, the last Queen of France before the French Revolution, and Marie Joséphine of Savoy (1753–1810), princess of France and wife of future King Louis XVIII. Fay's depiction of the Queen of France as unaffected, 'perfectly beautiful', and genuinely polite is pointed given the political hostilities between the two nations, and would have been still more interesting to her readers after the Marie Antoinette's execution in October 1793.

30 *"Ah! mon Dieu ... c'est joli"*: 'Ah! Oh, how charming! How pretty!' (French).

31 *Rotunda!*: The grandest building of the *Colisée* and a venue for grand spectacles, with an colonnade and two concentric circulation galleries reminiscent of St. Peter's in Rome. A central rotunda twenty-five metres in diameter served as a ballroom, and each evening the building was illuminated by 2,000 candles.

32 *his principle reason for quitting the Capital ... assassination*: Leon Poliakov suggests anti-Semitism in France was most conspicuous in this period on the part of religionists and bourgeois capitalists. Forbidden access to the Guilds, Jews in France – like elsewhere in Europe – were highly competitive merchants operating outside the Guild sphere, specialising in hire-purchase and credit arrangements, and frequently undercutting Guild-mandated pricing and quality controls. For these and other reasons, Jews often were more widely accepted at courtly and noble levels. Fay's relation of this wave of violence – and its apparent confirmation over the course of the next week as Anthony Fay seeks to settle a bet among the Parisians – suggests that overt and violent anti-Semitism was becoming prominent in Paris in the late 1770s and may have been connected with the nobility's pronounced philo-Semitism as popular opinion turned against the elites. See L. Poliakov, *The History of Anti-Semitism, Volume 3: From Voltaire to Wagner* (Philadelphia, PA: University of Pennsylvania Press, 2003), pp. 26–33.

33 *the Petit Chatelet*: A small castle, located at the southern end of the Petit-Pont and probably dating from the eighth century AD, Le Petit Châtelet was one of two fortifications protecting the bridges that connect the Île de la Cité to the banks of the Seine. It was used at various periods as a customs house, mortuary, prison, and place of summary execution before being demolished in 1782.

34 *the Lieutenant de Police*: The Lieutenant General of Police at Paris between 1776 and 1785 was Jean Charles Pierre Lenoir (or Le Noir, 1732–1807). Among his many duties, he seems to have given particular attention to the surveillance of foreigners and other 'undesirables' in Paris. He was unpopular and considered despotic by Parisians.

35 *Commodités*: Literally 'amenities', or toilets.

36 *feveretts*: Slight or brief fevers.

37 *We found the route totally different from what we expected*: Various difficulties of route and finance combine to create obstacles here for Fay and her husband. Expecting perhaps to travel by water from Paris, they discover that they instead must travel at a much higher cost by land: first to Chalons sur Soane, then to Lyons, and then onward to Marseilles. Travelling by road, their first option would be by the regular Paris–Lyon diligence, which charged 100 livres per person plus six sous per pound of luggage. For the Fays, this amounts to a cost of 200 livres plus luggage, or at least (by Paris exchange rates) eight guineas. See *Journal of Travels Made through the Principal Cities of Europe* (London: J. Wallis, 1782), p. 26. Faced with the prospect of these increased costs, the Fays elect to travel by private carriage to Marseille (with their fellow passenger Mr. B), purchasing two horses and a single-horse chaise for a total of twenty-one guineas. Their plan is to re-sell them on arrival, which they do, at a profit

of three guineas (see Letter IV). See T. Smollett, *Travels through France and Italy*, 2 vols (London: R. Baldwin, 1766), vol. 1, pp. 125–6; L. Denis, *Route de la Diligence de Paris à Lyon* (Paris: 1780), pp. 497–8; and P. C. Reynard, *Ambitions Tamed: Urban Expansion in Pre-Revolutionary Lyon* (Montreal: McGill-Queens University Press, 2009), pp. 143–4.

38 *no remittances till our arrival at Leghorn*: Eighteenth-century travel was financially complicated. With the risk of robbery making it unfeasible to carry large sums of money, travellers needed to secure credit abroad through letters of introduction. This meant that one's route needed to correspond with those places where one's letters secured financial and social *entrée*. As Fay's 2 July 1779 missive (see Letter V) explains, they must travel to Livorno because they have a 'letter of introduction from Mr. Baretto of London to his brother, the king of Sardinia's Consul at Leghorn', which procures them both hospitality and credit in Livorno. Through the Barettos they subsequently meet the Francos, 'eminent merchants' able to provide them with a further letter of introduction 'recommending us in the strongest terms to a Mr. Abraham, of Grand Cairo', thus guaranteeing the next leg of their journey.

39 *Duc de Chartres castle . . . scraped acquaintance*: Louis Philippe Joseph d'Orléans or Phillip Egalité (1747–1793). Fay presents himself uninvited at the stables of the Château de Saint-Cloud (now the site of the Parc de Saint-Cloud) in order to gain advice on the purchase of the horses. Fay's way of describing her husband's 'scraping an acquaintance' shows the embarrassment of currying favour with the Duc's employees for personal gain, even if they are countrymen.

40 *only a little touched in the wind*: A horse that is 'touched in the wind' or has 'broken wind' is suffering from chronic obstructive pulmonary disease (COPD), a respiratory disease or chronic condition of pulmonary bronchitis, not unlike asthma or allergic bronchitis in humans. It is characterized by noisy breathing, wheezing, and reduced stamina.

41 *six guineas*: Before Britain converted to a decimal monetary system in 1971, one shilling equalled 12 pence, and 20 shillings equalled one pound; one pound was thus comprised of 240 pence. Guineas were English gold coins first struck in 1663 with the nominal value of 20 shillings, but after 1717 they circulated at a value of 21 shillings (or 252 pence). The Royal Mint stopped making guineas in 1813.

42 *Azor . . . Zemire*: Fay's horses are named for the two leading characters of *Zémire et Azor*, a comic opera by the Belgian composer André Grétry first performed by the Comédie-Italienne at Fontainebleau on 9 November 1771. It enjoyed worldwide success and was part of the French repertory well into the 1820s.

43 *Bois de Boulogne*: Now the second largest park in Paris, the Bois de Boulogne was a royal hunting ground before being enclosed by a wall and eight gates in the second half of the sixteenth century. During the late eighteenth century, Louis XV and Louis XVI allowed the public access to the park, though both monarchs also used it as a hunting ground and pleasure garden. The land was officially ceded to the city of Paris in 1852 by Napoleon III.

44 *we had him bled immediately*: The practice of bloodletting, or the bleeding of a patient either by leeches or by an incision made by a physician or barber-surgeon, is an ancient treatment based on humoral theories of medicine and remained popular well into the nineteenth century. While it was – during the period of its use – perceived to be beneficial to the patient as a technique of 'rebalancing' blood with other bodily fluids, it was often very harmful, particularly if a patient was already in a weakened state.

45 *We have all necessaries with us*: Fay brazens it out in her description of their way of travelling – with most of their own provisions, avoiding inns except for necessary

overnight accommodation – but it is clear that the party are travelling with very little money and as modestly as possible.

46 *Fontainbleu*: A royal residence as early as the twelfth century, the Palace of Fontainebleau was expanded and renovated during the eighteenth century by Louis XV, who created lavish new apartments for himself and his Queen. After his marriage to Marie Antoinette, Louis XVI had the Queen's apartments redone in a Turkish style in 1777. Fay likely refers in this passage to the Treaty of Paris (1763), which ended the Seven Years' War (1756–1763).

47 *where Christina, Queen of Sweden, caused Monaldeschi her chief chamberlain to be beheaded*: Christina (1626–1689) became Queen of Sweden in 1632 and reigned from 1644 until 1654 when she abdicated, converted to Catholicism, and went into exile in Italy and France. Already notorious for her intellectualism, masculine appearance, and mannerisms, Christina scandalized the European courts and Vatican in 1657 by arranging for the execution of one of her party, in her presence, whom she suspected of betraying her. The marchese Gian Rinaldo Monaldeschi, her master of the horse, was stabbed multiple times, including in the throat, in the Queen's apartments (the *Galerie des Cerfs* or Gallery of Stags) at Fontainbleu. Fay's antipathy to Queen Christina is suggestive. Learned and opinionated, a Catholic convert, collector, politician and highly unconventional figure, Christina is judged by Fay to be 'an accomplished woman', but one who could 'never be called great, even by her admirers'.

48 *ornamented with box in a thousand fantastical shapes*: The gardens of the Palace of Fontainebleau were formal, laid out in orderly, geometrical style with box hedges shaped to resemble birds and mystical creatures. This style formed a marked contrast to English gardening, which drew from Chinese classical gardens and the paintings of Nicholas Poussin and Claude Lorrain to create a natural-looking, though idealized, pastoral landscape.

49 *set off Jehu like*: Driving like Jehu – driving like a madman, or wholly at one's own will. Jehu was the tenth king of the northern kingdom of Israel since Jeroboam I; the principal events of his 28-year reign are depicted in 2 Kings 9–10. In describing their manner of setting off as 'Jehu like', Fay likely refers not just to the aggressive nature with which Jehu claimed power, but also likely to the incident in which he had Queen Jezebel thrown from an upper storey of her house into the street and then trampled over her body with his horses.

50 *a thick sauce composed of eggs, butter, oil and vinegar*: Likely Béarnaise sauce.

51 *de grace un peu de viniagre!*: 'For God's sake a little vinegar!' (French).

52 *the book of roads*: A collection of maps used for navigating; the Fays are possibly using relevant sections of the Trudaine *Atlas*, often referred to in the period as 'Road Maps'. See S. J. L. Blond, 'The Trudaine Atlas: Government Road Mapping in Eighteenth-Century France', *Imago Mundi* 65 (2013), pp. 64–79.

53 *Mr. Fay had . . . received by weight twenty four livres ten sous*: 'Livre' is the French word for pound, and was a unit of currency in France between 781 and 1794. In 1779, the gold *louis d'or* coin had a fixed value of 24 livres. The exchange rate secured by Anthony Fay suggests near parity between the French *louis d'or* and the English pound, with guineas fetching still higher rates of exchange. Later at Chalons, however, Anthony Fay will be unable to negotiate a better rate for his guineas than 18 livres, and will elect to do without money until reaching Lyons.

54 *awfully terrible*: Both words here carry their late eighteenth-century meanings: 'inspiring awe' and 'inspiring terror'.

55 *they went so far . . . to expand my soul, and raise it nearer to its Creator*: Here, Fay relates an almost textbook encounter with the sublime, drawing most conspicuously from Longinus (213–273 AD, author of *Perì Hýpsous* [*On the Sublime*]) and Edmund Burke (1729–1797, author of *A Philosophical Enquiry into the Origins of Our Ideas*

of the Sublime and Beautiful [1758]) to describe her terrifying yet soul-expanding encounter with the 'cascades, torrents, and apparently air-hung bridges' of the Alps. As is typical of Fay, she signals her familiarity with the conventions of sublime description before moving to an even more arresting and less stylized account of her own feelings while travelling through the mountain passes of Cenis.

56 *go up across a mule*: To ascend Mont Cenis riding a mule, rather than as a passenger in the chaise, as Fay had been travelling until this point. Fay is also obliged to ride astride as they are not carrying a lady's side-saddle for her use.

57 *"still hills on hills, and Alps on Alps arise"*: Slightly misquoting line 235 of Alexander Pope, *An Essay on Criticism* (1711): 'Hills peep o'er Hills, and *Alps* on *Alps* arise!'

58 *vulgarly called notré Dame de Neige*: The early seventeenth-century chapel *Notre Dame des Neiges* ('Our Lady of the Snows') is described in *A Hand-Book for Travellers in Switzerland and the Alps of Savoy and Piedmont* (London: John Murray, 1841) as 'formerly visited by pilgrims, but of late abandoned on account of the risk and difficulty of the ascent' (p. 359).

59 *the Palace at Turin*: The historic palace of the House of Savoy built originally in the sixteenth century but transformed during the seventeenth into a baroque palace. It is now a museum and UNESCO World Heritage Site.

60 *a picture of our Charles the first . . . that unfortunate monarch's three children*: The portraits Fay viewed at the Royal Palace at Turin are likely *Charles I, King of England* (1627) by Daniel Mytens (c. 1590–1647/1648), featuring an elaborate architectural setting by Hendrick van Steenwyck (c. 1580–1649), and *The Three Eldest Children of Charles I* (1632) by Anthony van Dyck (1599–1641). Both now hang in Turin at the Musei Reali-Galleria Sabauda.

61 *callous libertine in Charles; nor the tyrant and bigot in James*: Fay here refers to Charles I's children Charles II (1630–1685) and James II (1633–1701), who reigned as kings of England from 1660 to 1685 and from 1685 to 1688, respectively. Known as the 'Merry Monarch', Charles II fathered at least 12 illegitimate children but provided no heir to the throne. The reign of his brother, James II, was characterized by early rebellions in 1685 by the Duke of Monmouth and the Earl of Argyll, both unsuccessful, and by controversies over his Roman Catholicism, which led him to attempt to repeal the Test Act in 1687. When Parliament and seven bishops of the Church of England protested, he attempted to rule by decree. In response, seven high-ranking nobles invited the Protestant William, Prince of Orange, to invade England from Holland and claim the throne, which he did successfully in November and December of 1688.

62 *Martin Luther, and his wife*: Fay likely refers to the portraits of Martin Luther (1483–1546) and of his wife Katharina von Bora (1499–1552) painted in 1529 by Lucas Cranach the Elder (1472–1553) and procured in 1894 by the Museo Poldi Pezzoli in Milan. See G. B. Vittadini, 'Novità Artistiche del Museo Poldi Pezzoli in Milano', in *Archivio Storico dell'Arte*, series II (1895), vol. 1, p. 216.

63 *Here is a terrible representation of . . . Sir Thomas More*: We have been unable to identify the painting seen by Fay of Thomas More (1478–1535), who was tried for treason and executed for refusing to take the Oath of Supremacy, by which one swore allegiance to the monarch as Supreme Governor of the Church of England. The daughter depicted in the painting is likely Margaret Roper (1505–1544), English writer and translator, and considered one of the most learned women of sixteenth-century England.

64 *the cave of Trophonious*: A cave of horrors. Trophonius is an Ancient Greek hero from the Boeotian city of Labadia; Fay's reference to him derives from Pausanias's *Description of Greece* Book 9, Chapter 39, which describes the process by which someone may consult the oracle of Trophonius: lodging in a house for several days;

engaging in purification rituals and sacrifices; drinking first the water of Forgetfulness and then of Memory; ascending the mountain and descending into the cave where he will learn the future. After the experience he is removed, usually paralysed with terror and unaware of his surroundings, and first questioned by priests and then taken home by relatives, where he eventually recovers from his horror.

65 *a faithful portrait of Petrarch's Laura*. Laura is the subject of the poems comprising Petrarch's *Rime Sparse* and, later, *Il Canzoniere*. While it is not certain to which portrait Fay refers, it is likely the one attributed to Simone Martini, a friend of Petrarch (1304–1374) who reportedly painted Laura shortly after Petrarch began writing poems to her. As Alexander Lee attests in 'The Look(s) of Love: Petrarch, Simone Martini and the Ambiguities of Fourteenth-Century Portraiture', *Journal of Art Historiography* 17 (2017), 'no trace of this work – if it existed – has survived', yet Petrarch's 'fulsome praise' of it has rendered it the subject of legend, and likely generated a number of wishful attributions (p. 1).

66 *Venus of Apelles*: Apelles of Kos (fourth century BC) was a renowned painter in ancient Greece; the famous mosaic of Alexander at the Battle of Issus is said to be based on a painting by him. His painting *Aphrodite Anadyomeme* ('Venus Rising from the Sea') is described by Pliny the Elder in *Natural History*, Book XXXV.

67 *"my mind's eye" than "I to Hercules"*: Quoting from Act 1, scene 2 of William Shakespeare's *Hamlet* (1601).

68 *the King of Sardinia*: Vittorio Amadeo II (1726–1796), who ruled Sardinia from 1773 to his death.

69 *The Theatre*: Opened in 1740, the sumptuous *Teatro Regio* (Royal Theatre) could seat 1,500 people and boasted five tiers of boxes and a gallery. As Fay's description of stages accommodating 50 to 60 horses at once attests, it would have been one of the largest theatres in Europe at this time.

70 *smaller theatre*: Likely the *Teatro Carignano*, which opened in Turin in 1757.

71 *the royal gardens*: The *Giardini Reali*, begun in the second half of the sixteenth century when Emanuele Filiberto chose Turin as the capital of Savoy. At the time Fay visited, the gardens would have been highly formal, consisting of square beds and fountains, the most famous of which remains the Fountain of the Tritons (1758).

72 *Banditti, and assassins, that every horrible story*: Here, Fay either anticipates or postdates – depending on whether the passage was composed in 1779 or added later – the conventions of popular gothic fiction, whose stories of robbers, bandits, tyrannical lords and priests, and supernatural haunting became wildly famous in Britain in the 1790s.

73 *the Palaces of Doria, Doraggio, and Pallavicini*: The first and third palaces to which Fay refers are the Palazzo Doria-Spinola and the Villa Durazzo-Pallvicini; the second is untraced, and 'Doraggio' nowhere among the many *palazzi* mentioned in the *Storia Generale e Ragionata della Repubblica di Genova*, 3 vols (Genoa: Giovanni Franchelli, 1795).

74 *the Cathedral*: The *Duomo di Genova*, dedicated to San Lorenzo, consecrated by Pope Gelasisus in 1118, and completed in the seventeenth century.

75 *Jesuits' church*: The *Chiesa del Gesú*, located in the *Piazza del Gesú* in Genoa. Possessing one of the first truly baroque façades, it became a model for churches thereafter. It is famous for its chapel frescoes and for housing masterpieces by Peter Paul Rubens (*The Circumcision* [1605] and *The Miracle of Saint Ignazio* [c. 1619]) and Giudo Reni (*The Assumption of the Virgin* [1617]).

76 *the Virgin by Guido*: *The Assumption of the Virgin* altarpiece (1617) by Guido Reni (1575–1642).

77 *Corpus Christi day*: The Feast of Corpus Christi, usually held in late spring on the Thursday after Trinity Sunday. Originally proposed by Thomas Aquinas (1225–1274) to

Pope Urban IV (1195–1264), it celebrates the real presence of Christ (body, blood, soul, and divinity) in the elements of the Eucharist. On that day at the end of mass, there is usually a procession and then a benediction of the Blessed Sacrament.
78 *the Doge*: The Doge of Genoa ('Commander of the Genoese and Defender of the People') was ruler of the communal Republic of Genoa from 1339 until the state's extinction in 1797. At the time of the Fays' visit the office was held by Giuseppe Lomellini (1723–1803) for the customary two-year period of office, in this case 1777–1779.
79 *a man after committing half a score murders . . . remains in safety*: Fay refers to Genoa's standing as a free port – that is, as a space possessing its own economic policies where merchants could trade with little or no interference from state authorities. Developed during the Renaissance in Italy, free ports attracted trade by creating a neutral space for the exchange of goods. For this reason, they thrived in places like Hamburg and Genoa, surrounded as they were by smaller duchies, city-states, principalities, and kingdoms. Here, Fay notes one of the negative aspects of such free-trade zones, their relative lawlessness, since suspected criminals needed merely to find refuge aboard a foreign ship not subject to Genoa's jurisdiction to escape prosecution.
80 *Cicisbeos*: Also called a *cavalier servente*, a *cicisbeo* is a married woman's recognized companion or lover, their relationship tolerated socially by her husband and their mutual acquaintance. In the same year that saw the publication of Fay's *Original Letters*, the term was made famous by Lord Byron in his comic poem *Beppo* (1817), which culminates with Beppo's return after many years and his befriending the Count, who has been *cavalier servente* to Beppo's wife Laura while he has been away.
81 *that expression of the Psalmist "the* Fool *hath said in his heart there is no God"*: Quoting Psalms 14:1.
82 *Mr. Baretto of London to his brother*: In his notes to the 1925 edition of Fay's *Original Letters*, E. M. Forster identifies these brothers as 'probably' Joseph and Luis Barretto, two sons in a large Indo-Portuguese family with networks across South East Asia. Born in Bombay in 1745, Luis Barretto de Sousa ('The Prince of Business'), began as a money lender, later founding the merchant firm L. Barretto & Company. In 1796, together with his younger brother Joseph, Luis donated funds to rebuild the Portuguese Church in Calcutta. In 1797 the brothers founded the first insurance company in Macau, the 'Casa de Sequros de Macao', insuring other merchants and cargo in the developing China trade. In 1800, the family purchased two merchant ships of their own to capture trade between London and the Cape of Good Hope, and between Macau and Asia, and then extended again into merchant banking. Entrepreneurial and highly successful, the family's businesses combined to produce what Roy Eric Xavier has described as 'one of the earliest examples of "vertical integration"' in the Far East trade, linking traded commodities, insured by the family's firm in Macau, 'with a tightly controlled distribution network that pre-dated modern corporations by almost two hundred years'. See R. E. Xavier, 'Luso-Asians and the Origins of Macau's Cultural Development', *Journal of the Royal Asiatic Society Hong Kong Branch* 57 (January 2017), pp. 187–205.
83 *in the mole*: A mole is a massive structure built usually of stone, in water, used as a breakwater, causeway, or pier. The word comes from the Latin *mōlēs* (meaning 'large mass') via the Middle French *mole*. The ships Fay mentions – tucked in behind the mole – are thus protected both from weather and attack by other vessels.
84 *so many French Privateers*: In this case, armed vessels held by private individuals but holding a government commission (known as a letter of marque) authorizing the capture of merchant ships belonging to an enemy nation. France would remain at war with Britain until 1783.
85 *she has already eaten her head off*: A colloquial phrase in use from the eighteenth through to twentieth centuries to describe someone or something which costs, in keep

or maintenance, more than it is worth. In this case, maintaining the ship and crew at anchor is costing the Captain and owners more than the value of the ship and its cargo.

86 *Bowsprit*: The bowsprit of a sailing vessel is a spar or length of timber extending forward from the vessel's prow (or front). It provides an anchor point for the forestays, which hold the mast aloft, allowing the foremast to be located further forward on the hull. The daughter of a shipwright, Fay clearly enjoys using technical sailing terms in her letters to her family, including 'pitching' or 'driving piles' (the up and down motion of the bow and stern hammering into the water), 'striking the lower yards' (dropping the horizontal spars that hold square-rigged sails aloft on the mast to the deck, in order to lower the centre of gravity of the boat in the storm), and so on.

87 *Mr. Brandy . . . Consul for one of the German Courts*: Mr. Brandi; his full name and dates of birth and death are not known. He is described by Rosemarie Said as 'an Italian tailor who lived in the former English factory in Alexandria, and who occasionally acted as an agent for the British'. He was employed strategically by Sir Robert Ainslie, the British Ambassador to the Ottoman Porte, as his personal agent in Egypt. See Said, 'George Baldwin and British Interests in Egypt 1775 to 1798', p. 46, note 2.

88 *Pompey's Pillar*: Constructed in 292 AD, this immense triumphal column located in the Kom el-Dekka area of Alexandria dates not to Pompey (killed 48 BC) but to the Roman emperor Diocletian (244–311 AD).

89 *the most famous of all the conquerors*: Alexander the Great (356–323 BC) founded Alexandria in 332 BC while conquering the Achaemenid Empire.

90 *dwarf walls*: Low walls, frequently used in gardening.

91 *the Palace of Cleopatra*: Fay is likely mistaken in this case, given archaeologists' recent underwater discovery of a Ptolemaic palace on Antirhodos, an island in the eastern harbour of Alexandria that sunk in the fourth century AD.

92 *Cleopatra's needles*: The name of the three ancient Egyptian obelisks re-erected in the nineteenth century in London, Paris, and New York. The one currently standing on the Victoria Embankment in London was presented to Britain by Muhammad Ali, the ruler of Egypt and Sudan, in 1819, and finally transported from Alexandria to London and erected in 1878. Both obelisks observed by Fay were made during the reign of Eighteenth Dynasty Pharaoh Thutmose III (1479–1425 BC); its partner went to New York. Paris's originates from a different site in Luxor, where its twin remains.

93 *bedizened*: Overdressed, particularly in a gaudy or vulgar fashion.

94 *stranger in a strange land*: Quoting Exodus 2:22.

95 *The Bar of the Nile*: Located just off the coast of Rosetta, the bar of the Nile was a bank of sand blocking the mouth of the Nile except at high tide. See *Travels of Ali Bey in Morocco, Tripoli, Cyprus, Egypt, Arabia, Syria, and Turkey, between the Years 1803 and 1807*, 2 vols (London: Longman, Hurst, Rees, Orme, and Brown, 1816):

> The bar of the Nile is nearly four miles in the sea. The billows are generally very strong; for it is a bank of sand, against which the waters of the sea and the Nile beat with prodigious force. Ships find very little water; and the straits which are passable shift continually, so that there is a boat stationed upon the bar to indicate the passage.
>
> (vol. 2, p. 2)

96 *the country where, the children of Israel sojourned . . . story of Joseph and his brethren*: Fay here refers to the Land of Goshen, given to the Hebrews by the pharaoh of Joseph in Genesis 45:10: 'And thou shalt dwell in the land of Goshen, and thou shalt be near unto me, thou, and thy children, and thy children's children, and thy flocks, and thy herds, and all that thou hast'. The story of Joseph is told in Genesis 37–50.

97 *"like a tale that is told"*: Quoting Psalms 90:9 ('we spend our years as a tale *that is told*').

98 *It has been supposed by many that the Israelites built these Pyramids*: The Giza Pyramid complex was constructed during the twenty-sixth century BC; historians generally place the time of the Israelite slaves depicted in Exodus roughly a thousand years later.
99 *sarcophagus*: A stone coffin, usually decorated with figures and inscriptions.
100 *a little flat . . . astrological observations*: While there appears to be no corroborating evidence for her conjecture, Fay is correct that astronomy figured prominently in Egyptian culture. The pyramids were aligned with the polar star, and by the third century BC Egyptians were using a calendar of 365 days and observing the stars in order to predict when the Nile would flood.
101 *the sphinx*: The Great Sphinx of Giza, a limestone statue of a reclining sphinx, a mythical creature with the body of a lion and the head of a human, measuring 240 feet long and 66 feet high, believed to have been built by ancient Egyptians of the Old Kingdom during the reign of the Pharaoh Khafre (c. 2558–2532 BC).
102 *Mr. Baldwin*: George Baldwin (1744–1826), a trader and diplomat interested in the potential for connecting trade between India and Europe through Egypt. He is a key – though shadowy – figure in the events Fay describes. After many years' residence and trading in the Eastern Mediterranean himself, Baldwin offered his services in 1774 as agent to the EIC handling the transportation of cargo via Suez and the Red Sea. The only English merchant in Egypt and a fluent Arabic speaker, Baldwin's trade began competing with both the EIC and the Ottoman Porte. In 1774 the Porte had issued a *firman* prohibiting English boats landing at Suez, but trade was also being supported and encouraged by the Egyptian beys in defiance of their Ottoman governors. In 1775, a written agreement negotiated by Warren Hastings and John Shaw with Abu'l Dhahab Bey guaranteed free and reciprocal movement of ships, communication, and commerce between Great Britain and Egypt. Both the EIC and the Levant Company immediately protested this agreement as a threat to their own trade privileges. In May 1779, during this period of heightened tension, a European caravan from Suez to Cairo was attacked, resulting in the imprisonment of some merchants and the death of others. This is the event to which Fay refers, but about which she cannot speak openly in letters from Alexandria or Cairo. Baldwin became a hostage to secure the release of the imprisoned merchants. Escaping to Izmir in late 1779, he married Jane Maltass, the daughter of his agent, and travelled first to India and then Europe in the hope of restoring his fortunes. Always a powerful advocate of the strategic place of North East Africa in commerce, he was appointed to Egypt as consul-general in 1785 to balance the growth of French trade in the region, a post he held until 1796. At the period Fay encounters Baldwin, he was acting (like Mr. Brandi at Alexandria) as unofficial consul for British travellers through Egypt and was respected for his singular political and commercial knowledge of the region. A key resource for Baldwin and events in Egypt at the period of the Fays' visit is the research of Rosemarie Said Zahan in 'George Baldwin and British Interests in Egypt 1775 to 1798' and 'George Baldwin: Soldier of Fortune?', in P. Starkey and J. Starkey (eds), *Travellers in Egypt* (London: I. B. Tauris, 2001), pp. 24–40.
103 *my dress . . . for the House; but as I was going out*: The Egyptian clothing Fay describes here is the ensemble she is depicted wearing in the portrait that appeared as frontispiece to the *Original Letters*. Fay's written portrait of herself in 'oriental' dress almost certainly responds to Lady Mary Wortley Montagu's very famous account of her own 'Turkish habit' in the 1763 publication of her travel letters, although images of Montagu in this costume had also circulated widely in the 50 years before the published account, becoming a motif of women's travel in the eighteenth and nineteenth centuries. The detailed description of silk robes, coloured muslins, and silver ornaments is also characteristic of women's interest in fabric and fashion at this period. Fay, who is writing to her sisters and would become a milliner during one part of her career, describes textiles and trims throughout her letters, always with an eye to their

detail and commercial value. Unlike Montagu, who found Turkish dress comfortable and liberating (it allowed her to move inconspicuously in public spaces at Constantinople), Fay finds the clothing conventions hot and oppressive. From India, however, she reports more favourably that 'the Eastern dresses have infinitely the advantage over ours; they are much more easy and graceful' (see letter of 19 February 1780).

104 *a severe epidemical disease, with violent symptoms . . . which carries all off*: Fay's description of the symptoms and progress of the illness resembles yellow fever, suggesting this may have been one of a number of related mosquito-borne viral diseases of typically short duration, in which about fifteen percent of patients suffer a severe or mortal form.

105 *"la queue de la Peste"*: Literally 'the tail of the plague', a phrase also used in the *Memoires de Lord Clarendon . . . sous le regne de Charles II* (Paris: Béchet Aine, 1824) to describe an earlier epidemic at Oxford.

106 *the Beys*: Within the Ottoman Empire, 'Bey' or 'Beg' was the title given to a regional ruler, chieftain, or governor of a province. Fay here is referring to the elite Egyptian individuals or Mamluk households who effectively ruled Egypt as a semi-autonomous Ottoman province until the French invasion of 1798 under Napoleon.

107 *The Christians (who are called Franks)*: Originally the Germanic peoples of the Lower and Middle Rhine, the term 'Frank' was used to describe Romanized German dynasties within the fragmenting Roman Empire, becoming, by the Middle Ages, a synonym for Western Europeans of the Carolingian Empire and those associated with the Roman Catholic Church during the Crusades. 'Franks' was used by many Muslim and Eastern Orthodox communities in the eastern Mediterranean and North Africa – including the Mongol and Ottoman Empires – as a descriptor for Western and Central Europeans. Latin Christians living in the Middle East are still known as 'Franco-Levantines'.

108 *hautboys*: A wooden double-reed wind instrument of high pitch, having a compass of about two and a half octaves, forming a treble to the bassoon; it is now called by the similar-sounding name of 'oboe'.

109 *this famous Canal*: Fay refers here to the cutting of the Khalig Canal, a ceremony dating back to ancient Egypt in which the bar or dam between the river and the canal in Cairo is broken at a large festival, usually in August, once the Nile attains the height of sixteen cubits. Murray's famous nineteenth-century handbook for travellers describes a festival which – although recently diminished in Wilkinson's account – is much more grand and pleasant than Fay's:

> The opening of the canal at Old Cairo is . . . a ceremony of great importance, and looked upon with feelings of great rejoicing, as the harbinger of the blessings annually bestowed on the country by the Nile. . . . The ceremony is performed in the morning by the Governor or by the Pasha's deputy. The whole night before this, the booths on the shore, and the boats on the river, are crowded with people; who enjoy themselves by witnessing or joining the numerous festive groups, while fireworks and various amusements enliven the scene. . . . About eight o'clock A.M the Governor, accompanied by troops and his attendants arrives; and on giving a signal, several peasants cut the dam with hoes, and the water rushes into the bed of the canal. In the middle of the dam is a pillar of earth, called Arooset e' Neel, 'the bride of the Nile' which a tradition pretends to have been substituted by the humanity of Amer for the virgin previously sacrificed every year by the *Christians* to the *river god!*
> (G. Wilkinson, *Hand-Book for Travellers in Egypt*
> (London: John Murray, 1847), p. 148)

110 *St. Giles's*: Referring to the parish in central London bound by Tottenham Court Road to the east, Francis Street (now Torrington Place) to the north, Newman Street to the west, and Stephen Street to the south. Immortalized in William Hogarth's *Gin Lane*

(1751) and the *First Stage of Cruelty* (1751), St. Giles was one of London's worst slums throughout the eighteenth and nineteenth centuries.

111 *the only interesting subject*: Fay declines to write of the recent attack on the caravan travelling between Suez and Cairo because she suspects that her letter will be read by censors, and so waits until Letter IX (dated 13 September 1779) to provide a full account of the attack on the English and French traders.

112 *a most dreadful Desert*: Fay refers to the 80-mile stretch of the Egyptian desert extending east from Cairo to Suez; the reason for it being so 'dreadful' to her becomes clear in her subsequent letters.

113 *under the orders of Major Baillie*: Possibly Major Ewen Baillie of the EIC.

114 *Nathalia*: Flying under Danish colours, the *Nathalia* was under the command of the Dutch or German Captain Vanderfeld (or Van der Velden) and second mate Chenu (unidentified). She carried English merchants O'Donnell and Barrington, and French brothers Pierre Mathieu Renault de St Germain and Renault de Chilly, who were transporting lucrative cargo and personal fortunes from India. After arriving and unloading at Suez, the caravan of 12 Europeans with local guides and camel drivers set off for Cairo. They were attacked almost immediately, robbed, and left in the desert without water, food, clothes, or camels. O'Donnell and Chenu elected to return to Suez and survived; seven of the eight pushing forward to Cairo perished, with only Renault de St Germain arriving alive. Fay met him at a moment of further crisis in Baldwin's parlour in Cairo when a second Danish ship under the command of Captain Moore, another Englishman, was seized at Suez (see Letter IX, dated 13 September 1779). John O'Donnell's letter of complaint to the Supreme Council of Calcutta about the incident survives in the EIC records (*Consultations of the Government*, 12 June 1780), and is quoted at length by Forster in his terminal notes; see E. Fay, *Original Letters*, ed. E. M. Forster (London: Hogarth Press, 1925), pp. 274–5, note 13. Rosemarie Said Zahan's account of the attack on the *Nathalia* caravan from the perspective of George Baldwin supplements Fay's description and outlines the disintegrating relationships between various players in the Red Sea trade, including local beys, the East India and Levant Companies, the British government, the French, and the Ottoman Porte. See Zahan, 'George Baldwin: Soldier of Fortune?'.

115 *Serampore, a Danish settlement on the Hooghly*: Serampore (also called Serampur, Srirampur, Srirampore) is a city on the Hooghly river in West Bengal, north and slightly west of Calcutta (Kolkata). A precolonial settlement of several villages, it became a Danish trading post in 1755 before governance was transferred from the Danish Asiatic Company to the Crown in 1777. It was known as Frederiknagore between 1755 and 1845. Serampore was a very international settlement and became the centre of Baptist missionary activity in West Bengal, as, unlike the British EIC in Calcutta, it accepted missionaries. It is a telling point of connection between the experiences and narratives of Fay and Newell. After arriving in Calcutta, the Newells quickly relocated to Serampore in June 1812, accepting the invitation of the English Baptist missionary William Carey to stay at his home. The *Nathalia*'s putative 'Danish' identity – she issues from Serampore, sails under a Danish flag and is captained by Vanderfeld, who 'passed for owner of the ship and cargo' – allows the English merchants O'Donnell and Barrington to evade the British East India embargo on Red Sea trade.

116 *panniers*: Large baskets for carrying foodstuffs or other commodities carried by a beast of burden (usually one of a pair placed one on either side of its back).

117 *Egypt, then, is governed by twenty four Beys*: The Eyalet of Egypt describes the period of Ottoman rule of Mamluk Egypt from 1517 until 1867. After a period of revolt under Ali Bey, Egypt had been brought back under nominal Ottoman governance in 1773, but power was effectively in the hands of ruling beys Abu'l Dhahab Bey, Ibrahim Bey, and Murad Bey, with the authority of the Pasha mostly insignificant. As

Rosemarie Said suggests, the 'history of the government of Egypt during the last half of the eighteenth century is a complicated and anarchic mixture of factional opposition, last-minute desertions and sporadic *coups d'etat*'. See Said, 'George Baldwin and British Interests in Egypt 1775 to 1798', p. 12.

118 *Bashaw*: An earlier form of the Turkish title *Pasha*, denoting the provincial governor.

119 *Firman ... on behalf of the E. I. Company*: Any edict, official grant, licence, passport, or permit issued by a Sultan. Here, Fay reveals that general opinion at Cairo was that the British Consul to the Sublime Porte, Sir Robert Ainslie, had procured the *firman* in favour of the EIC in order to quash trade by non-Company merchants and travellers (like the Fays, Baldwin, O'Donnell, and Barrington) through Egypt. The Fays are only permitted to leave their detention (with a local Italian family) when the local beys are bribed with three thousand pounds (see the close of Letter IX, dated 13 September 1779).

120 *the* Bowstring: Execution by strangulation with the string of a hunting bow, or any length of tightly twisted string – commonly made of hemp, linen, or rawhide.

121 *We found Suez a miserable place ... carried off*: Arriving at Suez on the last day of August, the Fays proceed to the *Nathalia*, which had been impounded by the local authorities since its arrival and only very recently released to the new Captain Chenu.

122 *Mount Horeb*: The mountain at which Moses was given the Ten Commandments by God, recorded in Deuteronomy 5:6–21. Other sources give Mount Sinai, and Biblical scholars are divided over whether these are two names for the same place or different locations.

123 *vessels ... built for the conveyance of coffee*: A related group of shallow-draught coasting vessels moved coffee and other cargo (including slaves) around the Red Sea, and included the local *dhows*, two-masted *baghla* from India, and the smaller *sambuk* from the Gulf and Oman. See R. Barnes and D. Parkin (eds), *Ships and the Development of Maritime Technology on the Indian Ocean* (New York: Routledge, 2015), and D. A. Agius, *Seafaring in the Arabian Gulf and Oman: People of the Dhow* (New York: Routledge, 2005).

124 *Banian*: Or Banyan, 'A Hindu trader ... of the province of Guzerat, many of which class have for ages been settled in Arabian ports and known by this name ... The word was adopted from *Vaniya*, a man of the trading caste (*Hobson-Jobson*, p. 48).

125 *Rajaput*: 'The name of a great race in India, the hereditary profession of which is that of arms' (*Hobson-Jobson*, p. 571). Deriving from the Sanskrit *raja-putra*, or 'son of a king', the term *rajaput* describes a social identification of the Indian sub-continent, based on caste, kin and hereditary profession (a warrior class).

126 *Chevalier de St. Lubin*: The 'celebrated FRENCH ADVENTURER' and '*Chevalier d'Industrie'* (as the *European Magazine* described him), Joseph Alexis Pallebot de Saint Lubin (b. 1738) had been sent to India by the French naval minister Antoine Raymond Jean Gualbert Gabriele de Sartine on a diplomatic mission to Maratha states. His mission was to establish an alliance with the Marathas against the British in order to support the French recovery of territory and power lost during the Seven Years' War. Sartine hoped to use Britain's preoccupation with the American War to contest its power in India and restore some of the lucrative trade and status lost in the preceding decades. Saint Lubin was an unorthodox choice for a diplomatic mission. Not unlike the Fays, he was one of the scores of European adventurers drawn to India in the mid to late eighteenth century. Arriving initially as a surgeon's mate, he had reputedly entered the service of Hyder Ali as a general before defecting to the British (Hyder Ali's opponent) during the First Mysore War (1766–1769). The Fays seem to have encountered Saint Lubin in Mocha on his return journey from the appointment as Louis XVI's envoy to the Maratha leadership in Poona (his object there had been to provide 2,400 French artillery troops to the Maratha state under the pretext of a

commercial treaty). Arriving in splendour at Poona in March 1777, Saint Lubin's indiscreet negotiations aroused the active suspicions of both the British in Bengal and Hyder Ali, precipitating even greater instability in the region. Ordered home by the Maratha court to present the negotiated commercial treaty, he arrived at Paris in October of 1780. At this stage of their voyage, Fay is more concerned about the passage of her own letters home than the political gossip, and entrusts her epistles to the Chevalier's '*honour*'. Hand delivery of letters and documents was a highly-sought opportunity in the precarious circumstances of international post at this period. See 'Memoirs of a Celebrated French Adventurer', *The European Magazine* 18 (August 1790), pp. 122–5; and K. Margerison, 'Rogue Diplomacy: Sartine, Saint-Lubin and the French Attempt to Recover "Lost India" 1776–80', *French History* 30 (2016), pp. 477–504.

127 *the Monsoon being against us*: Shipping by sail across both the Red Sea and India Ocean is heavily dependent on prevailing winds, and the timing of the key route between Calicut and the Red Sea was well established by the Middle Ages: ships left Calicut for Mocha in January and arrived in the reverse direction at Calicut between August and November. The west coast of India was virtually unnavigable between June and September. The Fays are travelling very late in the season and, by all accounts, are lucky to have such an uneventful passage. See M. Pearson, *The Indian Ocean* (London: Routledge, 2003).

128 *The woman . . . is . . . one of the lowest creatures taken off the streets in London*: That is, Fay suggests, a prostitute. Forster notes in his edition that her husband was probably William Tulloh, a well-known auctioneer (Tulloh & Co., Tank Square, Calcutta) whose portrait John Zoffany used to depict Judas Iscariot in his large painting of 'The Last Supper' for the new St John's Church at Calcutta. If so, Fay's 'Mrs. Tulloh' is his first wife Jean Duncan, by whom he had six children, and whose death is recorded by *The Bengal Obituary* as occurring at Calcutta on 27 May 1799, the deceased 'aged 53 years and 6 months'. She and her husband were both born in Forres, Morayshire. Ironically, Tulloh & Co. were responsible for the sale of Eliza Fay's effects after her death. For further details of Tulloh's appearance in the Zoffany painting, see K. Blechynden, *Calcutta Past and Present* (London: Thacker & Co, 1905), pp. 139–41.

129 *Miss Howe's description of Solmes, in Clarissa Harlowe*: Referring to Letter XXVII of Samuel Richardson's *History of Miss Clarissa Harlowe* (1748), in which Miss Howe describes the countenance of Mr. Solmes as the product of 'three years . . . of continual crying; and his muscles have never been able to recover a risible tone'.

130 *Chenu . . . "Jack in office"*: Although 'Jack in office' usually denotes a self-important minor official, Fay here uses the term to denote someone of minor rank promoted to a position beyond their desserts or ken. The Frenchman Chenu, second mate under Captain Van der Velden, had found himself made Captain of the *Nathalia* for her return voyage to India after the debacle at Suez. In his letter to Eliza's parents informing them of their safe arrival at Suez, Anthony Fay had described Chenu as 'a very polite good-natured man, which is a great matter in a long voyage', but his wife denounces him as 'insolent and overbearing'.

131 *John Hare, Esqr., Barrister at Law*: John Hare was admitted as a barrister to the Court of Calcutta on 28 March 1780, rather before Anthony Fay (who had come to India without the permission of the Company and was admitted 3 July 1780). Anthony Fay would in fact go on to work with Hare, defending James Augustus Hicky, the editor of the *Bengal Gazette*, 'in a prosecution for libel instituted by Hastings' (*Bengal Past and Present* 30 [1925], 168). Transporting diamonds on his return journey to England, Hare was murdered in 1784. He made bequests in his will to Warren Hastings and Sir Elijah Impey: the latter survives in the form of a silver soup tureen and cover, made by James Young of London in 1784 or 1785, now owned by the Sterling and Francine

Clark Art Institute in Williamstown, Massachusetts. Hare's account of the group's imprisonment, written as a petition to Sardar Khan, is preserved in the EIC archives and is reproduced in *Bengal Past and Present* 12 (1916), p. 257.

132 *Quadrille*: 'A trick-taking card game for four players using a pack of forty cards, without the eights, nines, and tens of the ordinary pack' (*OED*).

133 *scorbutic blotches*: The skin lesions and unhealed wounds commonly seen on sufferers of scurvy. Noticed from the classical period, the disease of scurvy – caused by a deficiency of vitamin C – profoundly affected seamen and was a limiting factor in the length of sea journeys. During the sixteenth to nineteenth centuries, it is estimated that up to fifty percent of sailors died from scurvy.

134 *"he could not ope ... flew a trope"*: Quoting Samuel Butler, *Hudibras* (1663–1678), Canto 1, Part 1, ll. 81–2.

135 *Mr. Manesty*: The son of a Liverpool merchant and slaver, Samuel Manesty (1758–1812) first voyaged to India at the age of nineteen as an EIC writer at Bombay. He would go on to be appointed EIC Resident at Basra in 1784, marrying the daughter of a local Armenian family, Maria Anne Saurius, and building a lucrative personal trade in the Persian Gulf. He was then involved in a notorious diplomatic incident in 1804 in which he presented himself – without authorization – to the Qajar Court in Shiraz and Sultaniyyah as British Envoy. Despite censure for his presumption, Manesty was able to return to his position as Resident at Basra before being dismissed in 1810. He returned to England via Constantinople, reaching London in May 1812. Bankrupt and in disgrace, he died there a month later at the house of his friend, former Bombay merchant and banker Charles Forbes, probably by suicide. See R. P. Walsh, 'Manesty, Samuel (1758–1812)', *Oxford Dictionary of National Biography* (2010); and D. Wright, 'Samuel Manesty and his Unauthorised Embassy to the Court of Fath Ali Shah', *Iran: Journal of the British Institute of Persian Studies* 24 (1986), pp. 323–36.

136 *fallen into the hands of sharpers*: A sharper is a swindler, cheat, or professional gambler, especially at cards.

137 *between the Captain and H— the Barrister*: John Hare; apparently, Chenu and Hare were narrowly prevented from duelling to decide their quarrel.

138 *purser*: 'An officer on board a ship responsible for provisions and for keeping accounts, or (in later use more generally) for various other administrative matters; (now) esp. the head steward on a passenger vessel' (*OED*).

139 *"catch as catch can"*: A popular expression meaning to take what one can, or to seize a given opportunity for personal gain.

140 *Calicut, 12th February, 1780*: Kozhikode, or the anglicized Calicut, is a city in modern Kerala on the west coast of India known from classical antiquity through the Middle Ages as the 'City of Spices' for its central role in the Middle East and Europe trade. Famous also for its woven cotton cloth, Calicut gives its name to the fabric 'calico'. A Portuguese Factory was established there for a short period in the sixteenth century (1511–1525), with the English and French following in the seventeenth century. The Danish East India Company joined them in 1752. The capital of the Malabar District under English rule, Calicut was captured by Mysore under Hyder Ali in 1765. At the time of the Fays' arrival, Calicut was governed by Sardar Khan, brother-in-law and noted military aide of Hyder Ali, Sultan of Mysore. Fay provides her own description of the town in her journal entry for 10 December 1779.

141 *state of dreadful Captivity*: Writing some ten weeks after her last letter, Fay describes her imprisonment (along with Anthony Fay, Mr. and Mrs. Tulloh, John Hare and his servant Lewis, Mr. Fuller, Mr. Manesty, Mr. Taylor, and one other) at the English Factory and Fort at Calicut from 5 November 1779 to mid-February of 1780.

142 *suspended over my head as by a single hair*: Referring to the story of Damocles, who flattered his king Dionysius by calling him fortunate to hold power and to be

surrounded by magnificence. On accepting Dionysius's offer to exchange places with him for one day, Damocles found himself seated under a great sword suspended over his head by a single hair. Dionysius sought to impress on Damocles that with great fortune comes great danger.

143 *anchored in the Roads . . . no English flag up*: From the Roads outside the English Factory – usually an area of safe anchorage used by ships waiting to be admitted, or for the transhipment of some cargoes – the passengers of the *Nathalia* notice that there is no English flag flying and are quickly surrounded by vessels. As the Fays will learn, the English Consul Mr. Freeman had already fled in the face of deepening hostilities with Hyder Ali and his deputy at Calicut, Sardar Khan (what Fay calls in Letter XII, dated 12 February 1780, 'a misunderstanding' between Hyder Ali and the English).

144 *Mr. Passavant, the Danish Consul:* The Danish East India Company was founded in 1616 and had held a trading post or 'Factory' at Calicut from 1752. The Factor and Resident at this juncture is Leonhard Passavant, and he offers the English passengers of the nominally Danish ship (the *Nathalia*) protection onshore if they are prepared to pass as Danes. The other passengers (including the Tullohs) take up this offer, while the Fays choose to remain on board.

145 chit: A short official note, frequently recording a small sum owed, but here containing written orders.

146 *Seapoys*: 'A native soldier, disciplined and dressed in the European style' (*Hobson-Jobson*, p. 612).

147 *the English are coming to attack Calicut*: When word reached India late in 1778 that France had entered the war against the British on the part of the American colonists, the British responded quickly by taking French colonial outposts at Pondicherry and the port of Mahé (also known as Mahey and Mayyazhi) on the Malabar coast. Allying with Hyder Ali, whose brother-in-law Sardar Khan currently held power in Calicut, the French retook Mahé in 1780. It was thus in a situation of conflict on multiple fronts – and characterized by delayed communications between the various theatres of war – that the French Captain Chenu apparently offered the ship *Nathalia* to Sardar Khan to protect Calicut in the event of an attack by the British elsewhere in Malabar.

148 *a second Suez business*: Referring to the attack on the *Nathalia* caravan and the confiscation of the *Nathalia* and *St Helena* at Suez (see Letter VII, dated 27 August 1779).

149 *Captain Ayres:* Although only Fay's account of Ayres – a highwayman who ended up in the service of Hyder Ali – appears to survive, he is just one of many men (and some women) who were taken hostage or defected to indigenous communities in North Africa and India. Fay describes a second man, Captain West, 'of a pretty similar description', in Sardar Khan's service in Letter XII, dated 12 February 1780. See L. Colley, 'Going Native, Telling Tales: Captivity, Collaborations and Empire', *Past & Present* 168 (2000), pp. 170–93.

150 *a Gentleman Collector on the* Highway: A highwayman patterned on the notorious James Maclaine, known as the 'Gentleman Highwayman' because of the courtesy with which he treated the people he robbed. Maclaine was hanged at Tyburn in London in 1750.

151 *his General, who is Governor of this Province*: Sardar Khan.

152 Nabob's *name*: 'Nabob' is derived from the Erdu word *nawab*, which denoted historically a Mughal imperial viceroy. By the late eighteenth century, it and 'nabob' took on a broader use, frequently describing a British person who had acquired a large fortune in India. Samuel Foote's popular comedy *The Nabob* (1772) did much to popularize the term. Here, however, Fay refers specifically to Hyder Ali as the supreme ruler, with whom the British Crown and EIC had most recently negotiated commercial arrangements in Malabar.

153 *scymitears*: A scimitar is a sabre or backsword with a curved blade.
154 Blue lights: 'Bengal' or 'blue lights' were weapons made with sulphur, used to expose enemies at night. As Fay suggests and as other contemporary accounts of Mysore tactics show, they could also be used to distract and confuse the enemy under attack. Hyder Ali and his son Tipu Sultan were renowned for their use of 'mysore' rocket technology in battle.
155 *Hooka*: 'Hindi from Arabic *hukkah*, properly "a round casket". The Indian pipe for smoking through water, the elaborated *hubble-bubble*. That which is smoked in the *hooka* is a curious compound of tobacco, spices, molasses, fruit, &c' (*Hobson-Jobson*, p. 322).
156 *hobby-horse*: A favourite pursuit or pastime, made famous in this sense as an absurd or foolish project by Laurence Sterne in *The Life and Opinions of Tristram Shandy, Gentleman* (1759–1767).
157 *made Mr. Passavant a visit, to look at the strangers*: Hare, the Tullohs, and others are evidently staying at the Danish Resident's while the Fays have been imprisoned at the abandoned English Factory. When Captains Ayers and West go to investigate the newcomers at the Danish Factory, the group take the precaution of speaking in French so as not to be recognized as British, until Hare foolishly reveals the *Nathalia* to be English property (and thus an enemy vessel).
158 *"Suiting the action to the words"*: Paraphrasing Hamlet's advice to the players ('suit the action to the word, the / word to the action') in *Hamlet*, Act 3, scene 2, ll. 18–19.
159 *Sudder Khan*: Sardar Ali Khan (sometimes transcribed as Sudder ul Hoe Khan or Sudder ul Hoc Khan), Governor of Calicut. A key figure in the army of Hyder Ali and Mysore's occupation of Malabar from 1774, Sardar Khan had been appointed by the Nabob Mobarick ul Dowla to fill the station of *Naib* of his *Adawlet* (Court of Civil Justice) and *Phouzdarry* (Court of Criminal Justice). He was effectively the Governor or Commander-in-Chief of the region, although Malabar remained in a constant state of rebellion. The way in which this appointment played into the highly complex politics of the entire subcontinent is revealed in the records of the impeachment trial of Warren Hastings. Edmund Burke argued that Sardar Khan's appointment had been made specifically at the request of Hastings from Bengal in order to replace the Company's preferred candidate for *Naib Subah*, Mahomed Rez Cawn, and constituted evidence of his misgovernance and of his collusion with opponents of the Company and Crown. See Sir F. Philip, *A State of the British Authority in Bengal under the Government of Mr. Hastings. Exemplified in His Conduct in the Case of Mahomed Reza Khan: With a Debate Upon a Letter from Mobareck Ul Dowlah, Nabob of Bengal: From Authentic Documents* (London: Printed by H. S. Woodfall, 1780).
160 Beelzebub: In popular use, a name for the Devil or one of the princes of hell. In 2 Kings 1:2–16, 'Beelzebub' is the name of a deity worshipped by the Philistines; in John Milton's *Paradise Lost* (1667), he is part of an unholy trinity with Lucifer and Astaroth and is second only to Satan.
161 *feed them on dry rice*: A form of torture in which prisoners are starved, and then fed dry rice with large amounts of water. The swelling rice in the stomach and intestines causes excruciating pain.
162 *You will wonder how I came by all this information*: Fay reveals later that she had learned these details of their incarceration and Hare's behaviour from Captain West (see Letter XVII, dated 27 September 1780).
163 *chequins*: Or Ottoman *sequin*, a small gold coin modelled on the Venetian sequin, originally struck at Cairo. Used in the Mocha trade (from whence the Fays clearly had acquired theirs), it was generally known as the 'Mocha ducat'.
164 *the Nabob's prisoners*: Here, Sardar Ali imprisons the remaining passengers in the name of Hyder Ali as supreme leader or *Nawab*.

165 *Moors*: In this Anglo-Indian context, 'Moors' refers to the Urdu language (*OED*).
166 *gewgaws*: 'A gaudy trifle, plaything, or ornament, a pretty thing of little value, a toy or bauble' (*OED*).
167 *VENETIAN FIDDLE STRINGS!!!*: A highly regarded double twisted string made of gut in the Venetian tradition.
168 *Isaac, the Jewish merchant*: Isaac Surgun (d. 1792), a wealthy merchant originally from Constantinople and influential in trade at Calicut, Cochin, and Tranvancore. Surgun appears in the historical record from the 1760s in connection with local leaders and the VOC; he clearly spoke multiple languages, including Urdu and perhaps Persian, but not English. His conversation with Fay takes place through an interpreter.
169 *catty*: Caddy.
170 *like the Pharisees in Scripture*: The parable of the Pharisees and the tax collector at the temple (Luke 18:9–14) teaches that 'every one that exalteth himself shall be abased; and he that humbleth himself shall be exalted' (18:14).
171 *Nayhirs*: Also *Nairs*, a Hindu community of Malabar ruled by matriarchs that (to some extent) practiced polyandry. In 1779 when British forces took Mahé from the French, the Nayhirs rebelled (with support from the British) against Hyder Ali's rule, but were suppressed. In 1780 the French retook Mahé with the help of Hyder Ali. E. M. Forster's note to his edition of Fay's *Original Letters* adds, 'Mrs. Fay is wrong in supposing they were attacking the English. On the contrary the English had instigated them to rebel against Haider Ali, and their operations near Tellicherry were probably to this end. The rebellion was soon crushed' (p. 278, note 30).
172 *Tellicherry*: Modern Thalassery, a commercial city on the Malabar coast and an important hub of the millenia-old Arabian and European spice trade. The British had established a trading post and Factory there in 1694; it was a strategic port for them in the south west of India, and the location of a British garrison.
173 *Mahey*: Mahé.
174 *Angria the Pirate*: Also known as Canajee Angria or Sarkhei Angré, Kanhoji Angri (1669–1729) led the Maratha Navy against the British, Dutch, and Portuguese navies in the first decades of the eighteenth century. Though dubbed a 'pirate' by European forces, he remained undefeated until his death, often employing Dutch and Jamaican captains to command his best vessels.
175 *"remnant of all things"*: Untraced, but perhaps referring ironically to Zechariah 8:12 ('I will cause the remnant of this people to possess all these things').
176 *spinnet*: 'A keyed musical instrument, common in England in the eighteenth century, closely resembling the harpsichord, but smaller and having only one string to each note' (*OED*).
177 *gambols*: 'Originally: A leap or caper; more generally: a playful or high-spirited movement or gesture; a bout of energetic playful activity, as running or jumping about; a frolic, a romp (frequently in plural)' (*OED*).
178 *bolts*: Rolls of woven fabric of a specific length.
179 *"ancient solitary reign we had molested"*: Misquoting line 12 of Thomas Gray's *Elegy Written in a Country Churchyard* (1751): 'Molest her ancient solitary reign'.
180 *The Governor marched at the head of his troops toward Tellicherry*: The captives are witnessing preparations of the allies of Hyder Ali to attack the British garrison at Tellicherry, which they did from 30 December 1779 to 18 January 1782. The attempt by Mysore to secure influence and territory in Malabar failed, and Sardar Khan would ultimately die in the attempt. The Treaty of Saleby (1782) ceded territory back to the British.
181 *Zamorin*: 'The title for many centuries of the Hindu Sovereign of Calicut and the country round' (*Hobson-Jobson*, p. 745).
182 *King of Prussia... the great Frederick*: Frederick II (1712–1786) ruled the Kingdom of Prussia from 1740 until his death. His reign was distinguished for his early patronage

of learning and the arts, his repeated tactical genius in battle, his encouragement of freedom of the press, and his commitment to modernizing the Prussian government's bureaucracy and judicial system.

183 *stagnant water . . . fatal to Europeans*: Hare refers to the tendency of stagnant water to breed mosquitoes, and thus to spread diseases like malaria, typhoid, and yellow fever.

184 *Seringapatnam*: Srirangapatna, a town in the state of Karnataka near Mysore, was the de facto capital of Mysore under Hyder Ali and his son Tipu Sultan; Hyder Ali was resident there at this point in Fay's narrative.

185 *Mr. Taylor*: Taylor, of the *Nathalia* group incarcerated at Calicut, had been caring for Fay's wound, which she describes receiving while imprisoned at the Factory in Letter XII, dated 12 February 1780.

186 *The Doolies*: From the Hindi *doli*, a 'rudimentary litter or palanquin used by the lower classes in India, and as an army ambulance' (*OED*).

187 *Levée*: Here, with irony, a party or celebration.

188 *Mr. Church, Governor of Tellicherry*: Richard Church, Resident and English Factor at Tellicherry.

189 *chined*: Cut in half along the backbone. The slaughter of the cow marks not only Ayres' caprice and cruelty but underscores his loyalty to the Muslim conqueror of the region, Hyder Ali. Cows are held sacred in many religions, including Hinduism, and Ayres' act is thus deliberately provocative in southern India.

190 *nankeen*: A sturdy woven yellow-coloured cotton cloth traditionally produced at Nanjing, for which it is named. Sailors often had trousers and jackets made of the fabric.

191 *waiting for a lucky day*: Sardar Khan would seem to be waiting for an auspicious time to enter or re-enter his residence, perhaps a form of *Griha Pravesh* which is practiced by multiple faith communities in Kerala. Fay dismisses it as 'ridiculous superstitions'.

192 *the Nabob*: Hyder Ali.

193 *Cochin*: Or Kochi. The 'Queen of the Arabian Sea', Cochin is a major port city on the southwest coast of India. An important centre of the spice trade since the fourteenth century, it is home to the oldest community of Jews in India (who, in some accounts, settled there after the destruction of the Second Temple in 68 AD). Cochin was occupied by the Portuguese in 1503, becoming the first of the European colony in India. The Dutch held power in the city until 1773, when it fell to Hyder Ali in the conquest of Mysore.

194 *Mahometan robbers*: It is in this tribute to '*Isaac the Jew*' that Fay first makes reference to different faith communities on the south-west coast of India, and curiously, it is primarily to distinguish between the 'Mahometan' robbers (the forces of the Muslim Hyder Ali), the unsympathetic Christians among their fellow captives of the *Nathalia*, and the 'benevolent Jew' Isaac Surgun.

195 *good Samaritan . . . benevolent Jew*: Referring to the parable of the Good Samaritan in Luke 10:25–37, in which a man, having been beaten and robbed, is left for dead by a passing priest and a Levite before being aided by a man from Samaria, who shows compassion for him and dresses his wounds. The parable not only teaches that we should love our neighbour, but also extends the idea of 'neighbour' to include all people regardless of faith or origin.

196 Peekdanees: A phonetic rendering of the Bangla word *pikadāni*; a spitoon.

197 *chewing betel*: The leaf of the betel vine (*Piper betel* of the *Piperaceae* family*)* is commonly consumed in Asia and Asian diasporas as betel 'quid', or in *paan* with the Areca nut and sometimes tobacco. A sheaf of the leaves can also be offered as an auspicious gift and as a sign of respect.

198 *Mr. Moore*: Captain Moore of the *St Helena*, which had also been impounded at Suez before following the *Nathalia* to the Malabar Coast.

199 *all the spectators seeming to look upon me as a* self *devoted victim*: Fay makes oblique reference here to the historical Hindu practice of *sati* or *suttee*, where a wife sacrifices

herself on her husband's funeral pyre. She elaborates a more explicit – though no less polemical – comparison between the forms of sacrifice required in Indian and British marriages in a later letter (see Letter XX, dated 28 August 1781).

200 *Ceylon*: Sri Lanka; at that time a Dutch colony (with the exception of the Kingdom of Kandy). Ceylon was transferred to British rule in 1815.
201 *Point de Galle*: Now Galle, a port city at the south-western tip of Sri Lanka.
202 *beating up in the wind's eye*: The zig-zag motion required to sail a vessel directly into the wind.
203 *Captain Richardson of the* Ganges: Launched in 1778 as an East Indiaman, *Ganges* was making her first voyage for the EIC under Captain George Richardson.
204 *shell-lime . . .* chunam *as it is called*: 'Prepared lime; also specially used for fine polished plaster. Forms of this word occur both in Dravidian languages and in Hindi' (*Hobson-Jobson*, p. 168).
205 *various complaints . . . incidental to the climate*: Fay suggests here that many of the health issues experienced by Europeans in India might be caused by over-indulgence rather than climate. Of the numerous tropical and communicable diseases that faced travellers and colonial residents of this period, among the most prominent were plague, leprosy, cholera, and malaria; 'fever' in various forms was a leading cause of death.
206 *"the hardy regions of the North"*: Possibly quoting from line 270 of W. Tasker's *Ode to the Warlike Genius of Great Britain* (London: for the Author, 1778).
207 *Dubashees*: A phonetic rendering of the Hindi *dūbhāshiya* or *dōbāshī* (man of two languages): 'an Indian interpreter or commissionaire, employed in transacting business between Europeans and the local people, and as a guide, courier, etc.' (*OED*).
208 *Mr. and Mrs. Popham*: Stephen Popham (1745–1795). Born in Cork (and thus Mr. Fay's 'countryman'), Popham was educated in England and elected to the Irish House of Commons in 1776 as the Member for Castlebar. Facing financial difficulties, he moved to Calcutta and took up a position at the advocate-general's office as secretary to Sir John Day. Quarrelling with Day, he elected to resettle at Madras in 1778 and, after purchasing land there, began the reclamation of the area known as Black Town through an ambitious drainage project. He is also credited with establishing the Madras police in 1782. The vestiges of 'Popham's Plan' – which was presented to Madras authorities in January of 1782 – remain in the name of one of the major thoroughfares through the commercial centre of Madras: Popham's Broadway, formally *Prakasam Salai*, but still popularly known as 'Broadway'.
209 *Massulah*: Or *masula*, 'a large surf-boat used on the Coromandel Coast of south-east India, especially for conveying passengers and goods between ships and the shore' (*OED*).
210 *projector*: 'One who plans or designs an enterprise or undertaking; a proposer or founder of some venture' (*OED*). See note 208 for Popham's improvement activities at Madras.
211 *as an attorney . . . nothing here*: As the centre of British administration in India, the Supreme Court (with the Council) was established at Calcutta with the Regulating Act of 1773. It is therefore only in Bengal that Fay can practise as a barrister in India but, perhaps more importantly, it is where he perceives the greatest professional opportunities.
212 *St. Thomas . . . Brahmin*: Tradition has it that Saint Thomas travelled outside the Roman Empire to India and (in some accounts) even to Indonesia. According to legend, he was killed by hostile priests at St. Thomas Mount, in Chennai, on 3 July 72 AD, and his body was interred in Mylapore. See D. Farmer, *The Oxford Dictionary of Saints* (Oxford University Press, 2011), p. 418.
213 *Banian*: Or Banyan, the Indian fig-tree (*ficus religiosa*).

214 *'Temples not made with hands'*: Slightly altered from Acts 17:24 ('God that made the world and all things therein, seeing that he is Lord of heaven and earth, dwelleth not in temples made with hands').
215 Toddy: The term is a corruption of *tāri*, the Hindi word for 'the fermented sap of the ... palmyra ... and also of other palms, such as the date, the coco-palm, and the *Caryota wrens*; palm-wine' (*Hobson-Jobson*, p. 706).
216 *challenged*: Meaning 'challenged to a duel'.
217 *supercargo*: 'A representative of the ship's owner on board a merchant ship, responsible for overseeing the cargo and its sale' (*OED*).
218 Juggernauth: See Newell, note 196.
219 *"life and immortality were brought to light by the Gospel"*: Quoting 2 Timothy 1:10.
220 *"one fold, under one shepherd"*: Slightly misquoting John 10:16 ('and there shall be one fold, and one shepherd').
221 *Garden-reach*: A neighbourhood situated in the southwestern part of Kolkata. Located on a bend in the Hooghly River, it yielded the first full views of the city to an arriving traveller and was the location of many opulent country homes or 'garden houses' for wealthy residents of Calcutta to escape the city. These were often in the Palladian style made popular by Thames-side villas built between Richmond and Hampton earlier in the eighteenth century.
222 *snake boat*: Also known as a *pamban-manche*, 'a canoe used on the numerous rivers and back-waters, from 30 to 60 feet long, and cut out of a solid tree. The largest are paddled by about twenty men, double-banked, and, when pressed, they will go as much as 12 miles an hour'. See Admiral W. H. Smyth, *The Sailor's Word-Book: An Alphabetical Digest of Nautical Terms* (London: Blackie and Son, 1867), p. 515.
223 *Budgerow*: 'A lumbering keelless barge, formerly much used by Europeans travelling on the Ganges' (*Hobson-Jobson*, p. 91).
224 *Fort William*: The original Fort William was built between 1696 and 1706 by the British EIC and named for King William III. In 1756 the Fort was surrendered under siege to the Nawab of Bengal Siraj ud-Daulah. Survivors were imprisoned in the Fort's tiny holding cell, where up to two thirds died overnight from heat, suffocation and shock. The incident became infamous as 'the Black Hole of Calcutta'. After the recovery of Calcutta in 1757 under Robert Clive, Fort William was rebuilt in the open area Fay calls the 'Esplanade' (also known as the Maidan) at enormous cost. It was completed in 1781, precisely at the period the Fays saw it.
225 *Fort St George*: The first English fortress in India, built by the EIC at Madras during the 1640s.
226 *Sir Robert Chambers*: The East India Regulating Act of 1773 established a supreme council (under Governor-General Warren Hastings) and a judicature at Calcutta. Sir Robert Chambers (1737–1803) was appointed to the Supreme Court as second judge to Sir Elijah Impey's Chief Justice. After Chambers' arrival at Calcutta in 1774, tensions within the Governor General's Council, and between the Council and the Court, grew, as the latter sought to clarify and expand its jurisdiction. Their disputes (which Anthony Fay becomes caught up in) finally required Parliament to pass the Amending Act of 1781, which further demarcated the relations between the Supreme Court and the Governor General in Council.
227 *whose lady*: Frances Wilton (daughter of the sculptor and Royal Academician Joseph Wilton) had married Robert Chambers in 1774, just prior to his departure for Bengal. Samuel Johnson had reported the news to James Boswell in a letter as follows: 'Chambers is either married or almost married to Miss Wilton, a girl of sixteen, exquisitely beautiful, whom he has with his lawyer's tongue persuaded to take her chance with him in the East'. See H. E. Busteed, *Echoes from Old Calcutta* ... (4th edition, London & Calcutta: Thacker & Spink, 1908), p. 146.

228 *"She loves me . . . pity them"*: Quoting William Shakespeare, *Othello*, Act I, scene iii, ll. 168–9.
229 *Mrs. Hastings*: Marian Hastings, Anna Maria Apollonia Chapuset (previously Baroness von Imhoff). Warren Hastings had met the German Marian, then wife of Baron Imhoff, on a voyage to Madras in 1769. The couple began a relationship, apparently with Imhoff's knowledge and consent, and resided together in Madras and Calcutta. After the Imhoffs were granted a divorce, Hastings and Marian were married in India in July 1777, and Hastings adopted Marian's two sons from her former marriage. Marian returned from India with a massive personal fortune and was renowned for her glamorous appearance and extraordinary jewellery. At the time of Hastings trial, Frances Burney found her pleasing, lively, and hopelessly indiscreet: 'the most conspicuous figure wherever she appears'. See F. Burney, *Diary and Letters* . . . (London: Henry Colburn, 1842), vol. 5, p. 305.
230 *Mrs. Motte*: Miss Mary Touchet, sister of Peter Touchet (a school fellow at Westminster with Hastings) married Thomas Motte, diamond merchant and Superintendent of Police, in 1779.
231 *I had brought them on myself*: Fay perceives a judgement against her on the part of Mrs. Hastings – probably for her husband's private 'adventuring' (he had not sought permission from either the Company or the new administration at Bengal to come out to Calcutta to practice), and possibly for her own decision to follow a husband whose behaviour was consistently rash and thoughtless.
232 bijou: A jewel.
233 *tatties placed to exclude the hot wind*: An ingenious form of evaporative cooling; 'A screen or mat, usually made of the roots of the fragrant cuscus grass, which is placed in a frame so as to fill up the opening of a door or window, and kept wet, in order to cool and freshen the air of a room' (*OED*).
234 *Sir Elijah Impey*: Appointed Chief Justice of the Calcutta Supreme Court from 1774 until 1787, Impey (1732–1809) arrived in Calcutta in the wake of the East India Regulating Act of 1773. His tenure as Chief Justice was marked by cases that exposed tensions over jurisdiction between the Court and Governor-General Warren Hastings's Council. The most notorious of these was the Nandakumar affair of 1775, in which a Brahman of that name accused Hastings of corruption. Impey instead prosecuted Nandakumar, who was executed for forgery on 5 August 1775, becoming the first man to be hung under new British law. Impey's conduct in the case has been long debated; Thomas Babington Macaulay famously concluded Impey to be criminally partial to Hastings, while later historians have largely concluded his conduct to have been just and impartial. Impey and Hastings continued to try to find administrative solutions to ongoing conflicts between the Court and the Council; they collaborated on a plan of judicial reform in 1776, but North's government did not act on it. In 1780 Hastings tried to institute a number of their ideas via a different means, by giving Impey superintendence over the *sadr diwani adalat*, or central civil court, which until then had been run by a team of British councillors and Indian officials. This appointment led the House of Commons 1782 to recall Impey to London to answer questions. Impeachment proceedings began in 1788 with a motion concerning the Nandakumar affair; that motion failed, a short while later the rest of the charges were dropped.
235 en passant: 'In passing', or 'by the way' (French).
236 *Carnatic*: 'The eastern low country' (*Hobson-Jobson*, p. 126), encompassing the eastern coast of South India, extending in the late eighteenth century from Cape Comoria and Tirunelveli in the south, extending beyond Madras (Chennai) to the Krishna River in the north.
237 *Khansaman*: Or *Consumah*. 'In Anglo-Indian households in the Bengal Presidency, this is the title of the chief table-servant and provider . . . . The literal meaning of the word is "Master of the household-gear"' (*Hobson-Jobson*, p. 190).

238 salaamed *to my foot*: Meaning 'Peace be upon you', a *salaam* can also apply to the ceremonious act of obeisance accompanying this salutation.
239 *comprodore*: Also compradore, from the Portuguese word *comprador*, or 'purchaser', here denoting a steward who purchases goods necessary for the household and keeps accounts.
240 *anna*: 'The 16th part of a rupee' (*OED*).
241 *harpies*: A harpy is 'a rapacious, plundering, or grasping person; one that preys upon others' (*OED*).
242 *cowrees*: Also *cowry*, 'the porcelain-like shell of a small gastropod, *Cypræa moneta*, found abundantly in the Indian Ocean, and used as money in some parts of Africa and Southern Asia' (*OED*).
243 *Banians*: 'In Calcutta ... specifically applied to the native brokers attached to houses of business, or to persons in the employment of a private gentleman doing analogous duties' (*Hobson-Jobson*, p. 48).
244 writers: The most junior of employees, clerks in the service of the Company were known as 'writers'. They could be based in either London or India; those in Indian service often rose quickly through the Company ranks. Samuel Manesty, whom Fay met on her voyage out, had been appointed as a writer at the beginning of his career.
245 four in hand: Driving a carriage and four horses oneself. In the late eighteenth century, it became a vogue among young men to drive their own coaches, often recklessly and at high speeds. In the period, the most famous of these young coachmen was Thomas Onslow, and the type is satirized vividly in Thomas Holcroft's character Goldfinch in *The Road to Ruin* (1792), and in James Thorpe in Jane Austen's *Northanger Abbey* (1818). 'Four-in-hand' literally denotes having reins of four horses in one's hands, and in London it quickly became the name of a popular driving club, most famously named in the opening chapter of Walter Scott's *Waverley* (1814). See J. Timbs, *Clubs and Club Life in London* (London: Chatto and Windus, 1872), pp. 248–9.
246 *gold-mohurs*: 'A gold coin used in India from the 16th cent. onward. Also called *dinar*' (*OED*).
247 *Calcutta Gazettes*: The *Calcutta Gazette*, a Government newspaper, was not published until 1784; so, as Forster suggests, Fay is probably referring here to the much less reputable *Bengal Gazette or the Original Calcutta General Advertiser* which was launched by James Augustus Hicky in January 1780.
248 *"summer friend"*: One who is a friend only when circumstances make it advantageous to be so. Untraced, though perhaps from Act 3, scene 2 of Thomas Shadwell's *The History of Timon of Athens, the Man-Hater* (London: Herringman, 1703). The culprit here is Mr. Hare, with whom Fay had had such a strained relationship in Calicut.
249 *a duel between the Governor General and ... Mr. Francis*: Sir Philip Francis (22 October 1740–23 December 1818), Irish-born politician and writer, was appointed to the Supreme Council at Calcutta in 1773 and quickly clashed with Governor-General Warren Hastings. Francis was injured in the duel, which had been precipitated by a minuted slight on the part of Hastings against Francis (Hastings accused him of being 'void of truth and honour'). Francis survived and returned to England; as a Member of Parliament in the House of Commons, he was active in the impeachment charges brought against Hastings from 1785.
250 *the cutting off Col. Baillie's detachment*: Fay is referring to the Battle of Pollilur (or Perambakam) between forces commanded by Tipu Sultan (the son of Hyder Ali) and Colonel William Baillie of the British EIC. The battle, which only 250 of Baillie's 3,853 men survived, was the worst loss that the Company had suffered in India to that date. Baillie was seriously injured, captured, and died in prison at Seringapatam in November of 1782.

251 Sir *Eyre Coote*: Lieutenant-General Sir Eyre Coote (1726–83) was renowned as a soldier in British service in India. In 1779 he returned to the subcontinent to assume the position of Commander-in-Chief of the EIC forces and was instrumental in the Second Anglo-Mysore War against Hyder Ali and Tipu Sultan.

252 *West*: Captain West, a soldier in the service of Sardar Ali at Calicut, whom Fay initially dismisses in the same terms as Captain Ayres but then comes to trust. See note 162.

253 *Dr Jackson*: Rowland Jackson M.D., born in Ireland, graduated doctor of medicine at Rheims 16 August 1746. He was admitted to the College of Physicians in 1766 and practised for a period in the West Indies; Forster suggests that it was the loss of family estates in Ireland that prompted his move to India with his wife, eldest son Edward, Edward's fiance Phoebe Tuting, Miss Maria Chantry, and family; see Fay, *Original Letters*, p. 281, note 32. He died not long after Fay became close with the family, and was buried in Calcutta on 29 March 1784. Phoebe Jackson, his daughter in law, died a year later aged twenty-four.

254 *"children of the sun"*: Likely a reference to ll. 13–14 of James Thomson's 'Liberty': 'Let wondering Rocks, in radiant Birth, disclose, / The various-tinctur'd Children of the Sun'.

255 *"where the song . . . festive board"*: Untraced.

256 *Burdwan stew*: An Anglo-Indian dish in which leftover meat (lamb, beef, rabbit, or poultry) is cooked in a pan with onion, cayenne, vinegar, and anchovy, and then stewed in a sauce of beef gravy and wine. It is likely named for its connection with Bardhaman (or Burdwan), a city and district in West Bengal. See A. Hunter, *Culina Famulatrix Medicinæ: Or, Receipts in Modern Cookery, with a Medical Commentary* (London: 1806), pp. 185–6. For a more sophisticated recipe roughly contemporary with Fay, see Mrs. Dalgairns, *The Practice of Cookery, Adapted to the Business of Everyday Life* (3rd edition, Edinburgh: Cadell, 1830), p. 166.

257 *the Spanish Olla Podrida*: Literally meaning 'rotten pot', *olla podrida* is a stew of pork, beans, and various vegetables cooked slowly in a clay pot. The dish appears as early as the 1620s in Act 2, scene 2 of Beaumont and Fletcher's *Rollo Duke of Normandy*.

258 *Five card loo . . . Tré dille and Whist*: The most popular trick-taking game in Britain in the eighteenth and early nineteenth centuries, whist requires four people forming two sides, in which trumps are determined by the last card dealt. Like whist, five card loo is a trick-taking game employing trump cards, but it incorporates a number of features (a growing pot, the option of playing or folding) now more commonly associated with poker. *Tré dille* (or *tredille*, or *tradille*) is a modification of Quadrille for three people usually employing thirty cards.

259 *Mr. Hyde*: (1738/9–96), Supreme Court Judge in Bengal from 1774 until his death, and author of *Hyde's Notebooks*, which summarized cases and transcribed court testimony. A hospitable man, Hyde was satirized by James Augustus Hicky in the *Bengal Gazette* as 'Turkey Cram'.

260 *King's birth day*: The birthday of George III (1738–1820) was 4 June, a public celebration where it was customary, as Fay intimates, to wear one's finest clothes – from which the phrase 'birthday suit' derives, and from which the slang version of that expression (meaning wearing nothing at all) then arose.

261 *Harmonic*: This seems to be a reference to the 'Harmonicon Society' a series of concerts and assemblies supported by subscription and held at Mr. Creighton's Harmonic House or Harmonicon Tavern in Lai Bazar, Calcutta. Forster's note from the 1925 edition reads, 'THE HARMONICON – dancing house, concert hall, and tavern – stood in the Lal Bazaar, opposite the Jail' (p. 281, note 34).

262 *a Sonata of Nicolai's*: Probably the German composer Johann Michael Nicolai (1629–85), whose *Instrumentalische Sachen* (1675) includes eight sonatas, the most famous of which is *Sonata A2 in C Major*.

263 *Lady Coote and her inseparable friend Miss Molly Bazett*: Susannah Hutchinson (d. 1812), daughter of the former governor of St Helena, and wife of Sir Eyre Coote (1729–83), who served as Commander-in-chief in India from 1759 to 1762, from 1769 to 1771, and from 1778 until his death in 1783. Fay's *Original Letters* provide the only substantive information we have on Miss Mary (Molly) Bazett.

264 *The house was built by subscription*: Calcutta's first theatre opened in 1756; it was replaced by the New Playhouse, also called the Calcutta Theatre, founded in 1775 and funded by subscription shares of one hundred rupees each. It had a variety of ticket types: pit, box, upper boxes, and gallery. Forster's edition notes that 'Mrs. Fay, for her gold mohur, would have sat in a box'; see Fay, *Original Letters*, p. 281, note 36. Between 1776 and 1808 the theatre performed at least eight Shakespeare plays (including *Hamlet*, *Romeo and Juliet*, *The Merchant of Venice*, and *Richard III*), as well as many popular farces like *Neck or Nothing*, the musical *Entertainment of The Waterman*, and *Barnaby Brittle*. Its productions were reported regularly in the *Bengal Gazette*. The acting company for the theatre remained all-male until the founding of the rival Chowringhee Theatre in 1813. The Chowringhee's decision to employ women forced the New Playhouse to do the same.

265 *Venice Preserved*: By Thomas Otway (1652–85), first performed in 1682 and one of the most popular tragedies of the eighteenth century. Its obsession with military honour and conspiracy gives it a poignancy in this setting. Forster's 1925 edition notes that

> This particular performance of Otway's *Venice Preserved* made a stir. The *Bengal Gazette* of February 11, 1781, says of it: 'Captain Call played Jaffier admirably well, and may be styled the Garrick of the East. Mr. Norford played Belvidera with such an amorous glow of features and utterance – and was so characteristic in the description of madness – as to procure him (as usual) universal applause.'

(p. 281, note 36)

266 *Lieutenant Norfar*: John Norfar, made Lieutenant 6 July 1778.
267 *chief ruler*: Warren Hastings.
268 *she has lately added a son to her family*: Edward Colin Chambers (Lady Chambers's fifth child) was born 26 April 1781 but died at six months old of fever. Lady Impey and Councillor Edward Wheler stood as godparents at the ceremony Fay so dreaded.
269 *Colonel Watson*: Colonel Henry Watson (1737–86), Chief Engineer of Bengal (1776–1786) who created the first dockyards at Calcutta. He stood as Philip Francis's second in his duel with Warren Hastings (see note 249). Despite both Eliza Fay and Elijah Impey reporting that Anthony Fay was retained to serve papers or prosecute the case on Watson's behalf, it is not known whether he finally undertook this mission (Impey MSS, British Museum 16260, 31 August 31 1781). Fay, together with his involvement in the impeachment process, disappears from the historical record at this point.
270 *His secret*: The final cause of the rupture between the Fays in 1782 would seem to have been Anthony's fathering of a child with another woman at Calcutta. This is not made explicit until Letter III of Part Second, dated 19 February 1815.
271 *"Tis Conscience that makes cowards of us all"*: Quoting from Act 3, scene 1 of William Shakespeare's *Hamlet* (1601).
272 *Chinsurah*: A city 35 kilometres to the north of Calcutta, Chinsurah had been the site of a Dutch Factory from 1656. It was seized by the British once news of hostilities with Holland reached Bengal in July 1781.
273 *Mrs. Wheler*: Charlotte Durnford was the second wife (m. 23 December 1780) of Edward Wheler (1732–84), who served as a member of the Supreme Council of Bengal between 1777 and 1784.
274 *custom of widows burning themselves*: See Newell, note 143.
275 *Parias*: 'A member of a very extensive low caste in Southern India, especially numerous at Madras, where its members supplied most of the domestics in European service'

(*OED*), 'pariah' came to be applied to any member of a lower caste and by Europeans – as Fay does here – to outcasts or those of no caste.

276 *Brahma, the creator, Vistnoo the preserver, and Sheevah the destroyer*: Referring to the *Trimurti*, the triple deity of supreme divinity in Hinduism, in which the forces of creation, maintenance, and destruction are personified in three deities: usually Brahma the creator, Vishnu the preserver, and Shiva the destroyer.

277 *"Gods changeful ... or lust"*: Quoting Epistle 3, ll. 257–8 of Alexander Pope's *Essay on Man* (1733–1734).

278 *Pundaram*: Or Pandáram, a 'Hindu ascetic mendicant of the (so-called) Sudra, or even of a lower caste' (*Hobson-Jobson*, p. 507).

279 *Jogee*:

> A Hindu ascetic; and sometimes a 'conjuror'. From Sansk[rit] *yogin*, one who practices the *yoga*, a system of meditation combined with austerities, which is supposed to induce miraculous power over elementary matter. In fact the stuff which has of late been propagated in India by certain persons, under the names of theosophy and esoteric Buddhism, is essentially the doctrine of the Jogis.
> (*Hobson-Jobson*, p. 351)

280 *Seniases*: According to a late eighteenth-century encyclopedia, Seniases are ascetics

> allowed no other clothing but what suffices for covering their nakedness, nor have they any worldly goods besides a pitcher and staff; but though they are strictly enjoined to meditate on the truths contained in the sacred writings, they are expressly forbidden to argue about them. They must eat but once a day, and that very sparingly, of rice or other vegetables; they must also show the most perfect indifference about hunger, thirst, heat, cold, or any thing whatever relative to this world; looking forward with continual desire to the separation of the soul from the body.
> ('Hindoos', *Encyclopedia Britannica* (Edinburgh: A. Bell and C. MacFarquhar, 1797), vol. 8, p. 515)

281 *Charruk Poojah*: An ancient Hindu festival held in honour of the god Shiva, *Charak* or *Charak Pooja* involves fasting, and forms of penitential pain – including piercing the skin and tongue with hooks or needles, and swinging from the *Charak gachh* or pole.

282 *Rajah*:

> Originally the title given in India to a king or prince; in later times extended to petty chiefs or dignitaries (as *Zemindars*) or conferred as a title of nobility on Hindus, and adopted as the usual designation of Malay and Javanese rulers or chiefs.
> (*OED*)

283 *Mr. and Mrs. Hosea*: William Hosea, Resident of Murshidabad, and his wife Mary. They, together with their young daughter and Thomas Fitzmaurice Chambers (eldest son of Sir Robert and Lady Chambers), sailed with the East Indiaman *Grosvenor*, captained by Coxon. Strangely, Fay does not mention their fate: the *Grosvenor* was shipwrecked near Durban on the east coast of Africa in July 1782 and, although the majority of passengers and crew made it ashore, all the passengers subsequently disappeared.

284 *Mrs. Chambers*: Mrs. Anne Chambers, the mother of Sir Robert.

285 *Admiral Suffren ... Sir E. Hughes ... our vessels*: Admiral comte Pierre André de Suffren (1729–1788), French admiral who during 1782–1783 fought five battles against British Vice-Admiral Sir Edward Hughes (1720–1794) for supremacy of the Indian Ocean. As Fay's comment implies, Hughes had a reputation for caution; knowing that a decisive loss could mean the loss of British India, he avoided unnecessary risks,

while Suffren attempted several daring attacks. Although intense, each of the battles ended without a clear victor; news of the 1783 Peace of Paris ended the conflict.

286 *"Let her works praise her"*: Quoting Proverbs 31:31.
287 *Dutch had commenced hostilities*: Fay refers to the fourth Anglo-Dutch War, fought in various American, European, African, and South Asian theatres between 1780 and 1784. Hostilities broke out over Dutch trade with British enemies, particularly France, and led to the British seizure of Trincomalee, one of the finest ports on the eastern coast of Ceylon.
288 *prize money*: 'Money realized by the sale of a captured ship or its cargo, and distributed among the captors' (*OED*). In the late eighteenth century, the distribution of prize money for ships and cargo captured by the Royal Navy was formalized under the Cruisers and Convoys Act of 1708, which established an Admiralty Prize Court to adjudicate the division of money.
289 *scuttle*: 'A square or rectangular hole or opening in a ship's deck smaller than a hatchway, furnished with a movable cover or lid, used ... for purposes of lighting, ventilation, etc.' (*OED*).
290 *piquet*: 'A card-game played by two persons with a pack of 32 cards (the low cards from the two to the six being excluded), in which points are scored on various groups or combinations of cards, and on tricks' (*OED*).
291 *this romantic island*: St Helena.
292 *Ladder Hill*: Steep pathway winding up the side of 'Ladder' or 'Tower' Hill in St Helena. The original means of access to the fort at the top of Tower Hill was a rope ladder; the first path was cut around 1718.
293 *Lord North, and the Hastings*: The *Lord North* (an East Indiaman, launched in 1770) and the *Hastings* (details not known), both engaged in the China trade.
294 *The* Chapman: A 700-ton merchant ship of two decks, built at Whitby in 1777.
295 *the Dartmouth*: A British East Indiaman of 755–800 tons (built 1779), the *Dartmouth* ran aground and was wrecked on Car Nicobar; Fay had tried to secure passage on her for the return voyage in January.
296 *Carnicobar island*: Car Nicobar is the northernmost of the Nicobar Islands in the Bay of Bengal.
297 *"From hidden ... my way"*: Untraced.
298 *Mr Casamajor and his mother*: James Henry Casamajor (1745–1815), joined the Company as a writer in 1762, and by 1789 was Second in Council at Madras. The Casamajors were prominent for three generations in Madras; his parents were Rebecca (*née* Powney) and Noah Casamajor, a merchant.
299 *Scilly*: An archipelago of islands off the south western tip of Cornwall. In October 1707 Scilly was the location of one of the worst maritime disasters in British history, when six (of 21) Royal Navy ships travelling from Gibraltar to Portsmouth under the command of Sir Cloudesley Shovell were driven on to the Western Rocks, with the loss of over 1,500 lives.
300 *having no poop, looked so unlike an Indiaman*: An Indiaman vessel – 'a large trading ship belonging to the East India Company' (*OED*) or designed for long distance trade – had a distinctive shape created by a high deck at the very rear of the ship which formed the roof of the stern cabin. The *Chapman* was not constructed in this way so when she arrived in the Bristol Channel she was identified as an American ship (with whom the British had until very recently been at war).
301 *although the preliminaries of peace had been some time signed*: Referring to the preliminary treaty signed by Britain and the United States on 30 November 1782, which set the scene for the more intense negotiations that would shape the Treaty of Paris of 1783.
302 *The manuscript submitted to your perusal*: Manuscript copies of the 'First Part' of the published text, that is the letters until 7 February 1783. Fay proposes to relate her

ELIZA FAY, ORIGINAL LETTERS FROM INDIA (1817)

subsequent voyages and experiences as memoirs to her correspondent, in several letters or journal entries composed at Blackheath. Perhaps, in this instance, an entirely fictional set of 'letters' addressed to Mrs. L—, although long journal letters were common in the eighteenth and nineteenth centuries, and there is insufficient evidence to decide whether Fay's form of letters in the second part of her narrative is or is not genuine.

303 *"a howling wilderness"*: Quoting Deuteronomy 32:10.
304 *"the feast of reason and the flow of soul"*: Quoting line 127 of Alexander Pope's 'The First Satire of the Second Book of Horace'.
305 *my friend*: Mrs. Irwin.
306 *severe indisposition*: Fay had ongoing health problems which are not described in detail in her letters, but which were probably complications from the deep lacerated puncture wound she received to her breast while imprisoned at Calicut.
307 *the offer*: The offer made to Fay at Calcutta of establishing a school in partnership with another woman, as detailed in Letter XXII. Fay had declined, citing health reasons, but claims the woman 'proved herself a sincere friend'.
308 *Captain* Walker: Captain Thomas Walker had taken command of the *Lord Camden* (launched the previous year), an East Indiaman in the Company's service. The details of this voyage are preserved: she sailed from The Downs on 17 March 1784 (as noted by Fay); reached Johanna on 27 June; Bombay on 25 September; Madras on 28 September; and Kedgeree on 10 November. These dates correspond closely with those given by Fay in her memoir of the voyage to Bombay.
309 *Teneriffe . . . the year 1704*: Referring to Mount Teide on the island of Tenerife. While there was an eruption in 1704, Fay likely means the 1706 *Montañas Negras* eruption, which destroyed the town and principal port of Garachico and several smaller villages.
310 *we spoke a Danish ship*: To speak a ship is to hail and speak to its commander.
311 *trade winds*: 'A wind that blows steadily in the same direction for a long period (as a season), especially at sea' (*OED*).
312 *"and bore healing on their wings"*: Invoking Malachi 4:2 ('But unto you that fear my name shall the Sun of righteousness arise with healing in his wings; and ye shall go forth, and grow up as calves of the stall').
313 *roundhouse*: 'A cabin or set of cabins on a sailing ship, located below the poop on the after part of the quarterdeck' (*OED*).
314 lee lurch: A sudden and often violent roll which a ship makes to leeward in a high sea, particularly when a large wave strikes her on the weather-side.
315 *Cape L'Aquillas*: The southern tip of the African continent, Cape Agulhas is a rocky headland 170 kilometres southeast of Cape Town in the Western Cape, South Africa.
316 *shipped so many seas*: Here, to take what seems a sea's-worth of water on deck of a ship because of high waves or heavy swell; to take on a dangerous amount of water.
317 *Bay of Johanna*: Anjouhan (known historically as Johanna) is a volcanic island in the Indian Ocean close to the Mozambique Channel.
318 *Mr Lewin*: Thomas Lewin (1753–1843), of the Madras Civil Service.
319 *Old-woman's Island*: Also known as Little Colaba; one of the islands constituting Mumbai and forming part of historic Old Bombay.
320 *Mr Coggan*: Probably Mr James Coggan.
321 *the Governor (Mr. Boddam)*: Rawson Hart Boddam (1734–1812), who governed Bombay from 1784 to 1788, and his second wife Eliza Maria Tudor.
322 Perell: 'Sans Pareil' or the Government House at Parel; this building was originally either a Portuguese Franciscan or Jesuit Friary (there are contesting accounts), before being taken over as the official summer residence of the Governors of Bombay in the early eighteenth century. It is now the Haffkine Institute for biomedical sciences.

323 *Nesbit's*: H. C. Marine Commodore Andrew Nesbit (d. 1791), responsible for the defence of shipping at Bombay.
324 *Anjengo roads*: Inman's authoritative *Navigation Tables for the Use of British Seamen* (Portsea: W. Woodward; London: Richardson, 1821) places the Anjengo Roads approximately at latitude 8°39'N and longitude 76°50', on the coast of southwestern India at modern Anchuthengu (p. 441).
325 *Mr Hutchinson*: John Hutchinson (d. 1797), commercial resident at Anjengo, later Resident at Travancore and Cochin. From 1832 the Select Committee heard a petition from Hutchinson's nephew Mr Bury Hutchinson regarding the recovery of a large private loan (900,000 rupees) that had been made by his uncle to the Rajah of Travancore in 1784 but was never repaid.
326 *distilled water*: Here, water made by boiling and distilling seawater.
327 *Miss Hicks married Mr Lacey*: The register of St John's Calcutta records the marriage of 'John Lacey, a bachelor, shopkeeper, to Avis Hicks, single woman' on 19 March 1785.
328 Severn Packet: The loss of the *Severn Packet* was first reported in London in the *Morning Chronicle and London Advertiser* #5558 (8 March 1787), p. 4. Further details were provided through the correspondence of a William Loehead, mate of the *Juliana Maria*, who details the loss of forty-one people in the wreck, and the strange manner of one survivor

> being saved by means of a hog: this will appear strange to those who don't know how strong and swift those animals swim; but, true it is, the person got hold of the hog's tail in the water, and was conducted safe on shore.
> (*Gentleman's Magazine* 57 [March 1787], p. 265)

By this wreck in the mouth of the Hooghly River, Fay lost her friend and business partner Mrs Lacey (Miss Hicks), and the unnamed illegitimate son whom Anthony Fay had apparently already abandoned at Calcutta.
329 *unlucky year 1788*: After Hastings' return to England, several factors contributed to a significant downturn in trade and wealth at Calcutta in the late 1780s. Local markets were saturated with European goods, while the economy was in recession. Miniaturist Ozias Humphrey wrote that

> there never was known in Calcutta so much poverty or so much scarcity of money, as there is at this time. All the first families are withdrawn from it . . . there are scarcely twenty persons left in Indostan, whose fortunes would each amount to twenty thousand pounds.
> (Ozias Humphry to Mary Boydell, Calcutta, 29 December 1785, Humphry MSS, Royal Academy of Arts, London, HU/3/ 49–50)

See P. D. Rasico, 'Calcutta "In These Degenerate Days": The Daniells' Visions of Life, Death and Nabobery in Late Eighteenth-Century British India', *Journal for Eighteenth-Century Studies* 42:1 (2018), pp. 27–47.
330 *Mr Benjamin Lacey*: Brother of John Lacey, and brother-in-law of Avis Hicks (Fay's business partner in the Calcutta millinery business).
331 *Captain Jacob Crowninshield*: Jacob Crowninshield, born 31 March 1770, Salem MA, died 15 April 1808. The Crowninshield family were prominent in American maritime affairs; Jacob had gone into partnership with three of his brothers, commanding ships in trade between America and India. He was later elected to the Massachusetts State Senate and appointed to the position of U.S. Secretary of the Navy, but was never able to assume the latter role due to illness.
332 *given a girl . . . with her two children*: Forster's 1925 edition of Fay's *Original Letters* (London: Hogarth Press, 1925) condemns this episode as 'the worst action recorded

of Mrs. Fay', and describes Fay as having stranded a girl named Kitty Johnson in 1782 on St Helena, where she had been sold into slavery:

> discovering [in 1794] that her late mistress was passing by on the *Henry*, she went to the Governor and denounced her.... The Governor then summoned Mrs. Fay ... and told [her] she must either settle the matter or remain to stand trial.
>
> (p. 284, note 47)

Among other details, Johnson alleged that her abandonment had stemmed from Fay's intimacy with the ship's doctor, leading Kate Teltscher and David Atkinson to note, 'Rather than stand trial, Fay paid a £60 fine. To set this incident in context, it should be noted that any report of sexual activity on the part of a separated wife might jeopardize her maintenance allowance' ('Fay (*née* Clement), Eliza (1755/6–1816), writer and traveller', *Oxford Dictionary of National Biography*).

333 *my brother Preston*: The husband of Fay's sister Eleanor.

334 *man-of-war birds*: Any of the various seabirds, also called frigate birds, that attack other birds to steal their food.

335 *albercuore*: Albacore, 'any of several small and medium-sized tunas of the genera *Thunnus* and *Euthynnus*' (*OED*).

336 *distressing news of Ostend being in the hands of the French*: Fay refers here to the campaign in Flanders, which dominated the early years of the war between revolutionary France and British, Austrian, Prussian, Dutch, and Hanoverian forces. By 1795 Prussia had withdrawn from the conflict and France had conquered the Dutch Republic. As a French port, Fay would be unable to land her cargo in the Belgian coastal city as planned. Fay opts to dispose of her cargo in America under the superintendence of Jacob Crowninshield.

337 *my dear father*: Edward Clement (d. 1794), a shipwright of Rotherhithe, Surrey.

338 *Richard Crowninshield*: Fay becomes owner or part owner of the *Minerva* and enters into a partnership in the American-Indian trade with at least two of the Crowninshield brothers.

339 *Emigrants*: Fay refers here to the many *émigrés* fleeing the French Revolution, particularly after 1791, when the Terror and the mass deportation of priests caused thousands to leave France for England.

340 *"the times were out of joint"*: Misquoting from Act 1, scene 5 of William Shakespeare's *Hamlet* (1601).

341 *Newtown Park*: An early eighteenth-century house and park approximately two miles from Lymington, owned by the Plowdens: Henry Chicheley Plowden (1754–1821) and his wife Eugenia Brooke (1756–1845).

342 *great church*: The Cathedral of Funchal. This gothic and romanesque building, renowned for its carved wooden ceiling, is one of the few surviving structures from Madeira's early colonial period.

343 *American Consul*: John Marsden Pintard had been appointed Commercial Agent to Madeira in 1783; he was then made Consul to Madeira by George Washington in 1790. He was either the son or the nephew of John Lewis Pintard (1732–1797), a New York merchant who became a major importer of wine from the island.

344 *Convent of Ursulines ... Golgotha, or the chapel of skulls*: Likely the Convent of St. Francis, which Nicholas Cayetano de Bettencourt Pitta describes as

> the only one of the island in which men are received.... In this convent, there is a singular curiosity – a small chapel, called the chapel of Ghosts, the whole of which, both sides and ceiling is composed of human skulls and thigh bones; the thigh bones being laid across each other, and a skull placed in each of the four angles.
>
> (Pitta, *Account of the Island of Madeira* (London: Longman, Hurst, Rees, 1812), pp. 102–3)

345 *Mr. Murray's plantation*: 'Quinto do Prazer', the estate of Charles Murray, a Scottish merchant and British Consul at Madeira (1771 to 1801).
346 *Consul Mr. C – k*: Untraced.
347 *the road of Oratavia*: La Orotava, a town in the northern part of Tenerife.
348 *Mrs. Barry*: Untraced.
349 enbonpoint: Weight or heaviness (here probably in the sense of 'plumpness').
350 *Santa Cruz*: The site in 1494 of the landing of Castilian troops that conquered the island, Santa Cruz de Tenerife became one of the most important ports of the Atlantic and Canary Islands.
351 *Laguna*: San Cristóbal de La Laguna or La Laguna, located in the northern part of the island of Tenerife, was one of nine aboriginal Guanche kingdoms until its conquest by the Kingdom of Castile. The city was founded between 1496 and 1497 by Alonso Fernández de Lugo and served as the capital of the island until the early eighteenth century, when declining population saw the capital moved to Santa Cruz. The old city retains much of its historic colonial architecture, including important buildings such as the Iglesia de la Concepción, the former Convent of San Agustín, and the University of Laguna, founded in 1701.
352 pour surcroît de malheur: 'With the additional misfortune' (French).
353 *R – y in Santa Cruz*: Untraced.
354 *deserves the pen of Mrs. Ratcliffe*: Referring to Ann Radcliffe (1764–1823), the most popular and critically acclaimed gothic novelist of the eighteenth century, as renowned for her descriptions of sublime landscapes, particularly mountainous ones, as for her ability to craft thrilling romances with supernatural overtones. Her *Romance of the Forest* (1791), *Mysteries of Udolpho* (1794), and *The Italian; or, The Confessional of the Black Penitents* (1797) remain standards of the genre.
355 *Holy Writ . . . 'Laugh and sing'*: Quoting Psalms 65:14.
356 *the time of Lord Nelson's attack*: The assault by the Royal Navy on Santa Cruz in July 1797, led by Rear Admiral Horatio Nelson.
357 *Port Praya Bay*: Porto Praya, now Praia, is located on the southern coast of Santiago Island in the Republic of Cabo Verde.
358 *Signor Basto the Commandant*: Probably Luis Antonio Basto.
359 *Exchange . . . Theatre and Pantheon*: A mansion building in a large park owned by Hall Plumer which, by 1789, had become a Public Hall and Assembly Rooms known as the Pantheon. In a flush of enthusiasm for theatricals, a stage manager was commissioned from England and the building became the site of a theatre under the superintendence of Mr Rowbotham. The Pantheon remained popular well into the nineteenth century. Visiting in 1810 Maria Graham, later Lady Callcott, described her visit:

> I was two evenings ago at a public ball in the Pantheon, which contains, besides a ball-room, a very pretty theatre, card-rooms and virandas. During the cold season there are monthly assemblies, with occasional balls all the year, which are very well conducted. The Pantheon is a handsome building; it is used as a freemasons' lodge of modern masons, among whom almost every man in the army and navy who visits Madras enrols himself.
> (M. Graham, *Journal of a Residence in India* (London: Longman, Hurst, Rees, Orme, and Brown, 1812), p. 130)

360 *"his love met no return"*: Untraced.
361 *Fulta*: Or *Fultah*, on the Hooghly, approximately 32 kilometres south of Calcutta; the same place where British settlers fled in 1756 when Nawab Siraj ud-Daulah conquered Calcutta.
362 *dead-lights*: 'A strong wooden or iron shutter fixed outside a cabin-window or porthole in a storm, to prevent water from entering' (*OED*).

363 *Cooly Bazar*: A neighbourhood ghetto very close to the Fort and Hasting's Bridge that was home to the huge numbers of labourers and domestic servants required to service Company officials.
364 *a Guinea pig*: In nautical terms, an inexperienced midshipman – probably derived from 'Guineamen' or sailing ships involved in the slave trade between Britain, Africa, and the Americas.
365 *the free use of bark*: The *Cinchona calisaya* tree and its bark, in use from the seventeenth century to treat fevers.
366 *Dr Hare*: Dr James Hare FRSE FSA, originally of Calderhall, an eminent physician in India, and father to James Macadam Hare (1775–1831), who was surgeon to the President of Calcutta.
367 *kedging*: 'To warp a ship, or move it from one position to another by winding in a hawser attached to a small anchor dropped at some distance' *(OED)*.
368 *Vizagapatam*: Visakhapatnam (also known as Vizag and Waltair), part of the Northern Circars, is home to the only natural harbour, and oldest shipyard, on the east coast of India.
369 *Captain Hodson*: Perhaps Captain George Hodson and his wife Mary Rodgers (sister of Mrs Child).
370 *Captain Pitman*: Perhaps Captain Frederick Pitman (d. 22 May 1803) who commanded the East Indiaman *Skelton Castle* for her second voyage (1802–1803).
371 *Curricle*: 'A light two-wheeled carriage, usually drawn by two horses abreast' *(OED)*.
372 *vingt-un, at a rupee a fish*: Twenty-One, an ancient 'round' game of cards (of unlimited players) and an antecedent of modern Blackjack or Pontoon; a fish is a gambling chip.
373 *being two Jonahs*: Anyone or anything that brings bad luck.
374 *round the Cape*: Cape Agulhas, the rocky headland that forms the southernmost tip of the African Continent.
375 *False Bay*: A large bay on the Atlantic coast of south west Africa, and the site of Simon's Town – a key naval base and harbour on the Atlantic.
376 *the former Governor General Craig*: Fay arrives at Cape Town shortly after the Cape Colony (established by the Dutch East India Company in 1652) was occupied by British forces under Vice-Admiral Sir George Keith Elphinstone, Major-General Alured Clarke, and Major-General Sir James Henry Craig (78th Regiment of Foot). Craig became Governor between 1795 and 1797. Cape Town remained under British control until the Peace of Amiens (1802) when it was returned to the Dutch, but was reconquered by the British during the Napoleonic Wars.
377 *too much of a Yankee*: 'A nickname for a native or inhabitant of New England, or, more widely, of the northern States generally' *(OED)*.
378 *Egg Harbour*: A town in Atlantic County, New Jersey, historically also known as New Weymouth. Egg Harbour got its name from the Dutch explorer Cornelius Jacobsen May in 1614, for the remarkable number of birds' eggs he discovered in the grasslands at the mouth of the river.